INSIDE OUT

FIFTY YEARS BEHIND THE WALLS OF NEW JERSEY'S TRENTON STATE PRISON

BY HARRY CAMISA

AND

JIM FRANKLIN

Windsor Press and Publishing
PO Box 332
Windsor, NJ 08561
www.windsorpress.net

jacket design by Larry Petraccaro

book design and layout by Lynn Holl

Printed in the United States of America

Library of Congress Contol Number: 2002115335
ISBN 0-9726473-0-9

Dedicated to—

- Ginny, Darryl, Kim and Vance
- Haven and Alicia
- And all of the others who kept the faith

Photographer unknow.n. Library of Congress Historical American Buildings Survey (HABS)

Aerial photo of the old prison complex taken from the southeast *circa* 1930.

- A Front house lobby, built 1836
- B Grille gate
- C Armory
- D 7-wing, built 1905-7
- E 1-wing, built 1870-2
- F 2-wing, built 1836, remodeled into Auburn- type cells, 1877
- G original 3-wing, built 1860-1, remodeled into inmate dining hall, chapel/ recreation area, 1919.
- H 4-wing, built 1836
- I 5-wing, built 1865-7 for women;
- J 3-wing (new death row) created 1966
- K 6-wing, built 1895-6
- L Death chamber, built 1909
- M Death row, built 1909
- N Truck gate, sally port, added when original wall extended, 1884

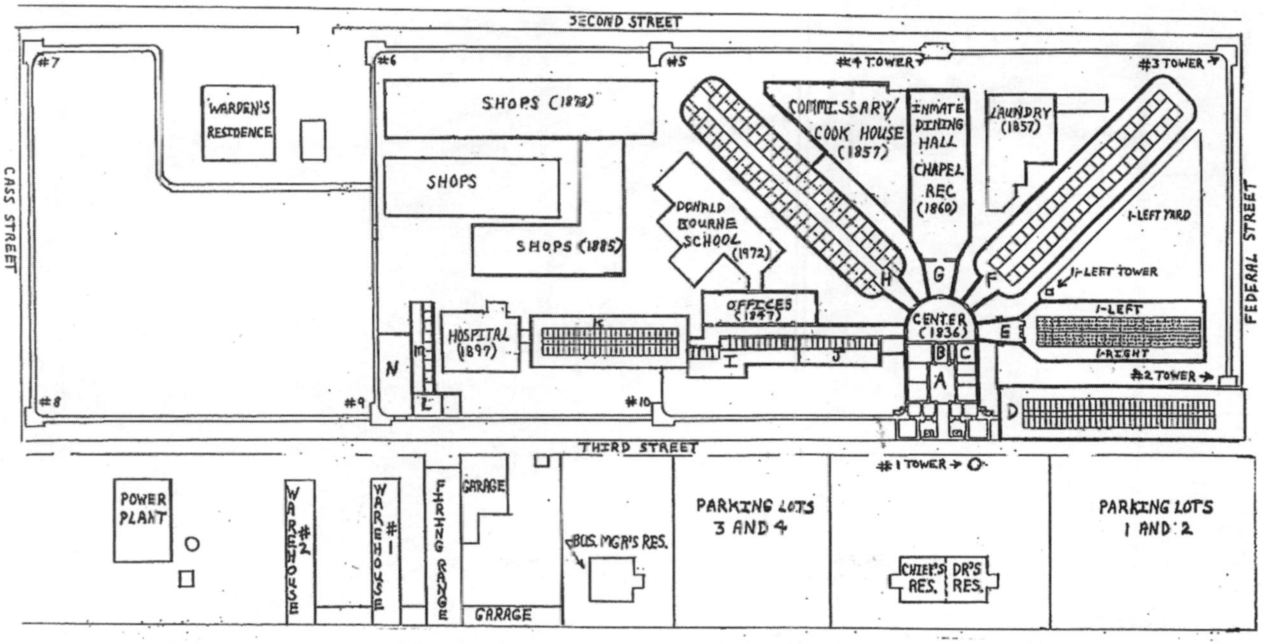

NEW JERSEY STATE PRISON, TRENTON 1974

(Original drawing by Lt. Donald Fiscor.)

Jack Boucher photograph, 1979

The front (east) wall of the old prison complex built between 1835-1907. This view down Third St. from Cass St. is now blocked by the new eight-story brick stucture built in 1981-1983 along this entire stretch of Third St. from Cass to Federal (see page 218). Inset: Harry in 1950.

CONTENTS

LIST OF ILLUSTRATIONS

Page

ACKNOWLEDGEMENTS

It's so difficult to even begin to thank all those who have been so helpful and supportive through this long process. . . . and we're bound to forget someone who was very important. To you—and we hope there is only one—thank you and we're sorry we forgot to mention you.

To the rest, in no particular order, thank you:

To Joe Butchko for finally getting us together to get this project underway.

To our families who suffered so patiently through those long hours of being deprived of our company: The Camisas—Ginny; Darryl and Pat and their daughter Megan; Kim and her husband, Larry Walker and their son Clint and daughter Blair; Vance and Ruth and their two daughters Holly and Sydney. The Franklins—Haven, Alicia, Alex and Kirsten.

To Teddy "The Bull" Roberts, who filled in a lot of gaps early on.

To those who read and edited—Laura Knight, Bruce Franklin, David Loscalzo, Joe Butchko, Caroline Pastore.

To good friends and other family members who offered important moral support: Pete Horne, Charlie Schlegel, Al Porter, Butch Miller, Noreen Duncan, Robin Schore, Charles Smith, David Collier, Bob Knight, Cynthia Lange, John Johnston, Al Gilligan, Jeff and Kevin Stull, Wells Walker, Bob Haisser, the late Alan Haisser, Jim and Andrea Petro, Adam and Lisa Winston, Dan and Michelle Suarez—and the two moms, Emilie Franklin and Jane Haisser.

To Tom Wilfrid, Tom Sepe, Eric Perkins, and the MCCC Board of Trustees for the much-needed sabbatical.

To employees of the prison, past and present, who helped in a number of ways: Windom Green, William Carhart, Charlie Donohue, Jack Malkin, Jr., Dorothy Masciotti, Vernon Stockton, Louis Pronesti.

To other members of the writing profession who provided advice and guidance: Henry Bryan, Kevin Coyne, Pat Yoczis, Reid Boates, Pablo Medina, Jon Blackwell, Paul Mickle, Carol Hupping, Lisa and Ed Leefeldt, Jean Hollander and the participants in the Trenton State College (TCNJ) annual writers' conferences.

To Brian Malone of the *Times* of Trenton for his generous support, and to Tony Russo for his permission to use his Joey Ernst article and his welcome advice.

To Lynn Holl, who designed and built the book and Larry Petraccaro, who designed the cover and helped in innumerable other ways.

To the MCCC library staff for their unflagging help with the research: Laura Ingersoll, Pat Wright, Pam Price, Frank Butorac and others; the Trenton Public Library staff, especially Charles Webster and Wendy Nardi. The staff of the NJ state library, the NJ archives and the Rutgers libraries and archives.

To Bob Harris for his advice and extraordinary photographs.

To the MCCC bookstore staff: Mike Massa, Pat Johnson and Ramon Sanchez.

To "The House of Wallace": Jim, Betty and Joanne.

To the NJ State Police: Stan Wojzkowski, Mark Falzini and Sgt. Jack Davis.

And lastly to all of those unsung reporters who live and record our history every minute, every day. You have no idea how important you are and how valuable your words will be fifty years from now.

Jack Boucher photograph, 1979

Front entrance of the 1835 prison.

1

CHAPTER ONE

IN THE BEGINNING . . .

I loved my job.

After fifty years of going to the same complex of buildings day after day, you'd think that I would have hated the sight of that huge red brick structure in the middle of Trenton, New Jersey. But I loved going there every day. Where else but Trenton State Prison (or as it is now more formally known, New Jersey State Prison, Trenton) could I sit down every day and talk with Rich Biegenwald, whose attorney argued against the death penalty by asking the jury to spare his life so that society could study the mind of a sociopath? Or walk into the law library and kid around with Big Rich Kuklinski, "The Iceman," who claims to have killed over 100 people and was convicted of killing four, keeping one of them in a freezer in a warehouse for two years. "It was strictly business," he says. Or move the pens on John List's desk and watch the mild-mannered former accountant meticulously rearrange them, just as he methodically lined up the corpses of his mother, wife and three children in the dining room of the Westfield mansion after he murdered them 25 years ago?

I was a prison guard at Trenton State Prison for twenty-nine years, starting on July 24, 1950 and retiring September 1 of 1979. During that time I completed an associate degree at Mercer County Community College and a bachelor's degree at Trenton State College. After taking some time off to use up accumulated sick days, I returned to "The Wall" in 1980 with the title of GED Proctor. I officially retired from the New Jersey Department of Corrections in the fall of 2002. In one of my last assignments I supervised the reprographics/print shop where two of my best workers were John List and Rich Biegenwald.

I watched thirteen men die in the electric chair, was taken hostage twice, and spent most of my life with some of the most violent criminals New Jersey has ever produced. I had threats made against my family and against me when I was the only witness willing to testify after a horrific Muslim bloodbath. I have felt the pain of losing two fellow officers, one a close friend, who were stabbed to death by inmates. And yet, I wouldn't trade my fifty years behind the walls of Trenton State Prison for any other job. I could never understand how some people can keep going to work day after day to jobs they don't like. I can honestly say there has never been a dull moment in my working life and despite the danger, violence and death, I can't conceive of doing anything else that I would have liked as much as working at New Jersey's oldest and toughest prison.

When I was a kid—seven years old or so—my family moved to Third Street in Trenton, just a block down the street from the front door of the massive sandstone and mortar century-old prison. I could almost hit the south wall of the prison with a baseball from the front stoop of our row house. I remember as a kid walking around and around those huge walls that took up about two square city blocks and wondering what it would be like to be inside.

Before we moved to Third Street, about 1932 or 1933 when I was four or five years old, we lived with my grandmother on Hamilton Avenue in Trenton. Each morning my grandmother would hold me in her lap by the window, and, even though this was a heavily traveled street, it was the Depression and we would sometimes wait for quite a while before the first car would go by. When that first car finally passed the house, my grandmother wrote down the license number and that would be the number she would play that day. She always played the number—everybody did—it was a big part of our daily lives.

Gambling was no big deal for me; my dad booked numbers. One day when I was about ten or eleven years old, my father had driven from our house on Third Street over to get some bread and pastries at the Italian People's Bakery in Chambersburg, the Italian section of Trenton, and on our way back home I noticed that my dad kept looking in the rear view mirror. Somebody must have tipped off the cops that my father had numbers on him.

Just before we reached the corner of Second and Cass Streets near St. Peter and Paul's School, about a block from our house (and right behind the prison), my dad handed me an envelope and said, "Harry, hold your arm down by the side of the car and toss this envelope into the gutter—but remember where you throw it. Then I'm going to let you out of the car. Run home and tell mom that I'll be a little late, and then run back here and pick up the envelope."

I didn't know exactly what was going on, but I did as I was told and after telling my mom, went back and got the envelope. Sure enough, when my dad got home, he said that the police had pulled him over just after I had gotten out of the car—in those days, the police had more respect for the family and wouldn't confront my dad until his kid was out of the car. Since they had no evidence, they had to let Dad go, but as far as I was concerned, the cops were butting into something that was none of their business.

I will say this about my father and the numbers, though: he never wanted any of his kids to get involved with gambling. I'll never forget him saying to me, "You know, Harry, in Italy where I'm from, they've got a big statue of the best gambler in all of Italy. And you know what, Harry? He's dressed in rags."

A few years later, after I had gone to work at the prison and was still living at home with my parents, I came home from work in uniform one day and my mother said, "Harry, your father got an important phone call, and he's down at the Neapolitan [pronounced *Nob li don*] club. Go tell him to call this number," and she handed me a slip of paper with a phone number on it. I drove over to the club, a small one-story brick building in the heart of "the Burg" and knocked at the front door. A burly guy in his fifties opened the door, and I said, "Is Ralph Camisa here?"

The guy looked me up and down in my blue cop's uniform, looked puzzled and said, "Ralph Camisa? Ralph Camisa? I don't know nobody by that name. You gotta the wrong address, kid," and he started to close the door in my face.

I got a little mad and I said, "Wait a minute, dammit. Look at this name plate," and I pointed to the name tag over my pocket. "I'm Harry Camisa. I'm his son, and I've got an important message for him."

Then the guy got all apologetic and started talking with those hand gestures typical of southern Italians. He put the tips of all his fingers together, hands pointed upward, shaking his hands up and down, and said, "C'mon kid, you come uh here in thata uniform—I don't know who you are. Wait a minute, I go get him."

That's the way it was. There was us . . . and there was them—the police. And now I was one of *them*.

So I would go into the prison every day, and I would see guys coming in with one to three years for the first gambling offense, three to five for the second and sometimes as much as five to seven years in a hellhole for something that I never thought was hurting anybody. I sometimes think of those guys who did so much time for gambling back then—Newsboy Moriarity from Jersey City, for example or Joe Adonis—and I wonder if they were alive today what they would think of the casinos in Atlantic City and the state-run lottery. Would they be bitter over having lost a piece of their lives for doing something that everyone accepts as a routine part of life today?

I got started at the prison because of my father. When I turned 21 in 1949, my dad started bugging me to get a regular job. I had a steady girlfriend, Ginny, and everybody in my family was telling me how I needed a regular job and some security. I wasn't ready to settle down yet; I still wanted to go out to the bars in the Burg and hang out with my friends, but my father had other ideas.

At the end of World War II and in the early fifties, Trenton was an important city in the northeast. It was the capital of New Jersey, and it was filled with all kinds of big manufacturing plants—ceramics, rubber, steel—and loads of smaller shops scattered throughout the neighborhoods. So jobs were around, but I wasn't moving very fast toward finding one. Back then, if a young guy like me didn't have much of an education and he wasn't a carpenter, plumber, electrician, mason or mechanic, in Trenton it was either take a job in one of the many factories or go to work as a prison guard—after all, the prison was, and still is, one of the city's biggest employers. Factory work and the building trades didn't interest me, so I told my dad that I would like to take a shot at being a prison guard and asked him to use his political influence to help me.

My father had been involved in politics for as long as I could remember. He had always been a low-level street worker for local Democratic politicians, and one guy in particular, George Page, would give my father $100 in "street money" every election to bring Italians to the polls. He would say to my father, "Ralph, here's a hundred dollars. Go and get all them Italians who can't read and write and bring 'em to the polls."

As soon as I said that I was interested in a job at the prison, my father started pushing the buttons to get me the job. I wasn't a big guy, about five foot, eight and 160 pounds, and at the prison they preferred big, beefy guards because so much of the job required physical strength—more so than today when manhandling of inmates is no longer as acceptable as it was back then. I was also Italian, which was an even bigger liability than my size.

My father's first call was to the office of the principal keeper (warden) of the prison—George Page. Page had been one of the five city commissioners in Trenton for years, partly through the efforts of immigrants like my father, and he swung a lot of political weight. In fact, Page had gotten the principal keeper job, a state position, mainly through his political connections. He was a pleasant man who was fond of going to the race track. In all the time that he was warden, I'm not sure he ever once walked through the jail, and I know he detested being required to be present at the electrocutions.

So, after my dad made the phone call to Mr. Page's office, here I was in July of 1950, walking down Third Street in Trenton along the grimy red sandstone wall that enclosed the huge compound. The prison sits in the middle of a residential neighborhood in the south ward of Trenton. Since I was still living with my folks on Third Street, it took me maybe three minutes to walk from our front door to the front entrance of the prison.

Across the street from our house was a huge factory complex, The Home Rubber Company. The prison stood catty corner to Home Rubber (in the early '70's an inmate sued the state, claiming he should be released because his civil rights were being violated by pollution coming from Home Rubber's smokestacks), and was bound by Third Street on the east side; Cass Street on the south side; Second Street on the west side; and Federal Street on the north side.

As I walked up to the front steps of the prison, I looked across the street at the officer sitting in a large concrete, steel and glass gazebo. The guard sat in his chair with a 12-gauge shotgun across his lap, watching me approach the front steps. The steps and front door of the prison were recessed off the street, enclosed within an alcove surrounded by those big reddish stone blocks stained by 120 years of industrial smoke from the nearby factories.

I climbed the five worn stone steps, thinking how unsure I was whether I really wanted to do this. I began to feel like I was being pushed into getting a steady job by my father, and I was worried about how a commitment like this was going to cut into my partying time. But I was here, so I pushed the brass button of the doorbell, made shiny by God knows how many fingers pushing that button over the last hundred years, and waited. After a few seconds I saw a cop's face looking out at me through an eight-inch square window in the massive wooden door. I could hear him putting a key into the big lock, and as he opened the door a few inches, I told him why I was here. He was a dour-looking guy who just nodded and swung the door open to let me in.

I walked into a lobby about thirty feet wide by maybe forty feet long. On my left, slightly to the rear, was the warden's office; on the right, also to the rear, was the office of the chief of security. Those two offices formed the sides of the alcove that I had been standing in outside.

The cop on the door showed me into the outer office of the warden and introduced me to Mr. Page's secretary, Mrs. Ryan. (I later became good friends with her and found out her father was Colonel Edward B. Stone who had been warden in the early 1930's.) After a few minutes, Mr. Page came out of his office. He was tall and heavyset with a pleasant, easygoing manner. Like a typical politician, he grabbed my hand, asked me how my father was doing, how the rest of the family was and so on as he guided me into his office. Page and I talked for several minutes, but because of my father's contributions to the party and the need for officers, it was pretty much a foregone conclusion that I was going to get the job. After Mr. Page was satisfied that I could see, hear, speak English and had all my limbs, he picked up the phone and called the chief of security, Captain Francis Fleming, into the office. In the fifties, all the cops had names like Fleming, Doll, Malkin—predominantly Irish, English or German. No Italians. I could tell right away that Fleming didn't like me because I was Italian and small, but Page was the boss and that was that.

I was hired at a salary of $2,400 per year—$200 per month. In 1950, the economy was strong, and people weren't beating down the doors to get jobs as guards because of the low pay—factory jobs, especially with overtime, paid a lot more. And the hours were lousy: all starting guards went on the night shift and worked six days a week, including weekends.

Since I was a rookie, my first assignment was in a tower. I was still partying pretty heavily and after about a month, I fell asleep one night and didn't ring in on the half hour, as required.

The next night when I reported to work, Captain Fleming called me into his office. He said to me, "What the hell did you do, you little guinea, go to sleep and fall off the tower?"

Being one of the first Italians ever hired at the prison, I took a lot of shots like that from those older Anglo cops: "Why ain'tcha sellin' bananas in the 'Burg, you little wop?"

And who was I going to complain to? Internal Affairs? They didn't come along until thirty years later. So I just took it and tried to keep my sense of humor. I understood, even then as young as I was, that these old guys had a big resentment seeing Italians come in as guards because so many of the inmates were Italian. I remember feeling a little bit the same way in the sixties when the inmate population became predominantly black and more and more black officers were being hired. Truthfully, though, when Bill Killingsworth, the first black cop, was hired in 1951, I breathed a sigh of relief because I figured now there was somebody else to take the heat.

So Fleming sent me in to see Warden Page, and Page said to me, "Harry, what happened?"

I had to be honest with him. I said, "Mr. Page, I'm 21 years old; I can't sleep during the daytime—there's too much that I want to be out doing. It's hard for me to stay awake out there when I've been up all day. I counted all of the sheets in a roll of toilet paper. I set up the bucket with the string through the cigarette so when the cigarette burns through the string the bucket drops to wake me up. It didn't work. I just can't hack the tower at night."

He said, "OK, Harry, I'll tell you what. I'm suspending you for three days, and then you can come in on days."

I thought he was going to fire me, and I don't think it was out of respect for my father that he didn't; it's just that they were short-handed and needed guards. Not many people wanted to work the lousy hours and be exposed every day to the potential violence from New Jersey's most hardened criminals for that kind of money. With that in mind, I even had the brass balls to ask Mr. Page to suspend me *with* pay. He almost threw me out of his office.

When I came back off suspension, I was assigned to center as one of the ten "extras" on the first shift (6:20 a.m.—2:20 p.m.). My job was to stay close to the central hub of the prison and during mass movements of inmates stand in the neck where the wing connected to the hub and hold the barred doors open to keep traffic flowing smoothly. Or if one of the wing officers needed to be relieved or an inmate needed to be escorted somewhere, I was sent to that part of the prison.

About six months after I started at the prison, I got drafted into the army for the Korean conflict, so from January of 1951 to January, 1953, I wasn't at The Wall. When I returned to work in '53, I went back to being an extra, and then one day in July I got a big break and sort of conned my way into working in the mailroom out in the front house.

Sergeant Nick Menkerell's son, Adam, had just started as a guard, and the sergeant had gotten the administration to put his kid in the mailroom because it was in the front house and therefore less dangerous than other jobs inside the prison itself. One morning during roll call, Sergeant Menkerell asked if anybody had ever worked in the mailroom because he wanted somebody to help his son learn the ropes. Never one to miss a golden opportunity, I raised my hand, even though I had never worked in the mailroom and didn't know squat about it. When I got in there, it took the kid about two minutes to see that this was a classic case of the blind leading the blind.

He said, "Harry, we have to censor this mail."

I looked at him and said, "Huh?"

Adam looked startled and said, "Harry, my father said you had worked in here. You don't know shit about the mail room."

I admitted to him that I had lied, but I said I would bust my ass to find out what to do and I would do a hell of a job. So between the two of us, we muddled through for a couple of weeks, and finally we got it under control. Adam and I stayed in there for the next seven years.

By 1960 I was considered a veteran cop—and I really was because the turnover rate was so high—so I was put in charge of the toughest housing unit in the prison—1-left lockup.

From '60 to '65, I was the first-shift officer responsible for the maximum security section of New Jersey's maximum security prison. This wing housed the institution's high-risk inmates, the guys who had committed offenses within the prison, ranging from homosexual activity to killing a guard. This unit housed guys like Jimmy Wilburn, who had broken the warden's jaw; Barney Doak, who had led a major riot; and George Zagorski, who had stabbed a guard to death.

In 1965 I was assigned to "The Star." This was one of my favorite jobs because I was always busy, always involved in the everyday action inside the prison. The star is literally that—a brass star embedded in a granite circle about ten inches in diameter in the floor of the prison rotunda, the central hub of the whole institution. The star officer is the traffic director in the old part of the prison; he has to watch the entrances to all of the wings as well as the entryway from the front house into the prison itself and tell everyone, mainly with hand gestures (what a job for an Italian!) when to move. During mass movements, like at mealtimes, the cops in the control booth (central control) and the wing cops watch the star officer for hand and voice signals to keep inmate traffic flowing smoothly.

From 1968 to 1977, I held virtually every other custody job in the prison: I was in charge of a variety of housing wings, shops, and so on. For about a year I was assigned to court officer duty, taking inmates to and from court appearances—another job I liked because I got a chance to drive all over the state on their time. Around 1978 the NJ Department of Corrections and Parole contracted with St. Francis Hospital on the east side of the city to set up a ward for prison inmates. I was assigned there for the last year before I retired as a corrections officer.

While I had been working as an officer, through the encouragement of my wife and my family, I attended courses first at Mercer County Community College and then Trenton State College and obtained an Associate in Arts degree followed by a Bachelor of Science degree in education. Since I had twenty-nine years in (with credit for the two years in the service), I decided to retire as an officer, and I was offered a job as a civilian employee in the education department. I jumped at the chance. From 1979 up to the fall of 2002, I worked at the prison with the title of Teacher II. Despite the title, though, I spent only about six months in a classroom. Most of my other duties involved testing inmates to see what level of education would match their backgrounds and abilities. As I mentioned before, I also supervised the print shop, a job connected to education since the art classrooms were next door to the shop, and the inmates we hired in the shop used the skills they learned in the art classroom.

I truly loved what I chose as a career. Watching the events and changes over the last 50 years has been a fascinating experience that I wouldn't trade for anything in the world. That decision way back in 1950 to become a prison guard opened the door to the greatest show on earth. It's a cliché, but as far as my career is concerned, there's never been a dull moment.

2
CHAPTER TWO

THE EARLY FIFTIES

After I served my suspension for sleeping in the tower, I started my job as an extra in center. This assignment made more sense to me for a couple of reasons. One was that I was able to move around the prison a lot more, filling in for an officer in a wing or escorting inmates to the hospital or to court-line (disciplinary) hearings. This way I got to know the layout of the jail a lot faster than if I was stuck in a tower.

I also liked this assignment because it fit my personality better. I was always outgoing and open to meeting new people. Being stationed in the central hub of the prison gave me the opportunity to see and meet a lot of interesting people—cops and inmates.

In those days, a big clock was mounted on the wall in the rotunda over the entrance to the mess hall. During every prisoner movement, while the cons traveled from one part of the prison to another—going to meals, to work, to yard and so on, a terrific five-piece inmate band would set up under the clock and play Sousa marches. There was also a jazz band that played in the mess hall during meals. Most of these guys had played professionally on the outside, and even the ones who hadn't were good. Back then, heroin was just starting to become a popular street drug, but it had been used by pop musicians for years, so it wasn't unusual to have several talented guys doing time in Trenton on drug convictions—even in the 1950's.

One day I was standing underneath the clock watching a movement, listening to the music and waiting for an assignment. I had asked one of the veteran cops to do me a favor—to point out a guy named Clarence Hill when he came through. After several minutes, the older cop nudged me and pointed to a short, pleasant-looking black guy wearing wire-rimmed glasses.

The cop said, "There's Hill."

I went over to Hill as he stood in line, waiting to go down the steps into the mess hall, introduced myself and told him that I was Rocky Buckley's nephew. My uncle Rocky had worked with this guy at Coleman's Poultry on South Clinton Avenue during the late 1930's. When Rocky heard I had a job as a prison guard, he asked me to look Hill up and say hello. I remembered that Uncle Rocky had told me about Hill six years before, back in 1944 when I was 16 years old, and had shown me Hill's picture in the newspaper. Clarence Hill was well known in the Trenton area as the "Duck Island Killer."

Clarence was short and stocky, about five feet, five inches tall, and had a big, friendly, toothy grin. Over time I would get to know him as a model inmate who never got into any trouble and was well liked by everyone who knew him.

When I told him who I was, Clarence stuck out his hand, and said, "Nice to meet you, Harry. How is Rocky doing?"

I was surprised at how soft-spoken he was and how gentle he seemed—especially given the violence of the crimes that had put him here.

I told him Rocky was fine and was still working at Coleman's. Then I told him I had just been hired as a guard a couple of months ago and had been out in the towers.

Clarence moved closer to me and said even more softly, "Listen Harry, these are tough guys in here. If they think you're a rookie, they'll try pulling a lot of shit on you to test you out. I'll tell them you've been in the system for a while and just got transferred in from Rahway. This way they'll show you some respect."

I said, "Hey, Clarence. That's nice of you. I appreciate that."

We talked a few more minutes about how he had worked with Rocky in the poultry shop. He asked me if I was married and some other questions like that—social chit chat as if we had run into each other on the corner of State and Broad Streets in downtown Trenton.

I didn't have to ask him how he was or how he came to be in Trenton State Prison. As "The Duck Island Killer," or the "Spooner Slayer," Clarence had picked up quite a few headlines in the Trenton *Evening Times* for three spectacular double murders in 1938, 1939 and 1940. Nobody even suspected that mild-mannered Sunday-school teacher Clarence Hill was the killer until he was nabbed in 1944 while serving stateside in the Army during the war. It was quite a story.

The first murder occurred on election night in November, 1938, on Duck Island, a remote and undeveloped section of Hamilton Township just over the city line along the Delaware River. Duck Island where the first two murders took place isn't really an island—it's just a marshy area near the river that's covered with underbrush and scrubby trees near the Trenton Marine Terminal. In one of the stories about the murders, the Trenton *Times* called Duck Island a "petters' paradise." A narrow paved road ran through the area with dozens of secluded little lanes coming off it where for years cars had been pulled off into the underbrush for romantic encounters.

Back then, the City of Trenton was a thriving metropolitan area surrounded by three suburban townships: Hamilton, Ewing and Lawrence. If you lived in one of the townships and wanted some excitement, you came into the city with its restaurants, movie theaters and bars. And if you lived in the city and wanted to go parking with your girlfriend or boyfriend, you went out to one of the townships. Duck Island was probably the most popular lovers' lane in the whole metro Trenton region when Clarence started his killing spree.

At 5:30 p.m. on Tuesday evening, November 8, 1938, 20-year-old Vincenzo "Jimmy" Tonzillo dropped his pregnant wife at the home of a relative and headed for his job at the United Sand and Gravel Company across the Delaware River in Morrisville, Pa. Instead of going directly to work, though, Tonzillo made the same detour he had been making for the past two weeks and picked up 15-year-old Mary Myatovich on Steamboat Street a few blocks from her house. Then the two of them headed for Duck Island.

Sometime between 6:30 and 7 p.m., while Tonzillo and Myatovich were parked, a short black man yanked open the back door of Tonzillo's car, told the couple to get out of the car and demanded money. When Tonzillo refused, the man fired a blast from a shotgun at point blank range, hitting Tonzillo in the shoulder and penetrating his lung. Mary Myatovich took off running, but the assailant chased her down and about 150 feet from the car brought her down with a blast that hit her in the left buttock and came out through her abdomen. After running her down and dropping her with the blast from the shotgun, the killer tore off the rest of Mary's clothes and raped her. Her torn clothes were found later by police near a blood-stained rock a couple of hundred feet from the car.

After the assailant left, though she was badly wounded, Mary was able to crawl back to the car. Jimmy Tonzillo's body was lying next to the passenger side with his feet under the running board. Mary dragged herself back into the front seat of the car, draped herself over the steering wheel and started crying out for help. Within about twenty minutes another couple driving along Duck Island Road heard Mary's cries and pulled into the lane. They found Mary, dressed only in stockings and a green sweater, covered in blood from the waist down. The young woman checked Tonzillo's pulse to see if he was still alive and then, with her boyfriend, drove back to a gas station on nearby Lalor Street to call the police.

Both the City of Trenton and Hamilton Township police departments responded to the call. Three officers wrapped Mary in a blanket and rushed her to St. Francis Hospital in Hamilton. She survived for 36 hours, dying from her wounds on Thursday morning. Before she died, Mary was able to tell police that the man who shot her "with a big gun" was a Negro, about five feet, seven inches tall wearing a suede jacket and a cap.

No arrests were made in the case, and the trail had pretty much gone cold when, ten months later, the killer struck again. This time, the woman victim was the one who was married and cheating on her husband with a neighbor. Early Sunday morning, October 1, 1939, 40-year-old Pemberton Wemmer was scouring the dumps on Duck Island looking for salvage, as he did every Sunday morning. He never knew what he would find—the previous week he had uncovered a woman's artificial leg. As Wemmer looked for deposit bottles and other treasures, he spotted what he at first thought was another artificial limb sticking out from under a pile of bundled newspapers. When he pulled the paper aside, he found the body of Katie Werner, 36, her face and head bashed in by a large, bloody slab of rock lying nearby. She had also been hit by pellets from a shotgun. Wemmer ran to the Trenton Yacht Club and called police.

When Trenton and Hamilton police arrived, they searched through the underbrush and found the body of Frank Kasper, 28, an unmarried neighbor of Katie and "Snap" Werner, sitting upright in the back seat of his car. Kasper had been hit by a blast from a shotgun fired at close range into the right side of his head and neck through the open rear window of his car, killing him instantly. Police theorized that Katie Werner had tried to run away and, after getting about 100 feet from the car, was knocked down by a blast from the shotgun and finished off with the stone slab. She had also been raped. Part of her right arm had been blown off by the shotgun charge and pellets were found in her chest. Kasper was still wearing his wrist watch and packages from a shopping trip were scattered around the car, so robbery was ruled out as a motive.

Police and newspapers profiled the killer a "sex-crazed maniac" who liked to spy on illicit lovers before he killed them. After several months of intense activity by investigators, this case also hit a dead end. No likely suspects were turned up, and the investigation trailed off.

Then, a little over a year later, on the night of November 9, 1940, the killer struck again, this time across the river in Morrisville. And again, the intended victims were a married woman and her unmarried boyfriend in a lover's lane. This time, the victim fought back and got a look at the assailant.

Just as 19-year-old Howard Wilson pulled into an isolated lover's lane outside of Morrisville, directly across the Delaware River from Duck Island, a Negro armed with a shotgun leaped from the bushes and yelled, "I told you to stay out of here! Now open that door!"

Wilson hadn't even had time to shut off the engine, so he threw the car into gear and drove right at the armed man. The man put the muzzle of the shotgun against the driver's side window and fired, nearly tearing Wilson's arm off. Wilson managed to speed away from the scene and drive to Bristol, PA, where he collapsed on the front lawn of Harriman Hospital. At first, he told police he had been alone in the car, to protect the reputation of the woman who was with him, but then he admitted there had been someone else in the car when he was attacked. Wilson told police the man with the shotgun was a Negro about 40 years old, five feet, five inches tall, weighing approximately 120 to 130 pounds. Again, though, the police were unable to make an arrest.

After the second set of murders in New Jersey, the Hamilton police had established a "spooner patrol" to watch the township's lovers' lanes. Since the killer seemed to be striking at regular intervals about a year apart, the police were especially alert in October and November of 1940, but they just missed him when he killed again on Saturday night, November 16.

This time, the shotgun slayer struck about three miles east and inland from Duck Island at another popular secluded parking area off Cypress Lane in Hamilton. The spooner patrol had driven through the Cypress Lane area around 7:30 p.m. and found it unoccupied. When they came back at about 10:30, they found the bodies of 35-year-old Louis Kovacs and his married lover, 27-year-old Carolina Moriconi in the back seat of Kovacs' car. It looked like the killer had yanked open the car door while Kovacs and Moriconi were "locked in an intimate embrace" and had fired point blank into both of them. Both bodies had powder burns around the wounds.

Kovacs had been hit by a load of buckshot in the chest just above the heart. Moriconi's left arm had been torn off by a blast, and pellets had pierced her heart and lungs. It appeared that both had died almost instantly. Kovacs was wearing a diamond ring, and his wallet was still in the pocket of his pants, so, again, police ruled out robbery as a motive.

Even though police knew from matching the shotgun casings found at the scenes of the attacks that the same man was doing them, they couldn't track him down. This killing also went unsolved.

Finally, in March of 1942, investigators got the break they were hoping for when the man struck again in Tullytown, PA below Morrisville. On the night of March 7, a soldier from Fort Dix was sitting in a car with a girl in a secluded lovers' lane when a man with a shotgun approached them and demanded money. The soldier, 25-year-old John Testa, resisted, and, as in the other cases, the assailant fired a blast from the shotgun, nearly tearing off Testa's arm. And, just as in the first two murders in Hamilton, the girl jumped out of the car and tried to run away. The killer ran her down, but this time, instead of firing at her with the shotgun, he clubbed her with it, breaking off a piece of the forestock containing a serial number. Testa, even though he was badly injured (his arm would later be amputated at the Fort Dix hospital), managed to start the car and drive toward the assailant, forcing him to run into the woods. The description of the would-be killer given to police by Testa and the woman fit the earlier descriptions, but police still didn't know exactly who the suspect was.

The broken piece of the shotgun was stamped with the serial number A-639. After more than a year of checking various records, the Hamilton and state police discovered that the gun had once been pawned and redeemed at Krueger's Pawn Shop on South Broad Street in Trenton. The man who originally had the ticket said he'd given it to someone he had worked with on a WPA project in the late 1930's—a medium-sized black guy from Hamilton Township named Clarence Hill. The police caught up with Clarence in the army, stationed in South Carolina. Hill was transferred to Fort Dix and then turned over to civilian authorities in February of 1944.

Clarence went on trial in the Mercer County courthouse in December of 1944 for the murder of Mary Myatovich. At first, it looked like Clarence didn't have a chance since he had supposedly told a colonel in the provost marshal's office at Fort Dix, "I did those killings."

The colonel, Lewis Sussman, said he asked Hill, "What killings?" and Hill said, "Duck Island."

Clarence had also given the Hamilton police two statements acknowledging that he had done the crimes and had even gone with authorities to Duck Island to try to help them find the murder weapon. I was 16 years old when Clarence was tried, and when Uncle Rocky told me he knew Hill, I followed the trial in the Trenton *Evening Times*. I remember reading the stories day by day and thinking, "Bye, bye, Clarence."

As the trial went on and the police testified, it looked more and more as if Clarence was headed for a date with the electric chair.

In his statements, the Hamilton police said Clarence told them, "I just went there to see if I could find any parked cars there with girls and fellows in them screwing and to see if I could get a chance to bother around with a girl."

In his statement about the Kasper/Werner murders, Clarence said, "I took a peep inside the car to see what was going on in there. I saw a fellow and a woman. They were on the back seat. To me, it appeared that they was having a screwing party.

"I jerked the door open and they both jumped up and I shot the fellow and the girl ran out the other side screaming. I shot her, I hit her in the arm, and she went down."

Clarence was dead meat.

Then he took the stand in his own defense.

When I knew Clarence, he wore wire-rimmed glasses because somewhere along the line he had lost the sight in his right eye. I'm not sure if he wore glasses when he testified, but if he did, they made him look even meeker, just like a Sunday-school teacher ought to look. With his soft voice and gentle, polite manner, Clarence might have made a good impression on the jury. When he took the stand, he told the court that police and military authorities had taken him out of the Fort Dix jail on a cold, rainy night the previous January and had driven him to the site of the Duck Island murders. There, he said, they had made him dig with his bare hands, in handcuffs, to search for the murder weapon. He also said that he told investigators he had never been on that part of Duck Island in his life, and when Colonel Sussman told him to indicate with his foot where Tonzillo's car was parked, he marked the ground with his foot only because he was a solider whose superior officer had given him an order.

Clarence went on to testify that the chief of the Bucks County (PA) detective bureau had struck him in the face during an interrogation at Fort Dix and said, "I hate a liar."

Hill said that a Pennsylvania state police detective had cautioned the Bucks County cop, "There'll be plenty of time for that later. We're on a military reservation."

Then, Clarence said, another detective made a gesture with his finger across his throat, indicating that Clarence would have his throat slit if he didn't confess to the murders.

Hill also said that he was confined in a "dungeon" at Fort Dix and denied access to a lawyer until police had finished questioning him. (This was long before Miranda Rights were ever heard of.) Clarence's attorney, Frank H. Wimberly, said that his client was brought to Duck Island "in chains" to look for the murder weapon and had been relentlessly questioned from 9 p.m. until 10 a.m. the next day on two successive nights at the Hamilton police headquarters before he signed the confessions. Wimberly described Clarence as a quiet, church-going young soldier with a wife and two children.

After a two-week trail, Clarence was found guilty of the Mary Myatovich murder, but the jury recommended leniency, so he wasn't sentenced to the chair. The newspapers said that the jury had given a lot of weight to the confessions in bringing in the guilty verdict. One theory about why the jury didn't recommend the death penalty was that Hill's confessions amounted to voluntary assistance to the police, helping them to solve the crimes, and he should get some consideration for that. Another opinion was that the lack of a murder weapon created doubts in some jurors' minds.

Two things about the Clarence Hill case always baffled me. The first was how Clarence—if he really was the killer—could have had the uncanny ability to pick out victims who were cheating on their spouses. Of the three couples he was said to have killed in the Trenton area, and two that he attacked across the river in Pennsylvania but didn't kill, in every case one of the two people involved was cheating on a spouse.

The other thing I could never figure out back then and cannot explain to this day is how a black guy gets accused of killing six white people in Trenton, New Jersey in 1944, gets convicted of one of the killings, and doesn't get the death penalty. The only thing I can figure is that the jury wasn't absolutely sure of his guilt when they decided not to give him the chair. I think maybe the prosecutor's office wasn't too sure about him either because they never brought him to trial on the other five killings. It looks to me like they were satisfied to put him away for 17 or 18 years rather than risk not getting a conviction on the other murders.

Whatever their thinking was back in 1944, Clarence went into the general population, and I saw him frequently until he was released in 1964. By the time he went out, he was in his fifties and in poor health—I heard he had throat cancer. Even though both New Jersey and Pennsylvania authorities had detainers against him for his other alleged crimes, so much time had passed and because of his health I'm sure they figured, "Why bother?"

He kind of disappeared after he left The Wall and lived quietly in the area until he died in 1973.

* * * * * * *

A couple of weeks after I first ran into Clarence Hill, I was back in center again, listening to the band play Sousa marches and watching the inmates step lively from the wing necks toward the mess hall. An older cop standing next to me nudged me with his elbow and pointed out a reserved, kind of distinguished-looking prisoner moving across center from one wing to another.

The other cop said to me, "Hey, Harry. See that guy? You know who he is?"

I didn't have the foggiest idea who the man was, so the older cop called him over and introduced us.

He said, "Charlie Workman, this is a new officer, Harry Camisa."

I still didn't know who this guy was, but he seemed to be quite polite and gentlemanly, not like most of the other hard-assed cons I had met in my short time on the job. Workman shook my hand and said quietly that he was pleased to meet me and hoped I would enjoy working at the institution. I was impressed by the man's bearing and dignity.

As he walked away, the older cop said, "You still don't know who he is? That's the guy who killed Dutch Schultz."

Then the other cop filled me in on Charlie Workman, the first of several "celebrity" criminals I would meet over the years.

Workman was convicted in the gangland slaying of Arthur Flegenheimer (Dutch Schultz) in 1941. Although Schultz had been murdered in 1935, Workman wasn't fingered and tried for the crime until six years later. Workman was about 40 years old when I met him in 1950 and had already been in prison for nine years. Charlie would go on to serve another 14 years (total 23) before being released in March of 1964, an unusually long "life sentence" by the standards of the day.

Under the laws in effect when Workman was sent to prison, a jury had two options when they brought in a conviction for first-degree murder: a recommendation for mercy meant a life sentence; no recommendation was an automatic death sentence. Under a life sentence an inmate first became eligible for parole after serving fourteen and a half years. No lifer I ever knew of got paroled after his first trip to the parole board; even if he had been a model prisoner, he always left the hearing room with at least a six-month "hit." Most life-sentence inmates who had clean records while they were in prison got one-year or 18-month hits and then went back before the board. Then they would "get a date" maybe another six months down the road. That usually brought the total time to somewhere around 16 or 17 years, the average life sentence in the '50s. If the parole board thought the inmate was still a threat to society or if he had a lot of institutional charges, especially involving violence, then he actually could be in prison for life. Unlike a one-to three for bookmaking or a three-to-five for burglary, a life sentence had no fixed maximum and release was at the discretion of the parole board. As far as I know, Charlie Workman never got into any trouble in the institution, so the only reason I can see for the unusually long time he spent in Trenton was the notoriety surrounding the crime.

Workman was known as "Charlie the Bug" on the street when he was hooked up with the mob, but I never heard anyone in the jail call him that; the other inmates respected him and left him alone. Unless Charlie Workman started the conversation, other inmates steered clear of him. (That's fairly typical of the way mobsters are viewed in any prison—they're at the top of the hierarchy, along with the "smart criminals," the ones whose crimes take some planning: jewel thieves, bank robbers, white-collar types; under them are the burglars, con artists and gamblers followed by the strong-arm and violent guys: murderers, armed robbers. At the bottom are the sex offenders, and at the very bottom are the child molesters, the "baby-fuckers.")

According to the testimony at his trial, Workman and another guy gunned down Schultz at about 10:30 on the evening of October 23, 1935 as Schultz and three other men sat at a table in a small dining room in the Palace Chop House and Tavern in Newark going over account books and papers. The newspapers said two unidentified gunmen walked into the restaurant and opened fire on Schultz and the three others with a tommy gun and a sawed-off shotgun. One of the other men with Schultz died of his wounds within a few hours, and Schultz died late the next day (after that famous photo of him "counting the bullet holes" was taken).

An hour and a half after Schultz was shot, one of his lieutenants, Martin Krompler, was gunned down in a barber shop in Manhattan, and the bloody gang war being waged over control of organized crime in greater New York and northern New Jersey escalated.

A lot of suspects were rounded up after Schultz' killing, but the hit was carried out so cleanly that the police had no real clues to the identity of the killers—this added to the respect that was accorded Workman in prison. Six years after the murders, early in 1941, two members of Murder, Inc.—Abe Reles and Albert Tannenbaum—made a deal with a New York City D.A. and said that Charlie Workman had bragged about killing Schultz. An Essex County (NJ) grand jury indicted Workman, who was known to be a gunman for the Louis (Lepke) Buchalter gang, but during the trial nobody could identify him as the gunman, so it looked like he was going to get off. Suddenly, an undertaker from Manhattan who had been Workman's alibi recanted his testimony, and Workman changed his plea to "no defense." It was commonly understood around the prison that Workman took the fall for killing Schultz in exchange for him and his family being taken care of while he was in jail.

Any time I would see him around the jail, Workman always looked neat and clean in his prison blues or khakis. He went about his business quietly, seldom mingling with the other convicts except for two or three other low-level mob guys also doing time. When I went out into the mailroom in 1953 after returning from the service, one of my responsibilities was checking in people coming in to visit inmates. Workman's wife, Catherine, visited him faithfully once a month; back then inmates were allowed only one 30-minute window visit per month, a total of six hours per year. Catherine Workman looked and carried herself like a classy lady, almost like Katherine Hepburn or Lauren Bacall. I always had the idea that she might have been some kind of actress in New York City before she met Charlie.

The word around the prison that Workman and his family were being taken care of by the mob (probably the Bonanno family in New York) got a boost when Workman finally got a date from the parole board and was scheduled to be released in 1964. A few days before his release date, a box from an expensive New York clothing store came into the mailroom for Workman. At this point, I was wing officer in 1-left lockup. I was on my way into work when one of the mailroom cops called me over and showed me what was in the box. I whistled and called my old buddy Adam Menkerell over.

"Adam. Look at this suit—it must have cost $500!" I said.

It would have taken me a month of overtime in 1964 to be able to afford an expensive continental-cut suit like that.

When he stepped out of the front door of the prison to freedom, at 54 years of age and wearing his new suit, Charlie Workman looked sharp—every inch a high-class mobster. Catherine (who had missed only a few visiting days in the 23 years that Charlie was in prison), and a few reporters were waiting for him on the sidewalk. Charlie kissed his wife, who was wearing dark glasses and, with her streaked blonde hair, looked more like a gracefully aging movie actress than ever, and the two of them walked silently to the curb. We had a guard with a shotgun and a pistol on his hip patrolling the area—just in case—as a dark blue Thunderbird driven by Charlie's son came speeding up to Charlie and his wife. They got into the car and took off, and that was the last I ever saw or heard about the man they said killed Dutch Schultz.

****

During the fall of 1950, while I was still being broken in as a rookie cop, the conflict in Korea that had started in June was heating up, and a lot of guys were being drafted into the armed services. I got my notice a few days after Christmas, and in January of 1951 I was sent to Fort Dix for basic training before being shipped to Europe.

A couple of months after I went overseas, I got a letter from Ginny along with some newspaper clippings that gave me my first taste of what the job at the prison that was waiting for me could mean in terms of violence—of how quickly any of us could become a front-page story in the newspaper . . . at least for a day or two.

During my six months at the prison, I had become friends with another guard by the name of Vic Vitterito, one of the few other cops of Italian descent at the jail. Vic was a couple of years older than I was, 25, and had completed barber school while he was working at the prison. He was good looking and personable and the two of us liked to kid around, especially about some of the shit we had to take because we were Italian.

Vic told me that he was ready to quit the prison job in a few weeks because the pay was so low—$2,400 per year at the time—and because of the lousy hours. Since we were both new on the job, we had to work every weekend and the normal work week was six days, so our only day off was Wednesday. Vic had been offered a job at a barber shop in Chambersburg and had jumped at the opportunity.

On February 28, 1951, about two weeks before Vic was scheduled to finish working at the prison, he and another officer, Lester Throckmorton, got an assignment to take an inmate named George Zagorski to Hackensack in Bergen County for sentencing on an armed robbery charge. Zagorski, from Jersey City, was already serving a sentence of 21 to 28 years for armed robberies he had pulled during a four-month spree in the spring and summer of 1950. He had admitted to nine armed robberies of building and loans in Union, Hudson and Bergen counties, netting about $30,000 in bonds, jewelry and cash. He had a jail record dating back to 1944 when he was 19, so he was already a career criminal. Vic and Throckmorton were taking him back to county court for another seven-to-nine-year sentence to be served tacked onto concurrently with what he already had.

Zagorski was 25, the same age as Vic. He was a handsome, well-built weightlifter and athlete with large, powerful wrists and hands. Vic and Throckmorton took Zagorski to Hackensack and then waited around to take him back to the prison at the end of the day. Transport duty is considered one of the better assignments in a prison because it gets you out of the everyday tension of being surrounded by inmates, and it's usually routine.

What Vic and Throckmorton had no way knowing, though, was that when the county jailers fed Zagorski lunch, they forgot to collect his spoon. In general, I found the county jail guards weren't used to dealing with the kinds of hardened criminals that we were used to in a maximum-security state prison, so they weren't as careful as we were. Also, back then, all utensils were metal. Today, after a lot of tragedies involving metal implements fashioned into shanks, eating utensils, plates and cups in the inmate mess halls are plastic and Styrofoam.

Zagorski went back to his cell in the county lockup and sharpened the top of the spoon handle into a shank. It was a lot easier in those older jails to sharpen a piece of metal because the walls were usually some kind of hard, rough stone, like granite, rather than the smoother concrete block of today's jails and prisons. It probably took him less than a half hour to make that spoon into a nasty weapon.

Once he had the shank made, Zagorski hid it under his mattress and then started making a lot of noise and complaining about having an awful earache. The county guards took him down to their infirmary where a nurse put ointment in his ear, stuffed it with cotton to keep the ointment in and put a piece of adhesive tape across the ear to hold the cotton in place. After they took Zagorski back to his cell, he took the piece of tape off his ear and used it to tape the shank in the hollow of his back between his shoulder blades.

Meanwhile, Vic and Throckmorton were waiting outside of the jail in the state car, unaware of all of this going on inside. The state transport cars, like the police cars of that era, had no inside handles on the back seat doors, but there was nothing—no Plexiglas shield, no screen—between the front and back seats. Since inmates were almost always transported with their hands handcuffed in front of them, prison officials figured this was secure enough. Today, in addition to the wire mesh screens between front and back seats in the cars and vans, prisoners are usually handcuffed with their hands behind their backs, even for short trips to county jails, especially if they're thought to be prone to violence.

After Zagorski had been sentenced, Vic and Throckmorton went into the jail to get him for the trip back to the prison. The two officers put the handcuffs on Zagorski, loaded him into the car and prepared to head to Newark to pick up two parole violators and take them back to Trenton. While the two officers were putting Zagorski into the car, he made an elaborate show of having a painful earache and kept his shackled hands cupped around his "bad" ear.

When the two officers got to Newark, they picked up two parole violators, Francis Finney and James Barton, and put them in the back seat, with Zagorski sitting behind Vic, who was in the front passenger seat. They started south on U.S. Route 1 and Zagorski kept moaning about his earache while keeping his hands up around his ear, working the ointment out of his ear and spreading it on his wrists. Because his wrists were so big, the cuffs weren't clamped down real tight, and by the time they had gotten down to Raritan Township near New Brunswick, Zagorski was able to work them off with the help of the ointment. All of a sudden, Zagorski reached over the back seat and pushed the point of the shank into the front of Vic's throat, in the hollow spot under the Adam's apple.

Zagorski told Vic to give up his revolver and pass it back to him. Meanwhile, the two other cons were sitting there, amazed at all of this. Nobody knows for sure exactly what happened next, but the story that made the rounds of the tables in the officers' dining room the next day was that when Throckmorton looked over and saw the shank at Vic's throat, he made a fateful decision: he slammed on the brakes. This was 1951 and cars didn't have seat belts, so, according to the story we heard, when Throckmorton hit the brakes hard, Vic flew forward and the shank plunged into his throat. As the car came to a stop on the shoulder of the road, Zagorski lunged across the seat back and was trying to pull Vic's gun out of the holster.

When he couldn't free Vic's gun, Zagorski slashed Throckmorton in the stomach, trying to disable him. As heavy traffic rolled by on Route 1, Throckmorton scrambled out of the driver's side door to get clear of the vehicle so that he could draw his weapon, a .38 caliber police revolver. Zagorski saw that without Vic's gun, he was in big trouble, so he clambered over Vic's unconscious, bleeding body, opened the passenger-side door and started running out into a field, heading for a small wooded area.

By this time Throckmorton had gotten clear of the vehicle, pulled out his gun and fired five shots at Zagorski. One shot hit George in the back of his left knee, but he managed to make it to the edge of the woods. Meanwhile, the two guys from Newark are sitting quietly in the car, watching amazed as this real-life scene from a movie is unfolding in front of them. A couple of truck drivers saw what was happening, pulled over onto the shoulder and started chasing Zagorski while Throckmorton, who was bleeding from the stomach wound, went back to the car to try to help Vic.

Township police and an ambulance came screaming to the scene, and while Vic was being loaded onto a stretcher, Zagorski, seeing the woods surrounded, gave up to the local police without a struggle. Vic and Throckmorton were taken to Middlesex General Hospital in New Brunswick while Zagorski was transported to the police station for questioning by Middlesex County prosecutors. After they had gotten his story, he was also taken to the hospital for treatment of the gunshot wound. In the meantime, Vic had died at the hospital from shock and loss of blood, but nobody told Zagorski about Vic's death.

The next day, Middlesex County arraigned Zagorski, and when the judge told him that Vic was dead, Zagorski's knees almost buckled; he grabbed the table and said, "Killed, Judge?"

Both *The New York Times* and Trenton *Evening Times* clippings that Ginny sent me said that Zagorski plunged the knife several times into Vic's neck and back in a vicious attack from behind. The word around the prison, though, was that when Throckmorton saw the shank in Zagorski's hand, he slammed on the brakes and Vic flew forward onto the shank. Zagorski's reaction when the judge told him the next day that Vic had died—his knees buckling—seem to corroborate the version making the rounds in the prison. If Zagorski had plunged the knife into Vic's back and neck, why would he be surprised when the judge told him that Vic was dead?

Middlesex County brought Zagorski to trial on a first-degree murder charge. Of course he was convicted, but when the jury came back with the verdict, they also recommended mercy, which automatically meant no death sentence for Zagorski. All of the guards at the prison and people in the law enforcement community were stunned—after all, the guy was a cop killer, and in those days, you just didn't kill cops. I was later told by a couple of other guards that during the trial one of the female jurors had fallen in love with the young, handsome, well-built Zagorski, and she held out for mercy. The jury was deadlocked on the death sentence and a unanimous vote was required, so Zagorski got life, tacked onto his armed robbery sentences.

When I got back from the army and was working in the mailroom, a young woman regularly came to visit Zagorski and brought him food packages and gifts.

As I got to know Zagorski's "girlfriend," a pleasant, attractive, slightly heavy blonde, she told me she had been on the jury during Zagorski's trial, so I always assumed she was the holdout for mercy. She visited regularly for a while; then, the intervals between visits got longer and longer, and finally she stopped coming altogether.

When Zagorski came back from Middlesex County after the trial, he went immediately into the hole on a charge of assaulting an officer. He was locked in a cell in the flats in the 1-left lockup wing for the standard ten days of bread and water, and then he was moved upstairs onto a tier where he spent the next 14 years locked in a cell 22 hours per day.

Back then, there was a law that said that all inmates, even the guys in lockup, had to be allowed the opportunity to work (at 25 cents per day). One of the few jobs available to inmates in lockup was Braille work because it could be done in isolation. The inmate was given a small awl, a set of instructions and either heavy paper or a pile of cards, depending on what he was making. I remember in the 1960's when I was 1-left officer watching Zagorski make Braille bingo cards and being amazed at how fast he could turn them out. Over time, Zagorski became one of the more respected inmates (by the other inmates) in the jail. The officers always despised him for murdering Vic, and I knew several who would have killed him if they could have gotten at him. By the time Zagorski became eligible for parole in the 1970's, he had developed a reputation for two things: the best Braille worker in the jail and an outstanding hooch-maker.

Throckmorton eventually achieved the rank of lieutenant before he retired. He never talked about the incident—I always had the feeling that he thought the other guards held him partly responsible for Vic's death.

Zagorski did about twenty-five years for the robberies and Vic's murder, got paroled, and then came back within a few months on a new armed robbery charge. Those years of being in prison hadn't taught him a thing—he was now in his late forties and he still wanted to be a thief. Being back in jail took its toll on him, and he was ultimately given a medical release because of his age (mid-sixties) and bad health. He died shortly after being released.

Here's a guy who spends his entire adult life, except for maybe a few months, in a rat-hole of a prison while another guy dies at the age of twenty-five, leaving a young, grieving widow. What a waste.

* * * * * * *

About a year after Vic's murder, in April of 1952 while I was still in the service, Ginny sent me more clippings that made start to rethink my career choice. Something must have been in the water or the air in New Jersey in1952 because it was a banner year for prison riots, with three major uprisings at Trenton and one at Rahway. It got so bad that the state's institutions commissioner, Sanford Bates, finally agreed to let the Osborne Association, a national penological welfare society, come in and report on conditions. This was five years after New Jersey Governor Alfred Driscoll made headlines in 1947 by ordering Trenton State Prison torn down and the land converted to parking lots for state employees. Driscoll said the prison was "hopelessly antiquated and inadequate." Every governor since Driscoll has made that same pledge when a disturbance hit the prison and guess what. It's still there. Behind the red brick facade of the new section, the old Egyptian prison still sits back there, housing 900 hardened criminals under the same conditions that have been causing problems for the last 150 years.

When I got the newspaper clippings from Ginny, I found myself sitting in Germany and looking at front-page photographs of guys that I worked with, like Albert Moon and Oris Robison. One day, I opened one of Ginny's letters with the clippings and staring back at me from page one of the Trenton *Times* was a guy I would get to know well eight years later—"Prison Riot Ringleader" August Bernard Doak.

Barney Doak, was a small, quiet guy, about five feet, six, maybe 130-140 pounds. When I went into the army, he was in his early thirties and had spent a good part of his life in jail. While he was in Trenton, he had already spent a fair amount of time in lockup for a couple of reasons. One was that he had disarmed and kidnapped a New Jersey state trooper—a definite no-no in any era. The other was that when he first came in, he had been identified as a potential ringleader and trouble-maker. He would live up to his potential in the '52 riots.

When I was hired in 1950, Doak had been in Trenton for four years after being convicted of kidnapping the trooper in 1946. Doak was from Michigan and while he was living in Detroit, he was supposed to have been a member of the notorious Purple Gang (giving him a large measure of respect in Trenton). He was doing time at the South Michigan Penitentiary in 1945 but escaped in September of that year and started on a cross-country trek that ultimately bought him accommodations in TSP's lockup wing.

Doak made his way from Michigan to Nashville, Tennessee and got a job there as a handyman at the House of the Good Shepherd, a—get this—girls' detention home. While he was working there and hiding out, he met a16-year-old resident, Constance Blondell. She was from New York City but had run away from home at age 13 and married a sailor. She was in the detention center because her parents couldn't control her.

Doak and Blondell took off from Nashville, stole a car and worked their way up to Elkton, Maryland by stealing cash out of the registers in motels and service stations. Somewhere along the line, Doak bought a pistol and stuck it in the glove compartment. When they got to Elkton, the happy couple got married, even though Doak still had a wife, Mabel, back in Detroit (Blondell's brief marriage to the sailor had been annulled because of her age).

After the ceremony, Doak and his child-bride continued toward New York, planning to visit Blondell's parents. As they were driving on Old York Road through Bradley Gardens in New Jersey, state trooper George Kell was patrolling the area on his motorcycle. Spotting Doak and Blondell, he pulled them over for a routine motor vehicle check. Doak told Kell that his driver's license was in the trunk, and as Kell walked toward the rear of the car, Doak took off.

Kell jumped on his motorcycle and pursued the car, pulling alongside; Doak flicked the steering wheel to the left and knocked Kell off the cycle. Doak grabbed the pistol out of the glove compartment, jumped out of the car and covered the stunned trooper. While Doak held his gun on Kell, Blondell took the officer's service revolver. The two then forced Kell into the car at gunpoint and headed south, down into Hunterdon County.

Doak started to get worried that the trooper would be noticed in the back seat of the car as they drove through the rural countryside, so when they got to Pleasant Run, Doak stopped the car.

"You're too much trouble," Doak told the officer. "Take off your shirt. I'm wanted, and I can't have you on my hands."

Doak forced the trooper out of the car at gunpoint, but instead of taking off his shirt, Kell kicked Doak in the groin and took off running for a nearby wooded area. Blinded by pain, Doak fired five shots at the trooper but missed.

Doak jumped back into the car, and he and Blondell sped south into the Sourland Mountains around Hopewell, near where the Lindbergh baby had been kidnapped. After he watched Doak speed away, Kell made his way to a farmhouse and called his headquarters in Sommerville. They had already been alerted by a woman who had seen Kell fall from the motorcycle back in Bridgewater, so two troops of state police, eighty officers, were on the road, searching for Doak, Kell and Blondell.

Doak ran a roadblock on Route 69 (now Route 31) near Hopewell and then jumped out of the still-moving car, abandoning it and his bride. Troopers captured Blondell as Doak scrambled away in a panic. Several hours later, trooper Louis Masin, who had been detailed to watch the Hopewell railroad bridge in the same patch of woods that had been combed in the search for the Lindbergh baby, spotted Doak walking along the railroad tracks, carrying Kell's service revolver. Masin crept up behind Doak and told him to drop the gun and surrender. Doak complied and within a few months he was in Trenton, serving a life sentence for kidnapping and attempted murder. The kidnapping plus the attempt to shoot Kell was Doak's ticket straight into lockup when he got to prison.

Whenever I would talk to Doak in later years while he was doing time in 1-left lockup for his role in the '52 riots, I found it hard to believe that this quiet little guy could be such a terror. I guess the old saying about a gun in your hand being the great equalizer was true in his case.

* * * * * * *

I got back to the prison from my tour of duty in January of 1953, and the other guards filled me in on the action in the '52 riots. The first disturbance started on the third shift at about 1:30 a.m. March 30, 1952 when an inmate in 5-wing complained of being sick, and a hospital orderly came into the wing to look at him. The orderly told the inmate that he wasn't seriously ill and to wait for sick call in the morning.

Other prisoners then started yelling, "Don't let him die, don't let him die here!"

At the time of the riot, the most destructive in the history of the prison, 5-wing was still being used as the segregation unit for the most dangerous convicts—

lockup. Barney Doak was in there, along with Jimmy Wilburn, who, the previous November, had punched Warden William H. Carty, breaking his jaw, and George Zagorski, who had killed Vic.

Once the riot had gotten up a full head of steam, it became apparent that putting the bad boys in 5-wing had not been a good idea. That wing, built in 1867, was designed as a special unit for women (they had long ago been transferred to their own prison in Clinton), and the bars and other furnishings had been constructed of lighter materials than the other wings. Thus, the toughest guys in the prison had no problem tearing the wing apart, yanking out toilets and sinks, and ripping apart iron-pipe bed frames. They made weapons out of newspapers soaked in water and wrapped in lengths of torn-out electrical wire.

The Trenton Police with 12-guage shotguns and state police and prison guards with automatic weapons stood guard in the streets around the prison as the Trenton Fire Department was called in to pour water into the wing. Since 5-wing is just on the other side of the east wall—the front of the prison—the fire department was able to put its ladders up against the wall and pour 1,500 gallons per minute into the wing through the broken windows on the east side of the building. Warden Carty was determined to keep injuries to a minimum, so he decided to play a wait-and-see game rather than giving orders to storm the wing.

At about 8 o'clock in the evening of March 31, Warden Carty got tired of waiting. He ordered the ten revolving ventilators on the roof of the three-story wing removed and tear gas grenades dropped into the cell block. The lack of electricity, heat and food, combined with the cold nights, and the water had worn down the rebels. The gas drove the last thirty holdouts down toward the door closest to center where they talked for about fifteen minutes through the door with Warden Carty. The inmates asked for some drinking water, and after several pitchers were passed through to them, they surrendered, filing one by one into center under the glare of a temporary spotlight; they gave up after holding out for 46 hours.

When the first disturbance ended, several of the ringleaders were transferred to Rahway, a move that angered the Trenton inmates and set the stage for the next disturbance. Just two weeks after the end of the first riot, on Monday, April 14, Barney Doak and a couple of others started another riot in the print shop, and 68 inmates took two guards and two civilian instructors hostage. The rioters barricaded themselves in the print shop building in the yard off the southwest end of 4-wing near the exterior wall that runs along Second Street. The major complaint in this flare-up was parole. The inmates wanted more consideration from the parole board and the right to address the board during the hearings.

This time, Commissioner Bates got involved with the negotiations because one of the inmates' demands was the removal of Warden Carty, a former guard who had worked his way up the administrative ladder. (Mrs. Ryan, the lady who was the secretary for all of the wardens in the '40's and '50's, never liked Carty because of his roughness. "He's so crude," she would tell me. "When he talks about 'contra-band,' he says, 'counterband.'" She would imitate Carty, talking out of the side of mouth like a tough guy, "'We gotta stop all the counterband from gittin' into this here institution.'" Then she would say, "I do wish that man would learn to speak properly.")

In addition to Doak, the other ringleader was William Dickens, who told Commissioner Bates, "We're sacrificing for what we want. We're outlaws from the word go. We're the scum of society."

Dickens also said to Bates, "Why don't you suspend Carty? We're not asking for no hotel. Give us the same thing they have in the federal prisons."

Other inmates later said that when they wanted to end the mutiny, Doak and Dickens threatened them with weapons made out of cutting blades torn off some of the printing equipment. Doak had never impressed me as a dangerous man, maybe because he wasn't a big guy—about five-foot, six, maybe 130 pounds soaking wet—but the fact that he had kidnapped a state trooper and fired five shots at him should have told me something. The strange twist here was that Doak had managed to get transferred out of lockup some time the previous year, so he wasn't in 5-wing when that riot kicked off. As a result of his role in the print shop riot, when it was over he was put into the new lockup in 1-left where I would get to know him and where he would eventually go nuts.

As the two sides negotiated in '52, Doak and Dickens gave Bates a list of complaints; some of them were standard—lousy food, not enough consideration during parole hearings. But a few of the grievances, which were made public by the Osborne Association, showed the outside world just how bad Trenton was:

Beatings—Dickens complained that three of the men who had been ringleaders in the first riot had been beaten so badly when they got to the isolation wing that they had to be hospitalized. The administration's response was, "We had to get them out of there (5-wing)."

The Hole—Dickens claimed that Trenton was the only prison in the country that still maintained a solitary confinement unit where the "toilet" was a hole in the floor and rats could come up into the cells. He also said that the prison was still using the same straw-type mattresses "that they used in 1835."

"The Baldy"—Dickens also claimed that Trenton was the only prison in the country that was still shaving the heads of new inmates.

Whether Dickens' claim that Trenton was the only prison in the country that still had these "features" is debatable, but there's no denying that what he said is totally accurate.

After three days of tense negotiations, the Trenton situation started to wind down. One of the hostages was Oris Robison, who had a history of heart trouble. During the second night of the takeover, Robison began complaining of chest pains. In the meantime, a couple of officers had managed to work their way into the loft over the print shop and had set up a microphone that was picking up everything being said in the shop below. Prison officials listened in while the inmates argued for almost five hours before agreeing to release Robison. Finally, the inmates phoned one of the administration negotiators, state institutions deputy commissioner Lovell Bixby, and said, "Robi is sick. We're willing to let him out through the window."

A couple of inmates held Robison under the armpits and lowered him from a six-foot-high window into the arms of three officers in the yard. He was able to walk out of the prison under his own power and later recovered. Concerned by the possibility of Robison dying and opening them up to charges of manslaughter, the inmates were coming to terms when word came in from forty miles to the north—Rahway, New Jersey's other maximum-security prison, had exploded!

Some of the leaders of the first Trenton riot had been transferred to Rahway and through that prison's grapevine helped engineer a sympathy revolt by a couple of hundred minimum-security inmates in one of the dormitories. Some of the inmates at Rahway and a couple of guards were slightly injured in the first hour or so of that uprising. Word also got back to Trenton that inmates were planning to set fires down at Leesburg Farm, a minimum security facility about 90 miles southeast of Trenton, down in Salem County. For a while it looked like the whole adult male prison system was in trouble. Nothing happened at Leesburg, though, and prison authorities concentrated on ending the Trenton and Rahway riots. Halfway into the fourth day, on Friday afternoon, the Trenton inmates gave up quietly and released the remaining three hostages. The Rahway uprising was also settled peaceably after four days of negotiations.

Then, in October of 1952, the third and potentially most dangerous disturbance flared up at Trenton. This one started in 7-wing, a 350-man cell block that faced onto Third Street and, after it was built in 1905-1907, formed a part of the front wall of the prison. Warden Carty was out of town when this one kicked off, and assistant warden Lloyd McCorkle planned and led the assault that ended this one quickly and violently.

Dr. Lloyd McCorkle was an interesting man. First of all, he looked like "Boston Blackie," a radio and movie detective out of the 1930's and '40's. He was slim and always impeccably dressed, even during prison riots. And he had one of those little well-trimmed mustaches that made him look even more distinguished in his tailored three-piece suits. The word around the jail was that during World War II McCorkle had been in charge of several prison camps in the states and overseas, and we knew he was highly regarded in the corrections field both in the U.S. and abroad. Later, when he became warden, he was away from the prison a lot, attending conferences all over the world and lecturing on penology and corrections. In general, the officers liked McCorkle because he didn't believe in "coddling" the inmates. Whenever there was a disturbance while he was in charge, it usually ended quickly.

A few minutes after 6 p.m. on October 12 all of the inmates had gone back to 7-wing after supper and were waiting to be locked in their cells for the night. One of the guys in the flats said he wanted to get a magazine from another inmate before the cell doors were secured. Vince Dawson, a guard who was in his early sixties, started down toward the inmate to tell him to get into his cell. Suddenly, Dawson was jumped by two other inmates with knives who had slipped out of their cells behind his back after he had gone by. Dawson said one of the convicts put a knife to his throat while the other guy shoved one in his back, took his keys and yanked his whistle off his uniform. Then they shoved him into a cell. Other inmates on tiers 2 and 3, when they saw what was happening, grabbed two other younger guards, Dennis Dunscombe and Paul Clayton, for hostages. The convicts then ran down the wing corridor to the end that connects to center. They piled tables, chairs, garbage cans and anything else they could pry loose to form a solid barricade between them and the rest of the prison.

Vince Dawson said that after the barricade went up, the three inmates who had lured him into the trap climbed up onto some refuse piled up under one of the high windows facing out onto Third Street and started cutting the bars on the windows with hacksaw blades that they had kept hidden in their cells. The blades weren't sharp enough, and after a few minutes they stopped sawing and tossed the blades away in disgust.

Meanwhile, Dr. McCorkle had been called and arrived at the prison. He mobilized the rest of the second-shift guards, called in officers from other shifts and had the armory officer hand out the Thompson submachine guns. McCorkle yelled through the barred entrance to 7-wing, ordering the inmates to dismantle the barricade and surrender. They yelled back, refusing, and saying they wanted the ringleaders of the April riots to be let out of lockup. McCorkle ordered two guards to stick the muzzles of the .45-caliber machine guns through the openings in the barred door leading into the wing and to fire short bursts over the heads of the rioters.

Those old Thompsons with the drum magazines were tough to control. When the lever was flipped to the "automatic" position and the trigger pressed, the weapon took on a life of its own—it instantly pulled itself up and to the right as the burst of six or eight slugs left the muzzle. As often happens in these situations, the inmates who got hurt—hit by ricocheting bullets—weren't even involved in the disturbance. They were only watching when the guards fired. John Dunphy got a serious wound in the chest and Al Visintins a superficial hit in the hand.

A couple of the ringleaders told Vince Dawson to yell out to the other officers to stop the shooting, but at that point Dr. McCorkle had given the order to force the barricades, and as the debris was pushed aside and the officers rushed into the wing, the rioters lost their nerve and surrendered.

As all of the action was going on inside the prison, city cops and state police from the West Trenton barracks patrolled the streets outside. The Trenton Fire Department also stood by in case they were needed as they had been in the April riots. This one was the last disturbance in a record year for riots at Trenton State Prison.

* * * * * * *

When I got out of the service and came back to Trenton, I proposed to Ginny. The army and being away from home had matured me, and I was ready to settle down. Ginny was a Protestant from a family of English ancestry and I was an Italian Catholic. Inter-faith marriages were a much bigger issue back then than they are now, especially for Catholics.

My family lived less than a block away from the yard of the prison. (As a kid in the summertime, my buddies and I used to hang around the outside of the wall, waiting for an inmate to hit a home run during their ball games. Then we'd run over and grab the ball and take off before the inmate trusty could get to it and toss it back over the wall.)

Our parish church, SS. Peter and Paul was on Second Street, almost directly across from the old colonial prison (1790's) that had been converted into the warden's house. I had been attending this church since I was a little kid and had been very active, including helping them out for years with Saturday night dances for the parish teenagers. So, naturally, after I "popped the question," I went around to see the parish priest, Father John, and asked him to marry Ginny and me. At first, he was very happy for me and congratulated me and all that, but as soon as I told Father John that Ginny wasn't a Catholic, I felt a chill enter the conversation.

Father John looked at me for a minute and then said, "Harry, why don't you go over to St. Joachim's. They do these kinds of marriages."

Boy was I ever steamed. But that's the way it was in those days, and Ginny and I were married in June of 1953 in the parsonage of the Groveville, NJ Methodist Church by the Reverend Louis Case.

The next time I would see Reverend Case, a little over a year later, he would be reading the 23rd Psalm in the death chamber at Trenton State Prison.

CHAPTER THREE

BACK TO THE WALL

As I put one institution—the U.S. Army—behind me and settled back into another one—Trenton State Prison—I went from a routine of garrison-life boredom to one of life on the edge—and I loved it.

As soon as I got back to the prison in '53, I was again assigned to center as an extra. It almost seemed like I had never left. One Saturday not long after I got back, I was assigned to SB-1 (1-tower) across Third Street from the front door of the prison. Since I was still low on the seniority list, I was working six days, including weekends, and had one day off in the middle of the week. For several months running I drew 1-tower on Saturdays to replace the guy who had it during the week. SB-1 was a circular concrete, steel and glass building about 16 feet in diameter that sat on a cement foundation about five or six feet above ground level. The tower had floor-to-ceiling bullet-proof glass panels in its front half, giving the officer a 180-degree view of the front of the prison. The back half of the tower contained a small office and a bathroom. The tower officer sat directly behind a bullet-proof glass door (closed in winter, open in summer) in an office chair facing the front of the prison with a 12-guage shotgun resting across his thighs.

The primary responsibility here was to check out any suspicious-looking characters approaching the front door; monitor traffic coming out of the prison (being especially alert for inmates walking out in civilian clothing); and scan the block-long front wall to watch for convicts coming over the top (not likely in daylight). A visitors' parking lot was to the officer's right, and people not familiar with the prison would occasionally stop by to ask about procedures for getting inside.

The first Saturday I was out there, on a chilly day toward the end of winter, I noticed a short, heavyset man in a black coat and a black hat standing in the alcove in front of the entrance door. He stood there for several minutes, and just as I was about to get up and go over to check him out, somebody came up, pushed the brass doorbell button and went inside. The man dressed in black also went in. I figured the man in black must be legitimate and had been waiting for a friend.

The next Saturday, at the same time, the man in black appeared again and stood outside the front door, waiting. I assumed he was waiting for that same person to meet him so they could go in together, but this time the door opened to let a visitor out, and the man in black slipped in through the open door. Now I was curious. This same scene was repeated for the next few weeks, usually with the man in black waiting in front of the door for several minutes and then slipping in as the door was opened to let someone out.

After about six weeks of this, on a cold, rainy Saturday, I watched as the man in black stood waiting patiently inside the alcove. Nobody came in or out, and after about ten minutes, I couldn't stand it any longer, so, shotgun in hand, I walked over and asked him if he needed any assistance.

"Ah, how kind of you," he said. "Yes, could you ring the doorbell for me?"

I'm staring at him and thinking, "What is this, a joke? He's got two arms, two hands, he's not crippled. Why the hell can't he ring the doorbell himself?"

The man in black must have seen the puzzled, or annoyed, look on my face and said, "I'm the rabbi. I'm here for services, and I'm not allowed to use any mechanical devices on the Sabbath."

"Aha," I said. "Now it makes sense."

So I pushed the button for him and walked back to my post—wet, but satisfied.

* * * * * * *

One weekday a couple of months after I got back, I was hanging around center, waiting for an assignment when the same older cop who had pointed out Charlie the Bug Workman to me a couple of years before shuffled over, nodded and said quietly out of the side of his mouth, "Look over there. See that guy, the heavyset one?"

I looked over to where he was nodding and saw another distinguished-looking older inmate, also dressed neatly in prison khakis, with a starched, pressed white shirt buttoned up to the neck. I half expected to see a necktie.

I thought to myself, "What is this? Am I in some kind of time warp? Have I really been away for two years?"

This inmate was even more distinguished-looking than Charlie Workman. I thought he was a stock broker or businessman who had gotten nailed for some kind of white-collar crime. My confidante, though, whispered that this guy was even higher on the mob ladder than Charlie—it was Joseph Anthony Doto—Joe Adonis.

"Wow!" I said. "He <u>is</u> big-time. What's he doing in here?"

The other cop told me that Adonis had pleaded "no defense" to gambling charges in the spring of 1951, just after I left for overseas, and was serving a three-year sentence in Trenton. With time off for good behavior, he was slated to get out in a few more months.

I had first heard about Joe Adonis around 1950 when he was front-page news almost every day. When I was growing up in the 1940's, everybody in my neighborhood knew about the wide-open gambling in north Jersey, especially around Lodi; we knew where to go for high-stakes poker or craps. The New York mob had set up shop in Bergen County with the apparent blessing of local cops and politicians. By the late '40's law-enforcement authorities in both states, especially Tom

Dewey in New York, had finally recognized the situation was out of hand. They started making a serious attempt to shut the gambling down. Joe Adonis and his associates, Willie and Solly Moretti, were known to be key players in organizing and running the operation.

In the early '50's J. Edgar Hoover was insisting there was no such thing as "the Mafia." Senator Estes Kefauver from Tennessee, the chairman of the Senate Crime Committee, disagreed. He held hearings in Washington aimed at proving a well-organized underworld not only existed, but had infiltrated nearly every aspect of American society. Committee investigators identified Adonis as a major racketeer in the New York/New Jersey area and tried for months to get him before the committee. Adonis always seemed to be able to slip through the net. At the time, even though I was in law enforcement, I almost admired my fellow Italian for his ability to avoid the subpoenas. As I said earlier, I never thought that what these guys were doing—the gambling part—was all that bad. After all, if somebody wanted to give his money to these guys in a card game or shooting craps, who cared? Today, after everything we've seen about how the gambling is just one piece of a much larger and far more dangerous operation, my view of the mob has changed. But even back then I wasn't naïve; I knew that these were the same guys who were involved in strong-arming the mom and pop stores in my old neighborhood for protection money. I hated them for that. But still . . . .

While I was in the army, Joe Adonis' luck finally ran out. The pressure got to him and he figured it was time to quit dodging. After more than twenty years of wheeling and dealing, dating back to Prohibition, Adonis gave in and gave up. Considering what he had managed to avoid over the years, ranging from possible murder charges to investigations by the IRS, Adonis had led a charmed life. In the 1930's New York's Mayor Fiorello LaGuardia had called Adonis "a gangster and the leader of the underworld." New York DA William O'Dwyer predicted he would put Adonis in New York State's electric chair if he could get the evidence linking Adonis to Albert Anastasia's Brooklyn-based Murder, Inc. It never happened and Adonis kept on slippin' and slidin' throughout the 1940's. Up until he came into Trenton in the spring of 1951, Adonis had spent only a few hours in jail, only enough time until his lawyer and bail bondsman could get to the jails to get him out. He had paid a total of $625 in fines, including minor busts during the Prohibition years. I have to say it—I held a grudging respect for the guy. And now, here he was, in my jail.

Seeing Adonis inside reminded of my father Ralph's line: "Harry, in Italy where I'm from, they have a statue of the best gambler in the country . . . and you know what, Harry? He's dressed in rags."

I came back to work in January of '53, and Adonis was released in August, so I didn't get to know him well. When I did get into conversations with him before his sentence was up, I found him to be soft-spoken, intelligent, charming and funny. He spoke in low tones, barely above a whisper, and sometimes, kidding around, he would talk out of the side of his mouth, like a "real" gangster. Once he told me a story about an incident back in the 1930's when a couple of reporters from the *New York Times* came into his restaurant in Brooklyn, looking for Joe Adonis. The regular bartender was sick, so Adonis was filling in behind the bar. The reporters had never seen Adonis, and they asked the "bartender" if it was true that his boss, Adonis, had a lot of clout with the New York City politicians. Adonis kept feeding the reporters free drinks and phony information until they went sailing out the door filled with booze and bullshit, still not knowing they had been talking to The Man himself.

Adonis locked in 4-wing, the "Andrew Jackson" cell block with the big dungeons. The cells in 4-wing were so big (almost 8 feet wide by 16 feet deep) that the administration usually put four men in them. Adonis, though, locked with only one other inmate, a guy who laid the boss's clothes out for him every morning and ran errands for him. Like other high-level mobsters, Adonis never ate in the mess hall—he had his man prepare his meals from the monthly food package that came in from outside. When that was used up, the valet trotted down to the side door of the mess hall to buy (with packs of cigarettes) specially prepared swag meals. What Joe Adonis wanted, he got.

Joe Adonis and his meals are a good example of two important elements of prison life: how cigarettes are used as currency and how the black market and a "go along to git along" philosophy keep things running smoothly. First, no money is allowed in most prisons. Money can be used to corrupt guards, and it can give an inmate a big jump start on the street if he can manage to escape. Therefore, the medium of exchange is packs of cigarettes (most guards aren't interested in risking their jobs or a jail term for cigarettes). Money from the outside is mailed to the prison in the form of money orders and is deposited in an inmate's account. Then the inmate is given credit in the inmate store. Any money earned through work for State Use Industries, manufacturing license plates, for example, is also deposited in the inmate's account. Cigarettes are the most commonly accepted form of "cash" and the value of all goods and services is measured in packs or cartons. Gambling is a big inmate occupation in a prison, and all debts and winnings are paid off in cigarettes.

The black market, "swag," makes life tolerable for an inmate—if he's smart enough or has enough cigarettes to wheel and deal. Take Adonis and his meals, for example. In the early part of the month when he still had supplies from the five pounds of food allowed in each month from his people on the outside, his man would cook his meals to order. Cook? In his cell? To me, this whole scene was always one of the great ironies in the jail. Back then, two of the most popular items in the inmate store were eggs and cans of Dinty Moore stew, yet no inmate was allowed to have any kind of cooking device. Adonis, like half the population, had a swag hot plate in his cell. Why wasn't it confiscated? Go along to git along.

Here's a case in point. When I was wing officer in 4-wing some years after Adonis got out, I used to let the guys hang around outside of their cells when they were supposed to be locked in for count with the understanding that as soon as they saw a sergeant coming, they would duck inside and shut the door. One day I saw a sergeant headed toward the wing, and everybody but one guy did the drill. I went over to the inmate and told him to get into his cell, and he started giving me a hard time. OK. Harry doesn't forget and Harry always gets even.

The next day when the inmate went out to the yard, I went into his cell and confiscated his hot plate. He came in from yard and said, “Hey Harry, somebody took my hot plate.”

I said to him, “You got a hot plate, man? That’s against the rules. I’m gonna have to write you up.”

Case closed.

That’s the way it works. Almost everybody, on both sides, goes along to git along.

Like Adonis and his meals. When his food package ran out, Adonis wouldn’t bother to have his man go to the inmate store to get the eggs or stew. Instead, his flunky would head down to the side door of the mess hall and come trotting back with a specially cooked breakfast of eggs, bacon and toast for the boss. The civilian cook who runs the kitchen knows what’s going on, but why make an issue of it? What’s a few eggs and some bread—produced inside the system by State Use Industries—to keep the inmate cooks happy because they can pick up a couple of packs and to keep on the good side of a big-deal inmate like Adonis? Who knows when a little debt like that might come in handy? Then the flunky would go on down to the bakery and pick up a couple of pastries especially ordered by Adonis. What’s a little dough and some extra sugar? Who cares?

The same system that got him his specially prepared meals kept Adonis looking good, even in prison khakis. His pants were pressed with a sharp crease, and his white shirts were starched and crisp-looking; a couple of packs each week to the guys who worked in the laundry made sure of that. He also visited the inmate barber shop regularly. He always kept himself fed and looking like the don he was supposed to be.

Throughout the early ’50’s the Kefauver committee hammered away at organized crime, and Adonis was front-page news almost every day for weeks at a time. The year before I got back from Germany, in 1952, the U.S. Department of Justice started going after organized crime with a vengeance. Totally frustrated in their efforts to prosecute these guys because of the reluctance of witnesses to testify—for obvious reasons—the Justice Department decided to try a different tack: they reasoned that most of the mobsters were immigrants into the U.S. So Justice started going after the gangsters as undesirable aliens—even if they had become U.S. citizens. Justice attorneys found that several of the older Mafiosi had criminal convictions in Italy before coming to America and had lied on their immigration applications. Using that as leverage, Justice expanded the interpretation of the immigration laws and went after other non-native-born gangsters based upon their activities in this country.

Because Adonis was in the news so often, I sometimes cut out newspaper stories about him and filed them away. (A lot of us, guards and inmates, kept newspaper-clipping scrapbooks about inmates we had known who went on to become famous.) This is an excerpt from a *New York Times* article about Adonis from February 20, 1953:

Deportation Writ Issued for Adonis Marks Hoodlum's 3d Blow in Week

Washington, Feb. 20—The Department of Justice issued a warrant today for the deportation of Joe Adonis, the reputed czar of a former multi-million-dollar gambling operation in Bergen County, N.J.

The move was the third legal roadblock thrown this week in the path of the soft-spoken former Brooklyn hoodlum who had enjoyed a twenty-five-year rise to affluence, political ties and high rank in the underworld.

The warrant will be served on Adonis tomorrow at the New Jersey State Prison in Trenton, where he is serving a two-to-three-year term for operating dice games.

On Tuesday Adonis was convicted of contempt of Congress during the Senate investigation of organized crime and sentenced to serve three months in Federal prison. And on Wednesday he was indicted for perjury before a Bergen County grand jury investigating waterfront racketeering and gambling.

The deportation action apparently was another step in the campaign begun last year by former Attorney General James P. McGranery to rid the country of aliens and naturalized citizens who were prominent in underworld operations. The Government contends that Adonis, whose real name is Joseph Doto, was born in Italy and not in New Jersey, as he claims.

When the U.S. Attorney General started the campaign in 1952 to get rid of the Italian-born Mafiosi identified by the Kefauver hearings, Joe Adonis was a primary target, along with Albert Anastasia of Murder, Inc., Lucky Luciano, Vito Genovese and a slew of other prominent New York City/New Jersey mobsters.

Adonis's two-to-three-year sentence was nothing compared to the time most of the guys in Trenton were doing. If he had been anyone else, he would have been long gone from the prison when I got back from the Army in January '53 because he was a model prisoner who worked and never got into any trouble. But because the state and feds were putting so much heat on organized crime and their gambling operations in New Jersey, they used parole to put pressure on Adonis to cooperate. Joe Adonis was potentially a vital witness in a bribery case against another guy whose name actually was Adonis—an aide to Governor Alfred Driscoll named Harold Adonis. The Republican state chairman said he had information that Harold Adonis had been paid over a quarter million dollars by mobsters to provide protection for their gambling interests and that Joe Adonis was involved. So the parole board, despite his work record and his good behavior, said they were going to make Adonis do his full sentence, meaning he wouldn't get out until August of 1953.

Meanwhile, by April of '53, I had managed to con my way into the job in the mailroom out in the front house, working with Adam Menkerell, so I got a first-hand look at the government's efforts to get Adonis. The U.S. Immigration Department held hearings at the prison and brought a lot of witnesses in to testify why Adonis should be deported. Adam and I were kept busy checking these people in and out of the jail. I also got a look at how the mob takes care of its own. "The boys" figured that Adonis would be getting out in April, so they sent him a coming-out present—a $700 camel hair coat.

Are you kidding me? I had never even seen a coat like that, even in the windows of the best men's shops in Trenton, much less being able to touch one.

I don't know for sure that the coat cost $700, but that was the figure commonly tossed around by guards and inmates who saw it. It was a topic of conversation for weeks. That coat would probably cost well over $2,000 in today's dollars. I figured I would have had to work for about four months to afford something like that.

Adonis finally completed his full sentence in August and the state had to release him (in prison terms, he "maxed out"). After he got out of Trenton in 1953, Adonis continued to be front-page copy for the next couple of years. The immigration service made its case against him and ordered Adonis out of the country, but meanwhile he had other sentences hanging over him. Wrangling about who had jurisdiction over him and which sentences he should serve first, along with his own appeals, delayed his departure for a couple of years. Finally Adonis was forced to admit that he had lied about being born in America. To avoid more jail time being tacked on for perjury, he agreed to leave the country by January of 1956. After that, I lost track of him.

I can't say that I admired Adonis, but I respected him for the way he carried himself and the way he did his time—especially compared to somebody like the "Teflon Don," John Gotti, or his son. Whenever I read something in the papers about today's top mobsters, I always remember the one I knew—one with a lot more class—Joe Adonis.

P.S. In case I sound like I condone everything these guys were doing, Willie Moretti was gunned down in a gangland hit in 1951 and Solly Moretti died at the age of 47 in 1952 in the hospital at Trenton State Prison. Albert Anastasia never made it to the deportation hearings before he was gunned down in a barber's chair, so I never had any regrets about taking my father's advice about staying away from gambling (well, maybe just the number or the guards' football pool every once in a while).

****

I had been in the mailroom for about a year, in April of 1954, when an inmate named George Vaszorich made a desperate attempt to cheat the executioner and managed to escape from death row. He was stopped in his tracks, literally, by one of the toughest cops I ever knew, Captain Alexander Abbott.

When I was hired in 1950, Warden Page had introduced me to Captain Abbott, and I knew then that this was one tough character. He was six feet tall, lean and hard with a little paunch, red-faced and mean looking. He almost never smiled. Abbott earned the name he was to be known by until he retired, "Machine Gun" Abbott, when he shot Vaszorich off the roof of the laundry. The incident caused a nasty backlash among the administrators in the division of corrections (which really surprised me), and it almost cost Abbott and several other officers their jobs.

In the long history of the prison's death house, only three people managed to break out. In 1922 Guildford Young, a 28-year-old from Camden, climbed up a hot steam pipe to a skylight and made it to the roof, but he was captured there and executed as scheduled September 5, 1922. The only one who made it over the wall was Jack (Peg Leg) Gordon, who escaped in 1926; he was captured several years later but died of tubercular meningitis before he could be executed.

The third was George Vaszorich, a 21-year-old from Ocean Grove who, in December, 1951, had been convicted of killing a 60-year-old retired tavern owner with a claw hammer during a robbery in Wayside, Monmouth County. Vaszorich and his two partners, who admitted to 15 burglaries in the two months preceding the murder, had gotten $300 in the Wayside robbery/murder. The two partners were given life sentences, but Vaszorich was identified as the killer and sentenced to death. Vaszorich, only 18 years old when he was sentenced, had avoided execution for three years through appeals to the state courts and the U.S. Supreme Court.

Most trouble in a prison occurs during the second shift (in Trenton, from 2:20 p.m. to 10:20 p.m.). Because of the seniority system, the most experienced officers choose to be on first shift; and because of activities, work and yard, more officers are on duty from 6 a.m. to 3 p.m. Third shift is relatively quiet since almost all (except for kitchen duty) inmates are locked in and sleeping in their cells. So second shift officers need to be especially alert.

Around 6 p.m. on Sunday, April 10, 1954, Vaszorich called out to death house officer John Van Note and, according to accounts in the local papers, asked for a couple of aspirins because he had a headache. Standard death house procedures at the time for that kind of request required the officer to order the inmate to the back of the cell while the officer placed the requested material on the horizontal flat bar midway up the cell door. Van Note testified at the inquiry the next day that he let Vaszorich stay near the cell door while he, Van Note, put the aspirins on the door. Van Note said that as soon as he put the aspirins down, Vaszorich grabbed his arm through the bars, spun him around and stuck a knife fashioned from a metal chair bracket into the middle of his back.

Then Vaszorich said, "I'll stab you if you call out. I'm here for one murder and I wouldn't worry about another one. It's a choice between being electrocuted or taking my chances with being shot."

Vaszorich quickly wrapped strips of torn bed sheet around Van Note's arms and tied him to the bars of the cell. Then he called out to two other death row convicts, Joe Grillo and Silvio DeVita, to help him. Grillo and DeVita were both about the same age as Vaszorich and were scheduled to be executed in two weeks, the same week as Vaszorich. They had been convicted and sentenced to death for killing James Law, an off-duty Newark cop moonlighting as a security guard, in a holdup attempt at a supermarket.

Grillo took the long handle of the mop that was standard issue in all of the death row cells and pushed it through the bars, hooking Van Note's desk by one leg. He then slid the desk over to his cell and managed to work it around so that he could get access to the drawers. Here was Van Note's second mistake: he had put pliers and a screwdriver in one of the drawers. Grillo was two cells away from Vaszorich, so after he got the tools out of the drawer, he passed them to DeVita who gave them to Vaszorich. With Van Note bound to the bars, Vaszorich worked for about two hours on the cell door lock while the other death row inmates played their radios loud, sang and bounced their iron bed frames off the floor. Nobody came to investigate the noise. This is where officers other than Van Note were to get in trouble when the inquiry board was immediately convened the next morning: why hadn't center raised an alarm when Van Note didn't check in each half hour, as required; why hadn't anyone investigated the noise (though death row was quite a ways away from the center of the prison); but most important, why hadn't the officer in the tower that overlooked the death house roof reported anything out of the ordinary? Nine-tower, overlooking the truck gate and sally port, was connected to the death house by a catwalk, and there was a skylight in the death house roof so that the 9-tower officer could walk along the catwalk and look down into the wing, which he was required to do periodically. None of this happened that night.

After a couple of hours, Vaszorich managed to pry the metal plate off the lock on his cell door and then force open the mechanism. Holding his homemade knife, he pushed open the door, forcing Van Note back. Then he went over to the wooden pegs on the wall where officers hung their jackets near the door to the outside and grabbed Van Note's jacket and hat. He figured that if his escape attempt was discovered before he could make it to the wall, he might be able to mingle among the other guards during the confusion until he could come up with an alternate plan.

Moving quickly back into the middle of the cell block, Vaszorich passed the tools back to DeVita, who started working on his lock. Vaszorich then grabbed the keys to the death house doors out of another drawer in the desk. This was yet another breach of prison security rules, but it really wasn't Van Note's fault—all of the death house guards had been ignoring the rules for years. Officially, at the end of each shift, the death row guard being relieved was supposed to lock the relieving guard in the wing and take the door keys to the guard in 9-tower. This was a long hike, and over the years everybody who had death house duty ignored the procedure and just tossed the keys into the desk drawer until the end of the shift.

It was now well after 9 p.m. and dark, overcast and cold outside as Vaszorich opened the death house door leading out to the small open yard space near the execution chamber and started working his way toward the east wall of the prison. Meanwhile, after about 25 minutes, while Grillo and DeVita were still working on the locks on their cell doors, VanNote managed to work his way free of the strips of bed sheet and hit the alarm button. More than a dozen guards rushed to the death house and Van Note told them what had happened. Warden McCorkle was in Sweden attending an international penology conference, so acting Warden Howard Yeager was called in, and he and about 20 guards armed with 12-guage shotguns started frantically searching the prison grounds, looking for Vaszorich. Warden Yeager ordered all of the tower searchlights turned on, and they started sweeping the rooftops and yards.

Since Yeager wasn't sure that Vaszorich was still inside the prison compound, the state police broadcast a state-wide alarm for the inmate while Trenton police searched through the streets and neighborhoods around the prison. At about 11:30 p.m. Bill Young, one of the tower guards sweeping the rooftops with a searchlight spotted Vaszorich hugging the roof of the one-story laundry building about forty feet from the east wall. Vaszorich had thought he could jump from the roof of the laundry to the top of the twenty-foot wall, but when he got on the roof, he discovered the wall was much too far away.

When the sweeping light stopped on him, Vaszorich knew that he had been spotted, so he stood straight up. Since he was wearing a prison guard's uniform, he figured he could act like he was supposed to be up there and bluff his way out. Young wasn't fooled—he leveled his shotgun at Vaszorich and ordered him to surrender.

Vaszorich stood up and yelled at Young, "You can't hit the side of a barn," and took off running for the other end of the laundry roof. Young fired a blast, hitting Vaszorich with several 00 pellets. Assistant Warden Yeager and Captain Abbott were now in the yard near the laundry. Yeager yelled for Vaszorich to surrender and come down. He refused.

Yeager repeated his order and again Vaszorich refused, so Yeager shouted, "We'll shoot you if you don't come down."

Vaszorich looked like he was turning to run again, so Abbott raised his .45 caliber Thompson submachine gun and fired a nine-shot burst. Seven of the slugs hit Vaszorich in the chest, stomach and groin, and he collapsed onto the roof. As other guards rushed toward the laundry building with ladders, one of the older guys, Alonzo Lanphear, a tower guard who had just reported in for duty, collapsed and died of a heart attack.

Vaszorich was carried down from the roof and taken to the prison hospital where he was given the Last Rites; he died at about 2 a.m. Later that same morning, within hours of Vaszorich's death, Commissioner Sanford Bates convened a hearing to find out how Vaszorich had managed to get out of the death house. The panel members also wanted to know why Abbott had shot Vaszorich when the inmate was too far from the wall to get out of the prison compound. Van Note contradicted himself several times in his testimony about how Vaszorich managed to grab him. In a statement released to the press a couple of weeks after the escape attempt, Commissioner Bates said, "He [Van Note] made inconsistent statements under oath during the inquiry. He was persuaded unnecessarily to place his hands through the bars of the condemned man's cell and contends that he became bound. This precipitated the whole incident." Commissioner Bates recommended that Van Note be fired.

Scuttlebutt around the prison in the days following the incident was that Van Note and Vaszorich had been kidding around about who was putting on the most weight and Vaszorich had conned Van Note into putting both of his hands through the bars to measure Vaszorich's waist. That's how Vaszorich had been able to grab him so easily.

Bates also recommended a six-month suspension without pay for the lieutenant on duty that night in center control for not getting suspicious when Van Note didn't check in, and he ordered Abbott suspended for three months for shooting Vaszorich when he was too far inside the compound to make it to the wall.

All of the guards appealed and eight months later, in December of 1954, the state civil service commission reduced Van Note's firing to a six-month suspension without pay; the lieutenant's suspension was reduced to two months, and Abbott got 30 days without pay.

****

As Adam Menkerell and I got used to the routine in the mailroom, we found one part of the job was actually fun: checking out the inmate food packages for contraband. Back then, every inmate was allowed one five-pound food package per month, and since so many of the cons were Italian, I got to see if their moms could cook as well as mine. I also discovered that some moms will go to great lengths to take care of their boys.

In the 1950's, before drugs became so prevalent in society and in prison, the preferred high was from alcohol. In a prison, it seems like everybody and his brother makes hooch (this is still true today, even with all of the drugs coming in). One of the most sought-after jobs in the joint is working in the bakery because you can earn so many packs by stealing baker's yeast and selling it to the hooch makers. The most common routine for "the little old winemakers" is to have a steady source of yeast, cans of fruit juice from the kitchen and some other kind of fruit, like raisins or orange peels. Then they get some kind of fair-sized container, like a bucket, and a plastic garbage bag to contain the odor. Over time, the brew ferments and depending upon the talent of the manufacturer, the concoction becomes a tasty wine of about eight or nine percent alcohol. A pint of homemade wine usually goes for about five packs. But, if you can get the real thing from the outside, that's like dying and going to heaven.

One day Adam and I were going through the food packages, shooting the breeze and nonchalantly looking for contraband. It was a dull day so I was commenting on each item as I took it out of the cardboard boxes. At some point I picked up a bottle of maraschino cherries and said to Adam, "You know, Guido must have a thing for these cherries because his mama sends him a bottle every month. What in the hell does he do with them?"

Adam said, "Maybe he's putting them in his Manhattans."

We both laughed. And then I said, "You know what? These look good to me today. I think I'll take one. He'll never miss just one." I opened the jar, took out one of the cherries and put it in my mouth.

"Damn!" I said and spit it out. "This thing has gone rotten or something. It tastes sour." Then the taste hit home. The "cherry juice" was actually vodka. Each month, sweet old white-haired mom had been sending Guido his cherries swimming in a pint of booze.

A couple of weeks later, Adam and I were doing the same thing—checking out food packages—but now I was a little more alert. Another Italian inmate was getting food packages from his mom, and this particular month she had sent in a

Tupperware bowl covered by a lid that pressed down and locked over the rim on the bowl.

I pried up the lid and said to Adam, "Isn't this sweet? Mom is sending Tony a nice bowl of spaghetti sauce."

I said, "I'm Italian; therefore, I'm an expert on spaghetti sauce. Let's see if Tony's Mom can really cook."

I stuck my finger into the sauce, intending to dip out a little and taste it . . . but my finger hit something large and solid just under the surface of the thick red liquid.

I said to Adam, "Uh, oh. Mom must have put a giant meat-a-ball in the sauce. There's something solid in here."

I felt around a little more and came up with a red balloon almost the same color as the sauce. It was about the size of a fist and had something other than air in it. I took the balloon and walked across the front house lobby into the men's room. After I washed the spaghetti sauce off, I took the balloon back to the mailroom. Adam had already called the sergeant to come and check it out. The sergeant took the balloon out and had it sent to the state police lab. A few days later we heard that Mom had sent in several ounces of pure heroin to her son—a spicy meat-a-ball.

* * * * * * *

Just before Warden McCorkle was promoted into the central office (he would eventually become commissioner), some of the inmates in the tag shop decided to go on strike for a raise from the $.25 per day they were getting. I don't remember who the ringleaders were, but I sure do remember McCorkle's reaction. I never saw anyone make major decisions in the jail as quickly and decisively as he did.

As soon as McCorkle heard that the men were refusing to come out of their cells to report to work in the tag shop, he came storming out of his office and into center. He listened as Captain Abbott filled him in on what was going on, and then he walked briskly over to the neck from center into 1-wing. We had been using 1-left for lockup since the '52 riots, but the entrance into the wing was still through a big arch with a large barred door.

McCorkle said, "I want that goddamned entrance to the wing bricked closed so that there's only a small door to get in."

Captain Abbott, who had trailed along behind as McCorkle went charging across center, said, "Yes sir. We'll get a contractor and get started on it tomorrow."

"No, goddamn it!" McCorkle roared. "We have cops in here who can lay brick. And we sure as hell have enough inmates who were masons. Get those guys down here right now and get started!"

Abbott was stunned. All he could do was say, "Yes sir. I'll get right on it, sir."

Then McCorkle said, "And another thing. Get some painters in here with black paint and have them paint the windows in there black. If those sons of bitches aren't going to work, they're not going to see any sunlight for a long, long time."

As soon as the word got to the inmates in their cells, they knew McCorkle wasn't kidding around. The brick work started that afternoon, and all of the inmates were back on the job at seven o'clock the next morning. Sharp.

* * * * * * *

Toward the end of the decade, about five years after Joe Adonis was released, another mobster who would go on to make a lot of headlines came into the jail. This guy was at the opposite end of the mob spectrum from the soft-spoken, sophisticated Adonis—Harold Konigsberg was a real leg-breaking head-buster. "Kayo" Konigsberg (he was also called "Hersh") would later be described in a *Life* magazine article as "the most dangerous uncaged killer on the east coast." To this day I think of him as one of the most interesting paradoxes I've ever met in Trenton.

I say this because, first, Kayo Konigsberg was Jewish, second because he had had a short career as a pro boxer (thus the *Kayo* nickname), and third because he came from a family that had made a small fortune in construction in Bayonne. Add all of that up and you get an enigma—a Jewish strong-arm enforcer for the mob who's not in it for the money. After I got to know him, I became convinced that Kayo was involved in crime mainly for the romance of being a gangster and the thrill of rubbing elbows with other mobsters.

When I talk about Kayo, some of the stereotypes that we held in the fifties—and still do today to some extent—come out. Back then most people, me included, assumed that all Jews were smart. Kayo shot that one down in flames. And even though there had been a few great Jewish pro athletes like Hank Greenberg, Sid Luckman, Barney Ross and Benny Leonard, most people didn't connect Jews with sports, especially boxing. There had been a significant number of Jewish gangsters over the years (Dutch Schultz, Abe Reles, Louis Lepke, Bugsy Siegal, Meyer Lansky), but back in the fifties when most people thought about the mob, they thought of Italians—the Black Hand, the Mafia, La Cosa Nostra. So Harold Konigsberg stood out in a crowd (he also stood out because he was a big guy—about six feet, six-one and 240, maybe 250 pounds when he was in Trenton).

Kayo first came to my attention when his parents came to the prison to visit him, and I wondered what in the world would bring this quiet, elderly, obviously wealthy Jewish couple to a hellhole like Trenton State Prison. That's when somebody told me they were coming in to visit their son, Harold. I always tried to be as nice as I could to the parents coming to visit their sons because I figured but for the grace of God, these could be my parents coming to visit me. I also figured that it was bad enough that their kid was in a place like this; we didn't have to make their lives even more miserable by being nasty to them.

So I got to be friends with Kayo's mom and dad, especially his father. Later on, in the sixties, when I was wing officer in 1-left and Kayo was in there, he told me how much he appreciated my kindness to his parents. He also opened up a lot to me and told about his career as a criminal.

Kayo grew up in Bayonne where his father was a builder and investor in real estate. When he was in shape, Kayo was a rock-hard 180, 190 pounds and, being a Jewish kid growing up in a city, he was good with his fists. He first got involved with gangsters when he became a pro fighter ("The Bayonne Bomber"). After a short career as a boxer, Kayo got hooked up with Joe Zicarelli, "Joe Bayonne," the capo of the north Jersey mob in the Joe Bonanno Mafia family.

When he first got involved with the mob in the early 1950's, Kayo did small-time enforcing jobs, like collecting deadbeat loans for mob-connected shylocks. One FBI guy told *Life*, "Kayo was an animal on a leash for Zicarelli and others. All they had to do was unsnap the leash and he'd kill for the fun of it."

Eventually, the other shylocks started selling their bad loans to Kayo, figuring that maybe he could get some action on their "dormant accounts." I heard stories from other inmates that when he was on a rampage, Kayo would use anything he could lift up to work over deadbeats—ball bats, chairs, whatever. Kayo told me he almost always got results—if he didn't, the guy would never be able to borrow money again. In time, Kayo became known in law enforcement circles as "The King of the Loansharks" and was the most-feared enforcer in the greater New York City area.

When I first met Kayo sometime in the mid 1950's, he was about halfway through a 10-14-year bid for robbery that he started serving in 1949. Over the next few years I got to see first-hand what a mean and tough son of a bitch he was. Periodically he would take a swing at an officer and would be put in lockup—it seemed like he was always in and out of trouble.

Then one day I was out in one of the wings when the door from the yard flew open and there was Kayo, sweating and cursing, flanked by two cops holding him under the arm pits. I looked closer and sticking out of his lower back I could see the handle of shank. He had gotten into an argument in the yard with some inmate named Spain, and Spain had stabbed him.

"That son of a bitch!" Kayo is yelling. "Let me go! Let me go back and get that dirty son of a bitch!"

He's bleeding like a stuck pig with the knife still in him, and all he's worried about is going back out in the yard and getting the guy who stabbed him. He was one tough nut.

Partly because of his notoriety as a Mafia enforcer and partly because he had gotten into so much trouble while he was in jail, Kayo served about two-thirds of his sentence before he was paroled (one-third of the lower number is normal if a guy keeps a clean record while inside). By the time Kayo left he and I had become friendly. I always enjoyed talking to him when I wasn't busy with other duties—he was such a character—right out of *Guys and Dolls*. I was also fascinated by the relationship he had with another older, and lot smarter, Jewish inmate named Abie Prinz. At one point, Abie locked on the tier above Kayo and treated Kayo like he was a loyal dog. And Kayo, as tough as he was, put up with it. I never understood that.

I lost track of Kayo for the next few years except when I would hear a story here and there about something he was "allegedly" involved in. Ginny and I liked to travel sometimes to North Jersey to check out restaurants we had heard about. It wouldn't be unusual for me to run into some guy who had done time in Trenton and be treated to a drink "for old times' sake." Naturally, I would ask about this guy and that guy who had been in Trenton and was now out, and that's how I would hear about Kayo's escapades. Also, we had new guys coming in constantly from the Bayonne area, and they'd give me bits and pieces about guys I knew, like Kayo. I heard he was still doing his thing with the mob, and then in the mid1960's, his name started popping up on the front pages of newspapers again.

Like Joe Adonis, Kayo made good newspaper copy—except, unlike the cool, dapper Adonis, Kayo came across as a little bit loopy. In early 1965 Kayo was in the Hudson County jail, and a big scandal had broken involving visits by prostitutes to jail inmates. And there was good ol' Kayo, right in the middle of the brouhaha.

A federal grand jury was looking into allegations that a secretary for Kayo's attorney took a high-class prostitute into the Hudson County jail to visit Kayo "as a client." The "secretary" was Israel Schawartzberg, a long-time buddy of Kayo's who had been convicted of fixing college basketball games in New York City. The warden of the jail, Henry McFarland, was a good old boy politician and retired cop; he denied that the visit ever took place. But then the grand jury brought in inmates and ex-inmates who testified that prostitutes, liquor, uncensored mail and other favors were routinely purchased from the warden. They said that each week McFarland would set up shop in a room at the jail, and anybody wanting favors would go in and pay him off. Most of the charges against McFarland were dropped, but he did get convicted of perjury and was sentenced to 18 months.

Kayo meanwhile rolled along, doing his thing. Two years later, he was back in the news, but this time it looked like he had lost it and had turned informant for the FBI. Sometimes Kayo acted like he had taken too many punches to the head when he was a boxer, but I always thought it was an act. When he went on trial in New York State on a charge of extorting money from two stockbrokers (one of whom was found murdered just off the Long Island Expressway), he refused to hire an attorney and represented himself. Throughout the long trial, Kayo harassed the assistant DA who was prosecuting the case, peppering him with personal attacks and insults. The way he acted in court seemed to fit with his crazy act, but midway through the trial I saw a headline in the *New York Times* that made me believe Kayo really was nuts: "Konigsberg Tipped FBI to Grave Site."

It looked like Kayo, facing a possible 174 years in prison, had turned canary! I couldn't believe it. This wasn't the Kayo I knew—the guy who worshipped his mob "brothers" and would do anything for them. For about a week Kayo was front-page news as the papers told how he had led the FBI to an old chicken farm owned by Joseph Celso in Jackson Township, NJ near Lakewood. Celso and Kayo had been convicted in 1964 in federal court for possession of stolen goods and had done time together in Lewisburg. The feds and reporters were calling the farm a "Mafia burial ground." When they finished digging up the farm, the FBI had found two bodies and an orthopedic shoe and pieces of a third body. Kayo had told them five bodies were buried there, so the feds figured that some corpses had been dug up again and moved somewhere else. The shoe would pop up a year later when *Life* magazine connected Kayo to a U.S. congressman from New Jersey.

A month after the burial ground stories, Kayo, still acting as his own attorney, faced the jury in his extortion trial in New York. In his summation, Kayo spoke for nearly four hours and told the judge his constitutional rights were being violated. He kept telling the judge to "do what's right."

Kayo told the judge, "All you can give you should give me. I want you to be able to sleep at night. I don't want you to worry about me."

The judge didn't worry about Kayo . . . he also didn't give him all he could have given him, which was 174 years in jail, but calling him "a predatory jungle creature without pity or remorse," the judge gave Kayo a total of 30 to 44 years in the federal pen.

During the trial, reporters asked Kayo if he was cooperating with the feds to get a lighter sentence. Kayo was worried that "the boys" would think he was a rat, and he said, "I don't cooperate with no one except myself. I have no control over what they do with me or where they take me or what the newspapers print."

Just as the trial ended, the *New York Times* printed another story saying the FBI was questioning Kayo about the murder of a young salesman in New York City who had fingered Willie Sutton after Sutton escaped from Sing Sing. This guy was just being a good citizen: he had seen Sutton on the a subway train and had called the police. For that he got whacked. The authorities didn't think Kayo did the job, but they thought he might know the whereabouts of the hit man who did pull the trigger. All of this was going down about four years after Joe Valachi had given the feds detailed testimony about Mafia operations. I figured the mob must be super-sensitive about informers and Kayo was dead meat.

But I also knew Kayo had a lot of street savvy. He had been involved with the mob since he was in his early twenties, and he knew what the score was. The word around the prison was that the mob was upset by what they were hearing about Kayo and the FBI. Somehow, though, Kayo survived, maybe because he was confined at the Mental Center for Federal Prisoners in Springfield, Missouri and they couldn't get at him. We figured they put him in a hospital-type environment as a payoff for leading them to Celso's farm.

About a year after he was convicted on the extortion charges, Kayo was in the news again. Now he was trying to get an injunction against *Life* magazine, trying to stop them from printing an article linking him to Congressman Cornelius Gallagher from Hudson County. *Life* went ahead with the article, and the orthopedic shoe dug up on the Celso farm in 1967 linked Kayo to the disappearance of a small-time Bayonne loan shark named Barney O'Brien. *Life* claimed that federal wiretaps on North Jersey mobsters indicated that Barney O'Brien had died, possibly of natural causes, while visiting Gallagher at his home. The story alleged that Gallagher (who at one point in his career was being considered as a possible candidate for Lyndon Johnson's VP) had called Kayo and asked him to come to the congressman's home. When Kayo got there, Gallagher supposedly showed him the body of Barney O'Brien and asked Kayo to get rid of it. Kayo refused to do it until Gallagher got the OK from Joe Bayonne—Joe Ziccarelli. Then, according to *Life*, Kayo took O'Brien's body to Celso's farm, told Celso to take his wife to a movie, and buried the body on the farm. Thus the orthopedic shoe, which the FBI later traced to Barney O'Brien. Whether any of this is true or not is anybody's guess. When it comes to Kayo Konigsberg, Gallagher said it best in the *Life* article. "Kayo is a . . . Kayo is an original." I'll second that.

Recently I ran into a retired FBI agent who had worked in the organized crimes unit in New York City during the '50's and '60's. I asked him if he remembered

Kayo and if he knew where he was. This guy told me he remembered Kayo well, especially how tough he was, and he said the last he knew—as of 1998—Kayo was still in federal prison in Connecticut. The FBI man said that Kayo would never see the street again, that he would die in prison. Given the chicken farm caper, Kayo's life expectancy has probably been a lot better right where he is.

4
CHAPTER FOUR

WATCHING THEM DIE

I witnessed my first execution on July 27, 1954—a hot, muggy night. I was 26 years old and had been working at the prison for about two years (after the two-year stint in the army). I was working in the mailroom with Adam Menkerell, which I loved because I was out in the front house, and I got to meet all different kinds of people—families of inmates, lawyers, politicians. I wasn't dealing with only inmates and corrections people all day long. One of our duties was pat frisking (or if a woman was going in, using a metal detector) everyone going into the jail.

A few days before the execution Jack Malkin, now a captain, came up to me and said, "Harry, I need a guard Tuesday night for an execution. Do you want to make some overtime?"

My first reaction was that this was a good opportunity to get four hours of overtime pay because my wife Ginny and I had recently had our first child, Darryl, and my salary was still only about $3,000 per year. My second reaction was a nagging doubt as to whether I would be able to deal mentally and emotionally with watching someone die in front of me. In those days, though, we didn't say no to a "request" to work overtime, plus I liked the idea of the extra money, so I told Captain Malkin that I would do it.

Since Adam and I were the guys on first shift who routinely screened people for weapons and contraband, Malkin asked us to come in to screen the witnesses (more for cameras than weapons) and then escort them through the prison to the death chamber.

The inmate who was to die that first Tuesday night was a young black guy from Trenton, Theodore Walker. When I was first hired, I had been shown the death row cell block and the death chamber, but since then I hadn't had any occasion to go back there, so I hardly remembered what the room looked like. I was curious, but I was also apprehensive.

The first witness, a reporter, arrived at about 9:00 p.m. Witnesses for executions were usually members of the press, police officers, or employees in the corrections field. I wondered if maybe victims' families might be invited to watch the killer of their loved ones die, or maybe even a member of the family of the killer to say goodbye, but I never knew of any relatives of either side attending.

As the witnesses, all men, came in, Adam and I frisked them. We were especially careful to check around the ankles and shins and particularly careful with the reporters. In the forty-six years, from 1907 to 1963, that 160 electrocutions were carried out at Trenton State Prison, no photograph of an execution was ever taken or published. That was also the reason for the sheet of white canvas suspended waist-high between the witnesses and the electric chair in the death chamber—nobody was going to strap a camera to his leg and snap pictures as had happened in New York State when the New York *Daily News* ran that famous front-page photo of Ruth Snyder being executed at Sing Sing.

After I screened the 16 witnesses that Tuesday night, checking their passes and credentials thoroughly, and then pat frisking and running a metal detector over them, I politely asked them to wait in the warden's office located just to the right of the prison's front door. When I had the whole group together, I escorted them through 6-wing past the deathly quiet cells and out into the small yard between 6-wing and the death house.

When I had first started at the prison, one of the inmates, a friendly old-timer, had said to me, "Harry, you hear how goddamned noisy it is in here. If you're coming to work and it's quiet, don't come in. It means that something bad is gonna happen." I laughed and thanked him for the advice, but his words came flashing back into my mind as I escorted the witnesses through the normally raucous interior of the prison: the silence was eerie. I found out that it was always like this on execution night as the inmates waited for one of them to die.

After we crossed the small exercise yard, we came to the door of the death chamber, a small one-story brick building close to, almost touching, the front wall of the prison. The door that witnesses entered through was near a wide receiving gate used for large vehicles, such as food and laundry trucks, entering and leaving the prison. Next to the big gate was a smaller, solid metal door known as the sally port and up above and to one side of both the big gate and the sally port was guard tower number nine. After the execution was over, witnesses would be escorted out of the prison through this sally port.

Once we reached the death chamber, I opened the door and held it for the witnesses as an officer stationed just inside the door showed them to their seats. All of the witnesses had arrived between 9:00 and 9:30, so we had all of them frisked and into the death chamber by about 9:50.

Executions normally took place on Tuesday nights at 10:00 p.m. If only one person was being put to death, the proceeding was over within a few minutes; executions were carried out with an almost mechanical efficiency. Of the 13 executions I witnessed from July 1954 to July of 1962, I never saw any of the high drama of that 1938 Jimmy Cagney movie, *Angels With Dirty Faces.* In the movie, Pat O'Brien, playing the priest, has convinced the gangster played by Cagney to do something to discourage the kids back in the neighborhood from a life of crime. In the end of the movie, Cagney drops his tough guy image and, supposedly terrified, is dragged crying and yelling to the chair. When I saw the movie as a kid, that scene always stuck in my mind, but I never saw anything like that happen in the Trenton State Prison death chamber.

Before I saw Walker executed, I thought that the condemned men would at least be upset, maybe crying and pleading; or that they might resist being put into the chair, even try to bolt from the room when they saw the chair. In fact, none of this ever happened, and every one of the men I watched die walked, sometimes quite nonchalantly, straight to the chair, sat down, said nothing (with one exception) and was pronounced dead by the attending physician within four or five minutes of entering the death chamber.

At this first execution, I went into the death chamber with a mental image that this would be a dramatic, formal, somber ceremony—that the condemned man would be asked if he had any last words, that he might make a long speech, that the warden would read the death warrant and maybe intone "And may God have mercy on your soul" or something like that. In fact, the process was so smoothly choreographed, it was over before I had chance to come to grips with the idea that a life was being snuffed out in front of me.

The death chamber itself was a stark room, and, surprisingly, quite small—approximately 18 feet by 24 feet—for the significance of what occurred there. When all of the witnesses, officers, warden, executioner and condemned man got in there, it was packed; it seemed as if we were all on top of one another—a closeness that I found oppressive and depressing. The front row of witnesses, separated from the chair by a rope that went from wall to wall and from which hung the white canvas sheet, was startlingly close to the condemned man and the chair—maybe six or seven feet. The room was dimly lit by a few fluorescent lights suspended from the ceiling, and the windowless interior walls of the brick building were painted a dull green. The witnesses entered through a solid metal door at the south end, and the condemned man, escorted by four officers, entered from the prison wing designated as death row through another solid metal door with a peephole on the west side of the room. The chair, a large straight-backed wooden apparatus with a metal skull cap, sat on a slightly raised concrete slab about eight feet from the door through which the condemned man entered. From the witnesses' perspective, the executioner and the control panel, in plain view, were just behind and slightly to the right of the chair. The door through which the execution party with the condemned man entered was to the left of the chair.

Upon entering the death chamber, the condemned men almost always seemed to first glance to their right and look at the witnesses. They would then look beyond the seated witnesses at us, the 10 or 15 cops standing along the back wall with batons held diagonally across our chests. Since the condemned were so quickly guided to the chair and strapped in, they didn't see the executioner until he approached them from the side to put the mask over their faces and the sponge on their heads.

When Captain Malkin had first asked me to do death house duty, I had started wondering what the executioner would look like. I had a mental image of a big, burly guy with muscular, hairy arms and a black hood over his head so that nobody would know who he was if they saw him on the street. Actually, the executioner was about five feet-seven inches tall, balding, kind of meek-looking and dressed in a rumpled, dark business suit. His name was Joseph Francel from Cairo, NY, and he had the execution contract for New York State, New Jersey, and Pennsylvania.

At the time of the Walker execution, he had electrocuted over fifty people at $150.00 "per head" (at least that's the way we referred to it) and had somewhat of a claim to fame in that he had executed atom bomb spies Julius and Ethel Rosenberg in June of 1953. He was very proper-looking, very "English." Francel was a licensed electrician, the sole requirement for being New Jersey's executioner.

Another misconception that I had carried around for a long time was "throwing the switch." I always thought that the chair was activated by a large knife switch thrown when the warden nodded his head. At Trenton State Prison, it was actually a metal wheel about eight to ten inches in diameter with spokes. The warden did nod his head, and at that signal, the executioner quickly spun the wheel counter-clockwise. The wheel was a type of rheostat that, when 2,000 volts was reached, released the current, and the condemned man was hit with the deadly jolt of electricity.

The law required 12 witnesses, but usually a few more than that attended, maybe 15 to 20, depending on who was being executed. If he was a nobody from the sticks, like James Beard, who had killed his mother with a tire iron in an argument over a bottle of wine, there weren't as many witnesses as there would be for a well-known bad-ass like Hot Dog Roscus from Newark, who had grabbed a few headlines by constantly disrupting his trial. Since Walker was from Trenton and had killed a local woman, there were a few more witnesses than usual.

Walker's case is a good example of the speed of the criminal justice system back in the fifties. He had gone into 45-year-old Mollie Schlesinger's uniform shop on Montgomery Street in Trenton on the night of August 18, 1953, to rob her of the day's receipts. When Schlesinger resisted and tried to fight him off, Walker slashed her with a butcher knife. He grabbed $11 out of the till and ran but was captured almost immediately. Schlesinger died the next day from shock and loss of blood. Walker was convicted of first-degree murder on November 23, 1953 and was executed July 27, 1954—11 1/2 months from crime to execution.

On the night of Walker's electrocution, by 9:55 all of the witnesses were settled on narrow wooden folding chairs that, appropriately enough, looked as if they had been borrowed from a funeral parlor. The chairs were arranged in four rows of six chairs with an aisle dividing two groups of twelve chairs to the left and to the right.

At exactly 10 p.m., the solid metal door at the west end of the death chamber opened and Walker, head shaved, stripped to the waist (it was a hot, humid July night), and wearing a pair of khaki cutoff shorts, was escorted in by four officers, two in front of him and two behind. Walker looked resigned to his impending death and puffed on a cigarette while two of the prison chaplains, the Rev. L.M. Case and the Rev. H.C. VanPelt, walked in front of him; Reverend Case was reading the 23rd Psalm. Walker was a big, well-built guy, about 6 feet, 180 pounds; while he had been on death row, he had been lifting weights regularly and was in great physical shape—ironic given the circumstances. He had also "gotten religion," on death row (as did many of the men I watched die) and was wearing an outsized metal cross dangling from a metal chain around his neck.

Lloyd McCorkle was the warden at the time, and he was standing near the chair along with four officers. The escorting officers moved Walker directly to the chair, and he sat down. I remember thinking that this guy ought to look terrified, but his expression was more of an interested curiosity than fear. I think that was one of the reasons the process was carried out so fast—to keep the condemned man from thinking about what was happening to him.

The four officers standing near the chair, one assigned to each arm and leg, quickly buckled three-inch-wide leather straps around Walker's arms and legs. Then the executioner stepped over next to Walker, reached into a bucket of water sitting on the floor next to the chair and took out a small sponge—about two-inches by two or three inches. He placed it on Walker's head and placed the metal skull cap down over the sponge; the weight of the metal cap pushed it down snugly onto Walker's head and held it there. Simultaneously, an officer who had strapped one of Walker's arms produced a leather mask with a two-inch diamond-shaped opening to let the nose protrude through. He handed it to the executioner who placed it over Walker's face and secured it behind his head by buckling two small staps. One of the officers who had strapped a leg cinched another leather strap around Walker's chest. Everyone then stepped back away from the chair. The warden moved a few steps closer to the chair, looked Walker over, and stepped back. He then did a half turn toward the executioner, who had moved over to the big electric panel with the wheel and dials, and nodded. The executioner turned toward the panel with the wheel, grasped it and gave it one sharp counter-clockwise turn.

I expected to hear some kind of loud buzzing or whirring of a dynamo (Cagney movies, again), but the only thing I heard was the loud slap of Walker's bare chest smacking against the restraining strap as the jolt of electricity caused him to lunge forward. The executioner must have done a silent "one, one hundred; two, two hundred" count for about three or four seconds, and then he smartly spun the wheel back to its original position. He did this quickly four more times, and each time Walker's bare, sweaty chest smacked against the restraining strap.

Because of the heavy humidity and the perspiration on Walker's chest, the metal crucifix must have picked up the current and the cross started to glow; it looked like it was burning and embedding itself in Walker's chest—a grisly, but I have to admit, fascinating, sight. I thought, "God. What's happening? Is he splitting open?"

As the current was hitting him, Walker's powerful weightlifter's body strained against the thick straps, as if he was trying to get up out of the chair to escape the electricity. I told myself that Walker was knocked unconscious by the first jolt and he was not feeling anything; I still believe this to be true. Recently I have seen some scenes from TV dramas, one of them the execution of Ethel Rosenberg, in which the condemned person vibrates wildly in the chair for many seconds as the current is applied. In the electrocutions that I witnessed, the person was violently thrust forward against the straps, more like being shot in the back with an elephant gun at close range. Bam! Then, each time the executioner spun the wheel, the man's body was thrust forward for a couple of seconds and sagged back until the next jolt. About twenty to thirty seconds, five shots of electricity, and it was over.

When the current was cut after the last jolt, Walker's head dropped forward onto his chest, and his body sagged heavily against the straps. The prison doctor, Dr. Howard Weisler, had been standing between the warden and the executioner.

He stepped forward and placed a stethoscope on Walker's chest. I'll never forget those words—the first of thirteen times I was to hear them: "This man is dead."

I looked at my watch. It was 10:05 p.m.

I helped escort the witnesses out of the death chamber and then turned back to glance at the officers unstrapping Walker's body so that they could lift it onto a Gurney with a heavy slate slab on top. Between executions, the Gurney was stored in a small room directly behind the electrical control panel that held the wheel. In that room ran all of the heavy electric cables that carried the power from the outside, through the panel and into the chair. I left the death chamber before the four officers who had strapped Walker into the chair removed the skull cap, the mask, and the straps, but the next day a couple of them told me what always happened after the execution.

After the witnesses left, the four officers took Walker's body, lifted him up and laid him on the Gurney, his head fitting into a melon-sized depression in the slab. They then wheeled him into the small room to wait until a detail of inmates from the hospital would come down with another, lighter Gurney and take the body back to the prison morgue, adjacent to the hospital. The next morning he would be put into a plain wooden box made in the prison repair shop and be picked up by a local undertaker.

Usually the body of the executed man would be claimed by his family from the Trenton funeral home that had the contract to pick up the corpses from the death house, but sometimes nobody claimed them. In those cases, we had a mold out in the repair shop to make little rounded grave markers like on Boot Hill in the old West. Then the inmate's number, no name, would be cast on the cement marker, and he would be buried in the prison cemetery on Cedar Lane in Hamilton Township just outside of the City of Trenton.

That night when I got home, I was drained and, I guess, depressed, maybe even in some kind of a state of shock. I couldn't put a finger on how I felt, but it wasn't a good feeling. Ginny, asked me how it had gone, and I described it to her in broad terms—I didn't think at the time that she would be able to handle all of the details.

She said to me, "Honey, if you don't want to work there . . . ."

And I told her, "I'm not a carpenter or a plumber. This is what I am—a prison guard—and this is what I do."

Then we went to bed and I tried to go to sleep. Darryl was about eight months old, and he was sleeping in a crib in our room next to my side of the bed. The crib had one of those rubber sheets that are used in case the baby wets through the diaper. It was probably about three or four in the morning, and I was just starting to drift off to sleep when the baby turned over and slapped his arm against the rubber sheet; it sounded exactly like Walker's chest smacking against the strap across his chest! My eyes flew open, and I sat bolt upright in bed, unable to sleep for the rest of the night.

Watching Walker die had bothered me, but I figured it was part of my job and if I was going to continue as a prison guard, I'd have to get used to it. In the fifties New Jersey used the electric chair 16 times, most of them from 1954 on, so it seemed like we were executing someone every several months. In fact, it was only three weeks after Walker's execution, in August of 1954, that Captain Malkin again asked me to do execution duty, so this time I figured I would go and look at the next guy's jacket (the file that the prison keeps on all inmates) and see what he had done to get the death penalty.

His name was James Beard, 40 years old, from Camden; he had asked his 63-year-old mother for money to buy wine, and when she refused, he bludgeoned her to death with a tire iron. When they brought the 6-foot, 170-pound Beard into the death chamber, like Walker he appeared to be emotionless. In fact, he looked kind of stunned—glassy-eyed—as he was strapped into the chair. He was also pronounced dead at 10:05, after five quick shocks.

Knowing what Beard had done made it easier for me to watch him die, so from then on, each time I had an execution, I would go and read the guy's jacket to help me keep a perspective on the whole thing.

****

A month after Beard's execution, in September of 1954, we got another "celebrity." George White Rogers, "The Hero of the *Morro Castle* Disaster" came in to start serving a double life sentence for the murder of two of his neighbors. Rogers really was a celebrity for a brief time but went from being a hero to a bum in the span of a few years.

Rogers had become famous in September of 1934 when the Ward Lines' cruise ship *Morro Castle* caught fire off the coast of New Jersey as it returned from a trip to Havana. The ship's captain, Robert Wilmott, had died of a heart attack the previous evening, and the ship was under the command of Chief Officer William Warms. When the fire broke out in the passengers' library, Warms kept the ship steaming full-speed ahead, fanning the flames, while the crew tried vainly to put out the fire. Finally, Warms acknowledged that they needed help and allowed Rogers, the chief radio operator, to start sending out SOS signals. Rogers heroically stayed at his post for hours, puffing calmly on a pipe and sending out SOS calls as the ship burned. By the time help arrived, 134 people had died, and the ship's burned-out hulk washed up onto the beach in Asbury Park.

Rogers was awarded medals for heroism by the Veteran Wireless Operators Association and by the city council of his hometown, Bayonne. The city fathers also offered him a job as a patrolman in the police department, working with Lieutenant Vincent J. Doyle, who was in charge of the nation's first two-way police radio system.

Members of the Bayonne police department considered Doyle and Rogers to be close friends—they were both married and the two couples visited each other's homes. Doyle and Rogers also rode into work together. On the afternoon of March 4, 1938, Doyle and Rogers left the radio room over the police garage to drive home together in the lieutenant's car. As they were leaving the building, Rogers reminded Doyle that there was a package addressed to Doyle on a table in the office. The two men went back inside and Doyle found a package with an anonymous typewritten note attached:

> Lieutenant Doyle—This is a fish-tank heater. Please install this switch in the line cord, and see if the unit will work. It should get slightly warm.

Unwrapping the package upstairs in the repair room, Doyle found a metal cylinder about five inches long and three-quarters of an inch in diameter with an electric cord attached. At that point, Rogers suddenly remembered a letter in his pocket that he had forgotten to mail.

Doyle said to him, "Why don't you go down to the post office while I look at this."

When he got downstairs, Rogers stopped for a drink of water. A blast shook the building, and Rogers ran back upstairs. He found Lieutenant Doyle, conscious but in shock, lying on the floor with three fingers blown off his left hand and his left thigh broken. As soon as Doyle had plugged the device into a wall socket, it had exploded.

When the Bayonne police investigated, the evidence pointed to Rogers as the bomber. First he was suspended, and then a few days after the incident, he was arrested. Rogers waived his right to a jury trial, choosing instead to have Judge Thomas H. Brown hear the case. Rogers testified in his own defense, but Doyle's testimony pointed the finger directly at the "hero." The prosecution contended that Rogers attempted to kill Doyle to get the lieutenant's job.

The evidence against Rogers was convincing, and after a short deliberation, Judge Brown found Rogers guilty, Before pronouncing sentence, Brown gave a brief biography of Rogers. The judge said that when Rogers was a kid in California, he had been sent to an institution for being "unruly." While he was there, Rogers was charged with "an unnatural offense against a young boy." Rogers later joined the navy and went to sea. He was arrested in New York for the theft of $2,000 worth of radio equipment but made restitution. The chief of the probation department in Hudson County said that Rogers had denied any responsibility for the *Morro Castle* fire but refused to comment about an explosion in 1920 at the U.S. naval base at Newport, RI that had injured him and resulted in an honorable discharge from the navy.

In sentencing Rogers to 12 to 20 years in state prison for attempted murder in the Doyle case, Judge Brown said,

> This was a crime of a diabolical nature, only to be executed by one with the mind of a fiend. There is no doubt in my mind that the finger of guilt points unerringly to you. You claim a frame-up on the part of the Bayonne police. Nothing in the testimony was adduced to show this.

Rogers served only three years and ten months on this bid and was paroled in 1943, so he was long gone when I started work in 1950.

But wait. The story doesn't end there. Rogers opened a radio and TV repair business out of his home in Bayonne. He had a few run-ins with the law over the next ten years, but he managed to stay out of real trouble until July of 1953. Then, the bodies of William Hummel, an 83-year-old retired linotype operator and his 58-year-old spinster daughter—friends of Rogers—were found in their home in

Bayonne, their heads beaten in by a blunt object.

When police first questioned Rogers, he said he hadn't seen either of the Hummels on the day they were murdered. Then, under further questioning, he "remembered" that he had taken William Hummel to a bank to withdraw $2,400 the day of the killings. He had also had some business dealings with the elder Hummel and had apparently taken a sum of money from him over time. Rogers was indicted and based upon "overwhelming" circumstantial evidence, including bloodstained pants and a bloody sledgehammer, he was convicted on two counts of first-degree murder. The jury deliberated only three hours. Probably because of the nature of the evidence and lack of eyewitnesses, the jury recommended mercy, and Rogers was sentenced to life imprisonment.

I remember Rogers as a big man—about six feet, two, 250 pounds. He was a quiet inmate who went about his business and, like Charlie Workman and Joe Adonis, wasn't bothered by the other prisoners. Because of his background as a wireless operator and radio and TV repairman, Rogers was put in charge of the radio system that ran throughout the prison. Back in the '50's each cell had a jack for head phones and a switch that allowed the inmate to get one of three local AM stations. The radio receiver and point of transmission throughout the jail was located in a small room near center the hub of the jail. Rogers was assigned to monitor the system and keep the equipment in working order.

I would usually see him walking slowly either from his wing to his job or going from the radio room to the mess hall. I had a few brief conversations with him, and my impression was that he was quite bright, but there was something shifty about him. He was not the type of person I would trust. He did about eight or nine years on his sentence, and then one day I heard he had had a stroke and died in the prison hospital. After his second conviction, some newspaper writers did some digging into Rogers' background and the circumstances surrounding the *Morro Castle* fire and speculated that Rogers might have set the fire so that he could come across as a hero.

If he did, a double-life sentence at Trenton State Prison was pretty light punishment.

****

During the fall of 1954, the civil service commission was still reviewing the penalties handed out to Alexander Abbott and the other officers in the Vaszorich death house escape and the subsequent shooting. Before they could reach a decision, there was another attempted breakout from the death house, in October. This one was engineered by Joseph Grillo and Silvio DeVita, who had helped Vaszorich escape and whose scheduled executions in April had been put on hold while the courts heard their appeals.

Grillo and DeVita were joined in the escape attempt by Eugene Monohan, who was awaiting execution for killing two men in an Elizabeth tavern hold-up; Frank Roscus, also of Elizabeth; and Alfred Stokes and Albert Wise, who, along with Albert's brother, Harry Wise, had been sentenced to death for killing police Sergeant Clinton Bond in Union County.

The six condemned inmates managed to get hold of a broken piece of a hacksaw blade, most likely from the discard bin in the repair shop. How it was smuggled in to them is anybody's guess. Warden McCorkle figured that the six men took turns working on the bars of their cells while the other accomplices made covering noises, probably during the day shift when the surrounding prison is also noisy.

At about 2:30 in the morning on October 30, one of the six got the third-shift officer, Charlie Black, to go to the far end of the death house to get some hot water for him. While Black was down at the end of the cell block, the six guys simultaneously shoved hard against the bars of their cells and broke through, each creating a hole big enough to crawl through. Once they were out, they charged Charlie Black and overpowered him, tying him with strips of bed sheet to a chair and then tying the chair to the bars of a cell. Another officer, John Colligan, who was stationed in 9-tower overlooking the death house, looked down through the skylight and saw one of the inmates sitting in the guard's chair, with his feet up on the desk. Colligan turned in the alarm, and while the inmates were planning what to do next, phone calls went out to Warden McCorkle and to off-duty officers to get to the prison immediately.

Warden McCorkle formed a party of 12 officers around four in the morning and then yelled through the door of the death house, telling the guys inside that he knew what was going on and ordering them to surrender. One of the men yelled back, "I don't think so, Warden. It's kind of stuffy in here, so I think we'll go out for a breath of fresh air and change of scenery."

Warden McCorkle, always an advocate of a swift, surprising use of overwhelming force in these situations, issued night sticks to the officers standing out in the corridor. Sergeant Gordon Doll was covering the death house door with a Thompson; Warden McCorkle told the officers that one man would unlock the door and rush in, followed closely by Sergeant Doll with the machine gun. Doll would brandish the gun while the other eleven guards, holding the night sticks high and poised to strike, would charge toward the inmates. The officers assumed that the inmates would fight back with the pieces of cell bars that had been sawed out. In fact, McCorkle's strategy worked so well that the inmates were totally surprised by the swiftness of the attack and surrendered immediately; Officer Black was rescued unharmed.

McCorkle's next move was typical of his response to inmate revolts: he ordered the five men to crawl back into their cells through the holes they had cut through the bars, despite the jagged edges on the ends of the bars. As one of the officers involved, Charlie Donohue, said to me, the inmates were "inspired to do this quickly" by the guards' use of the night sticks. Dr. Carl Franzoni was then called in to attend to any injured inmates. McCorkle ordered him to administer the stitches "cold turkey" (no anesthesia) to those prisoners who had been cut by the bars. The inmates were then transferred to other, secure, cells, and executions went on as scheduled: Roscus, Monohan, Stokes and his two cousins, the Wise brothers, all were executed in 1955. Grillo and DeVita never did go to the chair. After several years of appeals, they were retried in February of 1958 and were given life sentences. Both were paroled in the early '70's.

****

As the new year rolled in, January, 1955, I witnessed my third execution—one of the guys who had tried to break out of the death house with Grillo and De Vita and truly a tough customer. His name was Frank Roscus, a 34-year-old white guy from Newark. On the night of January 9, 1954, Roscus, a paunchy construction laborer, was drinking and playing craps in the bar of his Broad Street union hall when an argument over loaded dice erupted. Roscus, the father of three kids, was a known troublemaker around the Ironbound section of Newark. He had been in trouble since he was a teenager and had been dishonorably discharged from the army in 1947 for beating up an officer in France.

During the argument about the dice, Roscus, drunk and pissed off, left the union hall and went back to his house to get his sawed-off shotgun. He returned to the hall, looking for the small-time gambler he had accused of using the phony dice, a guy named "Trixie King" Cozzolino. When his buddies at the hall told him Cozzolino had left, Roscus went on a drunken rampage, firing six shells from the shotgun and wounding four of the guys at the hall. He managed to find Trixie a few minutes later at the Six Corners Tavern and killed him with a blast from the shotgun.

Roscus was picked up almost immediately and while he was awaiting trial, he tried to break out of the Newark Street jail, stabbing a guard in the shoulder during the attempt. During the trial, Roscus created havoc in the courtroom, alternately yelling at the judge, the jury and the lawyers. His defense was that he was too drunk the night of the killing to commit premeditated murder. His probation report did indicate that he was a chronic alcoholic, but the jury convicted him and sentenced him to death anyway.

The officers who worked the death watch that night told me that Roscus ordered turkey, sweet potatoes, ice cream, candy and a box of cigars for his last request. The cigar thing was common back then; the condemned man usually smoked a couple just before going to the death chamber and passed the rest down the cell block to the other guys on death row. When Warden McCorkle came into the cell block to ask Roscus if he had any last requests, Roscus said, "Yeah, let me out of here."

So Roscus had his last meal and asked the guard detail if he could finish his cigar on the way to the chair. They let him, and when the door into the death chamber opened, I watched as one of the prison chaplains, the Rev. Stephen Buividas, walked in followed by Roscus, swaggering like a big-time mobster and smoking that fat cigar. He turned toward the witnesses and, sneered, and flicked the lighted cigar into the middle of the 16 men; it fell harmlessly on the floor between the two sections of chairs. Then he turned and almost jumped into the chair—he was going out like the tough guy he had always been. As soon as he sat in the chair, though, and they started to put the straps on his arms, his whole attitude changed. I could see his expression change to fear—or at least apprehension—and his body sag.

Roscus was quickly strapped into the chair and the current was applied. He did the lunge against the straps and in about twenty seconds it was over. Normally, I left the execution chamber with the witnesses and didn't watch while the four-man squad undid the straps and removed the mask and skull cap, but this night I happened to stick around. Roscus had light brown hair, almost blond, and fair skin; when the officer removed the leather mask, a lot of blood vessels had burst around Roscus' mouth; the whole bottom area of his face was covered in blood—not a pretty sight.

Exactly one week later, Tuesday night, January 11, 1955, another one of the "Death House Six, " reputed tough guy Eugene Monohan, 45, went to the chair; but unlike the swaggering Roscus, when he came into the death chamber, Monohan looked like a tired, beaten, scared old man. I would have felt sorry for him, especially when, as he sat in the chair, he smiled weakly, lifted his hand and waved goodbye to Warden McCorkle. I had read his jacket, though, and I could never feel bad for someone who had done what he had to his son.

Monohan was a career criminal who had spent more than a third of his life in prison; he had also been training his son Michael to take over the "family business." In January of 1953, he and Michael were holding up the Shamrock Bar across from the Union County courthouse in Elizabeth when something went wrong and Monohan killed the 63-year-old bartender, Sebastian Weilandics and a 26-year-old customer, William S. Diskin.

Monohan and his son escaped from the murder scene, but Michael was later picked up for the attempted robbery of a Verona dress shop. Under questioning, young Monohan confessed to committing 150 robberies under orders from his father, including the one at the Shamrock. At first, Michael said that he had killed the bartender and the customer, but he later retracted his statement after his father was arrested and confessed to being the gunman.

A grand jury indicted both father and son, but the New Jersey Supreme Court said Michael's case had to be handled in juvenile court. He went before a juvenile court judge and was sentenced to an indeterminate term in the reformatory at Bordentown while dad got the death penalty.

While he was on death row, Monohan asked the prison's board of managers for permission to be remarried by a priest in the Roman Catholic church. He and his wife had been married years before in a civil ceremony while he was in the Essex County jail, and he wanted to be married in the eyes of the church before he died. The board granted permission, so Father Buividas married them through the bars of Roscus' death row cell in May of 1954, seven months before he was executed.

Then in October, Monohan hooked up with Roscus, DeVita, Grillo, Stokes and Albert Wise and tried to break out of the death house.

As he sat down in the chair the night of his execution in January, Monohan's pleading eyes wandered from Warden McCorkle to the witnesses to us in the back of the room. His expression seemed to be saying, "Please don't do this to me." Warden McCorkle returned Monohan's wave and smile, then turned away as the executioner fitted the mask over Monohan's face.

I witnessed my most memorable execution (other than Theodore Walker's because it was my first and because of the cross) in May of 1955, just a few months after Monohan, when three young Hispanics were executed, one after the other, for killing a diner owner during a holdup. This was a sad story all the way around because it was so senseless. Four guys were involved in the holdup, one a sixteen-year-old kid who was sound asleep on the back seat of the car. The other three, who were considerably older than the teenager and had criminal records, went into a diner in Camden and tried to hold up the owner, 69-year-old George Booris. When he refused to give them any money, they started firing wildly, hitting Booris in the chest, hands and arms with six shots, fatally wounding him. Then they reached into the cash drawer and took off with the "loot"—$21. They netted $7 each in a crime that cost them their lives. The sixteen-year-old, Gabriel Vega, even though he had no idea of what was going on, got a life sentence because he was at the scene of a felony murder. He came into Trenton at the age of 17 and got out when he was 35.

The night that the three men were executed was unusually hot and humid for early May. I never liked doing execution duty in that kind of weather because the high humidity and the perspiration on the person being executed always caused a smell of burning flesh, plus, when they took the straps off after it was over, you could see where the electrodes on the arms and legs had burned the skin.

The first one to come into the death chamber, led by a Spanish-speaking Roman Catholic priest brought in from Camden, was 27-year-old Felipe Rios. He walked in solemnly looking at the floor as the Rev. Aroque Longo chanted the liturgy. Reverend Longo had been asked to attend the executions because none of the three men spoke English. The prison's Roman Catholic chaplain, the Rev. Stephen Buividas, was also on hand. After four jolts, Rios was pronounced dead by Dr. Samuel Sica, who was on hand to assist Dr. Weisler.

The second man, 32-year-old Joquin Rodriguez was pronounced dead at about 10:20, also after four jolts. The third guy, Jose Cruz, was then brought in, wearing a kind of goofy half smile. Like Walker, Cruz had lifted weights while on death row and had developed a great physique—big biceps and a barrel chest. I had also heard from the death row officers that the pressure of waiting to die (ten months from date received to date of execution) had driven him crazy.

That night, two of my misconceptions were erased. The first was that they couldn't execute someone who wasn't in his right mind. Also like Walker, Cruz had gotten religion while on death row, so much so that he regularly pinned several religious medals to his chest—literally. The cops on the death watch had to tell him to pull three or four medals out of his skin before they took him to the death chamber that night. This guy was obviously a bedbug, but they went ahead with the execution anyway.

The other myth was that if the rope broke, they couldn't hang you again—that you had beaten the hangman. In this case, apparently because he was so powerfully developed, the four jolts didn't kill Cruz. I had never seen this before. After Francel had backed the wheel off after the fourth jolt, one of the officers went over, grabbed hold of the tee shirt on Cruz' chest and tore it so the doctor could put the stethoscope on him.

Dr. Sica said, "Uh, uh. This man isn't dead. His heart is fluttering." So everybody immediately stepped back away from the chair, and the executioner quickly turned the wheel three more times. This time they were successful. So I found out that when the state says you're going to die, you are going to die, even if the rope breaks.

Almost unbelievably, my next one was also a triple header—and only four months later, in September of 1955. This was the eighth triple execution since the chair was installed in 1907. The three men to be executed were all related: two brothers, Harry and Albert Wise and their cousin, Alfred Stokes. Stokes and Albert Wise had been involved in the death house breakout attempt the previous October.

By the time the Wise brothers and their cousin were sentenced to death, the capital punishment debate had really heated up. When Jose Cruz and the other two had been executed in May, petitions had been circulated and submitted to Governor Robert B. Meyner, asking for clemency, but Meyner had rejected the appeal. Now, the Wise brothers case became a *cause-celebre*—for both sides. On the one side were three young black men, victims of the white man's justice system, all slated to die on the same night, a clear case of "mass murder" by the state. On the other side was a dead Union County cop: these "kids" were cop-killers. In the streets around the prison that night protesters, monitored by armed correction officers outside the prison walls and Trenton police, marched with signs and maintained a hushed vigil as the hour of execution approached. Originally the three young men had been scheduled to die on Tuesday night, but they had been granted a stay until Gov. Meyner could review their case; he rejected their appeal for clemency and the execution was rescheduled for the following Friday night.

Albert Wise was 23 years old and his brother Harry was 21 when they were convicted of first degree murder with no recommendation for mercy in December of 1954. Their cousin Alfred Stokes was also 21. They had been convicted of holding up the Tuscan Dairy in Union and escaping with $1,400 after killing Union police sergeant Clinton Bond in the course of the robbery.

Watching three young men come into the death chamber one after the other like that wasn't easy, even though all three of them came in like this was no big deal. In fact, the Trenton *Times* reporter who covered the execution said in the next day's paper, the "cocky killers" seated themselves in the electric chair "with the aplomb of persons boarding a bus."

Alfred Stokes, the cousin, went first at 10 p.m. He was taken out of the chair at 10:06, put on the gurney with the heavy slate slab and wheeled into the room behind the control panel. I didn't see them, but I was told that those plain plywood coffins were back there and Alfred's body was slid off the Gurney into one of them. When Harry Wise was brought in by the same four-man squad at about 10:15, the Gurney was back in place. He strode into the chamber puffing on a cigarette, calmly flicked the butt to the floor, ground it out with his foot, and then sat down in the chair, looking like he was there to get a haircut. Harry was executed and removed by about 10:20. Albert was then brought in, led by Reverend Buividas (Harry and Albert had converted to Catholicism while on death row), and the whole thing was over by about 10:30.

Watching those three young guys die like that had tough, and by comparison the next one a little less than a year later, in August of 1956, was almost anti-climactic. His name was John Henry Tune, 24, from Newark. Tune had been convicted of strangling another man to death, and, like the Wise brothers, had converted to Catholicism while on death row. As he followed Reverend Buividas into the death chamber, Tune was chanting over and over, "Lord have mercy on me, Lord have mercy on me." When the first shot of electricity was applied and Tune lunged against the straps, a rookie guard's knees buckled, and he had to be helped out of the death chamber by a couple of other officers. Tune was then hit with four more jolts before he was pronounced dead.

After Tune's execution in '56, it almost seemed like a moratorium was declared on executions in New Jersey. The appeals process by now had stretched out to several years, and a lot of sentiment seemed to be building against the death penalty throughout the country. I wouldn't see another man die in the electric chair for another six years, in July of 1962.

CHAPTER FIVE

THE FIFTIES WIND DOWN

In the 29 years that I was a correction officer, three guys, Mario DeLucia, Bill Van Scoten and Terry Alden managed to go over the wall and escape from Trenton State Prison.

The first, in December of 1956, was Mario DeLucia, one of "Trenton's Own," a guy whose family we had known for years. I knew Mario's mother since she ran a corner store in our old neighborhood. Then, after Mario got busted, I saw her frequently when I was assigned to the mailroom and she was coming in to visit her son. I knew only a few words and expressions in Italian, and every time Mrs. DeLucia would come to visit Mario, I would haul out my few phrases to impress her.

I'd say things I had heard around the house, like, *Como sta, ma che fa* "How are you," *Que bella sei,* "How pretty you are" and *Ma che dice,* "What do you have to say?"

Then when she would start chattering at me in Italian and I couldn't understand a word she was saying, I'd fall back on my ace—I would put my hands up in front of me, palms up, smile and say something that sounded like *Do ay vavas a me,* "What, are you trying to make a fool of me?"

I'd laugh and she'd laugh and off she would go the window visit room to talk to Mario.

One day my mother, Rose, and I stopped at Mrs. DeLucia's store in the neighborhood, and Mario's mom started talking to me in Italian. My mother looked at her funny said, "Why are you talking to Harry in Italian?"

Mrs. DeLucia said, in Italian, "I always talk to Harry in Italian."

So my mother said to her, "Harry doesn't understand Italian."

When my mother said that, Mrs. DeLucia started shaking her finger at me and said, "Ahh, you son um beech, Harry. I breaka you neck."

Her son, Mario, was no bigger than a bar of soap. If he weighed 120 pounds, it was a lot. He was basically illiterate and had been in and out of jails since he was 10 years old. This guy could never get it together. Whenever I would see him on the street, between his stretches in the county jail or the prison, he always struck me as a pathetic little loser.

In December of 1956 he was doing a major bid for 14 burglaries, 32-45 years, but he was coming up for parole in two years. Whenever I would leave the mailroom to go inside and would run into him (he would zero in on me because he remembered me from the neighborhood), he was always bitching to me about how he got screwed by the DA and his lawyer, George Pellettieri, one of Trenton's most prominent attorneys.

"Harry," he would say. "You know them sons of bitches lied to me. They said if I pleaded, they'd give me a light sentence. You call 45 years light?!"

Mario would tell me over and over how he pleaded to the 14 burglaries because prosecutor Mario Volpe and Pellettieri had guaranteed him he would get a light sentence and look at him now—sick (he had bad kidney problems) and doing heavy time. He seemed to be doubly pissed off at Volpe and Pellettieri because they were *goombahs,* Italians like him. He was always whining and threatening to escape and "do something bad" to Volpe and Pellettieri. I never took him seriously. Then I heard that the little SOB really did manage to get over the wall—I couldn't believe he had the moxie.

Mario locked in 6 wing, one of the "modern" (1895) housing units, because it was connected to the hospital, and he needed frequent treatments for his kidney problems—one had been removed and the other was diseased. Six-wing is big: the metal cell blocks run down the middle of the large stone building and they're backed up: four tiers of 25 cells, 100 cells, on one side of the block; then, backed up to them is another set of four tiers, a mirror image, with a five-foot wide utilities space between them running behind the metal walls of the cells. The utility space starts down below floor level, where the sewer and water pipes run, and goes all the way up to the roof, in total about six stories high. The utility space is criss-crossed with pipes and electrical conduits, giving a little monkey like Mario a perfect way to climb up to the roof.

Each cell in 6-wing is seven feet high, five feet wide, and seven feet deep. On the back wall is a metal toilet sitting slightly back in a little recess, a rectangle 19 inches deep by two feet wide so that when an inmate sits on the toilet, he kind of has to lean forward a little to avoid hitting his back on a shelf above the toilet. In the recess behind the toilet a steel plate about ten by twenty inches is welded to the wall; the metal toilet is bolted to the plate.

When Mario got into his cell in 6-wing, he discovered he could loosen the bolts on the toilet—and being as little and skinny as he was, he figured if he could get that toilet off the wall, he might be able to slide through the opening and get into the utility space. He plotted, planned and worked on the bolts for almost five years. While he was working on getting the toilet off and back on again without arousing the suspicions of the wing officer, he was stealing blankets, tearing them into strips and weaving them into a rope. He also accumulated a store of chicken and beef fat from the kitchen to grease himself up for the slide through the wall.

The night before the actual escape, Mario slathered grease all over his clothes and did a dry run. After he got through the wall into the utility space, Mario used the water pipes running into each cell as a kind of jungle gym to haul himself up 40 feet to the roof where a found a catwalk under a barred and louvered ventilation window. Nobody figured that an inmate would ever get up there, so the welds on the bars were light enough that even a runt like Mario could work them loose. After pulling the bars away from the vent in the roof, Mario laid his blanket rope on the catwalk and went back to his cell.

Mario was worried that other inmates would catch on to what he was doing and rat him out or that the wing officer would find the loose bolts on the toilet, so he decided to go out on the Friday night before Christmas, December 21, 1956. The Trenton area was under a blanket of heavy fog and drizzling rain that night as Mario reached the ventilation window. He punched his hand against the loosened bars, freeing them, bent the louvers, and squeezed through the ventilation window onto the roof of 6-wing, five stories above the ground. He worked his way across the 6-wing roof, down onto the top of the three-story 5-wing and then to the roof of the front house, dragging his rope behind him.

Under the cover of the fog, Mario attached the rope to the roof of the front house and dropped the other end to the ground. Just as he started to climb down, Tony Tripodi in 10-tower spotted him and fired a blast from his shotgun. Tony missed, but the shot scared Mario so badly that he slid down a lot faster than he had planned, giving himself bad rope burns on his hands. He landed hard on the grass strip in front of the prison along Third Street. Mario hit the ground running and was gone, disappearing into the fog before Tony's called-in alert could get anyone out the front door quickly enough to go after him.

Mario had engineered a brilliant escape, but once he was over the wall, he had no clue. He had spent most of his life in jail; he didn't know anything but prison and the neighborhood, so he had nowhere else to go. He hiked through the freezing rain out onto Route 1 north of the city and holed up for the rest of the night and the following day, a Saturday, on the grounds of a factory that made concrete blocks. When darkness fell on Saturday night, he went back to one of his old hangouts, a bar on Brunswick Avenue in North Trenton and tried to borrow some money to "head west." Somebody in the bar recognized Mario and knowing he was supposed to be in prison, called the Trenton police.

They converged on the neighborhood and found Mario, cold, sick and hungry, wandering in an alley near St. James church. He said he was almost relieved to get caught. He was back at the wall Sunday morning, in time to celebrate Christmas with his buddies and facing another one-to-three for the escape tacked onto his robbery bid. Poor old Mario. He was eventually released on a medical when he was too sick to do any more burglaries, and he died not long after getting out.

* * * * * * *

Throughout the 1950's, the makeup of the population of the prison was changing to reflect the changes in New Jersey's demographics. Since I was a kid, the City of Trenton had always had a small, stable middle class black population. Blacks never came into the Chambersburg section—they knew it was too dangerous. The Italian community openly resented blacks. In the fifties in Trenton, it was safer for a white to walk through a black neighborhood than for a black male to walk through the

Burg. The situation was somewhat similar in New Jersey's other major cities like Newark and its environs and Camden where a lot of our inmates came from.

I said earlier that many of the older Anglo guards resented guys like Vic Vitterito and me when we were hired because so many of the inmates we were guarding were of Italian descent. Now I found myself feeling the same way about blacks. The complexion of the inmate population was steadily shifting from white to black as a tremendous influx of blacks changed the racial balance of New Jersey. I had been raised in the Burg amidst wide-open racism, and truthfully it was difficult at first for me to adjust to seeing more and more black inmates and officers coming into the prison.

Maybe it was the discrimination I had experienced when I was first hired or maybe it was just my personality, but my resentment toward black officers didn't last long. All it took was a few incidents of rushing into a cell block side by side with brother black officers to subdue violent inmates to build mutual trust and respect between the races. It was like the army—it didn't matter what the guy's skin color was when both of your lives were on the line, and you were depending on the other guy to cover your back.

White and black officers adjusted to each other relatively quickly because of the shared danger. The same couldn't be said of the inmate population. Even today, there is constant tension between whites and blacks inside the jail. And in New Jersey's prison system whites are a distinct minority—probably about 30 percent or less of the entire prison population.

In October of 1958 while I was still working in the mail room, we had a small-scale disturbance that the *New York Times* called a "racial battle" and Trenton's Sunday newspaper, the *Times-Advertiser,* called a race riot. While the fight out in the 1-left (lockup) yard definitely had racial overtones, it had its roots in a long-simmering dispute between two individuals: Tom Cooper and Skate Jones.

Willard "Skate" Jones, a 28-year-old black guy from Camden, was kind of flighty: he was always involved in some kind of con-job or another, and he was constantly getting into fights with other inmates for scams that he had pulled—that's why he was in 1-left. He and Tom Cooper, who was white, locked on the same tier, and over time the two had had some dealings with each other.

Skate had scammed Tom a couple of times. As I heard it, Skate had made a bet with Cooper for a couple of packs, and he was welshing on the bet. Cooper had asked Skate a few times for the cigarettes, and Skate just kept saying to him, "Later, man," and "Don't worry, man, you'll git 'em."

Finally, Cooper had enough, and every cop and inmate in the jail heard the story of what went down. The cells on the upper tiers of 1-left had angle-iron frame cots with coiled metal springs. According to the scuttlebutt, Cooper worked both ends of a couple of the coils until they snapped off; then he straightened out the coils and honed one end on his cell floor until he had two seven-inch knitting needles. Then he took two shoe laces and wound them around one end of the long, sharp pieces of metal to make handles; he was ready for Skate.

A few days after Cooper made the shanks, I was in the mail room when the second tier went out for their two hours in 1-left yard; Skate and Cooper headed out with about 15 other guys. When inmates go out to yard from 1-left, they're pat frisked, but over a period of time when there haven't been any incidents, the officers get complacent and they don't do a thorough search.

About 15 minutes after 2-tier had gone out, the trouble bell in center started clanging—three tower had called in a report of a fight between black and white inmates in the 1-left yard. I joined several officers in the rotunda and one of them tossed me a club and a helmet and yelled, "Here, Harry! Fight in 1-left yard!"

We ran from center through the wing toward the door to the yard, but it took a couple of minutes to open both of the barred gates and to get the chain off of the second gate. I was in the first wave of about ten officers with clubs and helmets charging into the yard.

When we got out there, the black and white inmates were fighting viciously, using their fists, rocks, and anything else they could get their hands on, including baseball bats. We started clubbing them to break them apart, and at one point the guard in three tower fired a blast from his shotgun at a white inmate trying to climb the chain link fence that ran from 1-wing to the back wall of 7-wing and closed in the far end of the 1-left yard. The buckshot hit inmate George Stolze in the leg and brought him to the ground.

When some semblance of order was restored, with the whites grouped at one end of the yard and the blacks at the other, I saw Skate sitting on the ground with his back against a wall, his eyes closed and his head slumped over to one side. A couple of baseball bats were lying on the ground nearby. When Lt. Donald Thoms and I knelt down to look at Skate, I didn't see any blood, so I figured somebody had hit him in the head with a bat and he was out cold. I called to a couple of other officers to get a Gurney, and we loaded Skate onto it and rolled him down to the hospital. He still hadn't opened his eyes.

When we got to the hospital, Doctor Weisler was on duty. He looked at Skate, unbuttoned his shirt, felt for a pulse, and said, "This man is dead."

I was flabbergasted. I said, "Doc, how can he be dead?! There's no blood, no sign of any kind of injury."

Dr. Weisler pointed to Skate's chest and said, "Look at those marks."

I looked closely and I could barely see two raised red dots on Skate's chest. The doctor said, "Those are puncture wounds. Somebody stabbed him with a very fine instrument, like an ice pick, and the wounds sealed off on the inside of his chest when the weapon was pulled out. This guy bled to death internally."

I later heard from some of the other inmates that when the disturbance kicked off, the blacks had gathered at one end of the yard and the whites at the other end. They taunted each other with racial slurs for a couple of minutes and then charged into one another. As the two groups engaged, the inmates I talked to said that Tom Cooper zeroed in on Skate. Tom punched Skate two quick, hard shots in the chest, both wounds near, but not in, the heart. But that's all it takes—it's over in seconds.

Then, in the words of my long-time inmate-friend, Teddy Roberts, "It's just another body."

After the brawl was over and all of the inmates had been taken to the hospital (nearly every one of them had some sort of injury—either from each other or from us), we scoured the yard for the weapon that had been used to kill Skate. Nobody had any luck. Then a couple of officers went out into Federal Street on the north end of the jail and found the two needle-like shanks with the shoelace handles. Nobody could ever prove that it was Tom Cooper, so no indictment came down, but it was common knowledge inside that he killed Skate.

Those kinds of killings in a prison, where the DA's office can't get any inmates willing to testify, either because of "the code" or because they're afraid of reprisals, often go unpunished. And society doesn't much care. It's just one bad guy killing another, saving the state the expense of keeping him incarcerated.

A few months after Skate's death, we had another stabbing, and it was the same story: everybody in the jail knew who had done it, but none of the officers or staff had actually seen it, and no inmate witness was going to testify, so nobody was ever charged.

I was breaking in a young rookie cop, and we were in 4-wing when I heard a commotion coming from about midway down the flats where the water cooler was. I ran down and an inmate named Jenkins was sitting on the floor, conscious, holding his stomach and breathing heavily. He was trying desperately to stop the flow of blood that was pushing through his fingers and making a big, spreading stain on his shirt and pants. I sprinted up to the head of the wing and yelled out to the star officer to get some officers into the wing, that somebody had been stabbed.

It took maybe three minutes for somebody to get the keys to the wing, get the gates open and then another couple of minutes to get a Gurney down from the hospital and get Jenkins loaded onto it. By that time, he had lost consciousness, and we could see he wasn't going to make it—he might even have been dead at that point. At any rate, blood now covered the whole front of his shirt, and his pants, down to the knees, were also soaked. The young cop watched as the other officers wheeled Jenkins out; then he turned to me and said, "Fuck this, Harry. I quit."

And he did.

* * * * * * *

In the spring of 1959, several months after Skate Jones's murder, a 19-year-old kid came in on a murder rap. He's still in the prison, back in on another multiple-murder conviction. He should have been sentenced to die in the electric chair in 1959, but because the victim's wife interceded, he wasn't. He did a life bid, got out, and went on another killing spree. This time he was sentenced to death, but he beat the needle when his death sentence was overturned—twice. Even though I talked to him every day for years, I don't think I'll ever be able to figure out what makes Rich Biegenwald tick.

I first met Rich in 1959 when I was working in the mailroom and his mother Sally used to come to visit him. Even though her son had killed a municipal prosecutor and was considered a cop killer, I still made it a point to be pleasant and helpful to Mrs. Biegenwald just as I had with Kayo Konigsberg's mom and dad. Rich appreciated my treating his mother with respect, so we always got along well throughout the years that I knew him during his first bid until his parole in 1975.

As I said, I could never figure him out. When we first got acquainted in '59, Rich was 19 years old. He seemed to me to be bright and articulate, and he was a good-looking young guy. He seemed like the type of kid who could have had a lot going for him on the street. Later on, he got into some trouble here and there in the institution, usually a fight with another inmate, and he was sent to 1-left while I was wing officer there in the '60's. That's when I got to know him better and over time he told me his story.

Back in December of 1958 when Biegenwald was 18 years old and living on Staten Island, he stole a car, picked up a buddy and drove over to Bayonne. While the friend, Jimmy Sparnroft, who was also 18, waited in the car, Rich went into a mom-and- pop delicatessen owned by a couple named Sladowski on Avenue B. Stephen Sladowski, 47, the husband, was alone in the store; he also happened to be an assistant municipal prosecutor in Bayonne. Sparnroft wasn't as tough as Rich: when the two were captured later in Maryland, Jimmy spilled his guts and ratted Biegenwald out.

Sparnroft said that while he was waiting out in the car, he heard a shot fired inside the store. Biegenwald came running out, carrying the money and the sawed-off shotgun that he had used to kill Sladowski. Before he got into the car, Rich fired another shot to scare away four kids who had heard the first shot and were running toward the store. Biegenwald jumped into the car and told Sparnroft to take off. He told Sparnroft the store owner hadn't wanted to give him the money. "I couldn't miss him at four feet," he said.

Sladowski, shot in the chest, died behind the counter of the store that he and his wife had bought four months earlier.

The day after the robbery, Biegenwald and Sparnroft headed south in the stolen car, and speeding through Salisbury, Maryland, got flagged down by a sergeant of the Salisbury police. As the officer approached the car, Rich fired two shots at him, one pellet (called a "pumpkin ball") grazing the sergeant's cheek.

As he was telling me this story, Rich chuckled when he said, "I had them Maryland cops runnin', man. I chased that one cop right into the woods."

Sparnroft and Biegenwald took off again at high speed and a little while later they got stopped again about fifteen miles outside of Salisbury by a Maryland state trooper, Lieutenant Carroll Serman. Rich fired two shots at him, hitting him in the thigh. Serman fired back with his service revolver, hitting Rich in the right cheek. Serman had balls: he charged the car while Rich was trying to reload the shotgun and kicked the gun out of Biegenwald's hands. Sparnroft wasn't in the same league as Rich, and "meekly surrendered." Serman took the two of them into custody.

(A couple of years ago I ran into a Monmouth County assistant DA They hate Biegenwald in Monmouth County because they tried him three times on his later crimes and couldn't make the death penalty stick. The DA said, "That's when we should have killed him. Those Maryland cops had their chance and blew it.")

Biegenwald and Sparnroft were brought back to New Jersey and arraigned. It didn't take a jury long to convict Rich, but then he got his first big break. During the death penalty phase of the trial, Mrs. Sladowski asked the jury to spare Biegenwald's life, primarily because of his age—he was 18 at the time of his trial. "There's been enough bloodshed already," she told the court, so Rich was sentenced to life.

When he first came into Trenton, Rich told me, he was "prime meat" for the older predators who wait for young, good-looking kids to come in. In one of our many conversations while he was locked up in 1-left, Biegenwald told me how it was for him when he first came in, back in the late '50's. He considered himself to be a street-wise kid, and he knew enough about jail to realize that he had to establish himself in a hurry.

Rich said to me, "Harry, I figured as soon as the first guy approached me looking for a boyfriend, I was gonna have to do somethin' quick and violent."

After five days, he got out of quarantine and was assigned to a cell in 6-wing. Sure enough, as soon as he got settled in, he was approached by a one of the biggest and toughest guys in the prison, a huge black guy named Theodore Gibson.

Biegenwald told me, "Gibson approached me and started making nicey-nice overtures. I told him to go fuck himself."

Gibson was probably the toughest guy in the joint back then—he was about six foot-five, weighed about 240 and lifted weights religiously every day. Rich said that when he told Gibson to fuck off, Gibson's eyes narrowed down and he said, "OK, asshole, I'll see you later, out in the yard."

This conversation took place on the third tier of 6-wing, about thirty feet above the concrete floor of the flats with only a pipe railing between Biegenwald, Gibson and outer space. Biegenwald said he knew he had a big problem. Gibson expected him to fight (Biegenwald was about five-eight, maybe 160 pounds at the time), and he said he fully intended to. He figured he might have to take a beating, but he was going to try to at least hurt Gibson as much as possible and get the word out that he was nobody to screw around with. That's how it works in a prison: when a kid like Biegenwald comes in, he either has to establish himself fast by tangling with a big, mean inmate, or he has to resign himself to being somebody's "girlfriend" for the duration of his sentence.

Biegenwald said, "The big problem was if Gibson decided to throw me off the third tier. I figured I could stand a beating, but I couldn't stand getting thrown off the tier."

Yard was called out and Biegenwald headed toward the stairs at the end of the tier . . . and there was Gibson, waiting. Rich said he didn't miss a step—he just put his head down, clenched his fists down at his side, looked at Gibson and kept on going. Finally, when Biegenwald was about twenty paces away from the end of the tier, Gibson turned and headed down the stairs. From that point on, Rich told me, the word was out: "Leave Biegenwald alone; if you cause him a problem, he'll fight."

And that was the end of it. Biegenwald said he found that once his point was made, he wouldn't have to keep on hurting people to prove himself. Any young inmate who has guts enough to take a stand—though he has to realize it may mean getting the shit kicked out of him while he hurts the other guy—will be left alone. So Rich Biegenwald established himself and, like me, settled in for the long haul. And he's still there forty years later . . . but that's another story.

****

When Rich Biegenwald first came in, his toughness was impressive for a kid so young. Another guy who came in around the same time, Fred Hartjen, was much older than Rich and probably even tougher. "Big Freddy" Hartjen was tall, about 6 ft., 2 in., and walked with an almost exaggeratedly erect posture. He always gave off an air of aloofness and seldom spoke to other inmates. A guy like this is usually left alone by other convicts because they're never sure what his angle is—what he's capable of. Hartjen was in his mid-forties when I first met him around 1958 and had been sentenced to Trenton for kidnapping, robbery and the fatal stabbing of a guy in Jersey City.

Hartjen was originally from New York State and had done heavy time in upstate prisons before we got him. His reputation preceded him because of a spectacular escape attempt in the Manhattan Criminal Courts Building while New Jersey was trying to extradite him for the Jersey City murder.

New York had detained him as a suspected parole violator, and New Jersey detectives had gone into the City to bring him back to face the murder charge. Three Jersey detectives, an NYPD detective and a New York State parole officer were escorting Hartjen to an extradition hearing in the courthouse when he broke away from them and bolted down a stairway from the second floor toward the lobby. The second-floor corridor was jammed with people, so the officers held their fire until Freddy hit the stairs; then they started blasting away at him. They chased him into the crowded lobby, firing a total of 11 shots at him as people screamed and ducked for cover.

Of the 11 shots fired, seven hit Freddy while a couple more nicked bystanders. Freddy fell to the floor in front of the lobby candy stand. With the cops standing over him, he gasped, "I had nothing to lose. I gave it a try."

They just don't make 'em like that anymore.

So we knew what Hartjen was made of before he even came through the intake gate. A year or so after he was in Trenton, Hartjen gave us the most impressive demonstration of iron-willed toughness I've ever seen. He got a resentment against one of the other inmates and decided to nail him. Hartjen was the silent type who would never let on who he ran with or who he was out to get—he would just kill the guy and that would be the end of it. We never did find out who he was after that night, but we definitely found out how he was going to do it.

Every Tuesday night a first-run movie from the street was brought in and shown in the chapel/rec hall, a popular break from the routine. On this particular night, Hartjen arrived early and took a seat on one of the metal folding chairs in a row near the back of the hall. As the other inmates filed in to take their seats, he continued to sit quietly until just before the movie was to start.

As the lights started to dim, one of the other inmates looked over at Hartjen, jumped up and yelled, "Holy shit!"

He pointed down at Hartjen's leg. Hartjen was still sitting quietly, unflinching, as blood ran down his leg, soaking his pants. A hole had been eaten away in the fabric covering his inner thigh, exposing a jagged, gaping wound. Acid was eating away his pants and the flesh from his thigh.

Hartjen had stolen some caustic soda crystals, either from the hospital, or more likely from the tag shop where acid was used for etching the license plates, and had mixed them with water. Then he had taped the container to the inside of his thigh and was waiting for the lights to go out so he could go after his target in the dark. Somehow, either the container broke, or more likely, the acid ate through it, and Freddy just sat there as the acid ate away his leg, almost down to the bone while blood poured down his leg. I often wondered if the other inmate hadn't noticed the blood, if Hartjen would have sat there until he bled to death.

They rushed him down to the hospital and patched him up. He maintained a stoic silence about the whole incident: he never admitted how he got the acid, and he never indicated in any way who he was out to get. In later years, like Barney Doak, Hartjen started to lose it mentally, and I think he may have died in prison or in the Vroom Building (the unit for the criminally insane out on the grounds of Trenton Psychiatric Hospital). To this day, though, I still remember Big Freddy Hartjen as one of the hardest and toughest of those old-time cons from the machine-gun mobster era.

* * * * * * *

A couple of months after the Hartjen incident, I was doing my job in the mailroom when I looked across the lobby and saw John Takach pulling the door open to let in two of the spiffiest-looking cops I had ever seen. I could tell by the look on John's face, even though I was about thirty feet away, that he was barely stifling a laugh because of the way these guys were dressed. They wore gray jodhpurs with a yellow stripe tucked sharply into knee-high spit-polished black riding boots. Over their tunics they wore black Sam Browne belts with holsters on their hips and Smokey the Bear type hats. But what got to John wasn't so much the clothing as the sidearm—pearl-handled revolvers! I could read John's mind. Here we were, two Trenton State Prison guards dressed in dark blue pants, light blue shirt, navy tie and a silver badge, clothes that we had probably had for five or six years at least—and the Trenton cops didn't dress much differently—being treated to the latest in cop *chic*.

John and I may have been amused by their appearance, but there was no joy on the faces of these two Georgia highway patrolmen—they were all "bidness." What went down with them, though, shows how widespread and vicious the racism was back then.

One of my responsibilities in the mailroom was to help process inmates in and out of the jail, either on intake, release, court trip, parole or transfer. These two state cops had driven all the way up from Georgia to bring one of our black inmates back to their jurisdiction—probably an extradition.

When two of our officers brought the inmate down to the front house, one of the Georgia cops said, "Y 'all goin' back where you belong, boy. Now git your ass in gear, and let's git outa here."

He made a couple of other remarks that were demeaning to blacks, and then told the inmate to put his arms behind his back so he could be cuffed. The inmate said, "Hey, you ain't cuffin' me with my arms in back for a ride all the way back to Georgia." I swear if I hadn't been standing there, the inmate would have been dead.

One of the cops turned to me and said, in that heavy southern drawl, “At what point do we officially take charge of this prisoner?”

I knew immediately what that was about, and it wasn’t something you’d see on *Andy of Mayberry*, so I said to him, “Look, as long as he’s in this jail, he belongs to New Jersey. There ain’t gonna be no ass-whuppin in here. Once you’re outside, what you do is up to you.”

Then I turned to the inmate and told him he ought to go to the bathroom before he left, and one of the cops said, “Thas right, boy, ain’t gonna be no piss stops for you for a long while.” The other Georgia cop grinned.

So the inmate went to the bathroom and came out; by now he was looking pretty shook up. He could see that dealing with us in a maximum-security prison in New Jersey had been a picnic compared to what he was going to put up with from these two for the next couple of days.

The cops put the cuffs on him, and he said, “Hey, those are on kind of tight, aren’t they?”

The Georgia cop looked at him with contempt and said, “Why, boy, if we’d have known we was gonna transport such a high-class fella as yourself, we’d have brought the fur-lined handcuffs.”

At this, the other cop burst into laughter, but I don’t think I’ve ever seen a sadder-looking inmate than that guy as they escorted him out through the front door.

6

CHAPTER SIX

1-LEFT

By September of 1960, with the high turnover rate typical of prison guards, experienced officers were in short supply. With about nine years of experience, I was now a senior officer. Captain Abbott called me into his office and asked me to transfer out of the mail room into what might be the toughest job in the jail: first-shift wing officer in 1-left lockup.

One-wing is a four-story brick building built in 1870-72 with the cells arranged in a large block running down the center of the structure. The block is divided into 1-left and 1-right, each section consisting of four tiers of 22 one-man cells, 88 cells per section and 176 cells total for the building. The entire 88-cell section called 1-left was designated as the lockup section. Every prison has to have a "jail within a jail" to house those inmates who violate institutional rules or even commit another indictable crime, such as the murder of another inmate or an officer. After the riots of 1952 when the inmates had torn up 5-wing, 1-left had been designated as the lockup section of the prison. So, if Trenton State Prison was the institution containing the toughest and meanest criminals in the state, it doesn't take much imagination to picture the type of outlaw that would get sent to 1-left lockup. And here was Capt. Abbott asking ol' Harry to become the CEO of the bad boys.

Just to give an idea of how tight the security was in that wing, when my shift began at 6:20 a.m., I would go through center and approach the bars that run floor to ceiling and wall to wall across the neck of 1-left. A smaller door-sized barred gate with a heavy mechanical lock was the first obstacle. All of the barred gates for the other wings coming into center were controlled by electronic locks activated by buttons on a console in the center control booth. Getting into 1-left was a different story altogether: first, an officer (usually one of the extras assigned to duty in the rotunda) had to go behind center control to a big board with keys dangling from hooks and get the set of 1-left keys; then, he and I would walk across the rotunda and he would unlock the gate to let the two of us in; then, we would get to a second barred gate about fifteen feet into the wing, and he would unlock a chain wrapped around the bars of that gate with a second key; then he would unlock another key-lock in the gate itself with a third key. After unlocking all of those locks, the officer would lock each one behind us as we worked our way into the wing. When

I was finally in the wing, he would turn around and repeat the procedure to let himself back out into center.

This kind of routine was a daily reminder of how serious the administration was about security and how dangerous the inmates were in that wing. As wing officer I was locked in at 6:20 a.m., let out for half an hour for lunch, and then locked in again until my shift ended at 2:20 p.m.

When an officer wanted to get out of 1-left, he would slap the wall next to the inner gate loud enough for the star officer to hear and call out to an extra to get the keys and come open the doors. If an inmate had to go somewhere in the prison, like the hospital or the social work office, four officers were required: an officer stood at the top of each of the stairways leading down from the tier as the wing officer unlocked the cell door, and a fourth officer stood by to act as escort. In the sixties, we moved these guys through the jail unshackled. Later, after a few of them attacked their escorts, the rule was put in that they were to be handcuffed and shackled whenever they were moved through the jail.

An inmate earned a transfer into 1-left lockup (tier two, three or four) in a variety of ways: assault on another inmate; physical or verbal threats on an officer; attempted escape—all of these would merit extended stays in 1-left lockup, sometimes lasting for several years. Although the potential capacity of 1-left (excluding the 22 cells in the flats, which were used for bread and water punishment) is 66 (three tiers x 22 cells each tier), it would be unusual to have more than 35 inmates in there at any given time. If there was a riot or significant disturbance at Trenton or one of the other prisons in the state, the wing might fill up; under normal conditions, though, the fourth tier sat empty, and the inmates were scattered throughout the other two tiers. All 1-left inmates were locked down 22 hours per day. They got out two hours per day for a shower and some yard. Typically, a tier would take yard together, which meant about fifteen to twenty men exercising in a little yard between 1-wing and the back of 7-wing.

Since we couldn't have tier runners under this kind of security, all housekeeping, including delivering meals to cells, distributing necessities such as soap and toilet paper, even mopping the floors, was done by the officers. Meals were brought into the wing by inmate food detail workers. Then the wing officer would bring the food on a small tray to the cells; each cell door had a slot with a metal ledge to set the tray on. If the officer was setting down a glass of milk or a bowl of soup, which was always cold by the time it got to the cell, it was considered bad form **not** to stick your thumb in the liquid as it was served to the inmate—just to remind him where he was and who was who.

Inmates normally came into 1-left through a "court-line" hearing. When an inmate violated an institutional rule, he was written up by an officer and given a hearing in a little room just outside of the office of the chief of custody. Usually the chief handled the hearing by himself or designated another "white hat" to do it. (Up until the murder of Sgt. Donald Bourne in 1972, officers of the rank of sergeant and above wore white hats while the rest of us wore blue.) Throughout most of the years that I was a blue hat ('50s, '60s, '70s), court-line outcomes were predictable. The captain read the report and then asked the inmate for his version. Nine times out of ten, the captain looked at the report, listened to the inmate, found him guilty and gave him some kind of punishment ranging from loss of privileges, to ten days' bread and water, to extended time in lockup. On a few occasions, especially if the reporting officer was known to be a little too free with write-ups (like a cop we called "Write 'em Up" Smith), the captain might let the inmate off with a warning—but this was rare.

When an inmate was sentenced to ten days' bread and water, he went into the hole, one of cells in the 1-left flats. The 22 cells on the ground floor of 1-left might be called "solitary confinement" in another prison, but we didn't use that term in Trenton; we always referred to that section as "the hole" or "bread and water." The bread and water cells were five feet wide by eight feet, eight inches long and seven feet high (pretty much the standard cell size at TSP). At the time I was assigned there, the first cell had been refitted as a small office with a desk, a lamp, a fan and a filing cabinet for the officer in charge of the wing.

Each of the rest of the 21 cells was furnished with a solid concrete pad about six inches high that, with a three-inch thick straw mattress filled with bed bugs, served as a bed. Over in the right rear corner, built up about eight inches off the floor was a triangular wooden platform about 18 inches deep with a hole in the center of the triangle. This "one-holer" was the toilet. The pipe dropped straight down to an elbow that connected directly to a sewer pipe with running water below. Since there was no trap, odors—and rats—came up through the hole. Guys confined in those cells have told me that between the bedbugs and the constant threat of rats, to get a full night's sleep in a bread and water cell, you had to be either very tough or very nuts—or both. A few years before I was assigned to the wing, they ran electricity into that first cell when it was converted to officers' use, but none of the rest of the cells in the flats had electricity, so the only light coming in filtered down from the narrow windows in the opposite wall. And the catwalk on the tier above cut the light down even more, so even if reading or writing materials were allowed in there, they wouldn't have been of much use.

During the years I was assigned to the wing, when an inmate was transferred to 1-left and put on bread and water, he spent twenty-four hours a day in the cell except for one hour toward the middle of his ten-day sentence when he was let out to take a shower. He was allowed one 16-ounce paper cup of water and four slices of institution-baked white bread for breakfast, the same for lunch and ditto for dinner. Every third day, he got a treat: a bologna and cheese sandwich for lunch. Sometimes people think I'm kidding when I say that an inmate was put on bread and water punishment for ten days, but it was no joke. Up until the late 1960's, when an inmate filed suit against the state, and the federal courts told New Jersey they couldn't do it anymore, bread and water was a standard punishment for a variety of offenses.

An inmate could be sentenced to the hole through the court-line hearing, or he might go in automatically for a certain type of offense, such as being caught in a homosexual act. This was an automatic ten days on bread and water. Bread and water punishment was limited to ten days, but once an inmate was in there, he had to watch himself because he was then at the mercy of the wing officer if he got out of line. For example, not too long after I became wing officer, an inmate was put in the hole for ten days, and on the ninth day he started giving me a ration of shit about something that I did or didn't do. I'm normally an even-tempered guy, and I let this go on for quite a while, even trying to kid around with him to get him back on track, but he wouldn't let up; finally, I told him to shut up or else, but he kept running off at the mouth, so two days later I let him out of the hole, as I was required by institutional rules to do, and I put him in lock-up, which meant moving him from the bottom floor to the first tier directly above. But before I let him out of the hole that morning, I called center and told them that he had been giving me trouble and that I was putting him back in the hole after I put him in lock-up for the one day. That's all there was to it—no new court-line hearing required. So if a guy wasn't careful, he could keep going in and out of bread and water like a yo-yo because once he got put on bread and water through court-line, his ass belonged to the wing officer.

If an inmate had committed some infraction and hadn't yet gone to court-line but was considered to be under lockup and was still in his own wing, a padlock would be put on his cell door to prevent the cell from being opened. This also let the wing officer on a shift change know that the guy was in lockup and awaiting either a court-line hearing or a transfer to 1-left.

One of the first guys I ran into after being assigned to 1-left was August Bernard "Barney" Doak. I remembered him from his picture on the front page of the Trenton *Times* that Ginny had sent me when I was overseas during the 1952 print shop riot. I had just about forgotten he was still in the jail because I never saw him—which is not so unusual since he had been in lockup and out of circulation for the past eight years for his role as a ringleader in the riots.

Being in isolation for so many years had taken a terrible toll on Doak, and he had deteriorated mentally. I always knew an inmate was starting to lose it when he became super-concerned about cleanliness and the way his meals were being served. When an inmate has reached that stage, the thumb-in-the-soup routine is enough to put him way over the edge, driving him into a rage while reminding him how helpless he is, locked in a five-by-eight-foot cage. I wouldn't do something like that to Doak. I never disliked the guy, and he had gotten so bad that I felt sorry for him.

I first noticed that Doak was starting to lose it when he asked me for extra soap and some detergent. Then, a few days later, he said to me, "Harry, could you get me one of them scrub brushes? You know, the kind with the real stiff bristles?"

I got him the soap and brush and then watched him meticulously scrub down the walls and the floor of his cell every day. It became a regular routine. I watched Jimmy Wilburn, the guy who had broken Warden Carty's jaw one day in center in the early '50s, go through the same process. Just before we would have to call in a squad to take Wilburn to the state mental hospital, as we often did, he would start scrubbing his cell just like Doak.

When I would bring Barney his food in 1-left, I would set it down slowly on the ledge in the slot midway down the barred door. He would look at the food carefully, cocking his head like a bird, making sure that everything was just so. God forbid that one type of food should be touching another.

Doak would always say the same thing to me: "Did you check this food out, Harry? There ain't no bugs under that hash, are there?"

Then he would take the napkin off the tray and methodically wipe under the tin cup and dish, followed by a thorough wipedown of the edge of his bunk where he was going to sit for his meal. Watching him made me edgy. He was definitely off his nut, but there was no way he'd get any help or treatment in this place. He would go on like this until he got bad enough to be shipped out to the state hospital or died. He was still in 1-left when I was transferred to a new job about five years later. Truthfully, I don't know whatever happened to Barney Doak. I can only assume he died in the prison infirmary or out at the state hospital.

****

About a month after I came into 1-left, while I was still getting used to the routine, a young guy named Roberts was transferred into Trenton from Rahway. Because he had broken a sergeant's jaw at Rahway, he was sent directly to lockup. The word was, "Watch out for this one."

Teddy Roberts, "The Bull," was 22 years old and had been sentenced to life for a murder during an armed robbery in Elizabeth. I already knew who Teddy was by his reputation and by an incident that had taken place in front of me. Not long after he had come into Trenton in 1957, while I was still in the mailroom, Teddy and his two partners, George Artis and Thomas Knight, were remanded back to Union County jail. They had been sentenced for the murder; now they were going back to have time added on for the robbery charge. Teddy, Knight and Artis were shackled and handcuffed, and the three men were being taken through the front house to go out to the state station wagon for the trip to the court house in Elizabeth. The escorting officers had drawn sidearms and were waiting for the three prisoners in front of the mailroom counter, so I was shooting the breeze with them.

The grille gate opened and the three shackled prisoners came shuffling through. I should explain that when an inmate was shackled for transport, he was handcuffed with his hands in front of him, and ankle cuffs connected by an 18-inch chain were put on, restricting the length of the steps the man could take. Another longer chain with a loop at either end was attached to the short length of chain between the handcuffs and the chain between the ankle cuffs, restricting movement even further. Normally, unless the prisoner was considered a serious escape threat, the ankle cuffs and the longer connecting chain were removed in the car for the inmate's comfort. The handcuffs were always left on until the man was safely in the cell at the county jail.

When Teddy and the others came into the front house that day, Sergeant Doll was on duty, and he stopped the three men to frisk them one last time before they went out to the street. Teddy was wearing his blue denim shirt that was a part of the required inmate uniform back then, and he had two cigars sticking out of his pocket. He had told his wing officer that he was bringing the cigars to smoke in county jail while he waited for sentencing.

Inmates commonly carried cigars or a pack of cigarettes in their shirt pockets, so nobody thought much about Teddy's cigars. Almost as an afterthought, Sergeant Doll said, "Wait a minute, let's take a look at these," and he took the cigars out of

Teddy's pocket.

Damn," the sergeant said, "they're heavy." The prison had recently been given an x-ray machine from one of the local shoe stores because the American Medical Association had come out with data showing it could be dangerous for people to be getting their feet routinely x-rayed. We had put the machine in the mail room and used it to look at the contents of food packages coming in for the inmates (looking for files in cakes—no joke).

Sergeant Doll put the cigars under the x-ray machine—inside each cigar was a needle-sharp shank. Doll was pissed; he walked up to the Bull, unlocked the handcuffs, grabbed Bull's arms and roughly 'cuffed him in the back. This meant a long, uncomfortable ride to Elizabeth for Teddy, sitting on the edge of the seat to accommodate his hands shackled behind him. In a case like this, comfort was not an issue. Doll then had the state police called in to pick these guys up and do the escort duty to the county courthouse. Since the state police didn't have to live with these guys the way we did, and in general considered all prison inmates to be subhuman, they would not be an inmate's first choice for escorts.

Of course, details of the incident in the front house between Doll and Roberts had made it all the way out to the tag shop in the far corner of the prison compound within about three minutes—that's literally how fast news travels in Trenton State Prison. So before he had even gotten settled in, Teddy Roberts had established his reputation.

I assumed for years that Teddy had planned to use the shanks to try to over-power the officers in the car and attempt to escape on the way to or from the county jail, like Zagorski had with Vic Vitterito and Throckmorton in '51. When Teddy was returned to the prison with the extra time for the robbery tacked on to his murder bid, he was given a court-line hearing and assigned to 1-left lockup for attempted escape.

Several years later, while Teddy was still in lockup (for another charge) and I had become wing officer in 1-left, I found out the real story. Teddy and I had gotten to know one another well and had developed a deep mutual respect. He opened up and told me how he had made the shanks for that trip back in '57. As soon as he had gotten out of new-inmate quarantine, Teddy had been assigned to the repair shop because of the skills he had learned as a construction worker on the street. One day, shortly before the trip back to the Union County jail while he was fixing one of the wooden folding chairs from the death house, he discovered that the dowels connecting the legs had metal rods in the core. He pulled three of the rods out, cut them down and made three nasty little shanks (sharpened needle-like pieces of metal with string or shoelaces wrapped around one end for a handle) to fit inside the cigars. Then he told me that he never intended to kill a cop on the trip, as Doll had thought. Artis had ratted on him and Knight and the shanks were intended for Artis. Teddy said he knew that he, Artis and Knight would be put in the same cell in the county jail while waiting to be called into court, and that Artis never would have made it into the courtroom. That's part of the code: you rat out your partners, you die. Simple. Neat. No further discussion.

But back to 1960 and 1-left. After a few years in Trenton (a couple of them spent in lockup for the shank caper), Teddy was transferred to Rahway to be closer to his family in Union County. Shortly after Teddy got there, a sergeant had put his hands on him, and Teddy had hit the man, breaking his jaw. This meant an automatic transfer back to Trenton, straight into 1-left lockup . . . again. Teddy's reputation was growing.

When Teddy got back to Trenton in '61, I was now the first-shift 1-left wing officer. Though I had heard about him, and I had watched him fight in the yard when he was working out with the other boxers (impressive), this was the first time I had actually met him.

Believe me when I say I was wary—I figured this was an unstable, dangerous guy. The word was that you didn't put your hands on Teddy Roberts in any way because to do so meant that you'd immediately be put on your back. Teddy is about five feet, seven inches tall, and, as his nickname implies, he's built like a bull. When I met him in 1961, he weighed about 190 pounds and carried himself like (and fought like) Joe Frazier.

As I got to know him, I realized that Teddy lived by a certain code of conduct. It's a code that people unfamiliar with crime, criminals, law enforcement and corrections would probably consider warped or even perverted, but a prison guard knows exactly what to expect from those inmates who live by it. It's the inmate who has no framework within which he operates, the one who commits violence suddenly and randomly with no apparent reason, that makes our work so dangerous. Inmates like Teddy Roberts can be violent when provoked, but they're predictable. If an officer knows and understands the code, he or she can usually stay out of harm's way.

Teddy bounced in and out of 1-left. After he did his time for hitting the sergeant at Rahway, he went back into the general population for a while and was put in 4-wing, the oldest wing in the jail. All of the other wings had stacked cell blocks with steep metal stairways leading to the upper tiers, like on a ship. Since 4-wing was 130 years old and had never been changed over to the "new" style of stacked cages, it had only two tiers with two long cement staircases on either side of the central corridor.

A few months after Teddy was assigned to 4-wing, one of our officers, a guy named Zielinski, made the mistake of testing the "Don't-put-your-hands-on-Teddy-Roberts" rule. Zielinski, had gotten a call to let tier two (Teddy's tier) out for yard. Zielinski went down the tier, opening each of the cells and letting the men out to head down to the steps at the end of the tier. Zielinski got the men lined up and started down the wide concrete staircase to the flats. Bull was at the head of the line, right behind Zielinski. Just as Zielinski got to the bottom of the steps, with the inmates filing down behind him, another officer yelled that yard was being held up and to put the men back in their cells.

Zielinski turned around and yelled at the last guy up at the top of the stairs to turn around and go back to his cell. All of the men turned around, bitching and moaning about not getting yard and about cops screwing up. Zielinski was right behind Bull as the line moved slowly back up the stairs. As Bull reached the top step, Zielinski said something to him about hurrying up, put his hand in the middle of Bull's back and shoved him. Big mistake. Bull spun around and without a second's hesitation, picked Zielinski up and threw him back down the cement stairs. Zielinski tumbled down the steps and rolled onto the floor of the flats. He got bruised from banging his elbows and knees on the steps and wall, but otherwise he wasn't hurt. He was, however, pissed off.

He wrote Bull up and Teddy drew another year in lockup for aggravated assault on an officer. Teddy was now going to be mine for a long, long time. In fact, because we were together for so many years, Teddy and I developed a remarkable rapport. Over the years, as I got to know him well, I developed a deep respect for Teddy Roberts; even though I could never condone his criminal acts or his violent behavior toward officers, I slowly began to understand where he was coming from.

He and I would talk about the "rule book" that governed our conduct toward one another when I was on the job. For example, it was understood that he had every right to try to escape. In fact, some inmates take this a step further and say that they have a responsibility to attempt to get out. They see themselves as guerrilla street fighters in a war between them and an oppressive society; they're prisoners of war with an obligation to do the honorable thing—get over the wall. It was also understood, and Teddy never had a problem with this, that if I was in the tower and saw him climbing the wall, I wouldn't hesitate to shoot him—no questions asked.

One day toward the end of my five years as 1-left wing officer, when The Bull and I had become good friends, an inmate runner came into the wing with a pass for T. Roberts to report to Captain ("Machine Gun") Abbott's office. The inmate's number wasn't on the pass, so I assumed it was for Teddy, forgetting there was also a Thomas Roberts in lockup.

I had to head out to center for some reason, so I went to Teddy's cell and said, "C'mon, Bull. Captain Abbott wants to see you."

I don't remember exactly what Teddy said, but I'm sure his response was something like, "Aw shit, what the fuck does that asshole want now?" as he hauled himself off his bunk.

Bull was now a veteran inmate and I was a veteran cop. Everybody in the joint knew both of us and knew we were friends. Bull was especially well known and respected for his boxing abilities. Before he had been transferred to Rahway, back in the late '50's, Bull and about ten other good fighters, including Hurricane Carter, could be seen every day during nice weather out in the yard putting on a show that fight fans would pay big money to see.

Because we were both so well known and I knew Bull so well, I didn't bother with the four-officers-to-bring-a-man-out-of-1-left rule, and Bull and I headed off to the captain's office. We went through the two locked gates, out of the wing, through center and into the anteroom outside of Captain Abbott's office, casually talking about nothing in particular.

We waited a few minutes outside of Abbott's door, and then the captain growled in his raspy voice, "Awright, Roberts, c'mon in here."

Abbott still looked like the tough cop he was when he shot George Vaszorich off the laundry roof. At six feet, maybe 200 pounds of muscle and a short, military-style crew cut, he definitely looked the part of the chief of custody and commander of the security force.

As Teddy and I walked casually into Abbott's office, the chief took one look at The Bull and said angrily, "Jesus Christ, I didn't want this Roberts, I wanted

Tommy Roberts!"

I figured it was the clerk's fault for not putting the inmate number and the full first name on the pass, so I wasn't bothered that Abbott was pissed off. I just turned to Teddy, put my hand on his arm and said, "Aw shit, c'mon Bull, let's get outta here."

"Crash!" Abbott literally leaped out of his chair, sending it crashing onto its back as his right hand shot down to his side, reaching for a sidearm that wasn't there.

"Jesus Christ, Harry, don't touch him," Abbott yelled. "That's Teddy Roberts, for Chrissakes!"

Bull and I just turned and stared at him like he was crazy and walked out of the office. As the two of us walked back through center, we had a good chuckle over the whole scene. I don't think either of us had ever seen Abbott lose his cool like that, and we both enjoyed it immensely for totally different reasons.

(Today, Teddy is out of jail—in fact, he recently retired after twenty years of working in construction and maintenance for the corrections department. He got to know the jail so well that when he was paroled, the state hired him to help maintain it. He's still rough around the edges, but he's one of my closest friends, and he frequently comes over to visit and have dinner with Ginny and me.)

* * * * * * *

Monday, January 2, 1961 was a holiday, and I was relaxing at home, watching the bowl games on TV. Newly elected President John F. Kennedy had created quite a stir by showing up unannounced at the Orange Bowl to watch Navy play Missouri. Kennedy and the people with him surprised everybody in the stadium, including the Secret Service guys, by taking seats right in with the crowd.

Just after dinner, as I was watching the game and listening to the commentators juggle the play-by-play with a running commentary about the newly elected president and his group of friends, the telephone rang. It was Chief Abbott.

"Harry," he said, "we've got a problem at Rahway, and I need you over here right away."

Ginny and I and the kids were living on Third Street at the time, about a block from the front door of the prison. At this point in my career, with about twelve years in, I was considered a veteran officer, and for the past few years I had frequently been called in for "goon squad" jobs. Back then, the goon squad wasn't a formal thing—not like these specially trained SWAT units or tactical operations teams they have today. We were just a bunch of officers who weren't afraid to mix it up with the inmates when there was a disturbance or when an unruly inmate had to be moved out of a cell and put in lockup or taken to Trenton Psychiatric.

I mentioned earlier that as a kid growing up in the projects of Trenton—the Donnelly Homes—I had gotten involved in the boxing program the city sponsored in a basement recreation area. Even though I wasn't a big guy like some of the other cops, for some reason—maybe the boxing experience—I was never afraid to respond to situations involving violence in the jail. Whenever the riot bell rang or I saw a fight break out, I seemed to get an adrenaline rush and respond before my head could get a chance to tell me that maybe this wasn't the smartest thing in the world to be doing. In the event of serious disturbances like this one, either at Trenton or one of the other institutions, guys on the goon squad were at the top of the call-list.

So when the chief called, I threw on my uniform pants and looked for my blue shirt. I can't recall if I didn't have a clean one or if I was just in too much of a hurry, but I remember kissing Ginny goodbye and going out the front door with a flannel shirt tucked into my blue pants.

After a brisk two-minute walk/jog, I reached the front door of the jail. It was dark, but I could see a yellow Department of Corrections bus (they were old school buses) parked outside the front door, with about five station wagons behind. The door to the front house was open and in the light from the lobby, I could see officers walking in and out of the prison. They were loading batons, helmets, shields, tear gas canisters, shotguns and Thompsons onto the bus through the rear emergency exit door—just like a high-school football team loading up to head out for an away game.

By 6:30 p.m. about 50 officers had been assembled and we started on the 70-minute drive north on U.S. Route 1.

At the time, Rahway was the only other adult-male New Jersey prison with a maximum-security designation. In New Jersey's prison system, both the institution and the inmate are classified as maximum, medium or minimum security. Trenton State and Rahway, for example, are maximum-security prisons, though an inmate confined there who has committed a non-violent crime and has stayed out of trouble could be classified as minimum security—a "trusty." Most minimum-security inmates do their time at minimum-security satellite facilities, like Jones Farm at Trenton, Marlboro Camp at Rahway or Leesburg Farm. These are prison camps, with barracks rather than cell blocks, and no walls or guard towers. Like Trenton, Rahway was, and still is, a classic old state prison with massive walls, guard towers, searchlights and hardened convicts.

On the bus we were told that the Rahway disturbance had started during the evening meal in the mess hall when a couple of groups of inmates started throwing food and trays at each other. It escalated from there into a wild free-for-all with separate fights breaking out all over the mess hall. When three Rahway guards were injured and the disturbance looked like it might develop into a full-scale riot, we were called in.

When we pulled into the parking lot in front of the massive old domed prison that (despite its name) sits in Woodbridge, we could see that the state police had also been called in to stand by in case they were needed.

Anyone seeing Rahway for the first time is immediately impressed by its huge copper-clad dome sitting on top of the old yellow brick structure. Most people connected with New Jersey's prison system usually refer to Rahway simply as "The Dome," just as they call Trenton "The Wall." Under the dome is a rotunda about seventy feet in diameter with a barred cage running all around the big round room approximately ten feet in from the walls. Rahway was built on a plan similar to Trenton with a central hub and wings radiating out like spokes in a half-wheel.

Rahway's front house is small compared to Trenton's. It's a one-story structure that runs about 100 feet across the front of the prison. After we disembarked from the bus, we formed up in the parking lot and headed into Rahway's front house. We marched in columns of two across the lobby with its a lounge/waiting room and administrative offices and entered the "tie-to," a corridor with windows on the left and right that connects the front house (a much newer structure) to the main part of the prison.

After going up a few cement steps, we came to a large brass doorbell button (a lot like Trenton's) to the right of a heavy wooden door with a 12-inch by 12-inch window. Under normal conditions, an officer would look out of the window and open the door with a large key. When we approached the big wooden door, it was pulled open as soon as we came up the steps. We stopped long enough for the officer in central control to check us out. Then he gestured to the cop on the door leading into the outer perimeter of the rotunda to let us in. We moved into the rotunda, and the barred door leading into the big cage was unlocked and held open by a Rahway officer.

When we got into the rotunda, I saw Lloyd McCorkle standing off to one side, talking to several white hats. McCorkle had recently been promoted from warden of Trenton State Prison to director of the Division of Correction and Parole and had come up from Trenton to run this operation personally. We were ordered to stand down and wait before going out into the wings to help subdue the rioters. I looked around the huge room we were in. We were flanked by rows of long, heavy wooden benches used during contact visits. Rahway had some medium and minimum security inmates inside the walls who were allowed supervised contact visits. Running around the outside perimeter of the cage was a corridor with the bars of the cage on one side and a plaster wall on the other. In front of us was another barred door (it was closed and locked at this point) that led into the prison proper. We could see through the bars the corridors and stairs that led down toward their mess hall and up to the auditorium. We could also hear a lot of yelling, cursing and threats to officers coming out of the wings.

As I recall, the Rahway warden, Warren Pinto, had been in New York at a play when the disturbance kicked off. He had been called back to the prison and was standing off to one side, letting the boss, McCorkle, run the show.

By the time we arrived at the prison, the Rahway officers had pretty much gotten the situation under control, so we stayed in the rotunda while they mopped up, forcing inmates back into their cells with shields and batons. After the inmates had been secured, we were ordered to get ready for the next phase.

While we waited around, still dressed in full riot gear—heavy jackets, helmets, shields and batons—McCorkle assembled the Rahway administrators and officers in the rotunda. He stood up on a visitors' bench and told the Rahway wing officers to go off to one side of the cage and compile a list of the ten troublemakers or leaders in each wing. He told the officers to get the list back to him within the hour while the rest of us took off our helmets, lounged around, smoked and waited.

Forty-five minutes later, McCorkle had his list, and the Rahway officers were dispatched through the wings to round up the inmates and bring them back to the entrance on the prison side of the cage. In the meantime, about 50 of us, still dressed in riot gear, put our helmets back on and waited for instructions. Within 45 minutes about 30 scared-looking inmates had been assembled just outside of the cage. Unlike today, most of these guys were white, with a few blacks and couple of Hispanics. They all looked dazed, confused and scared.

McCorkle didn't say a word to them. He told the Rahway officers to order the men to strip naked and form a line in the corridor that ran around the outside of the cage. The inmate at the head of the line was ordered to stop at the door leading into the cage from the front house. McCorkle ordered us to form two lines facing each other about four feet apart going from the door on the front-house side of the cage to the door that went into the prison, a distance of 50 to 75 feet. Then he had a captain of the Rahway officers order the inmates to move to the head end of the gantlet while a sergeant unlocked the door and held it open.

The officer standing next to me, "Doc" Kelly, was a big, solidly built black guy who also happened to be a minister in a church in Hamilton Township. When we would eat lunch together in the ODR (Officers' Dining Room), Doc would frequently use phrases like, "The Good Book says . . ." or "We're all brothers in the eyes of the Lord."

When I saw what was shaping up here, I nudged Doc and said, "Doc, this doesn't look so good. What are you gonna do?"

He looked at me, winked and smiled and said, "You know what the Book says, Harry: 'Spare the rod and spoil the child.'"

One by one, the naked inmates ran from the door on the front-house side of the cage to the door into the prison being held open by a couple of Rahway officers. While they tried to cover the twenty or thirty yards as fast as they could, we swung our three-foot-long batons at whatever portion of their anatomy offered the best target. The inmates didn't know whether to cover their manhood or their heads, and a lot of them tried to do both. Most of the cops aimed for knees and thighs. Head shots leave too much evidence, plus a well-placed baton strike in the thigh muscle can drop a guy like a sack of potatoes.

Some of the officers, especially the few who liked doing shit like this, yelled obscenities at the inmates—"C'mon, asshole, move it!" "Let's go, motherfucker—get your ass through here!"

Most of the inmates kept their mouths shut, not wanting to get the cops any madder than they already were. The cons just wanted to go as fast as they could from point A to point B and get the hell out of the line of fire. Naturally, with all of those sticks being swung, some guys did get hit in the head or face, and before long the concrete floor was slippery with blood, making it harder for the guys in the back to get through without falling down and taking hits while they were on the floor.

This was the 1960's and it wasn't unusual for punishments like this to be handed out when inmates dared confront the system. If McCorkle were around today and gave a similar order, he'd probably be brought up on charges and might even be indicted. In my years as a corrections officer, I was involved in my share of violence, but I have to say I never liked being a part of that kind of indiscriminate physical punishment inflicted on the inmates. I know that some of my old friends among the corrections staff disagree with me, but I think the restrictions on corporal punishment in place in the prisons today are a change for the better.

****

Throughout my long career at the prison, I prided myself on my ability to get along with even the toughest and meanest cop-hating inmates. And despite what I just said about not liking the physical abuse of inmates, when I was a young cop, I admit there were times that I lost it and reacted on their terms, especially when I was dealing with the type of inmate who got sent to 1-left. I was never bothered much by threats against me, but when an inmate threatened my family, then I felt an instinct to fight back with any means available. While I was a wing officer in 1-left, an inmate named "Wolfman" Schreiber got me so pissed off that I lowered myself to his level and went after him in kind.

Schreiber had been caught in a homosexual act, which was one of the offenses back then that drew an automatic sentence of ten days' bread and water. The start of the incident was as much my fault as his, and to this day I regret how all of this went down, but what has to be has to be.

I was working with a rookie cop, an amiable young black guy named Don Venable, and we had developed a good relationship. The morning that Schreiber was escorted down to the wing by a sergeant, Don and I were handling some of the routine chores, like mopping the floors and distributing toilet paper to the cells, that were done in other wings by tier runners.

When the sergeant got there with Schreiber, an officer unlocked the barred gate at the entrance to the wing, and they brought the shackled Schreiber into the foyer area. Don and I followed the normal procedure that included ordering the inmate to strip so that we could search him for any weapons or contraband before we issued him a pair of pajamas, one size fits all, with **FISH** stenciled in big black letters on the back. I stood in front of the naked Schreiber and went through the routine:

" Put your arms up; lift up each foot; open your mouth and stick out your tongue."

Then I told him to turn around, bend over and spread his cheeks. As I did this, I couldn't help thinking about the charge that had gotten him put in solitary, so I said something like, "Ohhhh, Baby!" I shouldn't have done this, but I was still a relatively young guy and prone to fooling around sometimes to break up the day.

I think Schreiber was already embarrassed enough about the homosexual charge, so he had to show Don and me as well as all the other inmates within earshot that he was macho. He spun around and said to me, "I'm gonna get you for that, you guinea bastard."

I said, "Hey, you can call me all the Italian names you want," and Venable said to him, "Just get in your cell."

Schreiber kept up a steady stream of abuse: "You guinea bastard. You dirty wop. I'm gonna kick your ass when I get out of this cell."

Then I got mad and got into it and started responding with things like, "You ain't kickin' nothin' little girl; just get in your cell."

Then Schreiber turned to Don and called him a Muslim son of a bitch and a nigger. Don said to me, "Maybe you can handle that Harry," and I said, "Hey, Ven, let him go. He's gonna get one cup of water and four slices of bread and every third day he gets lunch, maybe a bologna sandwich. Don't' sweat it. We're gonna go home, we're gonna be with our wives, scorin' and this poor bastard is gonna be on bread and water. Don't let that shit get to you."

At this point the sergeant had pushed Schreiber into the cell and locked the door, but Schreiber could hear everything I was saying to Venable, and now he was really pissed off.

He said, "You think you're a wise guy, Harry? I'm gonna get you because I know where your flower shop is, and when I get out, I'm gonna get your kids."

At the time Ginny and I owned a small flower shop about six blocks from the prison. We were supplementing my income as a prison guard because the one thing in the world that I wanted for my kids was a job better than working in a prison. At times other officers would say something to me about stopping by to pick up flowers, and Schreiber, overhearing some of those conversations, knew the shop was on Centre Street.

When Schreiber said that about my family, I said, "OK you son of a bitch. Now you have to die."

It never bothered me much when an inmate threatened me, but I wasn't going to accept a threat against my family.

I wrote up a charge against Schreiber for making a verbal threat against an officer and turned it in to the lieutenant in center. Then I told the lieutenant that Don and I were going to move Schreiber from the tier to the hole.

(For some reason Schreiber had been put in a cell on the first tier rather than going directly into bread and water, the usual punishment for getting caught in a homosexual act.)

An hour or so later Don and I went back to central control where the armory was and drew out a couple of billies. These billies dated back to the 1920's; they were shorter than the other type of batons used today, about nine inches long, and had lead in one end and a screw-on brass cap with a small hole in the center at the other end. The brass cap covered a hollowed out end piece designed to hold tear gas pellets; we had never used them that way in the time that I worked at the prison, but the little hole, a little bigger than the head of a finishing nail, was perfect for jamming into an inmate's belly and then twisting to catch his flesh. That usually got his attention.

Don and I got the key to Schreiber's cell and paid him a visit. Schreiber had been jailing long enough to know what this was about; as soon as the door opened, he jumped off the mattress and moved to the rear of the cell with his back against the wall. Don ducked down and went left, and I went up and to the right. In that small space, it didn't take long for two of us with billies to subdue him, and we proceeded to beat the shit out of him. I'm not a big guy—about five feet, eight and 145 pounds—but Don was about six foot, 190 pounds, and the billies gave us a big edge. After we finished, we called in a couple of other officers and told them they should get Schreiber to the infirmary. He was in there for a week—he got the message.

About two weeks later, the chief called me at home and said, "Harry, you've got

. J., THURSDAY, OCTOBER 24, 1935—36 PAGES THREE CENTS

Schultz Dying of Gun Wound, Two Aides Slain in Gang War

Exterior view of the Palace Chop House at 12 East Park street, where Dutch Schultz and his aides were "on the spot" last night.

Fourth Shot in Raid on Cafe Here, Fifth In New York

Amberg Link Seen

Dutch Schultz is dying at Newark City Hospital. Physicians this afternoon abandoned hope that he would live.

Two of his henchmen died from bullet wounds early today. A third is near death.

They were felled under a barrage of gangster bullets at 10:30 o'clock last night in a cafe at 12 East Park street. Two gunmen did the shooting and escaped. Two hours later another Schultz gang member was shot in Times Square, New York.

"Journey's End; This Is My Death," Says Schultz

The Newark News *ran the story of the mob hit on Dutch Schultz (Arthur Flegenheimer) on the evening of October 23, 1935 at the Palace Chop House in Newark. Charlie The Bug Workman was convicted of the killings six years later, in 1941. Workman spent 23 years in Trenton State Prison, an extra-ordinarily long life sentence during that era.*

(Story, photos courtesy the Newark Evening News/ Newark Public Library)

Police Comb 'Spooning' Area for 'Mad Killer' Clues

Cling to Maniac Theory; Slayer Linked to Other Similar Township Deaths

Township Women Terrorized; Plan to Ask for More Lights

Police Chief Declares Men and Women Should Realize Risks Involved and Stay Away From Crime Sectors

One of Victims

Mrs. Moriconi, 27, And Kovacs Are Latest Victims In Hamilton

A clean-up posse directed by police finecombed the area of the latest of Hamilton Township's spooner slayings today and uncovered a variety of shotgun shells.

Several other articles of possible value in the investigation were also picked up by the crew of men, who raked a network of peepers' paths winding through the underbrush along Cypress Lane, where the killer Saturday night shot down Mrs. Carolina Moriconi, 27, and her neighbor-lover, Louis Joseph Kovacs, 35.

Hill Guilty, Gets Life

Leniency Is Asked By Jury

Panel Out 5 Hours Before Reaching Verdict — Appeal Planned

Clarence Hill, 34-year-old Negro soldier, was convicted Friday night by a Mercer Court jury of the tryst killings on Duck Island. The jurors deliberated five hours and returned a verdict at 9:40 P. M. with a recommendation for life

Guilty

Clarence Hill

Clarence Hill, a resident of Hamilton Township, NJ, was convicted of "The Duck Island Murders," a series of lovers' lane shotgun slayings that terrorized the Trenton suburbs in the late 1930's, early 1940's. Hill did 20 years in Trenton and was released in 1964.

(Stories, photos courtesy The Times, Trenton, NJ.)

Duress Alleged By Hill

Murder Defendant Says Confession Wrung from Him By Third Degree

Hill at Scene of Duck Island Slayings

Fugitive Convict Caught After Kidnaping Trooper

Captor

Trooper Louis Masin

Kidnaper

August Bernard Doak

Victim

Trooper George R. Kell

16-Year-Old Bride Also Nabbed In Manhunt

The one-day honeymoon of an escaped convict and his 16-year-old bride ended abruptly last night when they were captured several hours after kidnaping State Trooper George R. Kell at gunpoint and holding him captive until his escape under a hail of bullets.

Their capture—near Hopewell—ended what police said was the most intensive Jersey manhunt since the same patch of wooded area was combed in a search for the Lindbergh baby.

Kell had stopped the pair near Raritan in Somerset County for speeding.

The first to be captured was the girl, identified by State Police Superintendent Charles H. Schoeffel as Constance Ethel Blondell Doak. She was taken when her husband fled on foot from their car as police closed in on them.

"Barney" Doak (above), reputed member of Detroit's Purple Gang, slowly went insane after years of isolation in lockup. (Stories, photos courtesy The Times, Trenton, NJ. Reprinted with permission.)

Convict Kills Guard, Stabs Another In Attempted Break On Auto Ride

Shot Twice, Prisoner Flees But Is Speedily Captured

A charge of murder faces a State Prison convict who fatally stabbed a prison guard and wounded another in a bold bid for freedom late yesterday.

The break for liberty occurred as the prisoner was being returned to Trenton after appearing in court at Hackensack on another criminal charge.

Victor Viteritto, 25, of 1312 Princeton Avenue, the prison guard, died several hours after the attack in Middlesex General Hospital of deep wounds in the neck and chest. He was a World War II veteran and had been a member of the prison staff since May 12 1947.

The other guard, Lester Throckmorton, 44, of the Crosswicks-Allentown Road, was wounded by the convict but was not seriously injured. He too, was given treatment at the same hospital.

Slayer Wounded

The convict George Zagorski, 25, of Jersey City, was shot twice in the leg by Throckmorton as he fled from the prison car on Route 25 in Raritan Township, just south of Metuchen.

Raritan Township police captured him a few minutes later. He is now confined to the prison hospital under guard until further action by State authorities.

Zagorski, when taken before Magistrate Christian J. Jorgensen of Raritan Township last night, was unaware that Viteritto had died.

When Jorgensen told him, Zagorski clutched a table for

Fatally Stabbed

Victor Viteritto

Wounded

Lester Throckmorton

Slayer

George Zagorski

Twenty-five-year-old officer Vic Vittorito (left) died from a stab wound in the throat in February of 1951 when George Zagorski attempted to escape during a ride back to prison from a court hearing. (Stories, photos courtesy The Times, Trenton, NJ. Reprinted with permission.)

Joe Adonis (above) the "Teflon Don" of the '30's, '40's and '50's, was finally snared in 1951 on gambling charges and did a short stretch in Trenton. (Photo courtesy The Associated Press)

Tear Gas, Water Fail To Rout Rioting Prisoners From Wing

Firemen Try Water Chaser On Prisoners

Trenton firemen set up hose-lines outside the State Prison wall today and poured tons of water into the cell block where the remnants of the rioting band of prisoners continued to hold out. Pictured are Joseph Muschal (alongside the engine); William Mostrangeli (alongside fireplug) and Edmund Schaller (in background). Other pictures on Page 18.

Pour 1,500 Gallons of Water a Minute Into Wrecked Prison Section; 30 Convicts In Barricade

58 Rebellious Convicts Still Hold Prison Shop

Prison Riot Ringleader

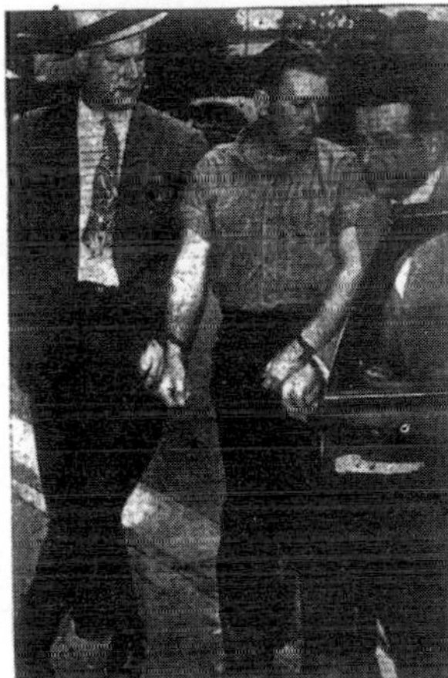

Officials Fear For Safety of Hostages

State prison officials at noon today were still trying to devise a plan to end the rebellion of 58 convicts who have barricaded themselves in the prison print shop without endangering the four employes who were being held as hostages by the inmates.

Following a conference with Governor Driscoll at the State House, State Institutions Commissioner Sanford L. Bates and Deputy Commissioner J. Lowell Bixby returned to the prison and met with Warden William H. Carty.

The officials discussed various courses of action that might be taken to cope with the explosive situation, but Colonel Bixby said later that each plan proposed had to be discarded, because of possible serious consequences to the four hostages.

The four employes at last reports were unharmed and apparently well. Colonel Bixby said the four were seen together inside the print shop shortly after 11 a. m.

No contact was made with the prisoners during the morning, Bixby said. There was considerable movement inside the shop and snatches of conversation could be heard, he said. The convicts have done "terrific" damage to printing equipment in the shop the deputy commissioner added.

Ready For Anything

Barney Doak hit the front pages again as one of the ringleaders in the '52 riots, the most destructive in the history of the prison. (Stories, photos courtesy The Times, Trenton, NJ.)

Condemned Killer Dies During Escape Attempt

John L. Vaszorich, awaiting execution on Trenton State Prison's death row, died early yesterday after he was hit by a burst from a guard's submachine gun on the roof of the prison laundry.

Vaszorich, 21, was felled by a slug in the lung and two in the stomach as he attempted to get over the 30-foot-high prison wall after overpowering a guard and taking his keys.

During the search for Vaszorich, after he made his way out of the death house wearing an officer's coat and hat, another guard, Alonzo Lanphear, was stricken by

JOHN L. VASZORICH
. . . cheats chair

Murder Suspect Gunned Down Attempting to Escape Custody

Frederick Hartjen, a suspect in the fatal May 5 knifing of Fiore Barile in Jersey City, was critically wounded yesterday attempting to escape from four detectives and a parole officer in the New York Criminal Court Building.

Hartjen, 43, was hit by seven shots as he tried to flee from custody in the lobby of the courts building. He had been paroled last August from Clinton State Prison in Dannemora, NY, where he was serving a term of 30 to 60 years on an armed robbery conviction.

Frederick Hartjen

John Vaszorich (above) died trying to escape the electric chair.

Indestructible Freddy Hartjen (right) was one of the toughest inmates in the prison in the 1950's.

Mild Little Man Who Staged Risky Jailbreak

Lieutenant Elliott Aldrich (in white shirt) dockets Mario J. DeLucia, 37-year-old State Prison escapee, minutes after he was captured Saturday night on East Paul Avenue. Others shown at the First Precinct desk are, from left: Patrolmen Frank Barelkowski and Charles Volk, DeLucia, Patrolman John McMahon and Night Captain James A. George. DeLucia's freedom was short-lived; he was nabbed 15 hours after the first successful escape from the prison in 25 years. Patrolmen Volk and McMahon, along with Sergeant Frank Dombroski, apprehended DeLucia.

Prisoner 'Home' In Cell For Christmas After Tame Ending Of Daring Escape

Tiny Mario DeLucia (above) staged one of the prison's most spectacular escapes. Protests against the death penalty (right), in the streets around the prison, gained momentum in the early '60's. (Stories, photos courtesy The Times, Trenton, NJ.)

Walker Dies In Electric Chair For Mollie Schlesinger Murder

Theodore Walker of Trenton died last night in the state prison electric chair for the murder of Mollie Schlesinger in her North Montgomery Street uniform shop last August.

Walker, 23, was the 147th man to die in the electric chair since it was installed at the prison in 1909. Walker was arrested after Miss Schlesinger died of wounds sustained during the robbery of her shop. He was convicted in November.

THEODORE WALKER
. . . death for murder

Trentonian Theodore Walker (above) killed Molly Schlesinger in August, was convicted in November and died in July of the following year—11 months from crime to execution.

Cool Con Stages Classic Escape

Puts Pajamas On Dummy, Hides In Little Hole

An inmate who fled the Trenton State Prison by going over the wall of a recreation yard is still at large today.

William Van Scoten, 32, of Bloomsbury, Hunterdon County, left behind in his cell a blanketed dummy with a plaster head that fooled two turnkeys who checked the cell seven times between them.

Bank robber and master escape artist Willie Sutton used the same ruse a number of years ago when he escaped

William Van Scoten

Bill Van Scoten (above) was the only inmate to get over the wall in the '60's. Officers were fooled by dummy (below) left by Van Scoten in his cell.

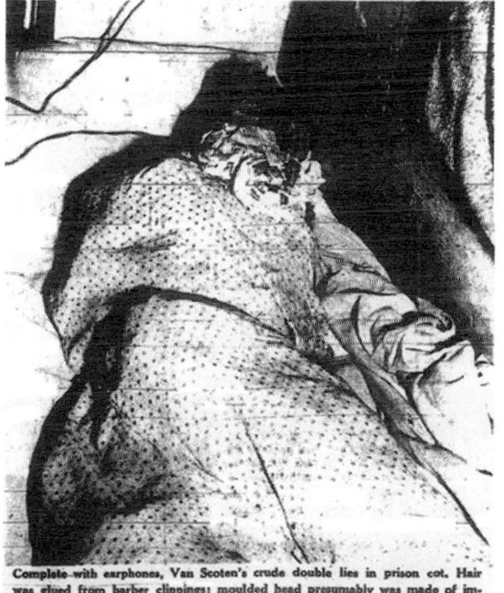

Complete with earphones, Van Scoten's crude double lies in prison cot. Hair was glued from barber clippings; moulded head presumably was made of improvised plaster

Big-time bookie Newsboy Moriarity (right) refused to acknowledge ownership of millions of dollars.

Police Gun Down TSP Escapee D. Kremens In Times Square

Daniel Kremens (right), convicted of killing a NJ state trooper, escaped from a minimum-security work detail. He was killed by a NJ State Police detective in New York City's Times Square.

DANIEL C. KREMENS
. . . death on Times Square

ARY 5, 1955

Flippant Until The End –

Defiantly Flings Lit Cigar At Death House Witnesses As He Walks To Electric Chair

Frank Roscus, shotgun slayer of a longtime buddy, died in the electric chair at the State Prison here last night after defiantly flinging his lit cigar at 16 official witnesses to his execution.

house. They were quickly herded back to their cells.

McCorkle said Roscus maintained his air of bravado during his last day. The warden said he visited Roscus yesterday and

kept the courtroom in an uproar, shouting at judge, jury and lawyers. He complained that state attorneys had mixed up the shotguns introduced as evidence and, at one point said he would not

Frank Roscus, another '50's tough guy, went to the chair maintaining his contempt for society and authority.

'Newsboy' Refuses To Discuss $2.4 Million Found In Car

Jersey City's Joseph "Newsboy" Moriarity yesterday declined to discuss with law enforcement officials $2.4 million in cash found in two leather bags in the trunk of a car in a garage he had rented.

Moriarity, 52, was convicted on gambling charges last July and was sentenced to three-to-five years in state prison.

The money, along with three handguns, a rifle and ammunition, was found by carpenters hired to renovate a row of 24 garages in Jersey City.

Hudson County prosecutor Lawrence Whipple journeyed to the state prison to question Moriarity about the cache, but Newsboy refused to acknowledge that the money was his or that he knew anything about it.

Joseph Moriarty

Police Capture Black Militant In Turnpike Trooper Slaying

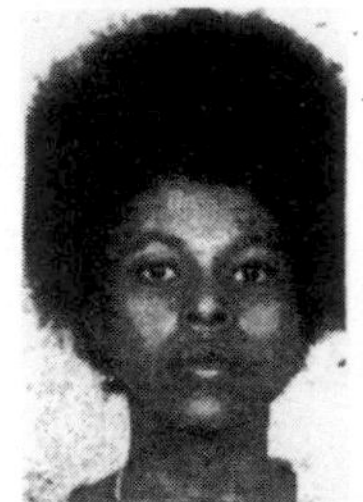

Joanne Deborah Chesimard

SEARCH FOR SHOOTER — East Brunswick Police stop cars and trucks on Rt. 18 at

Roadblocks (above) were used in the hunt for Clark Squire after a shootout on the Turnpike.

New Jersey State Trooper Werner Foerster (above right) died in a gun battle with Joanne Chesimard, Clark Squire (left) and the Black Liberation Army on the NJ Turnpike. (Story courtesy The New York Times. Reprinted with permission.)

Panther and Trooper Die in Shoot-Out

Continued From Page 1, Col. 3

heading ultimately for Washington, the police said. New York detectives who assisted the state police in examining the car found what they said appeared to be a list of potential targets for the black militant group. The list was stuck in the pages of a book.

Miss Chesimard was reported in serious condition at Middlesex General Hospital today with gunshot wounds in both arms and in a shoulder.

The dead trooper was identified as Werner Foerster, 34, who was serving as a back-up man to James M. Harper, 29, the trooper who stopped the car and who was wounded in the left shoulder.

Werner Foerster

booths down the line were alerted.

The suspects pulled off the road at milepost 78, five miles from the shooting scene. Trooper Robert Palentchar, the first to arrive, saw one of the male suspects standing 50 yards from the car. The trooper ordered him to halt, but the man ran into the wooded area along the toll road. Trooper Palentchar said he had emptied his gun at the man, but did not know whether he hit him.

The trooper then saw Miss Chesimard walking toward him from 50 feet away, her bloody arms raised in surrender. The body of James Coston was found nearby in a gully along the road shoulder where he apparently fell and died.

The New York Times

The suspects' car at the state police garage in East Brunswick. In the background is the car driven by James M. Harper, the trooper who was injured during turnpike shooting.

Inmate Slain, Guard Chief Wounded In NJ State Prison Escape Attempt

Robert Simmons

Trenton, NJ—A self-styled black revolutionary was shot and killed last night in a spectacular escape attempt and shootout in Trenton State Prison's 7-wing.

The prison's chief of security, Glenn Simmons, 39, was also wounded in what some law-enforcement authorities are viewing as an attempt by the Black Liberation Army to break one of its members out of the 150-year-old prison

John Clark

GUNBATTLE RIPS NJ STATE PRISON

The Trentonian

TRENTON, N.J. TUESDAY, JANUARY 20, 1976

2 Inmates Dead, 3 Guards Hurt

The Guns Were Going Off...

Prison officials' worst fears about the Black Liberation Army were realized in January of 1976. (Stories, photos courtesy The Trentonian)

The Evening Times — Bucks edition

Trenton, N.J., Tuesday, January 20, 1976 ★ 15 cents

Jailbreak foiled, 1 dead, 4 hurt

When the shots rang out, Trenton police moved in quickly to block off the streets surrounding the prison. For many cops it was a long, cold night

Arms-laden van found near scene

Trenton policemen ready their weapons and standby for a call from inside.

. . . and one is now dead

Two killers played key roles

CLARK E. SQUIRE

JOHN L. CLARK

JOHN DOUGLAS

Aerial photograph shows the violence-ridden Seven Wing section of Trenton State Prison.

Seven Wing failed as ultimate answer

(Continued from Page A1)

City policemen greeted by whining of bullets at prison

The shootout in 7-wing in January of 1976 resulted in the death of John Clark and the wounding of several correction officers. After the Turnpike shootings, Joanne Chesimard had been sent to the prison for women in Clinton, while Clark Squire was shipped to Trenton. Prison officials worried for months that the Black Liberation Army (BLA) would stage an assault on the prison in an attempt to free Clark Squire. When the violence erupted, Trenton police sealed off the entire area (above) and warned residents in homes around the prison to stay indoors and away from windows. (Stories, photos courtesy The Times, Trenton, NJ.

Jogger Finds Headless Bodies Of Two in Weequahic Park

Newark—A teen-age boy jogging in Weequahic Park this morning found the headless bodies of two young men, believed to be Muslims and possibly connected to the shotgun slaying of Muslim leader James Shabazz last September.

Shabazz, 52, and the father of 13 children was gunned down as he got out of his Cadillac in the driveway of his home on South Seventh Avenue. The slaying was believed by police to be connected to Shabazz' position as minister of Mosgue 25 in the Central Ward of Newark.

Open warfare between two rival Muslim sects in Northern New Jersey would culminate in the "bloody battle" indicated in The Trentonian *headline (right) of October 17, 1975.*

Raymond Dozier, 26, an inmate at Trenton State Prison, being returned to the institution

Jersey Police Scour Suburban Area For 2d Woman to Vanish in 8 Days

By JOSEPH F. SULLIVAN
Special to The New York Times

DEMAREST, N.J., Oct. 16—Teams of policemen using dogs and scuba gear scoured 17 acres of woodland and a pond on the Alpine Country Club today in a search for Susan Reeve, a 22-year-old woman who disappeared Tuesday after stepping off a bus near her home here. She is the second young woman to disappear in this affluent area of northeast Bergen County in eight days.

Miss Reeve is the daughter of Arthur H. Reeve, a lawyer and a former municipal judge.

On Oct. 6, Susan Heynes, a 26-year-old native of Britain, disappeared from the home in Haworth into which she moved with her husband seven weeks ago. The Heynes and Reeve homes are about two miles apart.

Abduction Feared

The police and members of the families of the two young women say they believe they have been abducted. The police in Haworth say they have found no clues to link the two disappearances, but they have not ruled out a connection.

"My daughter was an old-fashioned girl," Mr. Reeve said today. "If she was going to be 10 minutes late from work, she always would call us." The young woman, who works as a secretary for a New York

Associated Press
Susan Reeve

Associated Press
Susan Heynes

in a bag to enable the police dogs and bloodhounds to get her scent.

The dog teams from the Bergen County Police Department and the New York State Police began searching the woodland area around Orchard Road at dawn. by 3 P.M. the search teams had completed their sweep and were resting at police headquarters before returning for another attempt.

"After 48 hours it's very difficult to pick up a scent," Sergeant Powderly said. "It's still worth a try, but it becomes tough."

Policemen and volunteer firemen were scheduled to canvas homes in the area this evening to find anyone who may have seen the young woman on her way home. The volunteers also are going to conduct another sweep through the woods.

In addition, detectives from the Bergen County Prosecutor's office have been working with local investigators and plan to interview passengers on Miss Reeve's bus to see if they can provide any new clues.

Infant Reported Missing

The daylong search with the police dogs caused some concern during the early afternoon when the parents of a 4-year-old girl reported her missing.

"We were worried because

BLUE STREAK — BLUE STREAK — BLUE STREAK

PRISON SECURITY TIGHT AFTER BLOODY BATTLE

The Trentonian

Proudly Serving Historic Trenton and the Great Valley of the Delaware

VOL. 31 NO. 71 TRENTON, N.J. FRIDAY, OCTOBER [illegible] PHONE 989-7800 15 CENTS

Carter March Today

By STEPHAN ROSENFELD

Upwards of 15,000 demonstrators are expected to march in Trenton today, demanding the release of convicted murderers Rubin "Hurricane" Carter and John Artis, but they will not pass Trenton State Prison—the scene of bloody violence yesterday—as originally planned.

March sponsors agreed to change the path of the protest yesterday afternoon, after meeting privately with a N.J. Superior Court judge and three South Trenton residents, who sought an injunction to revoke the demonstrators' parade permit.

The march — to be led by world heavyweight boxing champ Muhammad Ali — was originally scheduled to wind through residential sections of South Trenton and circle the state prison, where Carter is serving a life sentence, before moving on to the state house.

The march itself is slated to begin between 10:30 and 11 a.m. at Cooper Park on the John Fitch Way across from American Bridge Co. Ali is scheduled to present Gov. Brendan T. Byrne with petitions containing thousands of signatures seeking executive clemency for Carter and Artis.

N.J. Superior Court Judge

(Continued on Page 28)

Related Stories And Pictures On Page Three

TALE IN BLOOD—Streaks of dried blood mark the walls of the downstairs classroom in Trenton State Prison where five of seven inmates were attacked with sharpened chisels and screwdrivers in an apparent Black Muslim power struggle yesterday morning. Two other inmates, one of whom was killed, were attacked at the same time in an upstairs classroom. (Trentonian Photo)

One Muslim Killed In 'Execution Plot'

By JOANNE MAYBERRY and JOHN TOTH

Trenton State Prison inmates will remain locked in their cells today while four law enforcement agencies continue the probe into the stabbing death of one inmate and wounding of six others there yesterday in what was described as a planned mass execution to revenge the murder of a Black Muslim leader.

Sources close to the investigation told The Trentonian late last night that 15 members of a Muslim splinter group had been earmarked for execution to revenge the 1973 slaying of Newark Muslim leader James M. Shabazz and also to get even for attacks on group members inside the prison.

The execution of leaders of the New World of Islam, also known as Bellies, had been planned for Wednesday, but they got wind of it and the showdown did not come off until yesterday.

Local officials and the organizers of a march by several thousand persons seeking the release of Trenton State Prison inmate Rubin "Hurricane" Carter have agreed to eliminate the prison from the march route this morning to avoid causing any additional problems for inmates and pris-

(Continued on Page 28)

BLOODIED GUARD

Officers Predicted Warfare at TSP

By JOHN TOTH

The bloody knife warfare between Black Muslim religious factions at Trenton State Prison was predicted by prison security officers several months ago.

Early in 1974, prison security officers took measures to keep certain Muslim factions apart.

Noting an increase in violent incidents between Muslim factions, Trenton State officials transferred several inmates outside the prison — to prevent a "bloodbath."

Those same inmates were returned to Trenton State Prison this year, at their own request.

Six of the inmates stabbed in a prison classroom yesterday (including Cleophus Mayers, who died) were among those who went back to the prison, officials confirmed yesterday.

Some of transferred inmates

(Continued on Page 28)

CLEOPHEOUS MAYERS

Daryl Curtis, (below) a convicted drug dealer, was trapped on the stairs and stabbed to death 90 minutes after entering the prison.

Inmate Slain within Hours Of Arrival at State Prison

The photo in The New York Times *above shows Raymond Dozier, one of the wounded victims in the Muslim bloodbath of October 16, 1975, being returned to the prison after being treated at St. Francis Hospital. Below the photo of Dozier the* Times *ran one of the first stories about the abduction and murders of two young women, crimes that would later be attributed to Robert Reldan.* (Story courtesy The New York Times/ photos courtesy the Associated Press.)

to come in right now. The FBI wants to talk to you."

I thought he was kidding around with me. I said, "Come on, Chief, what are you short of men? You want me to come in to cover for somebody?"

He said, "I mean it, Harry. The FBI is here and they want to talk to you. Come in, now."

So I went in and two FBI agents were waiting for me in an inmate-attorney conference room. Schreiber had filed an official complaint against Don and me for violating his civil rights (a new concept back then). I knew the older agent; I had seen him around the jail quite a few times investigating complaints when I worked in the mailroom, and he knew me. The younger one I had never seen before; I think he was new on the job.

The older guy asked me what happened, so I told him that Schreiber had been screaming obscenities and carrying on and that we couldn't have that in one-left with all of those bad guys in there, that he could get a riot started. So we had to go in and subdue him. I also told them what he had said about getting my kids. The other agent, the young one had the crew cut, the wing tips, the whole nine yards, and when he heard that he said, "You shoulda killed him."

The older agent turned abruptly and said to him, "You keep quiet. I don't want to hear another word out of you."

Then the older guy turned back to me and said, "How much force did you use to subdue Schreiber?"

I replied, blandly, "Only as much as was necessary."

He said, "Oh yeah, Harry? 'Only enough force as necessary' puts him in the hospital for a week?"

The older guy didn't believe a word I was saying. I got pissed off and told him he was on the wrong side, and should spend a few days in my shoes, dealing with these guys in 1-left.

At the adminstrative hearing on Schreiber's charges, I was glad that I had always tried to treat the inmates fairly as long as they didn't try to get over on me. The inmates in the nearby cells who had heard the whole thing said that Schreiber had threatened Don and me with bodily harm, and by the sounds that came from his cell, they could tell he resisted being taken out when we came to move him. So all of the charges were dismissed.

****

A couple of months after the Schreiber incident, one of the inmates in lockup pulled off a scam that was funny but almost got him killed. Ralph Urcolino was a recent immigrant from Italy who had gotten into some trouble almost as soon as he got to the U.S.—probably connected with gambling. He spoke little English, but he was an extremely skilled artisan—a genius with woodcarving. After he had been in Trenton for a while, he managed to accumulate a set of hobby tools that he kept in his cell and that he used to craft beautiful birdhouses. I don't remember what he had done to be put into 1-left, but after he had been in for a while, he asked to be allowed to have his woodworking tools, and the chief gave permission.

Urcolino built a birdhouse that was actually a trap, and he set it outside in a secluded corner of the 1-left yard with some bread crumbs as bait. After a couple of days, a plain old brown sparrow got caught in Ralph's trap. Ralph gently took the sparrow out and brought it back to his cell. Then he took the model paints that he kept alongside his tools and, using a picture from a book as a reference, he painted the sparrow green and yellow and sold it to another inmate as a "miniature parrot."

The other inmate was thrilled, thinking he was going to while away the hours teaching this "parrot" to talk. Of course, the model paint was toxic, and while the other inmate was asleep, the paint was being absorbed into the poor sparrow's body. The next day the guy finds the bird dead, realizes he's been scammed, and goes after Urcolino—all the way up on the third tier of 1-left. Ralph doesn't speak or understand much English, so as the guy who got conned is screaming obscenities at Ralph, Ralph is yelling back with his own obscenities in Italian, and the wing officer down in the flats, seeing this potential fight brewing up on the third tier catwalk hits the riot bell.

Five cops come running into the wing and head for the two inmates. The victim of the scam, when he sees the cops, calms down and backs away. But not Ralph. His Latin temperament is up and he directs his attention at the cops, screaming at them in Italian and waving his arms. They don't have any idea what he's saying; all they know is he's acting like he's crazy, so they knock him down and grab his legs, one officer to a leg.

Then they drag him, still screaming and yelling obscenities in Italian, the length of the catwalk, down the flight of metal stairs at the end, with Ralph's head going "boing, boing, boing" as it bounces off every step. He's still yelling and waving his arms, so he can't decide whether to protect his head or drive home his point. Meanwhile his head's going "boing, boing, boing." This goes on all the way to the bottom of the cell block so that by the time they get him down to the flats the back of his head is a bloody mess, and they have to take him to the infirmary. Hard-head that he is, though, despite all the blood, the damage is minimal and he's back in population within the hour, waiting to go to courtline on a variety of charges.

Urcolino came back from court-line with more time in lockup added on for refusing to obey an order. And, to add insult to injury, he came down with a bad case of diarrhea—probably something he picked up while he was in the prison infirmary getting stitched up. The officer on Urcolino's tier that day was known for his hard-line, sometimes even sadistic, attitude. As the cop was going from cell to cell distributing soap, tooth paste and toilet paper, Urcolino told the officer about the diarrhea and asked for an extra roll of toilet paper.

The officer said, "Well, hell, Urc, just yell down the tier and find out who's constipated and take his roll."

And he walked away with the rolls of toilet paper tucked securely under his arm.

* * * * * * *

One of the more interesting inmates I met during my assignment to 1-left was a bright but somewhat testy guy named Paul Fitzsimmons—"Fitz." Fitz was of average height, thin (almost gaunt-looking) with thinning white hair and a white mustache. He was serving a life sentence for murdering a 28-year-old rookie cop in Passaic in the late '50's.

Fitz and his older brother Gene had held up a candy store in Passaic when a foot patrolman, Robert Strone, confronted them on a dark street. Paul got the drop on the cop, disarmed him and as he told me in a flat, dispassionate tone, "I shot him in the back of the head while he was begging for mercy and telling me how he had a wife and family."

The cold and unfeeling way he talked about murdering a police officer was typical of Fitz' personality and temperament. I once told Fitz I knew an assistant prosecutor and Fitz said, "When I escape, I'll come visit you and shoot that son of a bitch in the head so we can watch him die on your front steps."

Those kinds of comments were typical of Fitz' everyday mood and outlook on life. Fitz told me that he and Gene should have gotten the death penalty, but the prosecutor had "fucked up" so here he was playing the big shot in Trenton State Prison.

Fitz got hooked up with another bright guy, Anthony Puchalski, who was also in for murder. The story I heard on him was that he and a partner had pulled off a series of armed robberies, but they were starting to feel some heat. Puchalski either got tipped off or just started to get worried that the partner was going to squeal, so he took the guy out into the woods for "a little talk" and shot the guy in the head. He told me he figured he didn't get the death penalty because he had killed another criminal.

Fitz claimed to have come from a well-to-do family in Connecticut and said he had gone to a fairly decent private school. He also told me he had attended Fordham University for a while. He seemed well-read and bright enough for that to be true. Later, in the '60's and early '70's, both Fitz and Puchalski attended college classes that were brought into the jail during Lyndon Johnson's "Great Society." Both of them did well in college. Puchalski eventually got out, and I heard he earned a master's degree and was actually teaching some college courses at a state college in south Jersey when he committed another murder and came back in. I saw him around the prison during his second bid, and then I lost track of him. I heard he died of a heart attack while still in prison some time in the early '90's.

But back in the early sixties, Fitz and Puchalski had difficulty accepting the fact that they were going to be spending a lot of time behind the walls of Trenton, so they decided to dig their way out. They hooked up with a handsome young Italian kid, and the three of them concocted a plot to start tunneling out of the prison from the hospital. The hospital was down at the end of 6-wing and consisted of two floors. Since Fitz and Puchalski were both good talkers, they managed to get themselves and the kid assigned to work in the hospital during second shift, from 2:20 p.m. to 10:20.

Only one officer was assigned to cover both floors of the hospital on second shift, and since both Fitz and Puchalski were bright, personable "bullshitters," they took turns keeping the officer distracted while the other one and the kid worked on an elaborate tunnel.

Over time they managed to steal a fan and a goose neck lamp and put together an impressive array of tools. They took the handle from the squeezing mechanism on a mop bucket and bolted onto it a flat piece of metal from the tag shop to make a small entrenching shovel. They also collected a variety of picks and chisels.

Initially, they opened a hole in the plaster wall behind a supply cabinet. It was easy enough to slide the cabinet to one side to let one guy into the hole to work for a while, and then slide it back. As with any tunnel, the big problem was getting rid of the dirt. Fitz later told me that the hospital generated a lot of garbage, and he and Puchalski got rid of the dirt by carefully distributing it among the medical waste. They probably couldn't get away with that today because of the way that waste is monitored by the state DEP, but it worked back then.

They dug for several months and constructed a substantial tunnel with cross bracing and ventilation, the whole escape-from-Colditz WW II routine. The scheme fell apart when somebody ratted them out. Fitz always thought it was the kid, but for some reason, neither he nor Puchalski ever went after him, even when they all ended up under my tender care in 1-left. The prison administration didn't pursue an outside indictment on the attempt-to-escape charge, but Fitz did a couple of years in lockup, and Puchalski did a long time there—several years.

Fitz bragged to me that they had done such a superb job of engineering and building the tunnel that when the prison maintenance people got in there and saw this marvel of construction, they put a cover over the hole in the wall but left the tunnel intact in case they might want to use it as a conduit tunnel for steam pipes at some future date. In fact, somebody would reopen the tunnel and try to use it fifteen years later, but running steam pipes under the wall wasn't exactly what Vasile Dovan, "The Mole," would have in mind.

****

About a year after I was assigned to 1-left, in June of 1961, an inmate named Bill Van Scoten managed to get over the wall—the first successful escape since Mario DeLucia's escapade back in '56 and only the second one to get out since I started work in 1950.

Out in the big yard was a rectangular concrete hole, two feet by three feet by three feet deep used for electrical connections; it was covered by a 300-pound stone slab. Van Scoten had eyeballed this pit for months and finally concocted a plan to use it as a means of escape. First, he accumulated several worn-out sheets that had been thrown out by the laundry staff. He made a thin but strong rope held together by tight little knots, and on the day he had set for the escape, a Saturday, he wore a real loose-fitting shirt with the sheet-rope wrapped tightly around his body and headed out for the yard. With that number of men (about 350-400) going out at one time, it was impossible to frisk all of them that carefully, so even though he was bulkier than normal, Van Scoten got out into the yard with no problem.

When yard was over and the officers headed toward the big double gate, a group of Van Scoten's friends gathered around the slab covering the conduit pit and screened him from the view of the officers over by the door and in the tower. To this day it amazes me that he involved so many people in this and stayed down there for the rest of that day and into the night, yet nobody squealed on him. With 400 men in the yard and a prison grapevine as fast and efficient as Trenton's, it's almost a given that somebody would squeal on Van Scoten to buy a transfer to Jones Farm or to gain some other kind of privilege. The only thing I can think of is that everybody figured, "Everybody in the jail knows he's down there, so somebody else must have already turned in the chit by now."

Whatever the reason, nobody ratted him out and Van Scoten got into the hole. We never found out for sure, but we figured that a couple of his friends must have helped him slide the slab to one side so that he could jump into the hole and then slid it back. They would have had to do this quickly so that neither of the guards in towers eight or nine would see him going into the hole.

Van Scoten stayed in the hole throughout the rest of the day and waited for nightfall. Up until the time of this escape, towers eight and nine were manned only during yard periods. After the inmates left the yard, the officers left the towers and moved back inside the jail to perform other duties.

Van Scoten wasn't big—about five feet, five inches tall, 140 pounds, but he lifted weights, so he was strong. Sometime during the night he got onto his hands and knees and placed his back up against the bottom of the slab; then he used his legs and back to push the slab up and over just enough to give him a space to crawl through. Before he went into the hole, Van Scoten had grabbed a 1 1/2-pound weight from the weight pile and brought it inside with him. He tied the weight to one end of his makeshift rope and moved over to the base of the wall that fronted on Third Street. Lined up along the wall were several heavy wooden benches that the inmates used for bench-pressing and as seats for the players in the baseball games.

By stacking seven of the benches, Van Scoten was able to get halfway up the twenty-foot-high wall near nine-tower. Fourteen feet above him was an iron railing extending out about ten feet from the tower along the top of the wall that the tower guard leaned on during yard as he stood on the catwalk and watched the men below. Van Scoten stood on the top bench and twirled the weighted end of the rope, flinging it upward and wrapping it around the iron railing. Then he pulled himself up to the top of the wall. Coiled on the catwalk was a length of sash cord that the tower guard used to haul food up in a bucket—this was faster and easier than having someone unlock the door at the outside base of the wall and climb up the steps inside with the food.

Van Scoten dropped the sash cord down on the outside of the wall and let himself down to the ground near the corner of Third and Cass Streets, about 400 feet from the nearest manned guard tower. Then he was gone.

The next morning when the first shift came in, there was the sash cord, dangling on the outside of the wall. When Lieutenant Tom Driber, deputy chief of custody, drove toward the parking lot on his way into work, he immediately noticed the cord. As soon as he got inside the prison, Driber went out into the yard and saw the benches piled up along the wall. Then he saw the slab out of place. He went back inside the jail, called the chief and ordered a count.

Every inmate in the jail was counted three times, and still nobody was coming up missing. The first-shift officer in 2-wing was Bob Hawk, an excellent cop who prided himself on never having been conned by an inmate; he went through his wing three times, and everybody was in his cell. By this time Howard Yeager had been named warden, and when Yeager was told three counts had been taken and nobody was coming up missing, he said, "I want a standup count. I want every sucker in this jail standing up and holding the bars."

So Hawk started back through the wing and when he got to Van Scoten's cell, there was Van Scoten, still lying on his bunk in his bathrobe in the same position he had been in when Hawk had done the first three counts. He was lying facing the wall with the earphones from the prison radio system on his head.

Hawk walked past Van Scoten's cell and said, "OK, Van Scoten, let's go. C'mon Van Scoten, get up."

Of course, "Van Scoten" wasn't moving, so Hawk opened the cell door and shook the inmate. Van Scoten's head rolled off onto the floor.

This was the best dummy I've ever seen in my life. Van Scoten had gotten the idea from bank robber Willie Sutton, who had used the same scam when he tunneled out of Eastern Penitentiary in Philadelphia a few years before. Van Scoten had made a plaster head and glued on hair he had collected from the floor of the barber shop. He had stuffed rolled-up newspapers into the pajama bottoms and filled the torso with his extra blanket. He wrapped the whole thing in his bathrobe and put the earphones on it. In defense of Hawk and the 3rd-shift officer, who had also been fooled ("Van Scoten" had been counted seven times during the two shifts while he was out in the hole and after he was over the wall!), the doorways to the cells in Trenton are narrow and the inside of the cells was dark back then. When an officer looked in, he didn't get a good view of the interior of the cell, especially if he had no reason to believe that the inmate wasn't really in there.

I was 1-left wing officer at the time of Van Scoten's escape and first thing Monday morning before the first shift headed out to their posts, Warden Yeager had everybody go to an area behind center where he had the dummy, bed and all, set up. He had every officer on every shift come and look at "Van Scoten" so they could see how easy it was to make a mannequin that could fool everyone in the jail. Even though I knew it was a dummy, I could have sworn it was a real person, it was that well done.

Van Scoten had a big jump on the pursuing cops because of the trick with the dummy, and he managed to stay out for a long time—almost five years. When he finally did come back in the mid-sixties, I heard they had caught him in upstate New York.

****

As I said in Chapter 1, I could never understand why the state spent so much time, effort and money going after gamblers—except maybe the ones who were connected with organized crime. Take Joseph "Newsboy" Moriarity, for example. What a character! Moriarity was a big-time gambler and bookie from Jersey City who was caught several times in those periodic sweeps that politicians initiate to make it look like they're doing something. Moriarity had become filthy rich from gambling, mainly the numbers racket, but the feds, the local prosecutors, and especially the IRS, could never prove how much money he was taking in.

In the early '50's Moriarity, along with the Moretti brothers, Joe Adonis, and other North Jersey gambling figures, had been hauled before congress to testify in the Kefauver hearings. Throughout the 1940's and '50's Moriarity would get busted for gambling and do short time, usually in the Hudson or Bergen County jails. Finally, in the late '50's, he was convicted on another gambling rap, and this time he was sentenced to two to three years in state prison. So he came to Trenton.

While Moriarity was in prison, the sale of a row of 24 garages in Jersey City in July of 1962 suddenly put him back on the front page of the newspapers of New Jersey. (The newspapers loved "Newsboy" because he was such a character and because he had gotten his start in the numbers racket as a paper boy, thus picking up his nickname. He learned early that he could make a lot more money taking bets from his customers than by selling them newspapers.) By the late 1950's, law enforcement officials estimated that Moriarity was doing about $10 million per year in a variety of gambling pursuits. Even with his talent for making money, though, the Associated Press described Moriarity as a "shabby, nickel-nursing loner with a gift for acquiring money but no knack for enjoying it."

In July of '62, Moriarity was 52 years old and had just started his two-to-three bid in Trenton. Before he came into the prison, Moriarity had rented a couple of private garages in an alley in Jersey City to store two cars while he was in jail. Unfortunately for the Newsboy, the owner of the property decided to sell the garages while Moriarity was in prison, and the new owner brought in seven carpenters to refurbish the buildings. Two of the carpenters saw Moriarity's 1947 Plymouth and started nosing around. Bingo! In the trunk of the car were three hand guns, a rifle, 150 rounds of ammunition, a metal tool box . . . and $2,421,580.00 mostly in cash neatly wrapped and piled in two leather bags. The bank wrappers on the bills, ranging from $5 to $1000 denominations, had dates from 1948 to 1961. The cops were also interested to find their own records on Moriarity, apparently lifted out of one of the local police stations.

The Hudson County prosecutor, Lawrence Whipple, came down to Trenton and talked to Moriarity. Whipple said to him, "You've just lost 2 1/2 million dollars," and Moriarity deadpanned and said, "Whatever you say, Mr. Prosecutor." He absolutely refused to acknowledge that the money was his.

When I first saw Moriarity walking around the jail, I couldn't believe this guy was worth millions. He looked and dressed like a bum off the Bowery. And what a cheap bastard he was. Everybody knew that he had a lot of money—he had proven it on a lot of occasions, usually by walking away from it when the cops found it. On the street he was well known for his plain, out-of-style clothes and the beat-up old cars that he drove.

While he was in prison, he actually ate in the mess hall! I never saw anybody who had that kind of money, usually high-class thieves, gamblers or mob-connected guys, not get elaborate food packages from the outside. But not Moriarity. He ate with everybody else, dressed like all the other guys, and worked—for peanuts.

I had Moriarity on a painting detail up at the state hospital. In the fifties and early sixties, we would take a detail of seven men up there, pay them each $.25 **a**

day and paint a ward a day for $1.75. Moriarity was on one of my painting details, and one day during a break I said to him, "You're no dummy. How did you get caught and end up here?"

He said, "Harry, ten years ago, everybody knew the heat was on. Kefauver was going after Adonis and Moretti and them other guys, and both New Jersey and New York was watchin' me. We told everybody to lay low. But my regulars would come to my door, knock, shove money in my hand and say, real quick, '162,' and then slam the door shut before I could give them their money back. That's how bad people want to gamble, Harry, and that's how I started to get caught. And once they're on to you, they never quit watchin'."

I guess one of the reasons Moriarity didn't want people to know he had money was that other thieves as well as the cops were always trying to take it away from him. One of the other inmates told me that one time a couple of strong-arm types snatched Moriarity and took him to an abandoned warehouse. The inmate said these guys beat the shit out of Moriarity, even burning him with lighted cigarettes and threatening to really burn him—with a blowtorch—but he still wouldn't tell them where his money was.

In the mid '50's Moriarity got shot. He drove himself to a hospital and checked himself in. When the police looked in his blood-stained car, they found $3,000 in cash. Moriarity said, "It's not mine. I never saw it before."

A couple of years later, Moriarity was standing on the street in Jersey City next to that same 1947 Plymouth the carpenters found in the garage. The police picked him up on a numbers charge and found $11,000 in cash in the car. He shrugged and said, "I don't have anything to do with it. It's not my car." (He had put the car in his girlfriend's name.)

He was always pulling stunts like that, walking away from hundreds of thousands of dollars over the years to keep his ass out of jail. But who was his gambling hurting? I don't know how many times Moriarity got busted for gambling, but if he was around today, he'd probably own a casino in Atlantic City and be a highly respected business man.

7

CHAPTER SEVEN

THE EXECUTIONS RESUME

On July 3, 1962, nearly six years after the last execution, New Jersey electrocuted 27-year-old Fred Sturdivant, another black guy from Newark. He was number 158 since executions started in 1907, and only two more would follow before the death penalty would be struck down by the U.S. Supreme Court in 1972.

I said earlier that after the Theodore Walker execution I had gotten into the habit of going into the files and looking at the condemned man's jacket before each execution to help me connect with the victim. This seemed to help put a mental and emotional shield between me and the man in the chair. After I read the description of the crime in Fred Sturdivant's file, watching him die was easier than most. He had been convicted in June of 1958 of sexually assaulting and then killing his four-year-old stepdaughter. Our daughter, Kim, had been born in 1957, the same year Sturdivant had molested and killed his wife's daughter, Yvonne Ragin, in their apartment in Newark. All I could think of was our Kimmy going through the kind of terror Sturdivant had put his stepdaughter through. I had no problem watching Sturdivant die.

I didn't witness New Jersey's last electrocution in January of 1963, a guy named Ralph Hudson from Atlantic City, but I did see the next-to-last one, Joey Ernst, on July 31 1962, just 28 days after Fred Sturdivant. Because of Joey Ernst's flip attitude and an article in a men's magazine, his execution turned out to be one that still holds a prominent place in my memory.

Some years after New Jersey had stopped using the electric chair and I was still a guard, probably sometime in the early seventies, somebody gave me a photo copy of a magazine article about an execution written by an inmate, Tony Russo. I had known Tony and his partner, Frank Bisignano, while they were on death row. I also saw Tony frequently later when the death penalty was declared unconstitutional, and all of the death row inmates came into the general population.

I hadn't seen the article at the time it originally appeared in *Man's Magazine*, but I was fascinated by it. I had never had death-watch duty, so I never knew exactly what went on in death row before a condemned man was brought into the execution chamber. I was also interested in the article because it was about Joey Ernst—and Joey was the last man I had seen die in the electric chair. He was number 159, and for some reason—I think I must have been on vacation or taken a sick day, I never saw number 160, New Jersey's last electrocution.

When I read Tony's article, I thought to myself, "Wow. Here's a guy who was on one side of the death-chamber wall, watching Joey Ernst go to the chair and then guessing what happened after Joey went through the death house door, while I was on the other side of the wall watching it happen."

I had known Joey Ernst only slightly. I knew he was just a kid who never had a chance. Tony Russo describes Joey in the article as "a tattoo-covered tough with a long police record." I remember Joey as a tiny kid who had spent most of his life in correctional facilities and was as hard as nails. After stints in reform schools, he had done three years in Yardville (a young-adult facility), going in when he was about seventeen. While he was there, I heard, he got a Dear John letter from his girlfriend. When he got out, he bought a .38, practiced with it, dyed his hair red, found the former girlfriend and killed her. Tony's article indicates that Joan Connor's death occurred almost accidentally when Joey fired through her door "to scare her." I remember hearing that the murder was a lot more premeditated than that.

I knew from officers who worked death row that Joey was real defiant all the time he was in there. They told me that when Captain Abbott and his squad of guards came to get Joey the night of the execution, he threw his ice cream against the wall of his cell and yelled, "Piss on you!" and a lot of obscenities at the cops.

When I was given the article that Russo wrote, Tony was no longer in the prison. After his death sentence had been commuted to life, Tony went into population and eventually got out on parole. Then, a few years after I read his article about Joey Ernst, Tony came back in with a long sentence for drug trafficking. When he came back, I ran into him and told him how much I had enjoyed reading his article; then I told him what had really happened in the death chamber the night Joey died. He was impressed with the way Joey went out.

This is Tony's article:

THE EXECUTION OF JOEY ERNST
by ANTHONY RUSSO

(Reprinted by permission, Anthony Russo)

EDITORS' NOTE: *Anthony Russo, who wrote this article, has lived on Death Row since July 8, 1961. He and two other men were convicted in Newark, New Jersey, of a tavern holdup in which an off-duty policeman was killed. Mostly through his own legal efforts, his conviction and death sentence were reversed in 1965 by the U.S. Court of Appeals in a landmark decision based on the right to counsel. The Supreme Court, however, set aside the decision, reinstating a death sentence for the first time in history. After 10 years and six execution dates, Russo remains on Death Row awaiting the outcome of his latest appeal.*

DEATH ROW WAS EXCEPTIONALLY quiet. The only sound I heard was the monotonous whir from a pathetically small fan in its feeble attempt to cool the stuffy mausoleum confines of the New Jersey death house. Glistening streaks of dawn slashed through the open skylights, casting barred shadows on the gray cement floor.

God, how I hated to see that day come . . .

Tuesday, July 31,1962, was six hours old. To most Americans, it was just the second day of a long work week. But for Joey Ernst, who lay on his narrow bed gazing blankly at the high ceiling, it was his last Tuesday. At 10 PM he was scheduled to become the 159th man to die in New Jersey's electric chair.

He puffed on a Camel cigarette, exhaled through his nose. . . as thoughts of the chair flicked through his mind. For the past three years, years of fruitless appeals, on every Friday when he was escorted by guards to the shower, he had peered through a peephole on the chamber door and studied the stark lines of New Jersey's legal murderer.

The execution chamber was usually dark, and he could just barely glimpse the chair's silhouette. But there always had been enough light for him to identify the round headpiece, chrome electrodes and thick, heavy straps that hung from the chair's arms.

But the sight of the chair never frightened him. Joey had prepared himself for it more than three years ago when a Camden (New Jersey) County jury found him guilty of the willful, premeditated murder of his girlfriend, Joan Connor. Now, he had little to live for. He was ready to die.

At one time, three years ago, things might have been different. He had loved his girlfriend dearly, and perhaps would have raised a family with her. At his trial he had little defense to the charge of first-degree murder and was easy prey for the skilled prosecutor. He never denied killing the 17-year-old girl . . .

His journey to death began on a cold March night in 1959. He had driven to his girlfriend's house where a quarrel developed. She demanded he leave, slamming the door in his face. Once outside, Joey felt contrite and asked to be admitted back into the house. But the girl refused. He pleaded, begged and pounded on the door. Still she would not open the door.

Now rage supplanted apology. Joey Ernst went home and returned with a loaded gun. Again he pounded on the door, this time demanding entrance. Again refusal. It wasn't Joey's intention to harm her, but in that maddened instant he found himself reaching into his pocket for the gun and firing through the door to—to frighten her.

A tattoo-covered tough with a long police record, Joey probably would never have won an IQ contest. He never stopped to think now that his beloved would be standing in front of the door, perhaps ready to open it. Three bullets had slapped into her body, and she was dead.

When she died, a part of tough Joey Ernst went with her . . .

Doomed by the State and by himself, Joey climbed from his cell bed and shuffled to the porcelain sink for a cup of water. From the corner of his eye he noticed the death watch sitting at a desk in front of his cell. The death watch's vigil had begun early last night. It was the elderly guard's duty to observe Joey's every action and move, anything that suggested a possible attempt at suicide or signs of insanity. An insane person cannot be executed. Nor can a dead man.

He gulped the water and returned to his bed to await the guards who would escort him to a barber's chair where his head would be shaved clean.

The day before he had joked with me, one of seven condemned men also awaiting execution, when the warden invited him to order his last meal.

"What shall I order, Tony?" he had called to me, four cells away.

"Order something you don't like because you're not gonna get the chance to eat it," I yelled back. "The governor's gonna give you a reprieve."

"Well, I'm ordering turkey, anyway."

Joey was a loner, a very temperamental man who did not get along well with most of the men on Death Row. In fact, he would speak to only two—myself and Edgar Smith, who became famous with his book *Brief Against Death* and has been on Death Row longer than any man alive.

A reprieve was Joey's last hope, but also the farthest thing from his mind. The chance for a reprieve was so slim he gave it little thought. Perhaps a year or so ago there would have been a chance, but when Fred Sturdivant walked to the chair, less than three weeks earlier, it opened the door for further executions.

Before Sturdivant was burned, New Jersey hadn't executed anyone in more than six years. During those years, at the request of the governor, Robert Meyner, a committee was formed to study the death penalty to see if it should be abolished. The committee had recommended its retention.

The governor, acting on the recommendation of the committee, had refused to grant executive clemency to Sturdivant. Joey felt the same fate would befall him. But, nevertheless, his attorney had petitioned Meyner for clemency, and he was now awaiting word of the governor's action.

Joey's disjointed thoughts were abruptly ended by the death-house door bell. He rose from his bed and watched Ernie Biachi, the dayshift guard shuffle to the door and grate a key in the lock. From outside, the act was repeated by another guard, and finally the large, iron-grilled door swung open.

Capt. Alexander Abbott, six solemn-looking guards, and an inmate barber stepped past Ernie Biachi and stopped at Joey's cell.

"Ready for your haircut and shower, Joey?" Captain Abbott asked. The captain, nicknamed "Machine Gun" Abbott by prisoners, had a reputation. Back in 1954, when inmate Jerry Vaszorich managed to overpower a guard, tie him to the bars of the cell and escape from the death house, it was Captain Abbott, a sergeant at the time, who, convicts told me, machine-gunned him off a roof.

"I've been up waiting for you," Joey mocked.

"Hear any news yet?" the captain asked.

"I'm not expecting any."

"Never can tell," the captain said, turning a key in the cell door.

The captain and the six guards flanked Joey as he headed for the green, straight-backed chair used by the barber.

"Tony, what're you doing up so early?" Joey asked, stopping in front of my cell. I didn't tell him I hadn't slept that night. He would have laughed.

"Just listening to the news, Joey." Trying to hear some good word for you."

"Don't waste your time. There won't be any good word for me." He had to remain tough. Nothing could make him turn to jelly now.

"Let's go!" said the captain. "The barber's waiting."

"Just a trim," Joey joked with the barber as he sat down. "Can't take too much off, got a date tonight."

With a few flicks of the wrist, the barber had his head shaved clean.

"Wow! What kind of a trim was that!" Joey said, running his palm over his smooth skull.

"Get a reprieve and you can grow it back," Captain Abbott replied, playing along with the gallows humor.

Joey stripped naked and stepped into the shower stall. Icy needles rained down on his slight, five-foot three-inch frame while he soaped himself and tried to rub away the goose pimples that formed on his pallid skin.

He toweled himself dry, then peered through the peephole on the death-chamber door. Nothing inside had changed, just that a few lights were on and an inmate clean-up detail was mopping the floor and dusting off the witness chairs.

With a new set of clothes—khaki pants, blue shirt and slippers—Joey returned to his cell, now almost bare. While he had been in the shower, the death watch had removed all his personal items and stuffed them in a cardboard box. He was left with cigarettes and two books: a Webster's paperback dictionary and a novel, *Let No Man Write My Epitaph.*

"I hope I don't have to come back tonight," the captain said, locking the cell door. "If you do," Joey scoffed, "I'll be here."

Captain Abbott and the six guards marched out of the death house. Breakfast was brought in. Joey took only coffee, black. Although he wanted to remain tough and in control of himself, butterflies whirled in his stomach. He hoped the black coffee would soothe his nerves.

The round wall clock over the deathwatch desk showed 10:30 AM when the Rev. Stuart Snedeker arrived at the death house and went to Joey's cell.

"How're you this morning, Joey?" the Reverend asked. "Have you heard any encouraging news?"

"Don't expect none," Joey replied, his back to the minister.

"Are you sure you won't change your mind and let me tell you the story of Jesus, how he died on the cross for our sins—"

"I told you before, I don't want to hear any of that holy-roller shit. Just leave me alone."

"It's a wonderful feeling when the spirit of Christ enters one's soul—"

Joey leaped from his bed and shouted, "Guard! Get this preacher the hell away from my cell! I don't want to hear any of his holy-roller shit!" Veins, blue as his tattoos, popped through his pale skin as he clutched the bars and glared malevolently at the minister.

The guard took the minister to the side and asked him to leave. It was the guard's duty to see that the condemned man wasn't disturbed.

Reverend Snedeker clutched his worn Bible and headed disconsolately for the door. "If he changes his mind and wants to see me, give me a call."

"Will do, Reverend."

Joey paced his cell, puffing incessantly on a cigarette. Preachers and religion! He detested both vehemently. When his mother had visited him two years before and began telling him about the Bible, he became enraged. Shouting and cursing, he demanded she leave. Since that time, his mother had written him, but he never replied to her letters.

For the first time in years, he wondered how she was getting along. She lived alone, his father having died when he was a child. For an instant, Joey had the urge to cry out for his mother, to ask her forgiveness for his cruelty. Then he set his jaw squarely, tried to turn his thoughts away from such "softness." He stepped to the front of the cell and glanced up at the clock. Time was moving swiftly.

Where's my mother . . . .

Lunch arrived, and once again he took only coffee. The butterflies still fluttered in his stomach.

It was 4 o'clock when the phone pierced the stillness of the death house. The guard picked up the phone, mumbled an "okay," then stepped to Joey's cell. "Your lawyer's here to visit you, Joey."

"Okay, thanks." A flicker of hope crossed his mind.

Moments passed before the lawyer arrived at Joey's cell. The lawyer was blunt. "I'm sorry, Joey. The governor declined to grant executive clemency."

Joey wiped the palms of his hands on his khakis. "I figured he would."

"I'm sorry, Joey. I did everything I could."

"Yeah, yeah, I know."

"Is there anything you want me to do? Anybody you want me to see? Your mother—"

"No! No, nothing."

"If there's nothing else—"

"No, nothing else. You can go."

"Goodbye, Joey." The lawyer, with head bowed, quietly left the death house. He seemed relieved to get away from the oppressive atmosphere of death.

The door bell rang, and the supper meal was brought in. Along with the meal, on a special cart, was Joey's. His last. A whole turkey, baked candied yams, salad, turkey dressing and gravy. With the meal was a gallon of ice cream. I hadn't seen many meals like that, but I eyed it without any appetite.

"Hey, Tony, do you want a leg or a wing?" Joey called, "Man, there's enough here for everybody—but just you, me and Smitty is gonna enjoy this meal.

"Just a leg, Joey," I replied.

Joey reached through the food slot in the bars and filled his dish with turkey. The butterflies were still raising hell in his stomach, but he had to show us that he was tough, he had to eat the meal. He sensed the guard watching him while he gnawed at the turkey leg. Although he couldn't taste the food, he managed to swallow it, gulp by gulp.

The death-watch eyed him. "How's the turkey, Joey?"

"It's okay, the best I had since I been here."

"They cooked it special for you," the guard said.

"Yeah, I guess so. It's about time they cooked something good."

"Jersey takes care of its condemned men." Damned, if he didn't sound proud!

"Hey! Tony, how you like the turkey?"
"It's good, Joey, but I wish it was under different circumstances."
The turkey leg lay on Joey's tray and got cold. He couldn't force any more down, tough guy or not.
"We'll save the ice cream for later," Joey called. "They sent a gallon in. I'm surprised, cheap as these bastards are."
In Warden Howard Yeager's office, the wall clock chimed nine o'clock. Witnesses, most of them newspaper reporters, sat sprawled on couches chatting to one another about the execution they'd witness in exactly one hour. The Warden walked to the large picture window and gazed out at pickets who marched in front of the prison with signs that read: END CAPITAL PUNISHMENT . . . ONLY GOD CAN TAKE LIFE . . . SPARE JOEY ERNST.
Warden Yeager sighed and returned to his paper-strewn desk. He didn't appreciate carrying out executions, but it was the state law. He'd abide by the law. Tonight would be his third execution as warden.
Joey lay on his bed, puffing on cigarette after cigarette. For 23 years he had been a nobody. Now, tonight, he was news. He was someone special, called upon to play a part for society. Tonight he'd be the main attraction. Without him there could be no show. He'd have the stage to himself and, by God, he'd play his part well. He'd die tough like he always dreamed of dying. After all, Joey Ernst was a *man.*
Where's my mother . . .
A half hour went by before Captain Abbott and ten guards, each clutching a small blackjack, arrived at the death house.
"I'm back," the captain addressed Joey.
"I told you I'd be here. Hey, guard!" Joey called. "Bring me my ice cream and give some to Tony and Smitty."
"How do you feel, Joey?" Captain Abbott inquired .
"What's the difference? According to that clock on the wall I got less than a half hour to live."
Captain Abbott moved from Joey's cell and huddled with his men. He gave out orders, and the guards spread out and formed a line from Joey's cell to the death-chamber door. At the captain's direction, one guard positioned himself at the door leading into the execution chamber. He and the captain synchronized their watches.
Warden Yeager and 40 witnesses entered the execution chamber. The witnesses were solemn as they took their designated seats. They sat in uneasy silence, waiting to see Jersey justice in action. Before the warden took his place at the left of the electric chair, he stopped to have a word with the prison physician and the electrocutioner, who would work the controls that would snuff out Joey Ernst's life. To the electrocutioner, it was a job worth $150; to the warden it was just a job, too; but to society it was revenge.
Reverend Snedeker arrived at the death house and spoke to Captain Abbott. "Sir, would it be all right if I stayed and said some prayers?"
Captain Abbott shrugged. "I have no objection, but you know how Ernst feels."
"Yes, but I feel it's my duty to pray for his soul and to be near him when he walks to his death."

"If Ernst doesn't complain, you can stay."
"Thank you and bless you."
The captain watched the minister move from cell to cell urging the death-row men to pray for the soul of Joey Ernst. But his real attention was focused on his wristwatch. The instant the second hand read 9:55, Abbott's head nodded. The guard positioned at the chamber door went rigid.
"We're ready for you, Joey," Abbott said. Methodically, he slid the key into the cell block and turned it.
"Soon's I finish my ice cream," Joey replied calmly.
"We're ready for you now!" barked the captain. His voice seemed like another man's. The guards nervously converged in front of Joey's cell, black jacks at the ready.
"Why don't you let the guy finish his ice cream, you rat bastards!" an inmate shouted.
"I hope your mother dies of cancer!" someone else called.
Joey flung his ice cream against the wall. "I'm ready, too." His jaw muscles tightened, and his small hands balled into fists as he stepped from the cell and shook off a guard's attempt to assist him in his walk.
He had to be tough. It was his show, and he didn't need anyone's assistance.
With sure steps, Joey Ernst began his last mile walk, which was actually only 40 feet. Even though he hadn't gotten along well with most of the men on the row, he now stopped at each cell and shook hands.
Reverend Snedeker followed at a respectful distance: "*Yea though I walk through the valley of the shadow of death . . .*"
"Take it easy, Frank."
"Good luck, Joey."
" . . . I shall fear no evil . . ."
"I'm praying for you, Joey . . ."
"Yeah, do that."
"Thou preparest a table before me . . ."
"Good luck, Joey."
"Take it easy, Smitty."
"*. . . in the presence of mine enemies . . .*"
Joey came to a stop in front of my cell, the last cell before he'd enter the death chamber. He offered his hand: "Take care of yourself, Tony."
"Good luck, champ." We clasped hands. "Go like a man, Joey."
"That's the only way."
He took three steps and was inside the chamber. "What do you think you're gonna see," he cracked, to one of the witnesses, sitting in the first row. "This ain't no big deal."
Outside the prison, pickets still marched. Fifty to a hundred of them. Some protesting the execution, others supporting it. The streets surrounding the prison were blocked off by city and state police who stood between the two factions with riot guns at ready. All around, red lights blinked DANGER. A siren howled in the distance.
He was in the chair, held in place while the glittering electrodes and thick, black

straps were fastened. The headpiece was brought down to his head and strapped firmly under his chin. A guard knelt and fastened the electrode to his bared ankle.

With bulging, bloodshot eyes, Joey Ernst glared at the witnesses. Then darkness came as the hard, black-rubber mask closed over his face. Witnesses saw a shiver pass through Joey's body before he brought himself under control again and became as inanimate as a statue.

If the witnesses came to see a man cry out, they were disappointed. If the officials expected a man to beg for mercy, they were frustrated. If society wanted a man to repent, it was cheated.

Good or bad, Joey Ernst died the way he lived—tough, scornful, returning cruelty with cruelty, a man seemingly without feeling.

Where's my mother . . .

The warden raised his hand, then dropped it. Simultaneously, the electrocutioner pressed four black buttons, and the dynamo behind the chair began to sing its powerful tune.

The lightning hit Joey's brain first, knocking him unconscious and throwing him, tense and shuddering, against the taut strap. His mouth gaped open, almost breaking his jaws, in a horrible, silent scream. The lethal current raced through his body at 1,900 volts for five seconds. Then the tune of the dynamo changed, and 900 volts of lightning surged through him, burning and cooking. This for 55 seconds. His temperature shot up past the boiling point. His brain cooked to 150 degrees Fahrenheit.

And then came a sudden whining sound, like that of a car wheel spinning in snow. That meant the power was being boosted again to 1,900 volts for another five seconds before it dropped back to 900.

The witnesses stared in disbelief as the cadaver on the grim throne danced and twisted to the tune of the dynamo . . . Two full minutes that seemed like forever to those who looked on. A human being was dying, and the awfulness of the moment reflected in the eyes of the witnesses. With him part of them was dying, too.

Then the dynamo came to an abrupt stop. All eyes focused on the purple smoke that rose up over the head of the still figure in the chair.

At the warden's signal, the prison physician stepped forward and touched a stethoscope to the stiffened, twisted body.

"This man is dead," he announced.

The chair had struck.

One of the witnesses vomited. Another gave out a sigh of relief. The brutal act they'd witnessed was over. With a penny's worth of electricity, the chair had ended the life of a human being.

Society was avenged.

Joseph R. Ernst was one of the last men to die in the New Jersey electric chair... I hope.

That's Tony's article. Now here's what really happened in the death chamber the night Joey Ernst died:

When Joey came through the death-chamber door at exactly 10 p.m., I was standing along the back wall with about thirty other guards, each of us holding batons across our chests, as we always did to discourage the condemned man from thinking about bolting. I suspect that because Joey was known for his defiant attitude, we had almost double the usual number of cops on duty in the death chamber that night, plus a large number of witnesses, about 30, making the 18-by-24-foot room even more oppressive than usual. When Joey stepped through the door, he smiled—more like a sneer—at the cops and witnesses and did say something like, "What do you think you're gonna see," or "You ain't gonna see nothin." The two local newspapers reported that's what he said. But what they couldn't report, being family newspapers, was what he said immediately before that as he came through the door and looked at us, the cops, standing along the back wall. It was Joey's parting shot at his keepers: he came through the door, turned slightly to his right, looked at us and said, "Fuck you."

I thought, "Wow! What a cold man."

This execution was on a hot night in July, so Joey's prison-issue khaki shirt was completely unbuttoned, giving us a good look at the tattoo of a laughing mouse on his chest under the words, "The Devil's Playmate."

As Tony's story says, Joey wanted nothing to do with religion when he went to the chair, so the chaplain didn't enter the death chamber as he usually did. Joey looked cocky and defiant to the end. He was strapped into the chair, one guard to each arm and leg. Tony says that a guard knelt and fastened an electrode to Joey's leg, but the electrode was actually inside one of the leg straps. The face mask wasn't hard rubber; it was leather. And the warden, Howard Yeager, didn't dramatically raise his hand and then drop it—he just nodded. But these are minor details. Where Tony's story really takes off is in the description of the application of the current.

The "electrocutioner" didn't press four black buttons—he spun a wheel. And no dynamo "began to sing its powerful tune." The current hit Joey like a bullet, and yes, it did throw him against the strap, but then the executioner, Joseph Francel, did to Joey what he always did—a three-to-five-second count, a quick turn of the wheel back to its original position, followed by, in this case, six more three-to-five-second hits. Then it was over.

Tony's account, however, continues—with a lot of drama but little accuracy. I don't know whether he wrote it that way to make electrocution appear even worse than it was, maybe to advance his own case for abolishing the death penalty, or if he just didn't know what exactly happened in the death chamber. Tony has the current racing through Joey's body at 1,900 volts for five seconds, then being backed off to 900 volts for 55 seconds to the ever-present "tune of the dynamo." Then he has the current being boosted back up for five seconds and lowered for another 55 seconds, "two full minutes . . . as the cadaver danced and twisted to the tune of the dynamo . . ."

In fact, Joey was hit with seven jolts (more than usual) of 2,200 volts in quick succession, each time making his body lunge against the restraining straps—total time less than a minute. The witnesses were on their way out of the death chamber and Joey's body was being unstrapped to be taken to the back room well before Tony's magazine execution grinds down to its grisly conclusion. And for icing on the cake, Tony has a plume of purple smoke rise up over the body. Dramatic, but pure fantasy. I never saw any smoke; a few times I did smell burning flesh, especially the hot and humid night that Cruz didn't die right away and had to be hit three more times. But even then, Cruz was hit for a total of about thirty-five to forty seconds. That was it. That was all it took.

Tony also has one of the witnesses vomiting. Something like that did occur the night John Henry Tune was executed and the rookie guard fainted, but nothing like that happened during Joey's execution.

Tony's description of the protesters outside the prison is essentially correct. Joey Ernst was executed in July of 1962, and at the time sentiment was growing against the death penalty nationwide. John F. Kennedy was in the White House, and the anti-death penalty movement had been gaining a lot of momentum. There had been clashes between groups opposing and supporting the death penalty in a number of states, so local and state police, as well as squads of prison guards, were routinely being deployed in the streets around the prison during executions.

Tony says at the end of the article that he hopes Joey would be one of the last people electrocuted by the State of New Jersey—it turns out that he was right. Joey's execution in July of 1962 was followed by just one more: Ralph J. Hudson from Atlantic County, executed on the night of January 22, 1963.

In 1972 the U.S. Supreme Court ruled the death penalty, as it was being applied by the various states, unconstitutional. New Jersey wrote new legislation and in 1982 reinstated the death penalty. Shortly thereafter, the legislature changed the method of execution from electrocution to lethal injection.

The chair now sits in a Department of Correction museum on the grounds of the central office complex on Whittlesey Road in Ewing Township, just outside of the City of Trenton, and New Jersey is still awaiting its first execution by lethal injection, with nearly 20 people now residing on death row.

8
CHAPTER EIGHT

THE STAR

Over the next ten years three major cases ending in the death of inmates or their partners who had killed cops would have the jail buzzing with rumors of police "death squads" and "executions" being carried out on the street by police. The first case involved Tommy "Rabbi Tom" Trantino and his partner, Frank Falco, in 1963.

Prison inmates in general are big on conspiracy theories, partly because they see themselves as victims of a giant conspiracy masterminded by a group of rich white men, including the Rockefellers and the Kennedys. And most inmates *know* that American law enforcement agencies, from the FBI on down, routinely employ specially trained death squads to "take care of" troublesome criminals out on the street. It's also an established "fact" in the minds of inmates that if an inmate is perceived by the administration as a threat, usually political, he'll be set up to be killed.

In corrections, we did use special teams throughout the fifties, sixties and seventies to transfer unruly prisoners or to quell disturbances. We always called these teams "goon squads"; now they're called "Special Operations Teams." Today they dress like local police force SWAT teams—dark blue shirts and pants bloused into black combat boots, blue baseball caps—and carry mean-looking automatic weapons. When I was on the goon squad, we wore our regular baggy-ass uniforms and, if it was a bad disturbance, carried a 1920's-era Thompson submachine gun with a big round ammo drum.

Also, the New Jersey State Police had a fugitive squad that was trained to go after wanted criminals and, in some cases, prison escapees. Most commonly, inmates who escaped in New Jersey took off from minimum-security details, like working on a grounds crew outside the walls; or they slipped out of minimum-security camps like Jones Farm or Rahway's Marlboro Camp. If they had achieved minimum-security status before they escaped, it wasn't likely that they would be threats to pursuing officers, so a couple of us were usually assigned to the chase detail. We would draw weapons out of the armory, normally a snubnose .38, go back to the guy's old neighborhood and start sniffing around. If the guy was black, African-American officers who knew something about the guy's home area would get the detail. In probably 90 percent of the cases, the escapee would pull a Mario DeLucia and we'd snag him in a bar in the old neighborhood. Most guys in prison don't qualify for membership in Mensa.

If the guy was a real bad ass and went over the wall, then that was a different story, and the state police fugitive squad would be called in to go after him. In all my years at the prison, though, I never heard of any squad being especially trained for or specifically having a mission to go out and kill a fugitive inmate.

Even so, most inmates and a lot people from organizations like the Fortune Society felt that Daniel Hogan was murdered by the administration in 1972 because he had information about the death of Merrill Speller in the Vroom Building. And a lot of inmates, Teddy Roberts included, felt that Clark Squire was set up to be executed in the 7-wing shoot-out in 1974 and that the administration got the wrong man when John Clark was killed. As much as Teddy and I would discuss this and I would point out the inconsistencies in his theory, he was (and still is today) unshakable in his belief in administrative conspiracies to kill certain inmates.

The first case that I remember making the rounds of the prison rumor mill, Trantino and Falco, happened while I was still wing officer in 1-left. In this one, everybody I spoke to, even other cops in the jail, believed that Falco had been tracked down by an NYPD death squad and executed in a Manhattan hotel room because he and Trantino had killed two police officers in Lodi. The rumors about this particular case made Tommy Trantino one of the most despised and hated (by the cops) inmates on death row in the sixties. Here's what happened, according to testimony in the case, and what we in the prison system *believed* had happened.

At the time of the murders, Trantino was 25 years old, an ex-con from Brooklyn, and a heroin addict. He had been in trouble all his life. He had done five and a half years at Great Meadows Prison in New York for robbery and had gotten hooked up with Falco and another guy named Anthony Cassarino, both ex-cons. After he was released from Great Meadows, Trantino got married and got a job as a roofer, but then he ran into Falco on the boardwalk in Coney Island and threw in with him as a robber and a burglar. Even though he was already married, Trantino started living with another woman (also married) in Allendale, NJ.

On a Sunday night in late August of 1963, Trantino, Falco and Cassarino robbed an apartment in Brooklyn and then went over to one of Trantino's New Jersey hangouts, the Angel Lounge in Lodi, to celebrate with four women: Falco's 17-year-old wife, Patricia; Trantino's live-in girlfriend, Mrs. Patricia McPhail, 23; Mrs. Farah Vander Fliet, 19; and Mrs. Norma Jaconetta, 20. According to the bartender, a guy named Nicholas Kayal, the after-hours party got pretty wild, and at one point, Cassarino pulled out a pistol on the dance floor and fired a shot into the ceiling. Kayal said that Falco told him, "Don't worry, we're only fooling around." A neighbor called the cops and complained about the noise.

Five minutes later, 40-year-old Detective Sergeant Peter Voto came into the bar to investigate the complaint. Voto confronted Cassarino in the hat-check room, checked his identification papers, and then let him leave the bar. As Voto went toward the bandstand, Trantino jumped him from behind, disarmed him, twisted his arm behind his back and propelled him out onto the dance floor. Trantino beat Voto with a gun butt and cursed at him while forcing him down to the floor. Falco opened the door and grabbed a young police appointee, 21-year-old Gary Tedesco, who was coming into the bar to assist Voto. Tedesco was unarmed because he was still a trainee. After beating Voto into near-unconsciousness, Trantino ordered Voto and Tedesco to take their clothes off.

While Trantino was beating Voto, Falco squatted on the bar in front of Tedesco with a gun in each hand, yelling at Trantino, "You're crazy! You're crazy!" Three of the women later testified that Trantino then fired two shots into Voto, who was on his knees, killing him. The bartender said he was crouched down behind the bar, praying, when he heard the first two shots.

Falco, still squatting on the bar, yelled at Trantino, "What are you doing?!"

Trantino yelled back, "We're going for broke!" and then two more shots were fired, killing Tedesco.

Later, when Trantino took the stand in his own defense, he said he had been drinking heavily at the bar and was high on Dexedrine tablets. When he was asked if he had heard any shots, Trantino said, "I was standing at the bar. There was a violent explosion right by the side of my head—just like a blast. Like a siren ringing in my head. I felt sick. Everything began to spin and spin and spin."

Trantino said that after the shootings he ran from the bar, rode for a while with a milkman making deliveries and then paid someone five or ten dollars to drive him to McPhail's apartment in Allendale. She drove him to Washington Heights in New York where he took a cab to his parents' house in Brooklyn.

Meanwhile, Falco slipped back into New York City and checked into the Manhattan Hotel near Times Square using the name J. Rello of Newport, R.I. By late Monday afternoon, cops from Bergen County were in New York teamed up with the NYPD and looking hard for Falco and Trantino. The next day an informant told the NYPD where Falco was holed up, and a squad of New Jersey and New York City police under the command of NYPD Lieutenant Thomas Quinn went to the Manhattan Hotel. Quinn told reporters he got a passkey from the desk at about 3:15 a.m. and while he knelt down with his revolver pointed at the door, he had one of his men quietly open it.

Falco was asleep in his underwear with the light on. Quinn said he put his gun to Falco's throat and said, "Wake up. This is the police. You're under arrest."

Falco jumped up "like a tiger," Quinn said, grabbed the detective's gun with one hand and hit him in the head with a beer bottle from the nightstand with the other. Falco then threw Quinn against the TV set, and Quinn fired at him. Falco wrestled with another one of the six cops who had followed Quinn into the room, and when he threw the officer onto the floor, Quinn and another detective fired a total of eight more shots at Falco, killing him.

Meanwhile, Trantino was hiding out in Brooklyn. As soon as he heard that Falco had been killed, Trantino ran to his lawyer, Enid Gerling, and told her he wanted to give himself up. Trantino told Gerling that he wanted to surrender right after Voto and Tedesco were killed, but he was afraid of Falco; now that Falco was dead, he wanted to turn himself in. To make sure he was surrounded by plenty of witnesses, Trantino's lawyer called an Associated Press reporter and photographer to accompany the two of them to a precinct house in Greenwich Village.

Gerling went up to the lieutenant on the desk and told him that her client wanted to surrender.

"For what?" said the lieutenant.

"For homicide," Gerling said.
"What's his name?"
"Trantino"
A detective coming down the stairs said, "We've been looking all over for you."
Meanwhile the reporter and the photographer are watching all of this.
Trantino later told the press, "The treatment I had is beyond belief. They treated me like a man. They treated me decent and like a man, and no other person could ask for anything more."

Trantino was extradited back to New Jersey, tried, found guilty with no recommendation for mercy, and sentenced to death. He came into Trenton early in 1964. As soon as somebody with a crime like that comes in, all kinds of stories race through the jail. Over time, a story developed that I heard repeated by a lot of officers and inmates that ran essentially like this: After Trantino and Falco got the drop on the two police officers and made them undress, they trained their guns on the officers and ordered them to perform sex acts with the women. When the two officers couldn't perform, Trantino and Falco, who were making fun of the two cops all the while, forced Voto down onto all fours and shot him. Then they killed Tedesco.

The prison version of Falco's death that I heard, especially from inmates, had Falco asleep in the bed, the NYPD and the Jersey cops kicking in the door and putting nine shots into Falco as he tried to get out of bed. No warning, no fight—just an "execution." Then, after Trantino ran back to Brooklyn and heard about the NYPD taking Falco out in the hotel room, he rushed first to a priest and then to his lawyer, and then the two of them went to a police station so that Trantino could give himself up in front of witnesses. Whether the version we heard is what really happened is anybody's guess, but being a cop killer combined with surrendering with his lawyer in front of reporters made all of the officers in the prison despise Trantino.

When Trantino came into the jail in early 1964 the executions had stopped, but the death penalty was still in force. Like Tony Russo, Joseph Grillo, Silvio DeVita, Edgar Smith, Frank Bisignano and the others on death row during that era, Trantino appealed for years until the death penalty was ruled unconstitutional in 1972. Trantino was put into population and that's when I met him. After he was moved from the new death row, a converted section of the old 5-wing, to 6-wing, I would run into Tommy periodically.

As soon as he went into population Trantino grew a long beard and shoulder-length hair. He tended to hang around with Tony Russo and Frank Bisignano, Italian *compadres* from North Jersey who had also been on death row. On the street, Trantino had been called "Rabbi Tom," but I never knew why. After he grew the long beard, I figured he might have had a beard like that at some point before he came to prison, and it did make him look like a Hasidic Jew. I started calling him Jesus Christ.

I have to say that, despite the particular nastiness of his crime, Tommy Trantino has the most engaging personality of any inmate I have ever known. Whenever I think of him, the word *charisma* comes to my mind—he comes across as a warm, caring, personable guy. When you talk to him, he looks you in the eye and seems to be hanging on every word. He acts like he's interested in everything you have to say and that he cares about you as a human being.

After he came off death row in '72, Trantino was in population at Trenton for a short time and then he was transferred to Rahway. He has been wrote books and articles and tried to win parole for 35 years. When I was on the road in the early '80's proctoring GED tests in institutions around the state, I ran into Tommy at Jamesburg reformatory. He was working in a special program to try to steer the kids away from a life of crime—using himself as a prime example of where it can eventually lead. At first I was surprised to see him there since it meant that he had been given minimum-security status at Rahway and was able to travel outside the walls. As I watched him working with these hard-assed young inmates, I was impressed. I could see that those same qualities of his personality that I mentioned earlier were working for him at Jamesburg—the kids were respectful and attentive as he talked to them. That's not an easy thing to achieve in a place like Jamesburg or Annandale.

Despite his good works, for many years every time Trantino came up for a parole board hearing, the families of the two dead officers (Voto's brother later became chief of the Lodi police), the police, and people from the prosecutor's office went to the hearings and testified against him. Finally, in 2002, the board quietly granted Rabbi Tom a parole. The last I heard, he was having a tough time finding a town to live in where the neighbors would accept him since virtually everyone in New Jersey knows who he is. If there is, or was, an NYPD death squad, Tommy Trantino escaped it, but his future on the outside of prison walls still doesn't look too promising.

****

While Trantino was on death row, appealing, appealing, appealing, I was still in 1-left. Toward the end of my 1-left assignment, we got a character named Preacher Jones, a short, rotund little roly-poly black guy who could talk a blue streak and cite scripture all while he was picking your pocket. Preacher ran more scams on the inside of the prison than anybody I can remember, so I can imagine what he must have been like on the street. Ultimately he got paroled to Texas and I heard that he got killed there. He probably tried to scam the wrong guy and got a cap in his ass.

One of preacher's favorite cons was to grab a new fish before the guy was issued the B-outfit, which included a pair of institution-made shoes. Back in the 1950's and '60's new inmates came into Trenton from the county jails on Wednesdays—"Fish Day." Station wagons or vans would pull up to the receiving gate on the north side of the prison, Federal Street, and pull into a garage-like area inside the wall. Big steel double doors would be locked behind them, and the new inmates, shackled, would be unloaded.

They would be marched into thc 7-wing flats where they would be deloused and given a shower and foot bath. They would be handed white cotton pants and a white shirt with a big, black **P** on the back. Then they were marched through 4-

wing, outside to the second floor of a warehouse where they would be issued two uniforms: blue wool pants with a yellow stripe down the leg and a blue denim shirt for cold weather; and cotton khaki pants with a black stripe down the leg and a white shirt for warm weather. They also got a tin cup, a metal spoon, a slop bucket, a sheet and a blanket, safety razor, toothbrush, and two packs of cigarettes. Then they were taken back to 7-wing to remain in quarantine for five days before going in front of the classification committee for assignment to one of the adult men prisons.

Preacher would watch for some poor kid coming in from a county jail with a pair of worn shoes, snag him and say, "Hey, Boy, them shoes ain't gonna make it through the rest of the day. Here, take a look at these—you can have 'em for a box (one carton of cigarettes)."

Then he would hold up a pair of shoes that he had rescued from the garbage and had refurbished using soap, paste, shoe polish and anything else they needed to make them look good. After the kid had the shoes, and Preacher had the cigarettes, as he walked away, he would turn and say over his shoulder, "By the way, Kid, don't go out in the rain with them shoes, "and then he'd be gone.

Preacher would also get another fish and tell him that his shoes needed new heels and soles and that he would fix him up for a couple of packs. Of course, the fish didn't know that the prison had its own shoe repair shop and that all inmate shoes were repaired for free. Preacher would take the fish's shoes and make a great show of putting a tag on them with the fish's name and prison number. Then he would take the two packs, payment in advance, and trot the shoes up to the shoe repair shop. It always amazed me that none of the fish ever got pissed off enough to kill him when they found out the truth, but I guess his personality carried it off.

Preacher was also a big-time baseball manager. The prison had a league of several teams that started playing as soon as it got warm enough, around late March, through late September when touch football got underway. Preacher's team was the Black Sox. Whenever a fish came in and the word went out that the guy was a good ball player, bidding would commence to get him onto one of the leading teams. It was like the major league draft with offers of cartons of cigarettes and other incentives to get the guy onto certain teams. Preacher was one of the best at spotting and grabbing talent. For years the Black Sox were a dynasty like the 1920's Yankees, and Preacher scored a lot of packs and cartons betting on his team.

One of his many scams got Preacher into a fight with one of the younger inmates, and both of them drew time in 1-left lockup. When Preacher came in this time (he was in and out of 1-left like a yo-yo), I did the usual routine:

"Awright, Preacher, strip. Bend over. Spread your cheeks. OK. Stand up. Turn around. Lift up your balls. Lift up your feet. Open your mouth." The whole strip search routine.

Then I started going through Preacher's raggedy-ass clothes, and when I got to his shoes, I almost had to call for help: they were funky. It was bad enough having to look up some guy's ass to see if he was holding cigarettes in the crack, (common practice for guys coming into 1-left), but looking in Preacher's shoes was even worse. Reluctantly, I reached my fingers into the toe of his left shoe and felt something.

I said to him, "C'mon Preacher, take whatever it is out and let me see it."

He got this real sheepish look on his face, reached in and pulled out an old, wadded up packet of chewing tobacco.

I said to him, "Preacher, if you've got balls enough to put that shit in your mouth after it's been in those shoes, you've earned it."

And that was one of the few times that I didn't go by the book, Rule # 19, that says nobody brings nothin' into 1-left lockup.

****

After my tour as wing officer in 1-left from 1960-1965, I was assigned to the star and stayed in that job for the next three years. In addition to my duties directing traffic through the central intersection of the prison, I had to monitor window visits. Contact visits didn't start at Trenton State Prison until the early '70s, so the only interaction an inmate had with family or friends was through a yellowed, scratched thick piece of glass about 18 inches square and a telephone handset. Visits were restricted to family members and friends on the inmate's approved mailing list for one half hour per month for a total of six hours per year.

(Back then, if mail came in for an inmate from someone not on his approved list, it was returned to the sender. All mail, incoming and outgoing, was read and censored, like in the military during a war, up until the 1970's. Today, all mail goes through to the inmate, uncensored, though it is opened to be checked for contraband. No approved list is required for mail, but it is still required for visitors. The administration can bar certain visitors, but they have to have a damned good reason to do it.)

As I stood on the star, the window visit area was to the rear of my left shoulder and to the right of the grille gate. A thick concrete wall stood between the lobby of the prison where the family member or friend sat on a round stool and the long narrow room on the inside of the prison where the inmate also sat on a low, round stool. A counter ran along the length of the wall under the windows for visitors to set pocket books and other belongings on; there was also a counter on the other side where the inmate rested his elbows as he spoke with the visitor. There were ten windows spaced about three feet apart with no partitions. Inmates usually hunched as they talked to the visitor to shield themselves from other inmates and presumably to simulate some kind of intimacy with the visitor. There were no doors on either the visitor's or the inmate's side of the two long rooms, so officers on either side of the wall could—and did—watch what was going on. One of my duties as star officer was to watch the visits on the inside as well as directing traffic, which, with nearly 1,000 inmates and scores of officers and civilian employees moving constantly through the jail, required a lot of concentration.

One day in the middle of a slow week, Charlie Price came down for a visit with his wife, and since there weren't many visitors that day, I let Charlie stay an extra half hour. When he had come through the star before the visit, he was sober as . . . , well, anyway, he was fine. When he came out of the visit room, he was lit. Blasted. Three sheets to the wind. I couldn't believe it! Charlie came staggering out of the visit room with a stupid grin on his face, and the lieutenant in the control booth behind me spotted him almost as soon as I did.

Lieutenant Connor called me over to the slot under the window in center and started chewing me out: "Harry, what in the hell is going on out there? Don't you see that man's drunk? Didn't you see he was drunk before you let him in there?"

I said, "Lieutenant, I swear to you, he was as sober as a judge when he came through here an hour ago. He was fine, honest."

We went back and forth for several minutes, both of us bent over and yelling at each other through a foot-long, six-inch high slot through the metal wall. Meanwhile, Charlie is standing off to one side, grinning happily and rocking back and forth. Connor called some other cops and they came and took Charlie away to lockup. Drinking alcohol was an automatic charge, usually bringing ten days in the hole.

The first chance I got, a day or so later, I went into 1-left and found Charlie's cell. I said, "Listen, you son of a bitch, you got me in a lot of trouble. How did you do that? You went in there sober and came out drunk. How in the hell did you do that?"

Charlie just laughed and said, "Harry, you'll never know."

Charlie had another three or four years left on his sentence, and every time I ran into him over the next few years, I would ask him how he had gotten drunk, and he always had the same answer: "Harry, you'll never know."

Then Charlie got a parole date, and I ran into him a couple of days after he had gotten the word he was going home. I asked him one more time, and he must have figured, "What the hell," so he told me. It seems that has wife had a fifth of Scotch whiskey in her pocketbook along with a long, thin, flexible piece of tubing. Naturally, in the window visit area there had to be a hole through the wall for the armored telephone cable to go through. A rubber grommet sealed the hole snug against the telephone line. Not snug enough. Charlie's wife managed to work the tubing between the grommet and the telephone wire, and all the time Charlie sat hunched over talking to his wife, he was pulling on that bottle of Scotch. The extra half-hour that I gave him was more than enough to "get the job done."

Up until this incident with Charlie, the mail room cop, whose job it was to search visitors before they went into the visit room, never bothered to check women's pocketbooks because they figured there was no way to get contraband to an inmate through that wall. After the Charlie incident, a new order came out that all bags and pocketbooks would be searched before visits. That's the way rules are born in prisons—first, an ingenious inmate finds a way to do something, and then a rule comes out to try to prevent it.

Charlie got over on me and got real booze that day, but most of the time inmates have to settle for homemade jailhouse "hooch." I think most people know that prison inmates find hundreds of clever ways to get around the rules against having alcohol in the prison, usually by making their own. The most common method is to steal fruit or fruit peelings from the kitchen or from the garbage and then bribe somebody who works in the bakery to get some yeast. Then the little old winemaker finds a container that will hold a quart or two of liquid but is small enough to hide or disguise. Then he seals it inside a plastic bag and sets it aside somewhere to ferment.

Periodically, sweeps are made through a tier, a wing or through the whole prison—usually on the third shift around three in the morning—to search for weapons or contraband, including hooch. One of the best at making and hiding hooch was Kayo Konigsberg's friend, Abie Prinz. Everyone in the jail knew that Abie was making and selling hooch, but no one could ever catch him. One white hat in particular, Lieutenant Jones, was hot to bust Prinz, but he could never catch him with the goods. I went with Jones on a couple of raids into Abie's cell, and it was always the same scene. Jones would take a couple of officers to Abie's wing at 2 a.m., yank open the cell door and kick Prinz's bunk, jarring him awake. Then, while Prinz was trying to wake up and figure out what was happening, Jones would shine a big flashlight in his eyes while a couple of us went through his belongings. Jones would order Prinz out of bed, and we'd tear the sheets and blankets off and dump the mattress on the floor. Nothing.

Every time we went into Prinz's cell, a bucket full of funky water was sitting over in one corner with his socks and underwear soaking near the surface. Abie's undershorts, with a brownish yellow stain, were always floating on top. None of us ever wanted to go near that bucket, but it wasn't until after we busted him that we remembered it was always there.

Finally, one night, Jones got so frustrated after we came up empty-handed again that he started screaming at Abie, "You son of a bitch, Prinz, I know you've got hooch in here somewhere!"

Then, really pissed off, Jones turned and kicked over the bucket of water. Strange to tell! Underneath a cleverly constructed false bottom holding a couple of inches of water and Prinz's dirty laundry was a compartment containing two quarts of fermenting hooch. The smell of the water hid the smell of the fermenting fruit. The yellow-brown stain on the underwear was actually spicy mustard that Prinz had been stealing from the mess hall. Prinz got thirty days in lockup and Jones finally got his man.

One day about ten o'clock in the morning I was on the star directing traffic when I noticed an inmate called Muskrat (I never did know his real name) sprinting through four-wing toward me. I knew there was a problem, but with all the activity and traffic, I couldn't sort out what was happening. I held up my hand to stop Muskrat, but he blew through my stop sign and ducked behind me. Then I saw what this was all about—Farmer Dog, another inmate who was Muskrat's boy-friend, was hot on Muskrat's heels, carrying a shank.

"Oh, shit," I thought, "just what I need today. A lovers' quarrel."

So here's Muskrat ducking, bobbing and weaving behind me, trying to keep me between him and Farmer Dog while Dog is reaching over and around me, slashing the air with the shank, trying to stab Muskrat.

"I'm gonna kill you, you sumbitch!" Farmer Dog is screaming. "I'm gonna cut your sorry black ass!" he's yelling as he flails away with the knife.

I'm doing some bobbing and weaving of my own, trying to stay away from the shank. Muskrat is holding onto the back of my uniform jacket, and I've got my hands up, palms outward, shuffling and bouncing from side to side, trying to cover the parts of my body I want covered, all the time yelling to the guys in center to do something.

Dog's yelling at Muskrat, "I'm gonna cut your balls off, you motherfucker," and I'm yelling at the cops in center, "Get your asses out here and help me!"

I found out later that for the first couple of minutes this was going down, the guys in center were completely unaware that Dog had a shank. Muskrat and I were blocking their view of Dog, and when you're in that booth, it's hard to hear what's going on outside because of the thickness of the steel walls and the bullet-proof glass. The guys inside, who had all known me for years, knew I liked to dance and that Ginny and I went out every weekend to various restaurants to have dinner and dance.

As I'm outside ducking and shuffling, they're inside laughing and pointing at me, saying. "Look at Harry. He's practicing a new dance—the Italian two-step."

While they're in there having a good time laughing at me, I'm scared out of my wits that Dog is going to cut me up before he gets to Muskrat. Finally, when I moved to one side, the guys inside center saw the shank in Dog's hand and started scrambling to grab night sticks and get outside to help. I don't think I ever heard a sweeter sound in my life than when I heard that big old grille gate door swing open behind me. I saw flashes of blue as the other officers subdued Dog, still out of his mind with rage and screaming at Muskrat that he was a lowlife and a rat and he was going to die. Farmer Dog was disarmed and dragged off to 1-left, still kicking and yelling while I pushed Muskrat away from me and sagged back against the wall of center.

The whole thing probably lasted only about 90 seconds, but I was wiped. My legs were rubbery and I was sweating like a pig. They got somebody to relieve me on the star for a little while until I got it together again. Dog drew time in lockup after a court-line hearing. After a few years, he went out on parole, did another crime and is back inside today. I would still see him every once in a while walking through the jail. Our eyes would meet, and neither of us had to say anything—we would just grin, two old veterans remembering the dance we shared in center some thirty years in the past.

A few months after Muskrat was attacked, there was a similar incident, but this one had far more serious consequences. I was directing traffic late one morning, a few minutes before the lunch movement, when an inmate came sprinting out toward center through 1-right. He was screaming and yelling and holding his hands over his face, obviously in a lot of pain. The guys in center saw him come running up to the gate, and they knew he was in trouble, so they hit the button that unlocked the door, and this kid—he was about 21 or 22 years old—came stumbling and screaming into the rotunda.

I thought that somebody had thrown boiling water in his face, so I yelled to a couple of extras standing in center to get him down into a shower and put him under cold water. But one of the other officers ran up to the kid and yanked his hands away from his face.

The cop said, "He's not scalded—look at the way the skin is peeling off his face."

I looked closely and could see the kid's skin was peeling downward in long, thin strips, and blood was starting to ooze through the raw, pink flesh underneath.

Meanwhile, the kid was still screaming, and yelling, "I can't see! I can't see!"

Two officers grabbed each one of the kid's arms and started running with him down 6-wing toward the hospital. When they got him there, Doc Weisler took one look at the kid and said, "Jesus! Somebody threw acid in his face. His eyes are burned out."

We started an investigation and found out the story. It turned out to be so stupid and petty but typical of the kind of trivial incident that leads to this kind of tragedy. An inmate named Chi Chi Walker and this kid locked in the same wing. The first-shift wing officer, a quiet guy who owned a bar in Trenton on the side, was known for being super-meticulous; he even measured the nameplate on his uniform shirt to be sure that it was exactly centered over his pocket.

One day, Chi Chi was looking for a piece of paper to leave a note for one of his buddies, and he rummaged around on the cop's desk. When the officer got back to the desk, he saw that his pens and notepads were out of place, so he started asking around. The kid had seen Chi Chi over by the desk, so he told the officer.

The officer raised hell with Chi Chi, and when Chi Chi found out who the snitch was, he said to the kid, "I'm gonna git you, man. You ratted me out."

That's all it was about. Chi Chi went to work in the tag shop and stole some of the acid to clean and etch the metal before the paint was applied to the license plates. He waited for the kid outside of the shower in 1-right. When the guy came out, Chi Chi said, "I told you I'd git you, man," and tossed the acid into the kid's face.

As it turned out, the kid not only lost his eyesight, but he had swallowed some of the acid and burned out his throat and stomach. Even though he was now completely blind, he was returned to population at Trenton for several months after he got out of the hospital, and then he was transferred to another prison. About a year or eighteen months later, I heard that he had died, at the age of 24, a direct result of swallowing the acid.

After the attack, Chi Chi was brought up on institutional charges and did about two years in 1-left lockup; but he was never charged outside of the prison, even after the kid died. I guess the state didn't think it was worth trying to get an indictment and conviction on murder charges since so much time had elapsed between the tossing of the acid and the kid's death. Besides, it was just one inmate killing another. Just another body.

****

After working in the prison for so long and seeing the way the legal system works, I've often said that if I ever got arrested, I would never plea bargain—I would much rather take my chances with a jury. Case in point: During the time I was assigned to the star, two guys tried to go out over the roof like Mario DeLucia. One of the guys, Eddie Sheffield, suffered from narcolepsy. Eddie was a small, stocky black guy who would fall asleep at the drop of a hat. Several times I saw him in the mess hall with his head down on the table, sound asleep, oblivious to all the noise and activity around him. He couldn't control it. When it hit him, out he went.

Eddie and another inmate were on kitchen detail preparing breakfast. They usually went into work around 1 or 2 in the morning—the equivalent of working the night shift on the street. Eddie and his partner frequently went back and forth from the kitchen to a storeroom behind the mess hall to pick up supplies. One day when they were on their way to the big yard, they noticed that the storeroom had large ventilators on the roof. They figured if they could make it up inside those ventilators, they could work their way out onto the front house roof and pull a Mario.

Each night when they went to work, Eddie and his partner made extended trips out to the storeroom. They went up into the loft and stacked cartons of supplies under one of the vents. While one of them stayed downstairs as a lookout, the other one would work for several minutes with a swag hacksaw from the repair shop, sawing the bars covering the inside of the vent. Then they'd use shoe polish to cover the cuts and go back to work.

After a few weeks they were able to break the bars, cut through the wire mesh and get access to the louvered opening. Working together, Eddie and his partner managed to bend the slats enough to get out onto the roof. They waited for a dark, overcast night and went out.

The cookhouse/storeroom butts up against the mess hall/chapel/rec building, and the two inmates were able to climb from the roof of the storeroom to the top of chapel/rec. From there, they were able to get onto the roof of the front house. Crouching low, Eddie and his partner worked their way across the roof toward the street-side without being spotted by a tower guard. The front house faced out onto the street, so all that was left was to lower themselves down onto the grass strip just like Mario had ten years earlier, hoping that the guard in 9-tower and the one down on the street in 1-tower wouldn't see them.

Just as they were about to lower their sheet-rope and start down, Eddie's narcolepsy kicked in. He lay down on the roof and went to sleep. Almost simultaneously one of the tower guards spotted them and hit the alarm button. All hell broke loose inside. Cops with riot guns and pistols came running out onto the roof, forcing Eddie's partner to surrender. And Eddie? He's out like a light.

Attempting to escape is an indictable offense, and Eddie and his partner went to trial in Mercer County Court. The partner pled guilty and drew an additional year (instead of a possible two-to-three). Eddie, however, decided to fight the charge. He took the stand in his own defense and told the jury that he was out on the roof because the air in the prison was stifling, and, because of his illness, he needed "a breath of fresh air." I swear that's what he said. I don't know if the jury believed him or simply thought that anyone with balls enough to come up a story like that ought to catch a break, but whatever the reason, they found him innocent. Trial by jury: the only way to go.

* * * * * * *

Anyone who knows even a little bit about history identifies the 1960's as the decade of turmoil. As we got deeper and deeper in Vietnam and several of our national leaders were assassinated, young people rebelled against authority, and blacks became much more militant in their demands for equality. The death penalty was under attack nationwide, and New Jersey didn't electrocute anyone after Ralph Hudson in January of 1963.

I don't think there is necessarily a connection between the absence of a death penalty (or in this case, a lapse in its use) and attacks on police, but as the 1960's closed out, three of our guys were involved in a blazing gunbattle on the street in north Jersey that would seem to be an omen of things to come in the '70's.

Charlie Trautman was one of the most intense officers I ever worked with. Charlie took his job seriously and could always be counted on by the administration to volunteer for extra duty and difficult assignments like escorting potentially dangerous inmates. He seemed to love the challenge of danger.

In August of '69, Charlie Trautman, Robert Nims and a young guy who had been on the job for only 15 months, George Paszkowski, were escorting two inmates from Yardville Prison to the Union County courthouse when they stopped for a red light in Elizabeth. Paszkowski saw a man wearing a Halloween mask sitting behind the wheel of a car outside of a branch of the National State Bank. The three correction officers, led by Trautman, swerved into a vacant lot and jumped out of the car with their .38 snubnoses drawn. When four bandits, heavily armed, came out of the bank pushing four women hostages in front of them, the three correction officers ordered the men to surrender.

The robbers shoved the women aside and started firing at the cops with high-powered rifles and automatic weapons. The officers and the bandits exchanged fire, and Paszkowski, who was behind a telephone pole, was hit in the chest by a shot from a rifle; he fell face forward into the street. The four robbers who came out of the bank jumped into the getaway car and escaped with over $26,000. They abandoned the car in Elizabeth. Paszkowski, 26 years old and the father of a three-year-old, died on the operating table in St. Elizabeth's Hospital.

The first suspect, Donald Wilkerson, was arrested within hours of the shootout when he went back to get the abandoned getaway car. Lester Gilbert was arrested a few hours later in Newark in a second getaway car. This had been a well-planned robbery with at least three stolen getaway cars planted along the escape route. Eventually all five were caught and convicted. Lester Gilbert would go on to become a Muslim minister while in Trenton and would be a peripheral figure in a war between two Muslim sects in the jail as life in the prison got really interesting in the '70's.

9

CHAPTER NINE

A WILD DECADE: THE '70S

When I talk to high-school and college-age kids today, they always seem to mention the '60's; they identify it as the era of sex, drugs and rock and roll—and rebellion. They hear about the Chicago Seven, the Panthers and Patty Hearst, and they think the kind of violence that got George Paszkowski killed was happening in the streets every day. In New Jersey's prison system, it wasn't the '60's that were so wild, but the '70's—maybe because what had happened in the streets at the end of the previous decade was now playing out inside the walls.

Throughout the '70's I held virtually every position a correction officer could have in Trenton State Prison, ranging from wing officer to outside-trip escort. My last job as a guard was as officer in charge of a special prison hospital unit at St. Francis Hospital, about two miles from the prison itself.

For me, the '70's began when Leroy "Duke" Snyder came back to prison in July of 1970. I've always been neutral on the death penalty, and Duke Snyder is one of the best examples of why I can't make up my mind. I first met Duke in the early '60's when he was doing a bid for armed robbery and assault. He was then in his early 30's, a short, stocky black guy with a pleasant personality and a good sense of humor. If I had met him while he was putting gas in my car or walking his dog in a park, I probably would have said hello and maybe kidded around with him the way I do with a lot of people and then forgotten about him. Whenever I would see him around the jail, that's exactly the kind of relationship we had—a little conversation, some kidding around, always pleasant, upbeat encounters.

Later, in the mid '70s, a few years after Leroy came back on this new bid, I helped my son Darryl get a part-time job in the prison law library to supplement the income from his regular job. His break happened to coincide with Duke's and they got to know each other; in fact, they became good friends. I would often see Darryl and Duke with their heads together, talking about their lives and telling each other jokes. I never felt any anxiety about their friendship, but I did make it a point to tell Darryl that Duke had "seven bodies." I wanted Darryl to know that while Duke might seem to be a harmless, funny little guy, he was capable of snuffing out seven lives. I said this before: I always judged these guys on the way they treated me after they came through the front door, not what they did to get here.

When Duke came back into the jail in July of 1970, the word on the grapevine was that he had committed a murder and then had stalked either the witnesses or some of the jurors and killed six more people. Nobody I talked to was sure whether it was witnesses or jurors he killed, but everybody knew the total body count was seven because Leroy kidded around about the number of life sentences he had.

I remember at one point errors were found in his sentencing and Leroy grinned and said to me, "Hey, Harry, I'm down to five life sentences."

He knew he'd never see the street again, so what was the difference? I finally got curious enough to check out the real story behind Leroy's seven life sentences, so I looked at his jacket. His story combined with my acquaintance with him as a fellow human being are exactly why it's so hard for me to make up my mind about the death penalty.

I don't know what it was like for Duke growing up as a kid, but his record has got to make the average person think, "Why does the state keep a guy like this alive?" Duke's record goes all the way back to the late1940's when as a teenager he was sent to the Annandale Reformatory on an assault charge. Since then, he never put together any significant time on the street. After he got out of Annandale, he did another four years in Bordentown Reformatory for threats to kill and attempted armed robbery, four years at Trenton for assault and battery and assault with intent to rob, and another nine years in Trenton for attempted armed robbery and threats to do bodily harm. This is not the record of a nice man.

Duke was released from Trenton in December of 1968 at the age of 38 after serving nine years of a ten-year sentence. Of his 38 years, 19 had been spent in various correctional facilities, all of the charges containing a common element—assault. When Leroy hit the streets of Camden in December of '68, he went on an eight-month killing spree that the Camden County prosecutor said was a "land-mark" in the history of crime in that county. The prosecutor, A. Donald Bigley, said that Snyder should be confined for the rest of his natural life.

In February of 1969, two months after he was released from Trenton, Duke went into a used furniture store in Camden operated by a middle-aged black couple, the Crawleys, and brutally murdered Mrs. Crawley. Mr. Crawley had recently broken his leg and was recuperating at home, so his 45-year-old wife Lula was alone in the store. Duke tied Mrs. Crawley's hands behind her back with twine and then stabbed her 13 times in the chest, neck and back. The medical examiner said that any one of the wounds was sufficient to kill the woman and the stabbing was the work of a "sick mind." The headline in the Camden County *Courier-Post* said, "Woman Slain by Sadist In Her S. Camden Store."

I believe Leroy's next two murders were the ones that caused the myth in the jail that he had committed a murder and then had gone out to dispose of six of the witnesses or jurors. What really happened was that he robbed and killed a young guy he was rooming with named Warren Wells for his paycheck. Then, he was afraid that a friend of Wells, Shirley Brittingham (who was six months pregnant), was going to identify him, so he stabbed her to death the next day. He dumped both bodies through a cellar window into the basement of an abandoned house where they were discovered by a guy scavenging for paint cans three weeks later. The faces of both corpses had been chewed off by rats.

Leroy did kill one potential witness, not six. Later, when Leroy pleaded guilty to the murders, he said that the motive for all of them except Brittingham was robbery. He said he killed her out of "fear of identification."

In May, Leroy killed Mrs. Lovie Williams and then in August beat Mrs. Vera Stevens to death. Finally, in September, his run ended when he raped and killed the 58-year-old operator of a linoleum store, Mrs. Gertrude Friedman. When Camden police finally caught up to Leroy, they found clothing and jewelry belonging to Mrs. Friedman in his room. They also charged him with the attempted rape of a South Camden woman the previous July. That's seven bodies in eight months—and Leroy pleaded guilty to all of them.

Like the Clarence Hill case back in the 1940's, I could never understand why Leroy didn't get the death penalty. It was still on the books back in '69 though it hadn't been applied in the last seven years. Maybe the prosecutors saw the handwriting on the wall and figured there was no use trying to get the death penalty because it was never going to happen. My understanding is that Leroy's attorney and the prosecutors entered into a plea-bargain arrangement, so even with the confessions and the brutal nature of the crimes, Leroy didn't get sentenced to death. Under the law in effect back then, a confession to murder was considered a mitigating factor during the death-penalty phase of a trial, but I can't believe a jury would have voted for life based on that alone, especially since the newspaper descriptions of Leroy's crimes contained words like "brutal," "sadistic" and "sick." I don't know exactly what happened, only that Leroy came into the prison with seven life sentences.

When the judge sentenced Leroy, he read pieces of the psychiatric report that said Duke was a "malignant sociopath" and "a threat to society." During Leroy's descriptions of the crimes in court in connection with his guilty plea, he was completely emotionless.

The judge said, "You have shown no remorse. It is apparent that each of these violent acts was deliberately intended and you exercised care to destroy the evidence against you."

This is the same guy that I kidded around with almost every day and that my son became friends with.

Leroy drew five concurrent and two consecutive life sentences. His attorney said it would be an exercise in futility to stand there and request anything less than a life sentence for Leroy, but he also said that consecutive life sentences would mean "imprisonment without hope" and this would "fly in the face of the state's parole act." Yeah? And your point?

✱ ✱ ✱ ✱ ✱ ✱ ✱

The following year, another case hit the headlines big time, and again I found myself examining my attitude toward the death penalty. I never liked Edgar Smith. I always thought he was a con man and a sleazeball. When Smith escaped the electric chair and was released in the spring of 1971, I, along with just about everyone in the jail who knew him, was pissed off.

Smith fooled a lot of people, including conservative columnist William F. Buckley, Jr. Even though I thought Smith was an arrogant, mean-spirited lowlife, I have to say that he was extremely bright. While he was on death row waiting to go to the electric chair for brutally murdering a 15-year-old girl, he read constantly and developed himself into an accomplished writer. Smith wrote a book claiming he was innocent and describing his battles with New Jersey's "inept" court system, *Brief Against Death,* that Buckley helped turn into a best seller. Smith's ability to express himself so well helped convince Buckley to support Smith's efforts to get out of jail.

Smith set the U.S. record of 14 years on death row, from 1957 to 1971, for killing Ramsay High School sophomore Victoria Zielinski in March of 1957. At the time of the murder, Smith was 23 years old and living in a trailer camp in Mahwah with his 19-year-old wife and two-month-old son. He knew Victoria Zielinski, who lived nearby, and had driven her home before without incident; she trusted him. On the night of the murder, Smith had borrowed a car from a friend of his, Joseph Gilroy, and had picked up Victoria as she was on her way home from her girlfriend's house around 8:30 in the evening.

Instead of taking her home, Smith drove Victoria to a sand pit, a local lovers' lane, and made sexual advances. She resisted, and Smith forcibly pulled her sweater up and yanked her bra down. The autopsy revealed human bite marks on her right breast. The autopsy also showed that Vicki had successfully fought off Smith and was still a virgin.

Police and prosecutors theorized (and Smith would confirm years later) that Smith became enraged when Vicki wouldn't give in. She jumped out of the car and started running along the dirt road back toward the entrance to the sand pit. Smith also jumped out of the car, grabbed a baseball bat from the trunk and chased Vicki down. When Smith caught Vicki, he hit her in the head with the baseball bat and dragged her to a small hill near the edge of the sand pit. There, using a couple of big rocks from the sand pit, he brutally beat her head in. Smith beat the kid so badly that he splattered her brains in the sand, broke her nose and jaw, loosened her teeth, and destroyed her left eye. Her body was found lying face down in the sand the next day by her father and the chief of the Mahwah police.

When Smith returned the car to its owner, Gilroy noticed spots that looked like blood on the seat cover and a floor mat. Gilroy asked a couple of other friends what he should do, and they advised him to go to the police. Smith became the prime suspect within 24 hours of the discovery of Vicki's body in the sand pit. When he was questioned by police, Smith admitted he had picked Vicki up in Gilroy's car and had driven her to the sand pit. He even admitted they had an argument and he had hit her, but he denied killing her. The investigation revealed that Smith's pants and shoes were stained with type O blood (Smith was type A, Vicki Zielinski type O) and that Smith had tried to get rid of the evidence by throwing it off a bridge into a river. During the questioning, Smith kidded around with police and said that apparently they needed a "fall guy."

After he was arrested, indicted and brought to trial for the murder, Smith revived the fall guy idea. During the trial, Smith took the stand and "modified" the story he had told police. He said that another friend of his, 21-year-old Donald Hommell, had been dating Vicki and that the three of them had gone to the sand pit that night. Smith said he hit Vicki when she told him his wife was seeing other men. Then Smith said that Hommell and Vicki went off to another part of the sand pit, and when they came back, Hommell had hit Vicki and she was bleeding from the head. As Hommell glared at him from the spectators' seats in the courtroom, Smith explained Vicki's blood on his clothes by testifying he had tried to comfort her and cradled her head while helping her wipe the blood off.

The jury didn't come close to buying Smith's story and deliberated for just under two hours before coming back with a guilty verdict with no recommendation for mercy—an automatic death sentence for the ex-Marine. The jury convicted Smith so fast that the prosecutor, Guy Calissi, didn't even get back into the courtroom from lunch in time to hear the verdict.

Smith came into Trenton in May of 1957. While he was on death row, he developed into an accomplished jailhouse lawyer and started corresponding with William F. Buckley, the editor and publisher of the conservative *National Review* and moderator of TV's *Firing Line*. Buckley had heard that Smith was an avid reader of the *National Review,* and the two of them became regular pen pals. Buckley helped promote *Brief Against Death*, putting it on the *New York Times* best-seller list; he also got prominent Washington attorney Edward Bennett Williams involved in Smith's case. Just about every cop in the jail was disgusted that someone of Buckley's stature would help this guy who had so brutally killed a 15-year-old girl. Added to that was the fact that Smith was a pain in the ass as an inmate.

On the few occasions that I spoke to Smith, I saw him as a cold, arrogant SOB who talked down to everyone he met. He seemed to believe he was some kind of superior being. When he was on death row, the only guys who would even give him the time of day were Tony Russo and Joey Ernst. Everybody else hated his guts.

A couple of the officers who worked in the death house told me that whenever Smith's wife, Pat, who was a beautiful lady, would come to visit him, Smith treated her like dirt. The other cops told me that Smith would order his wife not to wear underwear and to sit with her legs spread with her skirt pulled up enough for him to see. But, even if the rumors were true, he couldn't have seen much because of the mesh barrier between them.

Death row inmates couldn't have window visits like the regular population. They weren't allowed in any areas of the prison other than their cell block and its private yard. Someone visiting a death row inmate was escorted through 6-wing to the locked door of the death house. There, after the death row guards verified who the visitor was, he or she would be let in. The visitor was then escorted to a chair placed in front to the inmate's cell. Between the cell and the visitor one of the death house guards slid a large, heavy mesh screen into place; the holes in the mesh were quite small, maybe an eighth of an inch, so Smith couldn't have been getting all that much of a thrill when his wife visited.

Primarily because of Buckley's help, in 1971 a U.S. circuit court ordered New Jersey to retry Smith. Instead of going through a new trial, the state allowed Smith to enter a guilty plea, and he was sentenced to twenty-five to thirty years, with credit for time served. The rest of the sentence was suspended, and he was given four years' parole and released. When Smith left the prison in March, Buckley drove down from New York in a big, black limo and celebrated Smith's release with him with some Cold Duck and giant deli sandwiches in the back seat. All of us had mixed emotions when we saw him leave: I don't know of anybody who liked him, so everyone I knew was glad to see him go. But most of the other officers and I also felt that releasing him was putting a vicious killer back on the street. After he got out, Smith immediately went on Buckley's TV show and gloated about how he had beaten the New Jersey legal system, saying he pleaded guilty as a part of a plea bargain only to get out of jail.

It wasn't any big surprise to anybody at the prison when we heard that Smith had been arrested in Las Vegas by the FBI on a fugitive warrant five years later. He was 42 at the time and was accused of kidnapping a 33-year-old woman from the parking lot of the company where she worked in Chula Vista, CA.

After he got out of prison, Smith became a minor-league celebrity because of Buckley and all of the controversy surrounding his case. He moved to California, went on a $1,000-per-appearance lecture tour, hit the radio and TV talk-show circuit, and wrote two more books. His celebrity status didn't last, though, and by 1974 he was broke and working as a security guard at an apartment building. In the fall of 1976, Smith asked an editor at the *San Diego Union* for a job but got turned down. The next day he abducted Lefteriya Ozbun, a Greek immigrant working as a seamstress, from the parking lot where she worked while her husband waited for her in a car nearby.

Smith accosted Ozbun just as she reached the parking lot, put a butcher knife to her throat and forced her into his car. Ozbun figured by Smith's demeanor that she didn't stand much of chance of surviving this, so she decided to fight him—as Smith drove onto an interstate, the 100-pound woman kicked out the windshield with her platform shoes and grabbed the steering wheel. Smith plunged the knife into her upper abdomen, right up to the handle, puncturing her diaphragm and her liver. He missed her heart by a quarter of an inch.

Ozbun was one gutsy lady. She continued to fight Smith, stomping on the brake and fighting with him for the steering wheel, until he lost control on an exit ramp and skidded down an embankment. Ozbun managed to crawl out of the car, with the knife still stuck in her belly; a guy selling flowers at the end of the ramp ran over to help her. Smith took off in the car but witnesses got his license number. He dodged police for two weeks, going back to New Jersey briefly. Hearing Buckley was in Las Vegas, Smith went out there to try to enlist his help again, but Buckley was out of town. When Buckley's secretary called him and told him Smith was in Las Vegas, Buckley notified the FBI, who arrested Smith.

When he was arraigned, Smith convinced the judge to reduce his bail from $250,000 to $100,000. At least the judge didn't go for the $25,000 that Smith wanted. Smith told the judge that he wasn't trying to evade capture when he left San Diego for New York, using the assumed name Michael Mason. He said that the name was on his literary contracts "and any reasonably competent police officer" would know that he frequently used that name. I can just hear the arrogance and sarcasm in his voice when he told the judge that. It's comforting to know that he stayed the same swell guy we all knew and loved after he left us—that fame didn't go to his head.

Smith was convicted for the Ozbun abduction and sentenced to seven years to life. Smith told the court that while he was on the run and had gone back to New Jersey, he had visited Victoria Zielinski's grave. Then he admitted killing her. He also admitted to molesting an 11-year-old girl.

Smith said when he visited Zielinski's grave he had a revelation: "For the first time in my life, I recognized that the devil I had been looking at the mirror for 43 years was me."

* * * * * * *

To me, Smith's con job on Buckley and his beating of the system in '71 symbolized what was happening in the prisons—and in society—starting in the early '70's. Up until this decade, even throughout the "turbulent Sixties," custody ran the jails; services (medical, education, social work) ran a distant second. Partly as a result of what happened at Attica in September of 1971 combined with attitudes that had been born in the '60's, conditions inside Trenton State Prison seemed to change with mind-boggling speed. It seemed like one day the motto was "feed 'em, fight 'em, fuck 'em," and the next day we were giving them college courses and TV sets and stereos in their cells. Orders came down from above ending the censoring of inmate mail by the mail room officers; prisoners could now make unmonitored telephone calls to the outside; newspaper reporters were allowed into the jail on a regular basis; inmate interest groups were being represented by "committees"; <u>and</u> the old death row was converted into a contact visit hall!

And who could keep up with their changes in fashion? The convicts were no longer wearing blue pants with yellow stripes in the winter and khakis in the summer—now they could wear blue jeans and sweat shirts and flowered dashikis. Up until the changes of the '70s, an inmate's appearance had to match his mug shot in case he escaped, so hair length was kept within certain limits and beards and mustaches were out. Now, they could grow their hair down to their shoulders (which a lot of them did) and they could have beards and mustaches. All of this was incredible to me, now an "old-timer" at the age of 44.

I can't say whether these changes were a factor in the November 1971 riot at Rahway that kicked off on Thanksgiving eve, but I know for sure that New Jersey was reluctant to send in the state police after what had happened at Attica that September. Even though there was no apparent political motivation in the Rahway uprising, I can't help but believe that the changes going on in society and in the prisons played a role.

After it was all sorted out, the word that we got was that the disturbance was kicked off by an ex-professional fighter—not Hurricane Carter, who was there, but a guy named Clay Thomas. I never saw the full story of how it started in the newspapers, but several inmates from Rahway who got transferred back to Trenton after the riot told me what had happened. The story they told me was that Thomas, drunk on jailhouse hooch, ran to the front of the auditorium and threw a chair through the movie screen. Then Thomas, who was a big, well-built guy, lurched up onto the stage and started exhorting the inmates about parole and conditions in the jail. Thomas won the crowd over, and the revolt picked up momentum. Guards in the back of the auditorium saw the situation getting out of hand and following standard operating procedures, locked the doors to the auditorium, isolating the inmates—and five of their fellow officers.

The warden, U. Samuel Vukcevich, lived in a house directly across the street from the front of the prison. He rushed over and, concerned about the welfare of his men, did something that no warden should ever do in these cases: he had the guards outside the auditorium unlock the door, and he went in to try to reason with the inmates. Vukcevich went up on the stage and was negotiating with Thomas in front of the inmates. I heard that Hurricane Carter was trying to position himself behind Thomas and was planning to cold-cock him with a shot behind the ear, but before Carter could make his move, Vukcevich said something that set Thomas off. Thomas hip-threw Vukcevich off the stage, injuring the warden's back.

From that point on, the rebels were in control, and the rest of the prison was locked down while a negotiating team was sent up from the central office in Trenton. The state police were massed out in the Rahway parking lot, and we were on call to go up and assist if the decision was made to rush the jail. Trenton was also locked down in case our inmates decided to stage a sympathy revolt. The Rahway inmates held out for 24 hours until Governor William Cahill got involved in the negotiations while 150 state troopers waited out in the parking lot. I later heard from the inmates who were transferred down to Trenton after it was over that Attica was definitely on the minds of a lot of inmates, and they all wanted to see it end before the state police came in.

Generally speaking, there's a wall of resentment between correction officers and state troopers in situations like Rahway. While each side respects the job that the other has to do, correction officers tend to think that the state police have an attitude—they think they're the state's highly trained elite police force, far superior to grunts like us. CO's also have the feeling—and the inmates share this—that the troopers are just itching to get inside during a revolt to kick some ass. Most troopers I've met view inmates as animals and scum, and I've always had the feeling that they think that, since we live with them, a little of that rubs off on us. We always preferred to keep the local and state cops out of the jail if at all possible because if they do come in and shoot the place up, then we have to live for years with the resulting resentment and hatred of authority. Our job is bad enough as it is without that to contend with every day.

After the Thanksgiving Day uprising had ended, a lot of Rahway inmates were shuffled around the state, including several sent directly to 1-left lockup at Trenton. Also about 40 of them were shipped over to a special maximum-security section set up in Yardville, a medium-security facility for younger, less-violent inmates about 15 miles east of Trenton, to await trial on charges stemming from the riot. In June of '72 five of the Rahway rioters, including one guy that I knew well, escaped from Yardville.

I first met Alfred Ravenell when I was wing officer in l-left in thc early '60's. Of all the inmates I've met in the jail, this is one guy that I would have truly been afraid of if I had run into him on the street. Ravenell was a militant black Muslim who was doing a life bid for robbing and murdering an Elizabeth junk dealer in 1962. He was about six feet tall, slender and hard-looking. When I looked into his eyes, all I could see was pure hatred and disdain for anybody unfortunate enough to have been born white. I have absolutely no doubt that, given the opportunity, Ravenell would have killed me and any other whites he could get his hands on—no questions, no mercy.

Ravenell was all business: he had no tolerance for any finger poppin' or dancing by other black inmates—he considered such behavior demeaning to the black man. Several times when young black inmates were jiving and fooling around, I saw Ravenell give them a long, hard, cold look and quietly say something like, "Knock it off, man." The playing stopped immediately. Everyone, cops and inmates, knew that Ravenell was all business, so when he said to me one day, "Harry, if I ever escape out of here, I'm not gonna be taken alive," I believed him without question.

Ravenell and I got along because I respected his sense of discipline, and he knew I didn't play any favorites. As I said, I wouldn't want to run into him on the street, but he never gave me any trouble in the wing; I always knew exactly where he was coming from.

After doing close to ten years, Ravenell had been transferred to Rahway because he was from Union County and had maintained a clean record at Trenton for several years. The department tried, if possible, to put men closer to their families for visiting purposes as long as the inmate stayed out of trouble while in Trenton. After the riot, Ravenell was identified along with the 40 others as being a ring-leader in the riot. (Rubin Carter always maintained that when Ravenell, a Muslim with no tolerance for the drinking of liquor, was let out of his cell by the rioters and found out the riot was about hooch, not politics, he stayed out of it.) A few weeks after Rahway had returned to somewhat normal operations, Ravenell and the others were shipped to Yardville.

Ravenell and four of the other Rahway inmates escaped from Yardville mid-June '72. In October, Newark police were tipped that Ravenell was holed up in an apartment there. When a couple of Newark detectives, along with detective John Simpkins of the New Jersey State Police fugitive squad, went to the apartment, a gunfight erupted and Newark detective Anthony Spera, who knew and could identify Ravenell, was shot in the chest.

As Spera slumped in the doorway, Simpkins emptied his gun at Ravenell, but Ravenell escaped through a window onto a fire escape. Spera was seriously wounded but later recovered.

Now the heat was really on. A few days after the Spera shooting, more than a hundred Newark cops raided a house in Orange where Ravenell was reported to have been spotted, but he slipped away again. Then the cops got a break. While questioning people in the house, Newark detectives found two women who said they had driven Ravenell to Lancaster, PA where he had friends. Newark police alerted Pennsylvania authorities, and they surrounded the apartment house where the women said they had dropped Ravenell.

An off-duty Pennsylvania State Police detective who happened to live in the neighborhood of the house volunteered to join the warrant team and go into the apartment to look for Ravenell. The detective, Robert Lapp, offered to go into the building partly because he was the only officer on the scene with a bullet-resistant flak vest. Lapp and another officer, Joseph Wescott, cautiously searched the apartment and then approached the tiny, closet-sized bathroom. Suddenly the bathroom door flew open and Ravenell, with a .38 in one hand and a sawed-off shotgun in the other, burst out. He blasted Lapp point-blank in the face with the shotgun, killing him instantly. Almost simultaneously Ravenell fired the .38 at Wescott, grazing the other trooper's head. Wescott and another officer emptied their revolvers at Ravenell as they dragged Lapp out the door. Then the 50 state, local and county police surrounding the apartment house fired over a hundred rounds into the building along with several tear gas canisters. When there was no return fire, they rushed the apartment and found Ravenell lying dead in a pool of blood on the floor with bullet wounds in his head and chest.

When Alfred Ravenell said he would never be taken alive, he meant it.

10

CHAPTER TEN

LITTLE PUSSY

In the months between the Rahway riot in November '71 and Ravenell's death in Lancaster in October '72, it looked like the changes that had been occurring in the ethnic makeup of the prison population over the last decade had finally come to a head. In February of 1972, all hell broke loose in the mess hall on the second shift as a Mafia kingpin was attacked by a group of black inmates—a definite no-no. When Anthony "Little Pussy" Russo and several of his "associates" were jumped in the mess hall and stabbed by a group of black inmates, led by Theodore Gibson, the administration figured this was a racial incident. That interpretation made sense at first because by 1972 the balance of power in the prison was shifting. Blacks now made up at least 60 percent of the population, and with Hispanics thrown into the mix, whites were probably down to about a 30-percent, or less, minority.

In the 1950's and '60's blacks would never have dared to screw around with the Mafia—it was understood that you just didn't do that. All of us had heard stories, though I never actually knew of a specific case, about Mafia hit men intentionally getting caught committing a felony so they'd get sentenced to prison to carry out a contract on an inmate. In prison, it wasn't as much about the long arm of the law as it was about the long reach of the mob. But now it appeared that blacks were challenging the white power structure for control.

Pussy Russo, who was 55 years old at the time of the attack, was doing time for giving false testimony to a grand jury in Monmouth County. He had been identified as a major Mafia figure in the Jersey Shore area by FBI wire taps during the 1960's and had been called before the grand jury to testify about mob connections with corruption of officials in Long Branch. He was doing a three-to-five stretch in Trenton for perjury.

The trouble started in the mess hall during dinner hour on a Saturday evening, just about 5 p.m. Russo, Rosario "Babe" Miraglia, and three of their crew were sitting at a table in the mess hall when Teddy Gibson and two of his associates approached the table. No words were spoken. As Russo and the other four looked up, Gibson, John Tillman and William Eutsey attacked them with shanks.

Russo was stabbed twice in the lower back. Babe Miraglia was also stabbed in the back. Vince Fenick and Harry Schultz were stabbed and Charlie Heilig was hit in the head with a pipe. This was a planned and coordinated attack. While Russo and the others were being attacked in the mess hall, Stanley Mars was being stabbed in 2-wing. The next morning, Arnold Banks and Frank Williams cornered Mike Masucci just as he came out of the shower and hacked him, cutting off a chunk of his lip. An officer found the piece of Masucci's lip and it was sewn back on at St. Francis Hospital.

Paul Fitzsimmons, the inmate who was serving a life sentence for killing a cop and had dug the tunnel in the basement of the hospital with Tony Puchalski, told me he was on the balcony across from 3-wing looking down when officers carried Pussy Russo through on a stretcher on their way to the infirmary.

Fitz said, "I looked down and every time the cops took a step, a glob of blood would come out of Russo and go 'plop' on the floor."

As bad as it looked at first, all of the victims lived. The state police came in to do an investigation, and they confirmed something that correction officers had known all along—this wasn't about race and political power—it was about drugs. A couple of weeks before the stabbings somebody had stolen a lot of drugs from the prison hospital, and Russo and his boys had them. The word went out that bags of ten pills were available for ten packs, that is, if you were white. Blacks would pay 15 to 20 packs for the same bag. This didn't sit well with Teddy Gibson and his guys, so they decided to send a message to Russo and the rest of the mob that this kind of discrimination was no longer acceptable—"black power," baby. An inmate organization called the Black Inmates Protective Association later said that the motive behind the attacks on Russo and his guys was to rid the prison of drugs, that the white mob was controlling and victimizing blacks through the control of drugs and that Gibson wanted to "cleanse" the prison of drugs. That's their version. To me it marked a change in emphasis away from hooch toward drugs for getting high and the start of a shift in power from white to black; I don't buy any noble motives on anybody's part.

Over the next few months, the atmosphere was tense as the administration and the officers expected some reprisal killings: nobody messes with the mob and gets away with it. But the paybacks never came—at least not inside the prison. Russo and the others were transferred out of Trenton to Leesburg, the new medium-security prison ("the country club") down in south Jersey. The blacks were sent to 1-left, but none of them, as far as I know, was ever attacked in retaliation. BUT, word started to filter in about the brother of one of the black guys being found dead in the street in Newark, and the uncle of another one being mysteriously murdered in Elizabeth and so on. It looked like the mob had its own method of taking care of business.

* * * * * * *

Two weeks after the Russo stabbings, and totally unrelated, Sergeant Donald Bourne was stabbed and died within a few minutes on the steps leading down into the mess hall. There was a rational motive behind the stabbing of Russo; nothing about Bourne's death was rational.

Don Bourne had just installed some storm windows for Ginny and me in the house on Centre Street a couple of months before he was killed. Don was one of the nicest guys in the prison—I didn't know of anyone, cop or inmate, who didn't like him. When I got the phone call at home at about six o'clock the night Don was killed, I was stunned. My first thought was that this was somehow related to what had happened two weeks before.

To this day nobody knows for sure why James Monroe killed Don Bourne. We do know that Monroe had been taken out earlier in the day to enter a plea in Middlesex County court on a charge of stabbing an officer at Rahway 18 months before. Monroe and another inmate had been in a fight at Rahway in August of 1970 when officer Rocco Melillo tried to separate the two inmates and was stabbed. On the day he stabbed Don, Monroe had entered an innocent plea in Middlesex on the Rahway stabbing and had been returned to Trenton.

When Monroe got back to the prison in the early afternoon, he picked up the shank he had hidden in his cell and headed for the mess hall. When I saw the shank later, it sent chills down my spine: it was a long pail handle with one end sharpened to a point like a six-inch-long knitting needle. Monroe had bent the other end, about four or five inches long, into a U-shape to fit around his fist. He had wrapped that end with layers of adhesive tape to make a handle.

When Monroe got down to the entrance to the mess hall, he said a few words to Don, and then, without warning, he punched Don in the chest with the shank. The point punctured the area slightly above and to one side of Don's heart. Don was baffled as to why Monroe had hit him, and as he sank to the floor, he said to Monroe, "What did you want to do that for?"

As Bourne lay bleeding on the steps, two other officers, Rich Tucker and Harry Hontz, jumped Monroe and wrestled him to the floor. Before the doctor could get to Don, even though the hospital was only about three hundred yards away, Bourne had died from a severed artery—the whole incident had taken about three to five minutes.

As I said, nobody could figure out why Monroe had gone after a likable guy like Don Bourne. David Guy Baldwin, another one of "Trenton's own," a young kid who had "accidentally" killed two people and then had been convicted of killing a guy who was slated to testify against him in a robbery trial, was a member of the Prisoners' Representative Committee. Baldwin told the press that Monroe had told him that Bourne had been an escort on one of Monroe's trips to court in New Brunswick and had harassed him by not delivering some papers to the court. This was bull. Prison records showed that Don hadn't been an escort on any of those trips.

What was more likely was 1) Monroe was a whacko and 2) he was pissed off about the Rahway charge and was looking for the first white hat he saw to take revenge.

If Monroe had killed Bourne in the '50's or early '60's, there's a good chance he never would have eaten breakfast the next day: it's possible he would have been beaten to death by other guards during the night. But this was the '70's, "prison reform" was a hot topic, and Trenton, like all other prisons, was under a microscope. The way the officers saw it, New Jersey no longer had a death penalty, so now it was open season on correction officers because a guy already doing a life bid now had very little to lose by killing a guard or another inmate.

After being convicted of first-degree murder in the Bourne killing and having a life bid tacked on to his previous sentence, Monroe was returned to Trenton. Whenever he did something the least bit out of line, he was nailed. He did a few years in lockup and then went into 3-wing where he was caught with some crude escape paraphernalia. That combined with erratic behavior earned him a visit by a goon squad for a "night ride to the Vroom Building," the "max max" facility on the grounds of Trenton State Psychiatric Hospital.

After Monroe had been out there for a while, we got a call that he was acting up again, and I was one of ten or twelve officers sent out to subdue him. When we got to his cell, he was acting crazy, yelling and carrying on, and refusing to obey orders. One of the Vroom officers opened the cell door, and several of us pushed into the cell to restrain Monroe. He resisted and, seeing a clear shot, I brought my baton down hard on his collarbone. He screamed and dropped like he'd been shot in the head. A baton in the thigh muscle or on a collarbone usually convinces even the toughest inmate that it's in his best interests to cooperate. If nothing else, it knocks him down and distracts him long enough for other officers to grab his wrists and cuff his hands behind his back. I have to say that even though I was using "reasonable force" to subdue an unruly inmate, it felt awful good to get that lick in on Monroe as a sort of remembrance for one of the most likable guys I ever worked with.

In the twenty-nine years that I served as a prison guard, I was called in fairly frequently to be on goon squads for actions that required "special handling," such as taking an inmate like Monroe out to Vroom. They called on me not because I was big and tough but because I lived so close to the prison for so many years. The brass knew that I was available at a moment's notice; they could call me out in the middle of the night and I would respond quickly. Also, though not a big guy, I wouldn't run away from a fight.

When an inmate had been marked for the night ride, a goon squad of three to five officers (depending on how big and how difficult the inmate was) was assembled. About two or three o'clock in the morning, we would form up in center and be issued an 18-inch billy club, a curved Plexiglas shield about three feet high, and a steel helmet. Then, while the jail was locked down and quiet, we would walk quickly to the guy's cell; the wing officer would quietly unlock the cell door.

On a silent count of three started by a hand signal, one of us would fling open the cell door, and two guys would push through the narrow opening. One guy would yank the inmate out of bed while the other officer, usually a big, heavy man, would pin him up against the back wall with the shield. If the inmate offered <u>any</u> resistance, no matter how slight, one of us would give him a few shots with the billy, either driving it into his stomach or hitting him in the groin, shins or knees; we tried not to hit a man in the head or in the face because it could do too much damage and leave marks that would look bad in court if he decided to file suit. Also, a billy swung at head level in such close quarters could hit one of us, so we usually kept them low.

When we got the guy upright and subdued, we would order him to strip and then wrap him in a wet sheet that one of the squad brought to the cell. The purpose of the sheet wasn't to make the inmate uncomfortable, though it did have that effect; rather it was used to immobilize him. Try freeing your arms from a wet sheet—it's better, and quicker, than putting someone in a strait jacket. After we got him in the sheet, we would put ankle shackles on him and shuffle him out through center to a van waiting in the intake garage just inside the northeast corner of the wall near seven wing. If he was a guy like Monroe, a lot of accidents might happen to him as he went down the metal stairs from the tier because of those shackles. And the poor fellow would have a tough time breaking his fall with his hands and arms wrapped tightly in that wet sheet.

The Vroom Building was about a twenty-minute drive through the deserted streets of the City of Trenton. We would drive through the open gates of the grounds of the main hospital and pull up in front of the gate in the cyclone fence that surrounds Vroom. The building itself is one of those old dark stone dormitory buildings typical of state mental hospitals built in the 1800's. Originally, it had been modified to serve as a prison unit for the criminally insane. Vroom's best-known inmate is Howard Unruh, a World War II vet who had gone bananas one day in September of 1949 in Camden and had walked down the street picking off 16 people at random with a rifle. In the 20-minute shooting spree, Unruh killed 13 people, including a shoemaker, a tailor's wife, a barber and his 6-year-old customer, a couple who ran a drugstore, and a 2-year-old boy looking out of a window. Back then, Unruh's rampage had shaken the nation because it was the first incident of its kind. Today, late-night comedians make jokes about postal workers who shoot up post offices or nut cases who walk into fast-food joints with guns blazing. I guess we're still shocked when these things happen, but it's almost as if we now take them in stride.

In the 1960's, a cinder-block addition with modern cells was attached to the old Vroom Building. The addition has three tiers of cells and a walled yard. It was tagged the "Vroom Readjustment Unit," and it's the worst duty any officer can pull. When an inmate is off-the-wall, like Monroe, or is a constant troublemaker, like David Guy Baldwin, he ends up in Vroom. These guys are even worse than the ones locked up in 1-left. Cops who get on the bad side of the chief or the assignment lieutenant end up getting urine and feces thrown at them in the Vroom Building.

On one of those typical "night rides to Vroom," one of us would get out and go over to the small guard shack and identify the inmate; the guard at the gate would already be notified we were on the way. Once we got the inmate inside, one of us would unshackle him and unwrap the sheet while the other guys stood nearby with clubs poised diagonally across our chests, looking on menacingly. This usually made even the toughest, meanest inmate think at least twice (unless he was a real nut case) before trying anything once the shackles came off. Then we would escort the inmate to his new cell, sometimes encouraging him with the billies to step lively, and the Vroom wing officer would lock him in.

When the officers found the escape implements in Monroe's cell, he reacted very poorly to being asked to leave his cell at TSP and had to be convinced it was in his best interests. When he arrived at his new home in the Vroom Building, he was again reluctant to enter his cell, so he was convinced again that he should cooperate with the officers. Periodically over the next few years, he was visited and talked to by officers who had been friends of Don. Everyone knew who this guy was, so every place he went within the system, he got the same treatment. Eventually he was so whacked out that even the other inmates couldn't stand him. While he was at Vroom he was beaten up by inmates to the point that one of his legs was broken, and he had a permanent severe limp.

Not that he was ever wrapped too tight, but by the time Monroe left Vroom in the late '70's, he was spending most of his day staring into space and laughing occasionally at something only he saw. In the mid-1970's, several states had gotten together and entered into a contract called the "Interstate Compact." Since the federal system had institutions in most of the states, they routinely moved their inmate leaders and troublemakers from prison to prison in different states to prevent them from establishing a power base. Based on the federal model, a group of states entered into an agreement to trade difficult prisoners from state to state on a one-for-one basis. Monroe was one of the first New Jersey inmates to be moved to another state. I don't know for sure where he is today, but it's probably somewhere in the middle of a forest in Oregon.

As a result of Don Bourne's murder, and some other incidents around that time, the prison eventually stopped the practice of having officers with the rank of sergeant and above wear white hats while the rest of us wore blue. Don's murder more than anything else convinced the administration that the white hat created more danger for the ranking officers than it was worth for prestige and for marking who was in charge. Another effect of Don's death was the installation of an airport-type metal detector near the mess hall gate in center. All inmates heading into the mess hall, and those any officer suspected of having a shank, were ordered through the detector. It didn't stop inmates from carrying shanks, but it cut the numbers considerably.

11

CHAPTER ELEVEN

WHO'S CRAZY?

Before the new section of the prison was built in 1982-83, the state maintained a row of buildings across Third Street from the front of the older (1800's) structure. In addition to the power and heating plant, there were warehouses, an officer-training building with a firing range, a motor pool, and a couple of residences. A number of inmates who had earned minimum custody status were assigned to work over there. Minimum security usually meant the guy didn't have much time left on his sentence and could be assigned to work across the street or at the satellite facility at Jones Farm out in West Trenton.

I could never figure out why these guys would want to try to escape since it was almost a given they would eventually be caught and face another one to three years tacked onto their sentences. A prime example was this one guy, an excellent electrician, who was working on the wiring in one of the warehouses across the street. Doc Kelly ("Spare the rod and spoil the child") was standing in the front door of the building.

The electrician was up on the roof, and he yelled down, "Hey, Doc, hold onto this for me will you?"

The inmate dropped the end of a wire down to Doc. After several minutes, Doc realized that he was going to be holding that wire until he retired, so he started looking for the inmate and then sounded the escape alarm.

Just behind the prison was a big lumber yard, Apex Lumber, and this inmate, for whatever reason, had decided to take off. While Doc was holding the wire, the guy was over in the yard of Apex hot wiring one of the lumber trucks. In the meantime, I get a call at home to come in and draw a weapon and head down to Maple Shade, about 40 miles away in Camden County, to stake out this guy's house and neighborhood.

As I mentioned earlier, we had a house and a flower shop on Centre Street, not too far from the prison. Centre Street is probably two miles long and dead ends at River View Cemetery. Our house and shop were in the middle of the block just before the street stopped at the fence surrounding the cemetery. A lot of our business came from perpetual care contracts and from people visiting the graves.

So I've got my thirty-eight on my hip and another officer and I are in a state car heading for Maple Shade while the electrician is driving around town in the Apex truck trying to figure out how to get out of Trenton. I'm halfway to Maple Shade when the guy turns the truck onto Centre Street, sees it's a dead end, panics, and goes roaring right by the flower shop, through the fence and into the cemetery. Somebody calls the Trenton Police and before the guy can get the truck turned around, all kinds of cop cars have surrounded the area, and within an hour, he's back at the wall.

So now I'm in Maple Shade, staking out the guy's house, and he's been captured in front of my house and is back in his cell, waiting for the dinner bell. There's a lesson to be learned in there somewhere.

****

One of the buildings across Third Street from the front wall of the prison was a solidly built three-story brick duplex that served as home for the chief of custody on one side and the prison doctor on the other. In the early seventies when I was moving around from job to job within the prison, I was temporarily assigned to supervise a detail of inmates that had to clean Dr. Howard Weisler's house every three days. The first day that I went in there with the inmates, the doctor was over at the prison and his wife was out of the house. I walked into the kitchen while the inmates were, per the Doc's standing instructions, neatly folding each corner of the living room rug into the center of the room and cleaning the floor around the folded-up rug. Doc had been the prison doctor for over 40 years at this point (he would go on to put in 50 before he retired), and I knew he was set in his ways, but this seemed to me to be a little . . . eccentric? While the inmates were working, I went into the kitchen to have a cup of coffee and read the paper.

I was a little startled to see a big chain wrapped around the refrigerator and padlocked. I walked back into the living room and asked the inmates, who had been on this detail for months, what was with the chain. They told me the Doc did that every time they came into the house; he gathered up all his liquor and locked it in the refrigerator. That made sense to me, but then when they told me how insistent Doc was that his mattress be turned every time the house was cleaned, I drew the line. I told them that was stupid, that we didn't have time for that crap, and besides, how was he going to know whether we did it or not. They just looked at me and smiled, and we went back across the street to the prison.

The next day, I was talking to the star officer when Doc Weisler came in and started asking me who the inmates were who had been on the cleaning detail.

I said, "Jeez, Doc, I don't remember which ones they were. Why? Is something wrong?"

He said, "My mattress wasn't turned, Harry. This is not good. I left standing instructions that I want my mattress turned every time the house is cleaned. Please see to it."

I told him I would check into it and see if I could remember who the inmates on the detail had been. He walked away.

A few days later, I got the cleaning detail again, and this time I was determined to find out how he knew that we hadn't turned the mattress. I got the two inmates, and we went into the Doc's bedroom and went over every inch of that mattress. It didn't have any tags on it or any writing, so I couldn't figure out how he knew. Then I found it. The crafty old bastard had taken a tiny straight pin, like the ones used to pin new shirts, and had inserted it into the rim around the edge of the mattress at the foot of the bed.

"So that's it," I said. "Well, I'll fix his ass."

So, of course, every time I had that detail, the first thing I did was to go up to his bedroom and move that pin from the foot to the head of the bed.

****

A little while after my experience with Doc Weisler, I had an encounter with another doctor—the prison shrink, Doctor Sydney Fine. When Ginny and I had the flower shop, I used to go home from the prison at night and spend several hours watering the flowers. We had hundreds of sets planted, and if I was watering late at night with no traffic on the street outside, I could actually hear them popping through the surface of the dirt. Anyone who has ever been out in a cornfield at night in the spring knows what I mean.

One day, I was in the ODR, having a cup of coffee and talking with some of the other officers when I happened to mention hearing the flowers growing the night before. A little while later, I was standing out near the star when Doctor Fine came through and headed for his office in 3-wing. About ten minutes later, one of the other officers came over to me and said that Doctor Fine wanted to see me right away. I left what I was doing and headed for the Doc's office, thinking he needed some help with something.

I walked through the door and said, "What's up, Doc? You got a problem? You need something?"

He said to me, "Sit down, Harry, relax." Then he gave me this long stare and said, "Harry, how do you feel? Do you feel OK, Harry?"

Then I knew something was up, and I started to get a little steamed. I said to him, "I feel great, Doc. At least I'm not going around bitching about my brother-in-law all day the way you do."

But he was very calm, and he said in his most soothing tone, "So Harry, what's this I've been hearing about you and the flowers? You can actually <u>hear</u> them grow? This is interesting. Tell me more about it."

He didn't know that Ginny and I had the flower shop and the greenhouses, so he must have thought I was hearing them growing in Cadwalader Park or around the warden's house—I don't know what he thought, but I explained it all to him and told him it was just the boys' idea of a joke. He seemed to accept my explanation, but I was never sure. Several times after that I caught him staring at me, watching me—I don't think he was ever completely satisfied about my mental health after that.

A couple of months after the Dr. Fine incident, I met a teacher from Mercer County Community College, Joe Butchko, who would become a good friend and would share a lot of good times with me and members of my family. One day in late August a lieutenant called me over to central control and told me he wanted me to escort a biology teacher from MCCC into the jail and show him where he would be conducting his classes.

Bringing college classes into the prison was another one of those "Great Society" programs that reformers were trying out in the move to rehabilitate rather than just punish inmates. Some of the same federal funds that had gotten me started in college as a way to raise the education level of prison guards were being used to try to cut the recidivism rate of inmates. I thought it was great. But a lot of the guards, especially the old timers, hated having these civilian "do-gooders" coming into the jail.

On the day that I met Joe, I waited for him in the front house lobby, expecting to see a little skinny guy with horn-rimmed glasses and talking like Mr. Peepers (a meek, mousy science teacher from a popular television show in the '50s). Instead, when Joe walked in and we were introduced, I found myself facing a 6 ft., 2 in., 260 lb. ex-steelworker with a booming voice and a quick wit. I was the one who looked like Mr. Peepers next to this guy.

Joe told me that the college had bought a used Greyhound bus and outfitted it as a biology lab to bring science classes to inmates at Trenton, Rahway and Leesburg. He said that he and the chairman of the science department at Mercer had gone out to Cleveland where Greyhound had a facility to rehab old buses, and the two of them had driven this thing back to New Jersey. At Trenton, Joe would be driving the bus through the vehicle gate near the death house into the yard, and the inmates would do their lab assignments at work stations on the bus. I was impressed with Joe and with the whole operation.

Joe and I hit it off immediately. I liked his great sense of humor and he liked my easygoing manner. He told me that most of the cops he had had to deal with were hard asses who made it very clear that they didn't like all of this college-courses-for-inmates shit and that he was going to get only as much cooperation as the administration forced them to give.

While we were getting acquainted, Joe told me he had worked for sixteen years at the big U.S. Steel plant across the river in Morrisville, PA while he was going to school at night to get a bachelor's and a master's degree in biology. I liked the fact that this guy had gotten his degree the same way I was getting mine.

I said to Joe, "Let's go inside and I'll show you where classrooms are for your lectures. Then I'll take you out in the yard and we'll find a place for you to park the bus when you bring it in."

Joe said he was really looking forward to being in a maximum-security prison, and I could almost see his mighty steelworker muscles flexing under his shirt as we prepared to go through the grille gate into the jail. He was ready, man. He was pumped. He was going to face down New Jersey's biggest and baddest cons and let 'em know where it was at!

After we had been pat-frisked and the grille-gate officer opened the door into the central rotunda, Joe and I stepped in and stood several paces behind the star officer.

Boda bing, boda boom! Before we could even make a move toward the school wing, the riot bell starts ringing. The door to center is flung open and the cops inside start tossing out helmets and batons and yelling, "Fight in 1-left yard! Fight in 1-left yard!"

I grab a helmet and stick and turn to Butchko, "Get your ass against that wall and don't move!"

Joe's eyes bug out, and he plasters himself up against the rotunda wall.

Then I'm running with a bunch of other officers toward 1-left.

I don't even remember what the disturbance was about, but I know that it was over quickly, and I was back in center in about ten minutes. When I got back, there was Joe, standing at strict attention with his back against the wall, his face pale and his eyes still open real wide. He hadn't moved an inch. Not a millimeter.

Here's old 5 ft., 8 in., 140 lb. Harry telling the big, bad steelworker, "It's OK Joe, just a little fight in the yard. No big deal."

And off we went to see the school.

****

Not too long after the flowers thing, Dr. Fine resigned to go back to private practice (and no wonder—the prison job paid about $30,000 in the early '70's when a psychiatrist on the street could easily make three times that amount). In the fall of 1971 the prison hired Dr. Fine's replacement, Dr. William King, a tall, thin, red-haired man in his early 50's who seemed to me to be kind of frail. When I got to know him, Dr. King told me that he had had open-heart surgery, which probably accounted for my feeling that he was not real healthy.

I ran into Dr. King almost every day, and we had pleasant conversations on a number of topics—nothing heavy, usually just social pleasantries. Then one day I had a run-in with him over a kid from our neighborhood who had applied for a job as a corrections officer. Ginny and I and our three kids, Darryl, Vance and Kim, lived in a working class neighborhood on Centre Street. The flower shop that Ginny ran during the day was next door to the house with three long greenhouses out behind the shop.

Like most city neighborhoods, the kids "hung" in groups, and sometimes they got into trouble. Because of my connection with law enforcement, a lot of times I went to bat for neighborhood kids when they got into scrapes with the local police, and the kids appreciated that. In all the years we lived in the neighborhood, with all of that glass in the greenhouses, we never had a single pane of glass broken by any of the kids—not even on mischief night.

One of the toughest kids in the neighborhood was Mike Nawrocky. I liked this kid a lot, but I also felt bad for him. His father was a heavy drinker who would sometimes come home and cause problems, so Mike would come over to our house for refuge. We always took him in and let him stay overnight in Darryl and Vance's room. When Mike got to be a teenager, he started to get into more and more trouble at school and on the street. I got worried that he was headed for big-time problems—I was actually afraid that I might end up seeing him in the prison. Mike wasn't a big kid, about five feet, eight inches but a solid 170 pounds and hard as nails—and he loved to fight. I once saw him, with one punch, KO a kid who outweighed him by 30 pounds.

When Mike turned 18, he was getting into more and more scrapes and had wrecked a couple of cars I had let him borrow. I pulled him aside and said, "Listen. Either I'm going to have you killed, or you're going to get a job working with me as a prison guard."

He listened and took the civil service exam and filled out the application. They called him in for an interview, part of which was a visit to the shrink to determine his mental fitness for the job.

Enter Dr. King. Mike went to see King one morning, and later in the afternoon, when I had finished my shift, I went to talk to King about his evaluation of Mike.

As soon as I walked through the door of his office, King said, "What are you nuts, Harry? This kid is small, good looking, blond—how long do you think he's gonna last in here? He's not big enough, and he doesn't have the mental toughness to do this job."

"Doc," I said, "You gotta be kidding. Look at me. I'm no bigger than Mike, and I've held my own here for 25 years."

King said, "Yeah, but you come across like a guinea gangster—these guys are never sure whether you've got an ace in the hole. Plus they like you. I'm telling you, Harry, they'll eat this kid up."

"But, Doc," I said, "Mike is one of the toughest kids I know. He never backs away from a fight. I'd depend on him to back me up in here a lot sooner than most of the guys who are already working here."

"I'm telling you, Harry," King said, "that kid doesn't have what it takes. He'll be out of here within a month. It's not worth taking a chance on him and investing the money in the training."

I blew my stack. I jumped up and yelled at King, "All right you son of a bitch. I'll tell you what. I'll go get Mike and bring him back here and lock the door with you two inside. If you walk out, he doesn't get the job. If he walks out, he's hired." Then I stormed out of the room.

I don't know if King took me seriously or whether he just reconsidered his position, but he ended up changing his recommendation, and Mike got the job.

A few months after my confrontation with Dr. King, when he had been working at the prison for a little over a year, the whole place was rocked when a small detachment of state police and county detectives suddenly swooped into King's office and arrested him for plotting to kill his ex-wife, her husband and her sister. When state police detective Andy Andaloro told King he was under arrest for conspiracy to commit murder, the Doc fainted. Seriously. He actually passed out on the floor when Andaloro told him they were taking him to jail.

Just about everybody at the prison who knew King was shocked at his arrest—I certainly had never seen any signs that he was unstable enough to put out a contract on his ex-wife. As the details came out, though, it turned out that Trenton State Prison's resident psychiatrist had himself seen the inside of the mental ward a couple of times—as a detainee. Not only that, he had been arrested twice for making threats, plus he had never passed the board exams to become a certified psychiatrist. All of this posed a bit of a problem for the New Jersey Department of Institutions and Agencies, Division of Correction and Parole since Dr. King had processed roughly 400 parole applications in his tenure at the prison and had rejected a significant number. All of them would now have to be reviewed.

In the days following King's arrest, details came out that caused Institutions and Agencies even more embarrassment. After his divorce from his first wife in the mid-sixties, King apparently became obsessed with the idea that he had been treated unfairly in the proceedings, particularly in regard to the awarding of custody of his daughter. A couple of times he had become so belligerent that local officials over in Montgomery, PA, where both he and his ex-wife lived, had him arrested. He was fingerprinted both times, which, when that came out in the newspapers, was especially embarrassing to Institutions and Agencies since that's a key part of the background check on potential employees at the prison. (It turned out, though, that King had managed to get the arrest records expunged in Pennsylvania, so New Jersey didn't look quite so bad on that score.) He had also been confined briefly in two different Pennsylvania state hospitals for "observation and evaluation." When King filled out the employment application for the prison job, he said that he had no physical or mental defects and that he had never been arrested.

When one of the local newspapers talked to Dr. Fine, who had been on the hiring committee that had interviewed King, Fine said, "I had the feeling he wasn't the best man for the job. At the time, there was nothing to indicate that he was a mental case. We had no idea about the threats he had made."

After King was arrested, the details of the plot were laid out. About a year after he was hired, in the fall of 1972, King established a counseling relationship with convicted murderer Frank Bindhammer. Bindhammer was a big, well-built German kid—nice looking with a pleasant personality. It's funny, I always had the feeling that King was kind of a con artist, but it turns out that Bindhammer was even better at it than King was.

Over time, King got to a point with Bindhammer that he trusted him enough to offer Bindhammer a deal: if Bindhammer would make arrangements with his contacts on the outside to hire a hit man for King, King would see to it that Bindhammer got transferred to a minimum-security facility like Jones Farm.

Bindhammer seemed to go along with the plot, but instead of contacting a hit man, he went to the prison administration and started cooperating with them to trap King—Bindhammer had been in jail long enough to know who had the clout to get him out to Jones Farm and who didn't. The state police were called in, and they wired Bindhammer, telling him to meet with King to see if the psychiatrist was serious about having the three people killed. Bindhammer met with King and the conversation was monitored and recorded in a van parked outside of the prison. A second meeting between King and Bindhammer was recorded from an office next to the one they were in.

Bindhammer told King he was having a hit man flown in to meet with King at the local Holiday Inn and that King should bring a $1,000 down payment to the meeting. Those meetings with a State Police undercover detective were also recorded from a van parked outside of the hotel. King told the "hit man" he wanted a large propane tank that was attached to the house of his ex-wife and her new husband to explode while the ex-wife's sister was visiting from Georgia. King also wanted to make sure the explosion looked like an accident. Psychiatrists who examined King later said he was convinced the three were plotting against him, and his mental condition reached "a crescendo of vindictiveness."

Institutions and Agencies was embarrassed again a month after King's arrest when Frank Bindhammer escaped from Jones Farm, where he had been transferred as the payoff for setting up King. He was recaptured within a few days and brought back to The Wall.

King went to trial in 1974, using, what else, an insanity defense. The first trial ended in a hung jury. He was convicted in a second trial in 1975 and did some time, but that conviction was overturned on appeal in 1976. He was supposed to be tried a third time, but his attorney said that even if he was convicted again, he wouldn't do much time since he had already served all but 17 days of his sentence. I never heard anything more about King, so I think the prosecutors decided not to go to trial again and that was the end of the strange case of the weird psychiatrist.

* * * * * * *

A few months after King was arrested and while he was out on bail, in May of 1973, there was a graphic demonstration of the "rat me out and die" part of "the code": a new inmate, Darryl Curtis, was killed within 90 minutes of coming through the intake gate of the prison. Curtis was a 25-year-old small-time drug dealer from Jersey City who had turned state's evidence in a murder trial in Hudson County court, a case unrelated to his drug conviction. Two of the guys convicted in the murder case, the killing of a player in a card game during an attempted holdup in Jersey City, were in Trenton State Prison. The Jenkins brothers, Anthony and Randolph, were serving life sentences, and Curtis's testimony had helped convict them.

When Curtis was sentenced, he literally begged the judge not to send him to Trenton State because he knew the Jenkins brothers would be waiting for him. Somehow, though, the word never got from Hudson County to Trenton, and Curtis arrived at the prison just before noon with six other new fish. As soon as he came through the intake gate, the Jenkins brothers knew Curtis was in the prison.

After he was brought in from the county jail and turned over to us, our officers took Curtis into 7-wing, the normal procedure for orienting new inmates. He began his processing in 7-wing—delousing spray, foot bath, and so on, and then he and the six others headed out toward the warehouse in the yard off of 4-wing to pick up their prison clothes. Normally an officer would escort new prisoners out to the warehouse, but it happened that one of the other inmates coming in had been in Trenton before, so he volunteered to lead the other guys, including Curtis, out to pick up their shoes and clothing.

As the story got pieced together and passed along the grapevine, the veteran inmate walked the new guys through 4-wing, outside, across a small courtyard and up the steps to the second floor of the warehouse where new prisoners were given pants, shirt, underwear, socks and shoes. Just as the small group got to a landing in the middle of the stairs, two figures suddenly appeared at the top of the steps, each holding a shank, and another one popped out from around a corner near the bottom of the stairs to block that exit.

Curtis knew immediately what this was about and started screaming for help. The six other fish knew they better get the hell out of the way. The veteran inmate just faded into the woodwork, and the two guys at the top of the stairs started down after Curtis. He turned and tried to sprint down the stairs, but there was the other guy waiting for him at the bottom with another shank. Curtis never had a chance; he was stabbed nine times in the chest, two of the wounds puncturing his right lung and one the left. By the time officers got to the scene, Curtis was bleeding to death on the stairs and the guys who had done it were long gone. As the Trenton city police were rushing Curtis to St. Francis hospital in one of their vans, he named his attackers. He died a few minutes after reaching the hospital.

Teddy Roberts was working in interior maintenance when Curtis was killed, and he was detailed to go over to the warehouse to clean up the blood.

I said to him later, "Didn't that bother you, Bull?"

Teddy looked surprised and said, "Why? It was just another body."

That's exactly the value of a life in a maximum-security prison.

As a result of Curtis's deathbed statement and an investigation by the prison administration and the Mercer County prosecutor's office, five inmates were indicted: Anthony and Randolph Jenkins, Stanley Harris, Richard Williams and Euther Presha. We figured this was an open and shut case of a payback execution, but it turned out to be anything but a cakewalk for the Mercer County prosecutor's office. The investigation into Curtis's death was long and difficult because nobody from the prison staff had seen the actual killing, and the inmates obviously weren't talking.

The trial that began with pre-trial motions in early December of 1974 and lasted until the first week of April of 1975 was one of the longest in Mercer County history.

The defense attorneys claimed that the prosecutor's office had withheld evidence from them and they filed for a dismissal of the charges. The judge found that both sides had made mistakes, but that everybody was acting in good faith, so he refused to dismiss the charges. The prosecution submitted a list of potential witnesses with the names of 175 guards and 20 inmates. Then, during all of this legal maneuvering, one of the local newspapers ran a series on the prison written by a reporter, John Toth, who had worked undercover as a prison guard for nine months. In one of the articles, Toth said that some of the guards had prison records themselves. The defense jumped on this to impeach the credibility of the prosecution's witnesses. What a mess!

At the end of the trial in April, after deliberating for 41 hours, the jury acquitted Harris, Williams and Presha and couldn't reach a verdict on the Jenkins brothers.

Even though the word throughout the jail was that Tony and Randy Jenkins had planned and carried out the killing, they ended up walking. Since there were no staff eyewitnesses and the other new inmates on the stairs that day had gotten the point of the lesson, the prosecution couldn't make the charges stick. The prosecutor's office called more than 40 witnesses, most of them guards and staff, but all of the evidence was circumstantial and the jury just didn't buy the state's case.

****

As much of a bad ass as Tony Jenkins was, he had a funny side. Before the Curtis murder, Tony was assigned to the Officers' Dining Room (ODR) as a busboy. Tony was a tough, black supremacist type, and he made it obvious that waiting on tables and cleaning up after white officers was offensive to him. One day, they were serving pork chops, and Tony, being a Muslim, didn't even like picking up the dishes the pork had been on. As he picked up my dish, he leaned down, took a long look at the pork chop bones, looked me straight in the eye and said, "You are what you eat, Harry."

I thought it was pretty funny, and I said, "Awright, Jenkins. You got me. But just wait. I have a long memory."

The death penalty had just been ruled unconstitutional and as I mentioned, monumental changes were sweeping through the prison—including something a lot of us never thought we'd see at Trenton: contact visits. The building that housed the old death row had three tiers of six cells each, total 18 cells. Sometime in the mid-sixties, condemned men number 19 and 20 had come in, and the administration had put a wall in 5-wing, creating a new wing with 27 cells. This new area, designated 3-wing, was the new death row. The old death row sat empty for several years until the central office sent word down that we would be allowing contact visits. Our administration scrambled around to find space for the visits, and the only area large enough was the old death row. Why not? It even had a kind of macabre charm.

On contact visit day, the competition to be the first one to get down to the holding room was intense. The trick was to be one of the first six inmates into the contact visit area because the two officers assigned to monitor the visits usually stayed down in the flats at either end of the tier. Thus, the absolute best place to be was in cells 3 and 4 (the middle two cells) on the third tier; next best was 3 and 4 on tier 2, and so on. The worst places were cells 1 and 6 on the flats because the two officers spent most of their time right outside these two, occasionally leaving to walk the tiers to make sure nothing too physical was going on. But believe me, a lot of physical relationships were consummated on those visits. I hated doing the inmate strip searches after these encounters because of the still-wet underwear and the semen smeared in various places on the bodies of the inmates.

So after Jenkins had nailed me in the ODR with the "You are what you eat" line, I was thrilled one Monday morning when one of the officers who had been on contact visit duty the day before came up to me and said, "Hey Harry, you'll never guess who I caught with his face buried in his wife's crotch yesterday."

I said, "Don't tell me. Let me guess. Tony Jenkins!"

The officer nodded, grinned, and said, "Yup. And I even wrote him up. He's gotta go to courtline later this week."

I whooped and took off for Tony's wing. He was still locked in, lying on his bunk and waiting for the morning count to clear when I got to his cell.

"Hey, Jenkins," I yelled at him. "I just heard about the charge you got yesterday. You are what you eat, motherfucker!"

He just looked at me, smiled and shook his head. Ah, sweet revenge.

* * * * * * *

In May of 1974, my daughter Kim graduated from Mercer County Community College and, after a discussion with Ginny, decided she wanted to transfer into a four-year school for speech therapy. I had also gotten my associate degree from Mercer and then transferred to Trenton State College where I earned a bachelor's degree in education. I knew that Trenton State had a reputation for having one of the best speech pathology programs in the state, so old Harry, figuring he had all kinds of connections at his *alma mater*, made some phone calls to several contacts at the college.

I got the same line from everyone I talked to: "Sorry, Harry. You're a swell guy, and I'm sure your daughter is a bright student, but that program is extremely selective, and it's all closed out."

Being the hard-headed Italian that I am, I refused to take "No" for an answer. I went home from work early one beautiful May afternoon a few weeks before Kim was slated to graduate from Mercer, picked her up at the college's campus in West Windsor, and the two of us headed out to Trenton State to see if the personal approach, with Kim in tow, might work better than the telephone.

I dragged poor Kimmy all around the campus as I went from office to office, wheedling, cajoling, pointing out her superior grade point average, trying every con that had ever worked in the jail—*nada*. In every office we heard the same story: the program was closed out, no transfers or new applicants were being accepted. One dean even told me that the Governor's daughter wanted to get into the program and they weren't even accepting <u>her</u>.

As Kim and I walked back across the campus toward the parking lot, I was amazed to see a familiar figure heading toward us—Frank Bisignano. I had known Frank since the early 1960's when he and Tony Russo had been sentenced to death for killing an off-duty police officer in a bar holdup in Newark.

I couldn't believe my eyes when I saw Frank striding toward us from the parking lot like he was the king of the campus.

"Frank," I said. "What in the hell are you doing here?" I almost thought that maybe he had escaped and was on the lam.

He looked at me and said, "Harry! What are you doing here?"

It was funny because each of us thought that the other was the last person in the world he would expect to see on the campus of Trenton State College on a beautiful day in May.

As Kimmy stood next to us, trying to figure out what was going on, Frank told me that he had been paroled a couple of months before and was now working in the public relations office of the college. I was stunned. Frank went on to explain that he and Tony had been appealing their death sentences since 1961, all the while, of course, living on death row and awaiting electrocution. That's how I knew the two of them. Every once in a while I would be assigned to 3-wing, and Tony and Frank were bright, interesting guys, so I would often talk with them to pass the time.

Both Tony and Frank were accomplished writers. Each of them had had stories published in magazines (Tony had that article on Joey Ernst published in *Man's Magazine,* among others), and Frank had published several articles in the *Village Voice*.

Frank said that he and Tony had managed to win stays of execution several times, and the longer they stayed out of the chair, the better their chances became because the political climate in the country was steadily swinging against the death penalty. Finally, in early 1972 when the Supreme Court struck down the death penalty, saying that it was applied inconsistently and unconstitutionally, 3-wing was converted to a regular cell block, and Frank, Tony and 20 other guys on death row were transferred out into the general population.

Then, Tony said, he started the paperwork to get his sentence commuted by Governor Cahill. Apparently because Bisignano was such an accomplished writer and had gotten noticed outside of the prison through his articles, Governor Cahill commuted his sentence to 45 to 48 years, making him eligible for parole. When the parole board let him out, he was the first condemned man in the history of the state to be granted parole.

Frank had gotten out about a month before Kimmy and I ran into him in May. He told us that he had taken courses in Mercer's and Trenton State College's prison education programs and had done well. Because of his good grades (and because it was good PR for them), Trenton State had offered him a job in their public relations office. Frank told me that he had been written up in the *New York Times,* and the story of the murderer-turned-PR-man had made the wire services, giving Trenton State all kinds of great publicity. He was the man of the hour on campus.

After Frank finished telling me why he was on campus, he asked me why I was there. Neither of us knew that the other had taken courses at both Mercer and Trenton State. I explained to him that I had graduated and was using my contacts to try to get Kimmy into speech pathology but we had struck out.

He said, "Come with me."

Frank led us back onto the campus and into the office of one of the deans. Within 20 minutes, we had Kim registered in the speech pathology program. It amazes me to this day that a hard-working prison guard like me, who had gone to school at night for years and had earned his bachelor's degree at that institution, couldn't get his daughter into the speech pathology program, but an ex-con, a convicted murderer who had beaten the system, could. I guess that's one of the things you learn when you've been around a prison long enough: it's not who's right or wrong or good or bad—it's those who can use the system the best who ultimately win the game.

12
CHAPTER TWELVE

CONSPIRACIES? DEATH SQUADS?

When Tommy Trantino's partner, Frank Falco, was killed by the NYPD in 1963, most of Trenton's inmates thought that Falco had been executed without benefit of a trial because he and Trantino had killed two cops. Then, when Alfred Ravenell was gunned down in Lancaster, PA, the word around the prison was that he had been tracked down and killed by a death squad—"they put 100 bullets into him" was the way we heard it. A little over a year after Ravenell was killed, another TSP escapee was gunned down in the middle of Times Square in New York, and the inmate take on this killing was that it was more of the same.

In April of 1973, Albert Gray was named warden of Trenton State Prison. The former warden, William Fauver, had been appointed commissioner of Correction and Parole by Governor William Cahill and Gray was brought in from the outside. Gray had retired as a lieutenant from the New Jersey State Police, and we saw him as a no-nonsense, by-the-book administrator who advocated strict discipline among the inmates.

A couple of months after Gray's appointment, minimum-security status was granted to Daniel Kremens, 40, who had been convicted in December of 1966 in the killing of state trooper Anthony Lukis, Jr. This seemed like a strange move to a lot of us.

According to the evidence presented at Kremens' trial, Kremens was sleeping in his car on the shoulder of the New Jersey Turnpike about a mile from the Mount Holly exit when Trooper Lukis pulled over to see if he needed assistance. While Lukis was questioning Kremens, he discovered two hand guns and ammunition in the car.

Lukis confiscated the weapons, but a scuffle broke out and Kremens managed to get one of the guns back. Lukis was then shot six times—four times in the back and twice in the head. Kremens took off in the trooper's car—with Lukis still in it. Kremens was caught about four hours later, hiding under the porch of a vacant house in Paulsboro. One of the newspapers down in south Jersey ran a front page photo of Lukis' pregnant wife with their four other children. Kremens was not exactly the poster boy for the PBA widows and orphans fund.

Kremens was convicted and sentenced to die in the electric chair, but his death sentence was voided and he was resentenced to life imprisonment when the Supreme Court struck down the death penalty in '72. Shortly after Gray was named warden and Kremens was given minimum-security status, he was assigned with 17 other inmates to an outside detail working in one of the warehouses across Third Street from the front wall of the prison. One November morning in 1973, in the seventh year of his sentence and with prospects of ever seeing the street again pretty dim, Kremens walked.

At first, when it was discovered that Kremens was missing, the search concentrated on Furman and Centre Streets near the prison because someone reported seeing a man wearing prison khakis near a bar in that area. Ultimately, though, investigators theorized that Kremens had jumped from the warehouse onto a slow-moving freight train that was passing by and continued on to the freight yards in North Trenton. A 13-state alarm was broadcast and the state police fugitive squad was brought in.

Sixteen days after he got away, an informant tipped police that Kremens had made arrangements to buy a gun and was picking it up in Times Square. The informant told the cops Kremens would be driving a 1964 Oldsmobile that he had stolen earlier in the Glendale Section of Queens.

Three detectives from the Midtown South precinct and Detective Sgt. Andrew Andaloro (the same guy who had busted Doc King) of the New Jersey State Police fugitive squad set up a stakeout in Times Square. A few minutes after midnight they spotted Kremens sitting in the Oldsmobile on 40th Street near Eighth Ave. Andaloro took the lead and, revolver drawn, eased up alongside the back door on the driver's side of the Oldsmobile. Andaloro yanked open the door and yelled at Kremens to surrender.

Startled, Kremens spun part way around and swung his arm at Andaloro in a backhanded shot at the detective's head. Then he ducked down, looking to Andaloro like he was reaching for a weapon under the seat. At the same time, Kremens threw the car into drive and hit the accelerator.

Andaloro jumped clear and fired three shots at the back window of the car. One of the slugs hit Kremens in the center of his back. Kremens slumped over the wheel as the car continued down 40th Street for a couple of hundred feet before coming to a stop against a fire hydrant in the middle of the block. No weapon was found in the car.

The killing of Kremens was the second incident in New York City within a few days involving a stakeout and the death of a fugitive. Just four days before, Twymon Ford Myers, a reputed member of the Black Liberation Army, was killed in a gun battle with the NYPD and FBI following a stakeout of his apartment in the Bronx. Ford was being sought in connection with the murder of police officers Rocco Laurie and Gregory Foster in 1972 in the East Village. Several months later, the BLA and Joanne Chesimard would be in the headlines following a shootout on the New Jersey Turnpike. The aftermath of that incident would have a major impact on us at the prison—and get everybody buzzing again about conspiracy theories.

But before the BLA/Joanne Chesimard drama would play out and work its way down the Turnpike to us in Trenton and just about a month after Kremens was gunned down in Times Square, Daniel Hogan's bizarre death in 4-wing added fuel to the conspiracy fire. Hogan's death raised one of the greatest storms of controversy I've ever seen in my years at the prison.

* * * * * * *

Just after Christmas in 1973, Daniel Hogan started raising a ruckus in his cell in the flats of 4-wing, the oldest housing unit in the jail. This wing was completed in 1836, and the cells in the flats had thick wooden doors with a six-inch square opening at the bottom, originally designed to slide food through. These were doors that we would never see today, about two inches thick, solid oak with heavy metal strapping, studs and huge wrought iron hinges. (After the doors were ordered removed, some of the administrators had coffee tables made out of them.)

For years before Hogan was moved into 4-wing, the cells on one side of the flats, primarily because of those wooden doors, had been used to confine unmanageable inmates or those who had gone crazy and were slated to be transferred to the Vroom Building. The doors could be closed, muffling the yelling and carrying on of the zanies. When we put an inmate into those cells, we unlocked the wooden door with a huge old metal key and swung it back on those big metal hinges; those doors always reminded me of the dungeons in stories like *The Man in the Iron Mask.* After going through the wooden door, which was only about five feet, eight inches high, the inmate would be in a cell considerably larger than the average TSP cell; today four men lock in most of them, sleeping on hinged bunks that fold up against the wall. These stone dungeons are about eight feet wide, nearly eleven feet high and 16 feet deep.

On the other side of the wooden door from the corridor, about three feet in, is a nine-inch step down so that the floor of the cell inside is almost a foot lower than the floor of the hallway outside. Sometime after the original construction of this wing, a set of bars had been installed at the top of the step. So, after ducking down a little and going through the wooden door, the inmate would be in a good-sized room facing a set of bars; he would then go through a regular barred door to get into the cell and then step down the nine inches into the cell.

In December of 1973, nine of these cells were being used for solitary confinement and to hold the psychiatric cases, even though the administration had circulated a memo the previous month saying that inmates should no longer be placed in them. So on the night of December 27th when Hogan was transferred into 4-wing, the kid got caught in a fatal administrative snafu.

Hogan, who was 21 years old, was known to have mental problems. He had been in and out of institutions, some of them psychiatric, since he was eleven years old. He had originally been sentenced to four-to-six years for robbery and possession of a firearm in Union County. He had been sent to Rahway, but he was causing problems there, so he was transferred to Trenton Psychiatric Hospital in early December for an evaluation. On the 19th he was shipped to Trenton. Everyone knew that Hogan wasn't wrapped too tight—a couple of times he had been disruptive, but two nights after Christmas he got really wacky and started cursing at the officers in the wing, screaming and yelling so much that the other inmates complained they couldn't get any sleep.

After he had been locked in the cell, Hogan continued to yell and scream and carry on. The third-shift wing officer that night was a relative youngster, 25-year-old William Jaichner from Bordentown. During the first part of the shift, Jaichner responded to Hogan's screaming and his cries for help, but each time he found Hogan was OK. Finally Jaichner got tired of opening and closing the heavy wooden door, so he stopped responding and just let Hogan yell and carry on.

Later, Jaichner told one of the local newspaper reporters who frequently covered the prison, Jack Knarr, that Hogan was continually yelling obscenities and telling Jaichner to "get your ass down here." Jaichner said that he stopped checking on Hogan about 3:15 a.m., though he also said that he knew as early as midnight that Hogan had done something to flood his cell.

Apparently, when Hogan had seen that his ranting and raving was being ignored, he started on a different tack to get attention and stuffed a blanket or a towel into the toilet. Since those cell floors are lower than the surrounding corridor floors, when the toilet started to overflow, instead of the water flowing out into the corridor where the officer would notice it, it was trapped in the cell and started to form a pool. Evidence indicates that Hogan saw what was happening and tried to unjam the toilet, but it was old, and he had broken the feed pipe.

The prison compound, being in the middle of a city, is such a tightly packed complex that when modern heating was put in, the heating plant, a relatively large building in its own right, was built outside of the walls. It was located on the other side of Third Street, and superheated steam was piped into the buildings through conduits under the street and beneath the east wall. Since Hogan was confined in the oldest wing, the steam in the radiators of those cells was about the hottest in the whole prison; the steam came directly from the heating plant into that wing before being piped into the other, newer wings, cooling down some as it traveled.

The radiators in the cells in the flats were just a couple of inches off the floor, so as the water rose in Hogan's cell, it started to come into contact with the hot radiator pipes. At that point, as the water started turning to steam, Hogan must have known he was in real trouble. The whole area became like a shallow concrete swimming pool filled with super-heated water. Apparently Hogan was frantically trying to get rid of the water, or at least trying to avoid it by climbing up onto the bunk and screaming for help, but by this time Jaichner had heard enough from Hogan and had gone off to attend to other duties.

As the cell filled with steam, Hogan must have been unable to breathe, passed out and fell into the pool of boiling water. Finally, at about 5:30 a.m. when Jaichner had finished with his other responsibilities, he stopped by Hogan's cell again. At this point, Jaichner said, he became suspicious because he could feel the heat coming from behind the wooden door. He told Jack Knarr that he started thinking, "Boy, this guy must really be cooking in there."

Jaichner opened the wooden door and through the cloud of steam, he saw

Hogan's body, as red as a boiled lobster, floating face down in the bubbling water. Jaichner called for help and then waded in and pulled the body out. Dr. John F. Marshall, the Mercer County medical examiner was called in and said that Hogan had been scalded to death and had died of multiple first, second and third-degree burns. Marshall also said that Hogan had fluid in his lungs.

Later, during the investigation, some inmates, especially Theodore Gibson, claimed that the officers knew what was happening, that Jaichner had seen the steam coming out of the food slot at the bottom of the wooden door and ignored it—the administrations wanted Hogan dead, according to Gibson.

I don't believe it. I don't care how much an officer might be pissed off at an inmate, I never knew any cop who would deliberately let a sick inmate like Hogan die—especially like that.

This was the seventies and prison reform was a big issue; an incident like this was just what the reformers wanted. All of the officers, me included, thought it was bullshit when Jaichner and Lieutenant Robert Maddox, the lieutenant in charge of center on the third shift that night, were suspended without pay pending the outcome of a full-scale investigation. Ann Klein had just been named the new commissioner of Institutions and Agencies by Governor Brendan Byrne. We knew she wanted to get off to a quick start and look good to the press. At one point, four separate investigations were going on simultaneously: the prison administration, the Department of Institutions and Agencies, the Trenton Police Department and The Mercer County prosecutor's office were all looking into Hogan's death.

In addition to the official investigations, several prison watchdog groups jumped into the case. The most visible group was the Fortune Society headed by David Rothenberg. In March of 1972, a 34-year-old inmate named R. Merrill Speller had hanged himself out at the Vroom Building with a pair of socks. Hogan was in the Vroom Building the night Speller died and had written a letter to Rothenberg, saying that he had information about Speller's death. Speller, who, like Hogan, had a history of mental problems, especially depression, had also written to Rothenberg shortly before his death, saying he knew he was "being set up to be iced."

Rothenberg, a lawyer, was also looking into the death of 32-year-old Wilfred Hardman, who had died while in custody at the Vroom Building in January of 1972. Rothenberg and two Newark lawyers said that Hogan had been slated to be a key witness in a suit filed against state officials by Speller's family. Rothenberg said that it was a strange coincidence that Hogan was the third inmate to die in custody under what Rothenberg termed "mysterious" circumstances.

At the same time that inmate-advocacy groups outside the walls were focusing on these incidents in the prisons, inmate committees inside the walls were also becoming much more vocal. By now, the reforms started the previous year after Attica and Rahway were having far-reaching consequences inside the jail. A number of successful lawsuits filed by "jailhouse lawyers" and an atmosphere in American society favoring rehabilitation over punishment had given inmates a sense of power in an environment of powerlessness.

So when Hogan died, Trenton Prison's most prominent inmate spokesman, Theodore Gibson, jumped into the controversy. In a letter to Rothenberg, Gibson and two other inmates said that, according to other inmates confined in 4-wing, Hogan had continually cried out in the early morning hours on the day of his death, "Let me out of here! You're trying to kill me!" and the inmates had heard a guard yell back, "You can die for all I care," and "I'll close the door on you so nobody can hear you." Gibson's letter then alleged that the guard closed the solid wooden door to Hogan's cell "with the steam steaming out of the cell."

Acting Mercer County prosecutor Wilbur Mathesius said that his office had been concerned about certain conditions at the prison prior to Hogan's death. Mathesius said, "This was the catalytic agent for something we've been on the verge of for a long time. His death just exposed a lot of problems." Mathesius said he was pursuing an aggressive investigation. Institutions and Agencies announced that a board of inquiry convened at the prison and headed by Warden Gray had recommended the dismissal of both Jaichner and Maddox.

Mathesius presented his findings to a Mercer County grand jury, which could have indicted the two officers, but the grand jury failed to bring any charges, and the potential for any criminal proceedings against the guards ended.

Jaichner and Maddox lost their jobs and Daniel Hogan lost his life. As the Bull says, "Just another body, Harry."

* * * * * * *

I was hoping the new year, 1974, would be a little more peaceful than the previous three had been, but no such luck. In April, I got a first-hand look at what kind of cop Mike Nawrocky had turned out to be after Doc King had tried to put the screws to him. I was working in a wing one morning when we got a call that several Vroom inmates had gone on a rampage and were tearing up one of the cellblocks. This had started the day before when nine guys had refused to come in from yard because they said one of them had been beaten by an officer. At first, the administration was going to wait them out and let them come in when they got cold and hungry, but then the inmates armed themselves with bricks and steel rods and started smashing in the basement windows. Tear gas was lobbed into the yard, and that was the end of that.

The next day, though, when they were let out for breakfast, they started up again. They were smashing plumbing and electrical fixtures, setting fires in the corridors and tearing up their cells. We got the call to go out there, and I found myself sitting on the bus next to Mike Nawrocky. This was going to be Mike's first experience with this kind of thing.

When we got to the front door of the Vroom Building, we were issued fiberglass shields, helmets with curved Plexiglas face plates, and batons.

I pulled Mike to one side and told him, "Here's how we do this. We form up in squares of ten guys: two rows of five guys each will be in the first wave; then you and I will be in the second group of ten. When we push open the door, they'll go in first and push the inmates back, and then we'll come in right behind them and start swinging."

I told Mike to stick close to me and I'd show him how to do it. As soon as the door opened, the first two rows charged in, and before I could move or say a word, Mike bolted ahead of me, through the door and into the middle of the fight. The sight of twenty cops behind shields swinging night sticks intimidated the inmates, and it was all over in a matter of minutes. After we had herded the inmates into their cells, I looked around for Mike and saw him leaning against a wall in the corridor.

I ran over to him and said, "Don't you ever do that again! You're lucky you didn't get killed."

He just smiled and looked embarrassed. This wasn't the end of it, though. Mike was going to find out about payback a few months later as attacks on officers, and vice versa, continued to escalate throughout the year.

* * * * * * *

Just two days after the we put down the Vroom uprising, Mike again demonstrated that I was right and Dr. King had been wrong when Trenton State Prison's most accomplished tunnel engineer, Vasile "The Mole" Dovan, ran us around the maypole for a couple of days before Mike and a couple of other officers found him in Paul Fitzsimmons's "marvel of engineering" under the hospital. Apparently Dovan had found the entrance to the tunnel Fitz and Anthony Puchalski had dug back in the early '60s that had been closed off by a trapdoor with a heavy padlock.

Dovan looked like a mole. He was about five feet, seven inches tall, weighed maybe 180 pounds and had a pale complexion and receding hairline. He was originally from eastern Europe and often told people he had tunneled out of a Rumanian concentration camp in the 1950's and escaped to Canada. He had worked his way down to Brooklyn and in 1968 he was involved in a wild shootout with police during a bar holdup in Union County. A bartender and a patron were killed in the crossfire, and Dovan was convicted of murder. In this escape attempt, Dovan hooked up with the unlikeliest of partners, a black guy named John Clark; it was common knowledge throughout the jail that Dovan despised blacks.

John Clark was six feet, two, 165 pounds, with brown eyes, black hair, and very black complexion. He would be killed less than a year later in an attempted breakout engineered by the Black Liberation Army. By definition, BLA members are not generally fond of whites. These two constituted the oddest odd couple I've ever seen at Trenton State Prison. The only thing they had in common was they were both in for murder. None of us could ever figure out how in the world they got together in the first place and then how they could stand to work side by side in a small tunnel when each of them despised the other's race. A whiff of freedom can make strange bedfellows.

One theory about the Clark-Dovan odd-couple routine that made the rounds of the joint was that Clark had found out about the tunnel and told Dovan, "Either I go with you or the cops find the tunnel."

I'd put my money on that version.

Dovan had gotten his nickname "The Mole" because his appearance fit so well with his fondness for digging tunnels. First, he said, he had tunneled out of the Soviet Union. Then, when he was in Rahway, he had tried to tunnel out of there, getting him transferred to Trenton. A year before this tunnel, Dovan had been spotted in the utility space in 7-wing when an officer just happened to glance through the porthole into the lighted area and saw The Mole dart behind some pipes. After Dovan was hauled out of there in '73, we found a 25-foot tunnel heading for the street. Working alone with a two-foot metal bar and a knife, he had about 50 more feet to go to get to the wall when he was caught.

The whole crazy story of the Dovan/Clark partnership started on a Sunday night in April when an officer discovered a bar covering a window in the bathroom next to the auditorium had been sawed through and bent outward. It looked like somebody might have gotten out through the window and headed for the front house roof. The second-shift center commander ordered a count, and Dovan and Clark came up missing.

Because of the hole in the bathroom window, the first assumption was that the two of them had gotten out onto a ledge, climbed up onto the roof of chapel/rec and headed out over the front house roof, like Mario DeLucia in '56. Working against that theory, though, was the fact that there was no blood around the broken window glass, and there had been a bright moon on Sunday night—it would have been tough to get over the wall without being seen by a tower guard; besides, under the wall not over it was a better fit with The Mole's MO.

But, not taking any chances, the acting warden, Richard Seidl, called in the Trenton police with bloodhounds and armed a squad of correction officers to go outside the walls and look for Dovan and Clark. The bloodhounds got fooled, too, taking the searchers all the way down to River View Cemetery before they sat down, indicating a cold trail. Meanwhile the jail was locked down, and guards with .38s and shotguns were posted near all of the known other tunnel attempts just in case Dovan and Clark were in an old tunnel.

As it turns out, they were. Dovan and Clark both worked in the school, not far from the hospital. They must have used their school passes to get near the hospital and then slipped down into the basement where Fitz and Puchalski had dug their tunnel in the early '60s. When Charlie Trautman, now a lieutenant, sent a squad of officers into the basement of the hospital to check out the small trapdoor that had been used to cover Fitz's tunnel, they found they didn't need a key for the padlock used to secure the wooden cover: the tumblers had been removed.

Mike Nawrocky and John Golden pulled the trap door open and found a makeshift flashlight—three batteries taped together with a bulb on top. They shined their own flashlights into the old tunnel, and behind a pile of dirt, they thought they saw somebody moving. The officers called Trautman.

Trautman came down into the basement and yelled into the crawlspace, "We know you're in there. We'd like you to come out now."

No answer.

Trautman: "If you force my hand, we'll put gas in there."

No answer.

Trautman to Officer Barry Coan: "Go to the armory and get some tear gas. Get permission from the chief."

Dovan: "We're coming out now, one at a time."

Seidl had a prison photographer standing at the entrance to the tunnel to document the escape attempt. When Dovan crawled out and the flash went off, he said, "What is this, Candid Camera?"

After interrogation, Clark and Dovan were sent to 1-left lockup.

* * * * * * *

Dovan and Clark were caught in April of 1974. Three months later, Vroom erupted again over the long Fourth of July weekend when five inmates already out in the yard demanded that all 50 Vroom inmates be let out for yard at the same time. The shift commander was Captain Bill Killingsworth, the first black officer hired back in the 1950's who was now in charge of the Vroom Readjustment Unit. Killingsworth basically told the guys in the yard there was no way in hell that he was going to let everybody in the unit outside at the same time. When the cons heard that, they started tearing the wire mesh away from the windows and snapping off three and four-foot-long pieces of angle iron from the frames holding the mesh. Then they started smashing in the windows with rocks and the angle iron.

Killingsworth gave the inmates five minutes to get back inside the jail. They refused, and more officers were called in for support. I was off because of the holiday, but the guys who responded used the same battle formation we had used a few months before: 20 officers, two groups of ten. Before they went into the yard, about ten rounds of tear gas were fired in, but a breeze blew the gas away and it had no effect whatsoever on the inmates.

The cons used the wire mesh for shields and armed with the angle iron met the 20 officers head on in the middle of the yard. This time the inmates weren't intimidated, and the fight went on for about ten brutal minutes before they surrendered. A day or two later the cops involved told me this was probably the toughest battle they'd ever been in. The first wave got the worst of it. As the five cons swung the pieces of angle iron, they knocked shields out of the cops' hands and actually split a couple of the helmets. Bob Griffith got a nasty broken arm and was hit in the head, sending him to St. Francis Hospital. Melvin Spruill was also hit in the arms and head and hospitalized, and the two "Pogo" brothers, Ted and Walt Pogorzelski, along with seven other cops (total 11), were treated for cuts, bruises and tear gas burns. All five of the inmates needed hospital treatment.

Just another day at the office, honey.

* * * * * * *

Mike Nawrocky's payback came on Veterans' Day at the end of October of '74. Between The Wall and Vroom this had been a particularly bad year in terms of violence—both ways: inmates on guards and guards on inmates. That morning, Mike, who was now 23 years old, was on duty as wing officer in 6-wing when Jim

McGaney, a convicted murderer, told Mike he wanted to go to the prison hospital.
Mike said, "This is a holiday. No doctor is on duty. You'll have to send a special request to the nurse."

McGaney told Mike what he could do with that, and when Mike again told McGaney he couldn't leave the wing, McGaney blew up and punched Mike in the side of the head, breaking his cheek bone. As Mike staggered back, McGaney pushed him against the wall and tried to strangle him. A couple of other cops jumped on McGaney and pulled him off. Mike was taken to St. Francis and McGaney went into 1-left. Mike was OK—in fact, he got a paid vacation for a few weeks. He just had to watch how he chewed.

Around the same time that Mike got punched, my assignment was on the second floor of the school. The desk where I sat was located midway down the second-floor corridor that ran from the stairs at one end to a big art room at the other. Directly across from the desk was a short alcove-type corridor that ran into two recessed classrooms. Just to the right of that was a men's room.

One morning around the time of Mike's run-in with McGaney, I was sitting behind the desk and Teddy Roberts was sitting on one corner. We were involved in a conversation when a young black inmate came sauntering down the corridor and flipped his school pass onto my desk.

I said to him, "Hey, Man. Don't do that. How about a little respect here? Don't throw the pass at me—hand it to me."

The inmate said, "Fuck you, old man."

Teddy looked over at the kid and said, "Hey, don't talk to Harry like that."

The inmate stared back at Teddy and said, "Fuck you, too, old man."

Teddy looked at me, I looked at Teddy. I said, "Whatdya think, Bull?"

Teddy said to the kid, "Why don't me and you go into the bathroom over there and talk this over?"

The kid, who was about 19 or 20, tall and well-built from lifting weights, looked at Teddy who was now in his mid-thirties, stood at about five-eight and had a pretty good belly on him, and said, "Let's go."

I got up and followed the two of them across the hall, positioning myself in front of the doorway. An inmate came out of one of the classrooms and headed in the direction of the bathroom.

Assuming my official cop's stance, legs spread apart, arms folded across my chest, I blocked him and said, "You don't want to go in there. Somebody just threw up. I'm waiting for maintenance to come clean it up."

The inmate looked disgusted and headed down to the bathroom on the first floor. I watched him start down the stairs and then ducked into the bathroom to see the action. Just inside the doorway was one of those big marble slabs that block people from looking in; I pulled myself up and looked over the top.

The kid was dancing, bobbing and weaving and flicking jabs at Bull's head. He <u>was</u> pretty, I have to admit. Bull had his fists up in front of his face in the peek-a-boo style that Joe Frazier had just made popular in his series of fights with Muhammed Ali. The kid was up on his toes, dancing and shooting left jabs at Teddy's head while Teddy moved in on him flatfooted, like a bull, forcing the kid back toward the far wall. When the kid couldn't go back any farther, Bull hit him one shot hard in the belly, doubling him over, and then nailed him with a nasty right uppercut. The kid's head snapped up, his whole body straightened up against the wall, and he slid, just like a sheet of paper, down the wall onto the tile floor—out like a light.

I said, "Jeez, Bull, I hope you didn't kill him."

Teddy said, "Nah, he's OK. Just give him a few minutes."

We went back to the desk and about five minutes later the kid came out of the bathroom, still looking dazed, walked over to the desk, picked up the pass, and handed it to me. I thanked him, and that was the end of it. I hope he's still treating his elders with respect.

13

CHAPTER THIRTEEN

HURRICANE

Rubin "Hurricane" Carter was a pro boxer who fought three great fights in his career. The first one lasted under three minutes when he knocked out the welterweight champ, Emile Griffith, in the first round in Pittsburgh. The second one went 15 rounds in Philadelphia when Hurricane lost the middleweight title in a close decision to Joey Giardello in Giardello's home town. The third fight lasted 21 years and got him out of prison when it looked like he was going to be an old man before he saw the street again.

Rubin is a remarkable guy who went from rags to riches and back to rags; from jail to top-ranked middleweight contender, back to jail. Truthfully, I was never sure whether or not he was guilty of the murders he was charged with; but when I look at the whole story now, some thirty years after the crime, I have to say I think that he and his partner, John Artis, were probably set up and framed.

This story burst into public view in the fall of 1974 when a reporter for the *New York Times*, Selwyn Raab, wrote a front-page story questioning Artis and Carter's convictions on a triple-murder charge. The controversy over their guilt or innocence and the issue of racial discrimination in the American justice system would make front-page news off and on for the next 14 years.

When I say Rubin Carter is a remarkable guy, I'm talking about a man who first went to jail at the age of 11; who reached the top of his class as a boxer; who taught himself how to write well enough to publish a book; who studied law and became such an expert on *habeas corpus* that he was invited to lecture about it at Harvard; and who fought the Passaic County prosecutor's office like a pit bull for over 20 years until he won his freedom. It's a hell of a story.

I first met Rubin in the late 1950's when he came into Trenton on his first bid for robbery and assault. He was about 19 or 20 years old at the time, and I can't say that I ever got to know him then or that I remember him all that well. He was just another young black kid from North Jersey coming in for a serious crime in the streets. Teddy Roberts and Rubin did become good friends at the time, and Teddy says that he helped develop Rubin as a boxer.

In his book, *The Sixteenth Round*, Rubin mentions Teddy as one of the toughest fighters in the jail. He says,

> As good as I was, I *knew* I wasn't ready yet. They had some mean mister humdingers out there [in the yard] in those boxing gloves, some real bad motorscooters! I mean, the kind that could make you dance bowlegged, put you to sleep, make you dream, and then wake you back up before you knew you was even hit. Jimmy Isler! Booker Washington! Donald Bird! Fitzgerald! Teddy Roberts! Shannon! Northfleet! Chuck Carter! Bo Jingles! All of them, some bad motherfuckers!

Later, when Carter came back to Trenton on two murder convictions, it was partly through Teddy that I got to know him well.

Carter was born in Clifton, NJ and raised in Paterson, an old industrial town near Newark. In his book, Rubin acknowledges that he was out of control as a kid, though he blames growing up in a racist society for most of his problems with the law. He started running with one of Paterson's street gangs, the Apaches, when he was around nine years old, and his first contact with the police came when his father turned him in for a shoplifting incident involving him and members of his gang. When he was 11, Rubin was transferred to a special disciplinary school for all of the hard to-handle juveniles in Paterson. That was also the year that he got into real trouble with the law.

Rubin always maintained that the incident was caused by a homosexual assault made on him by an older white man. The juvenile authorities saw it as a mugging of a respectable white man by a gang of black hoodlums. Rubin said that the man was trying to pull down the pants of one of the black kids at a local swimming hole and that when he intervened, the man picked him up and threatened to throw him off a cliff into the Passaic Waterfalls. That's when Rubin pulled out his pocket knife and stabbed the guy in the head repeatedly to the point where he thought he had killed the guy. I have a problem with Rubin's story when he said the guy first held out his gold watch to entice the kids and then took off his gold wedding band and threw it at Rubin and hit him in the chest with it. At any rate, one of the other kids was caught with the man's watch, and he fingered Rubin as the guy with the knife. The three other kids involved drew nine-month sentences. Because he had done the stabbing, Rubin was sentenced to ten years in the New Jersey reform school system and was sent to Jamesburg in the farmlands of central New Jersey.

After doing six years at Jamesburg, Rubin said, the superintendent promised to release him if he could stay out of trouble. Instead, he said, he was double crossed by a member of the custody staff and was slated for transfer to the next step up on the juvenile justice ladder—Annandale. So he escaped and, on foot, worked his way back to Paterson, forty miles away. His family helped him get to a cousin's home in Philadelphia where he joined the army, volunteering for the 101st Airborne, the "Screaming Eagles."

Rubin went through basic training at Fort Jackson, South Carolina in 1955. When he was sent to Germany, Rubin was introduced to two significant influences on his life: Islam and boxing. Rubin said that his friendship with a Muslim from Sudan who was trying to earn citizenship through serving in the army helped open his eyes to the importance of black pride (something that would later be viewed by whites as Rubin's philosophy of black supremacy). In the amateur ring, he won 51 (36 by KO) and lost 5, winning the European light-welterweight championship twice. He was invited to represent the army in the Olympic tryouts, but that would have meant re-enlisting. He was anxious to get home, so he passed up the shot at the Olympics and returned to Paterson in the summer of 1956—where he was almost immediately arrested for the escape from Jamesburg and sent to Annandale.

Now Rubin was really pissed off. He figured that he had turned his life around and had achieved a big measure of respect in the army. Here he was back in New Jersey and back in jail. One of the first things he was hit with at Annandale was the news that three of his friends from his Jamesburg days, the two Wise brothers and their cousin Alfred Stokes, had died in the electric chair while he was in the army. He also received a letter from the government telling him his rights to the GI Bill had been rescinded because he had entered the service illegally (he had lied about his place of residence to cover up his police record). Rubin said in his book that when he was released from Annandale ten months later, he was a "walking, ticking, short-fused time bomb ready to explode upon contact with an unsuspecting public."

When Carter returned to Paterson, he got a job in a plastics plant and started hanging around with an old friend from his days in Jamesburg. In July of 1957, after spending the evening in a bar with his buddy, Rubin did something that he said he will never be able to fully explain and that left him feeling more humiliated than anything he had ever done before: he left the bar and snatched a purse from a woman—a black woman. Then, as he ran down the street, he punched two men. He was arrested the next day and, after pleading guilty to the charges, was sentenced to three-to-nine years in Trenton for robbery and assault. He came in around the same time as Teddy Roberts and Rich Biegenwald, in the summer of 1957.

While he was in Trenton on his first bid, Rubin worked on his fighting skills with Teddy and the other guys he mentions in his book. He also became acquainted with Bill, "Bucky," Leggett, a former professional lightweight fighter who was one of the three or four black guards working at The Wall in the late '50s.

Rubin was paroled in September of 1961, after serving four years. Bucky Leggett had been watching Carter work out with the other guys in the big yard and knew that Rubin had a lot of potential as a boxer. When Rubin got out, Bucky helped him find a place to live in Trenton and, acting as his manager and trainer, started getting pro fights for him in Philly and north Jersey. Rubin said Bucky asked him to go to Maryland to *watch* some fights the night after he got out of prison. Before he knew what was happening, he was in the ring, fighting—and winning—his first professional match.

After a few months of an uneasy relationship, Rubin and Bucky had a falling out, and Rubin started fighting under a new manager and trainer early in 1962. In *The Sixteenth Round*, Rubin talks about an incident before the split with Bucky where Leggett signed a contract for him to fight Holly Mims, the top-ranking middleweight contender in the country, for Rubin's second professional fight.

In the book Rubin said, "Holly Mims was the top-ranking middleweight in the country, one of the best fighters in the world. Without even taking off his robe or working up a sweat, he could undoubtedly splatter my stupid brains all over the arena."

Rubin found out about the Mims contract by accident when it was mailed to his apartment rather than Bucky's house. He also found out that Bucky had received a cash advance of $300—money that Rubin said he never even got a whiff of. Rubin was broke, living in a cheap apartment in Trenton with no heat and no food on the shelves. When he found out Bucky had gotten the advance and hadn't given him a penny, he was pissed.

Later, when he was back in prison, Rubin said to me, "Harry, Bucky had me eating hot dogs. I couldn't live and train for fights on hot dogs. I needed steak. I needed real food to build me up."

From his first pro fight in September of 1961 through June of 1963, Rubin fought 24 times, winning 20, 14 by knockout. Television was just starting to have a big impact on the fight game when Rubin got out of jail, and a young, talented unknown like Hurricane Carter could get enough exposure on TV to move up fast in the rankings. Rubin shaved his head, grew a beard and a droopy mustache and played the part of the mean ex-con out to dismantle every opponent—no mercy asked, none given. I think the image he developed as a "black avenger" in the ring may have really hurt him later when he was accused of murdering three whites. A lot of sports writers at the time started comparing Rubin to Sonny Liston, the title holder in the heavyweight division. Both fighters were extremely hard punchers with wicked left hooks; both looked like contract killers, using the stare-down technique to intimidate opponents; and both had done hard time in state prisons.

After Rubin had more experience and did get in the ring with the top-ranked Mims in December of 1962, Rubin knocked him out in the tenth round.

Then, in December of 1963, Rubin stunned the boxing world by knocking out welterweight champion Emile Griffith in the first round in a fight in Pittsburgh. After a decision over Jimmy Ellis in New York and a first-round knockout of Clarence James in Los Angeles, Rubin signed a contract to fight Joey Giardello for the middleweight championship in Philadelphia in December of 1964. Rubin Carter was on top of the world. In the spring of 1964 he was listed by *Ring Magazine* as the number-one middleweight contender in the world.

He was also number one on the Paterson Police Department's shit list. By the time he signed for the Giardello fight, Rubin had become a hometown hero to Paterson's black community. Paterson is one of New Jersey's oldest industrial cities and, like Trenton, Camden, and Newark, it was having problems in the transition from majority white ethnic European to majority black. Rubin had established a reputation in Paterson as a black activist and an outspoken critic of racial discrimination and police brutality. As he said in *The Sixteenth Round,*

> While earlier in my career my concern was for the welfare of all prize fighters, it later narrowed down only to black fighters, and then came to be for black people in general. I had no religious convictions to define my position, no moral feelings to explain away my attitude. I only knew that white people always stuck together, no matter what the cause, in order to break the independent black man.

In the '60s in New Jersey's cities, conflicts between the virtually all-white police departments and the black communities were an everyday thing, with a lot of complaints from blacks about lack of respect and excessive use of force on the part of the police. As the number-one middleweight contender, Rubin was hot copy, and he didn't hesitate to use his position to accuse white cops of brutality and unprovoked violence against blacks. Rubin didn't make any friends in law enforcement when he was frequently quoted in magazines and newspapers, blaming the cops for the civil disturbances of that era and for "murdering black children."

In confrontations between blacks and police, Rubin could be counted on to tell a reporter something like, "Hundreds of sadistic policemen arrived on the scene with their pistols drawn, and started kicking and cuffing and beating those little [black] children over the head with their billy clubs until they were lying out in the streets, torn and bleeding like the abused lumps of helpless humanity they were."

Comments like these didn't win him any get-out-of-jail-free cards from the local PBA. Like his contemporary, Malcolm X, a lot of Rubin's public comments gave him the reputation of being anti-white and anti-police.

At the time of the Giardello fight, Rubin was making big money, probably ten times as much as the average Paterson cop, because he was fighting every chance he got. And he didn't hesitate to show off his success, tooling around town in a big Cadillac Eldorado. Maintaining a low profile wasn't Rubin's strong suit, and after he had made a number of "sadistic-police-beating-black-children" type comments, he began to get the idea that he might be *Ring's* number-one contender, but he was also number one on the Paterson/ Hackensack/Newark cops' pick-up list.

In late spring of 1964 Rubin was arrested for a bar fight. He claimed he was trying to rescue a friend, one of his sparring partners, from three whites who had backed the friend into a corner in the Kit Kat Club, a white-owned bar frequented by blacks. Rubin said,

> The cracker who owned the nigger ginmill called the police and charged me with assault and battery to himself and one of his flunky Negroes—the bartender who had a billy club in his hand. But neither one had to be rushed to the hospital in dire straits, so that proved it couldn't have been me put my hands on them. Because if I had, they would have been ruined. Forever.

Rubin had to post $5,000 bail on the assault charge. While that was still pending, he got arrested again in a gambling bust. Rubin saw these scrapes with the law as set-ups by the local police.

In October of 1964, two months before the Giardello fight, Rubin gave an interview to *The Saturday Evening Post* that both he and I think did a lot of damage. The *Post* writer, Milton Gross, said that, with his shaved head, beard and "Mongol-style moustache," Rubin looked "sinister."

Gross also said, "In the ring, glaring from under a monk-cowled robe as he listens to instructions from the referee, Carter hopes to terrify his opponent before the fight."

Today, none of that sounds unusual—it goes on all the time in the ring. Back then, though, Liston and Carter were the only fighters acting like killers and using the stare-down technique to intimidate opponents. With all of the civil unrest of the mid-'60s a lot of whites saw Carter and Liston as representative of the evil and violence that lurked under the exterior of every black man. Eldridge Cleaver, Stokely Carmichael, George Jackson, Malcolm X, Liston, Carter . . . these were the guys who were encouraging their brothers and sisters to tear up the cities of America. Even Carter's hometown newspaper, *The Newark Evening News,* called Rubin "another one of boxing's rehabilitation cases."

In the *Post* article, Rubin told Gross that when he got out of Annandale, he had lost his car, his job and his GI Bill.

He told Gross, "My partner and me, a fellow I knew in Jamesburg, we used to get up and put our guns in our pockets like you put your wallet in your pocket. Then we go out in the streets and start fighting—anybody, everybody. We used to shoot at folks."

When Gross asked, "Shoot at folks?" Rubin said, "Shoot at people. Sometimes just to shoot at 'em, sometimes to hit 'em, sometimes to kill 'em. My family was saying I'm still a bum. If I got the name, I play the game."

Gross also said that during riots in Harlem in the summer of 1963, Rubin was kidding around with his old friend Elwood Tuck and said to Tuck, "Let's get guns and go up there and get some of those police. I know I can get four or five before they get me. How many can you get?"

After the article appeared in the *Post,* Sugar Ray Robinson called Rubin and raised hell with him about the things he had said to Gross. Rubin said that he was quoted out of context, but Sugar Ray knew that the comments about the police fit with Rubin's philosophy and repeated some of the things Rubin had been saying all along to reporters from the local north Jersey newspapers. To this day, I'm convinced that Gross's article, along with Rubin's reputation for black militancy among whites in Paterson, helped sway the all-white jury toward conviction in his first murder trial. And I believe the publication of his book in 1974 may have had a similar effect in his second trial.

About two months after the *Post* article, in December of 1963, Rubin fought Giardello for the middleweight title in Giardello's hometown of Philadelphia. I remember getting together with a bunch of my fellow guards from the prison to watch that fight on TV in a local watering hole. All of us had known Rubin as an inmate and were happy to see him making it big as a fighter. Better Joey Giardello in the ring than one of us in 2-wing.

The Carter-Giardello fight was a classic. Rubin took the fight to Giardello all the way, constantly boring in on the champ while Giardello danced and jabbed. Giardello was a tough street-wise fighter just like Rubin (he had also done some jail time), and several times he stopped dancing and went toe-to-toe with Carter. It was a hell of a fight. All of us in the bar that night thought that Rubin had won hands down. When the ring announcer read the cards and said it was a unanimous decision for Giardello, we couldn't believe it. Neither could some of the fans—a lot of them booed, and the TV announcer said that somebody threw a whiskey bottle into the ring. I read in the paper the next day that the UPI sports writer scored it 69-67 for Giardello, and when he polled the other writers at ringside, they agreed 12-4 with the judges' decision. All the writers had it scored as a very close fight.

In the 18 months following the loss to Giardello, Rubin fought 15 times, with seven losses, seven wins (six by knockout) and one draw. One of his losses was a ten-round decision to number-one contender Dick Tiger, the former middleweight champ that Giardello had beaten for the title.

By the summer of 1966 tensions between whites in the old ethnic working-class neighborhoods of Paterson and blacks in "the ghetto" were at their height. Rubin's boxing career was also at its height as he waited to hear about a rematch with Giardello or a fight with Dick Tiger, the new champ. Late in the evening of June 16th, 1966, a black man, Roy Holloway, who had recently bought the Waltz Inn tavern in Paterson, was killed by the former owner, a white man. A few hours later, in the early-morning hours of the 17th, two armed black men walked into the Lafayette Grill in a white, working-class neighborhood that was in transition from white to black and Hispanic. Fifty-two-year-old James Oliver, a part-owner of the tavern, was behind the bar. Oliver had a reputation for not liking blacks; police had been called to the bar a few times by blacks who complained that Oliver refused to serve them. Without saying a word, Oliver hurled a bottle at the two armed men as they walked into the bar.

Also without uttering a word, the two blacks opened fire on the bartender and customers with a sawed-off shotgun and a .32-caliber pistol. Oliver was killed instantly by a shotgun blast that severed his spine. One customer, 60-year-old Fred Nauyoks, was hit by shotgun pellets and .32 caliber bullets. He died at the scene, still sitting on his stool with his head resting on the bar. Fifty-one-year-old Hazel Tanis was knocked off her stool onto her back on the floor by a blast from the shotgun. She died of her wounds a month later. The only other customer in the bar that night, 42-year-old William Marins, was hit in the left temple by a .32-caliber bullet and slumped unconscious, head down on the bar. He survived.

A woman who lived over the bar, Patricia Valentine, was asleep in front of the television when she was awakened by the gunshots in the bar below. She heard a woman's voice yell, "Oh, no!" and then she heard more shots. Valentine went to her bedroom window and saw two black men running toward a white car with blue and gold license plates. Both Pennsylvania and New York State used blue and yellow or gold license plates at the time. New Jersey used cream and black. A few minutes later, someone called the Paterson police and reported the shootings.

At 2:35 a.m., five minutes after the attack in the bar, two Paterson police officers, Theodore Capter and Angelo DeChellis, driving a patrol car about seven blocks from the scene, heard the radio report and spotted a white car speeding toward Route 4, a busy highway. The officers tried to intercept the car but lost sight of it. At 2:40 a.m., about 14 blocks from the Lafayette, the same two officers stopped a similar-looking white car driving slowly in a different direction from the first car. Inside were three black men: Rubin Carter, John Artis and John Royster. Artis was driving the 1966 white Dodge Polara with New York plates that had been rented by Rubin Carter—his "expense car." The police checked the registration and Artis's license and let the three men go.

After getting a more complete description of the car outside the bar, Capter and DeChellis believed that Carter's vehicle might be it, so they drove around looking again for the white Dodge. A little before 3 a.m. they came across Carter's car, this time about 15 blocks from the Lafayette. Carter and Artis had driven Royster home, picked up some money at Carter's house and were on their way back to a bar, the Nite Spot, about six blocks from the Lafayette. The two officers radioed for assistance and five patrol cars, sirens screaming, converged on the scene. The police cars ringed Carter's rental and ordered Artis, who was driving, to follow the lead police car.

In *The Sixteenth Round*, Carter describes the scene. He says an angry white mob had gathered in front of the Lafayette as the cavalcade of police cars screeched to a halt in front of the tavern. The crowd was pushing against the police, straining to get a look at the bullet-riddled bodies lying on the floor inside. Cops with shotguns jumped out of the cars and surrounded the white Dodge, ordering Carter and Artis out of the car and up against a wall.

Carter asked what this was all about and was ordered to shut up and get against the wall. One of the cops pulled his pistol out and cocked it. The crowd fell silent, watching. A paddy wagon and several ambulances arrived on the scene as Carter and Artis were being frisked. Another officer had the trunk of the Dodge open and was searching for evidence. Carter says he still didn't know what all of this meant.

Carter and Artis were pushed into the rear of the paddy wagon and driven over to St. Joseph's Hospital. The two men were escorted into the emergency room where they saw doctors working on a balding, middle-aged white man who had been shot in the head. The bullet had exited through his left eye, leaving a jagged, gaping wound. The police asked the doctors for permission to briefly question the victim, William Marins. When he was asked if Carter and Artis were the men who shot him, Marins stared at the two men with his one good eye for several seconds. He looked intently at Carter, then at Artis, and back to Carter. Finally, he closed his eye and shook his head from side to side.

The cop who had brought Carter and Artis into the emergency room asked Marins if he was sure that these were not the men who shot him. The officers seemed terribly disappointed when Marins couldn't identify Carter and Artis. Rubin said at that moment, it hit him full force what this was about—that the Paterson police desperately wanted him and Artis to be fingered as the killers.

Marins later told police that the man with the shotgun was a light-skinned black about six feet tall, 175-190 pounds, with a pencil-line mustache and no beard. He didn't get a look at the guy with the pistol. Before she died, Hazel Tanis gave police a similar description. Artis was about six feet tall with a lighter complexion than Rubin and clean-shaven. Carter was about five foot, eight with a solid build, a drooping mustache and goatee and a dark complexion.

Carter and Artis were brought back to Paterson police headquarters and questioned for 17 hours. After talking for several hours with the lead detective from the Passaic County prosecutor's office, Vincent DeSimone, Rubin agreed to take a lie-detector test. DeSimone called in a New Jersey State Police expert, Sergeant McGuire, to administer the test. When they were finished, Rubin said McGuire called him over to the machine and spread out the polygraph charts on the table of him and several of the local cops.

McGuire said, "See this long line running straight through there? It measures your respiratory reaction to the questions given. It indicates your answer to my question, 'Have you ever been inside of the Lafayette Bar and Grill?' Your answer was 'No.' The lines on the chart continued on uninterrupted, so that was the truth. All the answers for the questions on the lines are the same."

Rubin said that McGuire then turned to the Paterson police captain standing in the group of officers and said, "So you can turn him loose, Captain. And Artis, too. Both of them are clean. They had nothing to do with the crime."

When Rubin and John Artis got down to the police garage after being released, they found the rental Dodge had been torn apart by the cops who searched it: the interior door panels were off, the seats had been pulled out, the radio was hanging out of the dashboard by its wires. Rubin said he was so glad to be getting out of police custody that he decided not to go back upstairs and raise hell about it.

The murders had rocked the local community. Paterson's mayor, Frank Graves, Jr., announced a $10,500 reward for the arrest and conviction of the killers. In August, while the investigation was continuing, Rubin flew to Argentina where he lost what would be his last professional fight, a ten-round decision to Rocky Rivero. When he got back to the states, he signed a contract to fight the new middleweight champion, Dick Tiger. Before he could fight again, on October 14, 1966, Rubin Carter, 29, and John Artis, 21, were arrested and charged with triple murder.

After being held without bail in the Passaic County jail for six months, Carter and Artis were brought to trial in April of 1967. The state's case was handled by assistant prosecutor Vincent Hull Jr. Rubin considered hiring F. Lee Bailey as his lawyer, but because of the racial overtones of the case, he felt he needed a black attorney, He asked his wife, Mae Thelma, to get in touch with prominent black defense attorney Raymond Brown who agreed to take the case for $20,000—$10,000 for Rubin and $10,000 for Artis. Arnold Stein from Brown's firm was Artis' lawyer. The judge was Samuel A. Larner.

Jury selection took a month as 377 potential jurors were questioned. Rubin said he began to see where Larner was coming from during the *voire dire* when Larner dismissed a prospective black woman juror because she had only a sixth-grade education. When Brown tried to dismiss a white man who had recently been mugged by a black, Larner refused. Rubin said when Brown pointed out that this man had only a fifth-grade education, Larner cut him off and seated the juror. In New Jersey criminal cases, fourteen jurors are seated. When deliberations begin, two of the jurors are chosen by lot to be non-voting alternates. The Carter-Artis jury consisted of four white women, nine white men, and one black man—a West Indian.

The trial began on May 9, 1967. In his opening, Hull told the jury the state would prove beyond a reasonable doubt that at 2:30 a.m. on June 17, 1966, Carter and Artis parked Carter's 1966 white Dodge with New York license plates several feet from the curb and entered the Lafayette Grill. Hull said Carter was armed with a shotgun, Artis with a .32-caliber pistol. Without saying a word, the two armed men came toward the bartender and the customers and Rubin Carter fired a shotgun blast into the left side of the back of the bartender, James Oliver. Oliver fell to the floor, dead, near the open cash register.

Hull continued, the state would prove beyond a reasonable doubt that John Artis, armed with a revolver, fired a bullet into the head and brain of Fred Nauyuks, who was seated at the bar. Hull said that Nauyuks died seated on the bar stool, his head slumped over the bar.

Hull said that Artis then fired a bullet through the head of William Marins, who was seated at the bar. The bullet entered into the left side of Marins' head and exited through his left eye. Marins lived but lost the sight of his eye because of the shooting.

Hull then said that Mrs. Hazel Tanis, seated down at the end of the bar, was fired upon by both defendants. He said that Carter fired a shotgun blast at Tanis, part of it hitting her in the left arm, the rest striking the wall behind her. Hull said that Artis then fired five shots at Tanis, one missing completely and going through a window behind her. The other four shots hit her, knocking her to the floor in front of the air conditioner. She was later removed to Paterson General Hospital where she died on July 14, 1966.

Hull said that Carter and Artis then left the tavern and appeared on Lafayette Street, laughing. They then got into Carter's car and fled the scene. About ten minutes later, Officers Capter and DeChellis stopped the car and found three black men inside: Rubin Carter, John Artis, and John Royster. The officers checked the license of the driver, John Artis, and the registration and then let the car go.

The officers then went to the scene of the murders and talked with Alfred Bello, who said he was outside the Lafayette when the killers left the bar. Based on information from Bello, Capter and DeChellis again stopped Carter's car at 2:55 a.m. about 15 blocks from the scene. At this time only Carter and Artis were in the car. With the assistance of other officers, the car was escorted back to the Lafayette. Carter and Artis were removed from the car, placed in a police van and driven to police headquarters.

Rubin claimed here that Hull left out the fact that he and Artis were not taken at first to police headquarters but to the hospital where Marins said that he could not identify him and Artis.

In his opening, Hull continued that Carter's car was taken to the police garage, impounded, and searched by Paterson police detective Emil DiRobbio.

Rubin said that at this point both Brown and Stein jumped up and objected. The murder weapons had never been found. Both defense attorneys knew, though, that Hull was going to claim that during the search in the police garage, DiRobbio had found a live .32-caliber bullet and an unfired 12-gauge shotgun shell.

Larner thought for a while about the objection and then overruled it, allowing Hull to tell the jury that DeRobbio had found a live Western 12-guage shotgun shell in the trunk of the Dodge lying among some boxing equipment. He then said that DeRobbio had found a live .32-caliber Smith and Wesson bullet under the front right passenger seat. Hull went on to say that the state would prove that Oliver had been killed by a blast from a 12-gauge shotgun and the bullets removed from the brain of Nauyuks and from Hazel Tanis were .32-caliber Smith and Wessons.

Hull continued to tell the jury the story of that morning in the Lafayette. He said that money was taken from the open cash register, but it wasn't taken by Carter or Artis. Hull said two other men were in the vicinity of the bar that morning: Alfred Bello and Arthur Bradley. The two men were in the neighborhood attempting to break into the Ace Sheet Metal Company about a block and a half away from the Lafayette. He said the men heard the shots and went to the bar to see what had happened and that they would testify to what they had seen.

In his opening, Brown said that Bello and Bradley were ghouls who looted the cash register in the Lafayette while standing over the bodies of the murder victims. Brown also said that Bello and Bradley had long criminal records and their testimony would lack credibility. He questioned why Rubin hadn't been told that the bullet and shotgun shell had been found in his car and asked to explain how they got there. He pointed out that Carter and Artis had been released after questioning and hadn't been arrested until four months after the crime. Brown said that race and pre-trial publicity, because of Rubin's prominence as a professional athlete and outspoken critic of the police, were significant factors in his arrest.

When William Marins testified, Brown tried to pin him down on discrepancies in the statements he had given to police over the four months between the crime and the arrests. Both Marins and Hazel Tanis had told police that the man with the shotgun was about six feet tall, light-complexioned with a thin mustache, and the second man was about the same height but darker.

When Mrs. Patricia Valentine was called to the stand, she said that she was awakened by a loud noise from the tavern beneath her apartment, like a door slamming. As she got off the couch and went to the front window, she heard two more loud noises and then saw two colored men running to a car parked away from the curb. She knew the men were colored because she saw the back of the neck of one of the men. She said that the license plate on the car was blue with yellow and gold lettering and that the taillights were shaped like triangles or butterflies, wider on the outside.

She threw on a bathrobe and went downstairs. When she got there, Alfred Bello, whom she knew, was already there. He told her to stay by the door. When she saw the bodies of the victims, all of whom she knew, she screamed and ran back upstairs to call the police. As she was leaving, she saw Bello heading around the bar toward the cash register.

The state then called Ronald Ruggierio, a white draftsman who lived near the bar and had seen two Negroes in the car speeding away from the scene. Ruggierio was also a sometimes boxer, so he knew Rubin and had ridden in his car. Ruggierio testified that he hadn't gotten a look at the men in the vehicle but that he thought the car was a white Chevrolet.

In the third day of testimony, the state brought in its key witness: 23-year-old Alfred Patrick Bello. Hull immediately had Bello confirm his lengthy arrest and conviction record for assault, robbery, larceny, and breaking and entering since Hull knew that Brown would make it an issue in the cross-examination. Bello also said he had done time in Annandale and Bordentown reformatories. Bello testified that he, Arthur Bradley, and another man were attempting to break into the Ace Sheet Metal Company in the early-morning hours of June 17. Bello said he was acting as lookout when he decided to walk down to the Lafayette to buy some cigarettes. Before he got there, he heard the gunshots. Bello said he was about twenty feet from the front door of the bar when two armed black men came around the corner (the Lafayette had a "ladies' entrance" on the side of the building), talking loudly and laughing. Bello said that he looked at the two men and then turned and ran back up the street with the two men chasing him briefly. They gave up the chase when he ducked out of sight into an alley.

In the courtroom, when Hull asked him if he could identify the two men, Bello said, “Right there,” and pointed at Carter as the man with the shotgun.

When Hull asked him if he could identify the man with the pistol, Bello said, “Right there,” and pointed at Artis.

Bello said that he saw a white Dodge go speeding by with “two Negroes inside,” and then he returned to the Lafayette. Going inside, he saw the bodies and headed around behind the bar, intending, he said, to get a dime from the cash register to call the police. When Mrs. Valentine appeared at the side door, he told her to stay there. He said she looked at the bodies, screamed and ran back outside.

Bello testified that when he got behind the bar, he stepped over the body of James Oliver and instead of taking a dime out of the register, grabbed all of the money—about $62. He said he later gave it to Arthur Bradley.

Rubin said that when Raymond Brown began his cross examination of Bello, he stood behind Rubin's chair to make sure Rubin didn't jump up and go after Bello. When Bello had taken the stand, Rubin saw that he was wearing high-heeled shoes, and Hull's questioning had confirmed that Bello was wearing high-heeled shoes the night of the murders. Rubin is sitting there thinking, “How in the hell could a jury believe that this fat, little guy in high heels could outrun me, a professional boxer and John Artis, a high-school track star?”

In fact, under Brown's cross examination, Bello admitted that he had lied about being chased. Even though he had told Ruggierio, a newspaper reporter and the police that the two black men had chased him, Bello was forced by Brown's questioning to admit that it never happened. When the two armed men came around the corner, Bello immediately turned and ran back up the street. Then Brown pressed him hard on the identifications. He asked Bello if he had told the police on the night of the crime that he had recognized Rubin Carter and John Artis. Bello hedged. Finally, Brown produced the statement Bello had given to police on the night of the crime in which he said, “I didn't see their faces.”

Brown forced Bello to admit that he had not identified Carter and Artis as the gunmen when he was first questioned. It was under police questioning in the weeks following the crime that Bello said that Carter and Artis were the killers.

During the cross examination of Bello, which went on for a day and a half, Brown and Stein pressed Bello on whether the prosecutor's office had offered him anything in return for his testimony. Bello wouldn't budge on that issue and said he had never been offered any deal with the prosecutor's office. Not only that, but he didn't know about the $10,500 reward for the arrest and conviction of the killers.

Bello was followed to the stand by his partner, Arthur Bradley, a 23-year-old convicted thief. Bradley testified that his current residence was the Morris County jail. He basically repeated Bello's version of the events except that he said while he was trying to force open the door of the factory, he heard the gunshots and went looking for Bello. He spotted Bello near the Lafayette and then saw the two Negroes come around the corner. He testified that one was short and one was tall. He could see that one had a shotgun in his hand, and the other had something in his hand but Bradley couldn't see what it was.

When Hull asked Bradley if the man with the shotgun was in the courtroom, Bradley said he was and pointed to Rubin.

Judge Larner said, "Pointing where? Tell us again."

Bradley pointed at Carter again and said, "That *Negro,* right there."

Rubin said Bradley wanted to say "nigger" so bad, his lips were trembling.

Under cross examination, Bradley admitted to Brown that he didn't identify Rubin as the man with the shotgun until October, after Carter and Artis had been arrested for the crime. Bradley said that Paterson police drove down to Bordentown, where he was incarcerated, and showed him pictures of Carter and Artis, and he identified Rubin. He also testified that when the police interviewed him at Bordentown and he identified Carter, pending charges against him included four armed robberies, two breaking and entering, a car theft, and possession of stolen property.

Detective Emil DiRobbio testified that when he searched Rubin's rental car in the police garage a few hours after the murders, he found a live .32-caliber bullet on the floor under the passenger seat and a live shotgun shell in the trunk. He said he put the bullet and shell in his pocket and turned them into the police property clerk the next morning. A state police ballistics expert followed DiRobbio on the stand and testified there was no way of matching the live rounds DiRobbio said he found in the car to the spent bullets and the casings found at the scene. Larner refused to admit the shotgun shell into evidence, but he did allow the .32 caliber bullet to be admitted.

Brown called a number of defense witnesses to establish an alibi for Carter and Artis. Rubin had told police that on the night of the murders he had been in a local bar, the Nite Spot, and around the time of the murders he had driven a friend of his, Cathy McGuire, and her mother home. In rebuttal, Lieutenant DeSimone testified that McGuire signed a statement saying that Rubin had driven her home in the early morning hours of June 18th , not the 17th, the morning of the murders. McGuire testified that DeSimone had intimidated and confused her and that she had made a mistake on the date during questioning.

Brown also had one of Bradley's crime partners, Hector Martinez, brought to court from the Bordentown Reformatory. Martinez testified that Bradley had told him he was "going to play the Rubin Carter thing for all it was worth because he had worked out a deal that would go light on him."

On the 27th day of the trial Rubin took the stand in his own defense and denied having any involvement in the crime.

Carter said, "I had nothing to do with the killing. I had nothing to do with it."

Rubin also said that when he and Artis were brought before William Marins at St. Joseph's Hospital on the morning of the murders, Marins had said, "No, they're not the men."

John Artis also took the stand and said that he never owned a shotgun or a pistol, never had one in his possession, had never been in the Lafayette Grill and did not know any of the victims.

"I never shot anyone in my life," he said.

During his summation, Hull dumped three bags of bloody clothing on a table in front of the jurors. Then he leaned 8 x 10 photos on the clothing showing the three dead victims on slabs in the morgue. Hull said that Carter and Artis had "forfeited their right to live" and asked the jury to "extend to them the same measure of mercy they extended to the victims." He asked the jury to bring in a verdict of guilty with no recommendation for mercy.

In his summation, Raymond Brown called Bello and Bradley jackals and ghouls. He said that Carter and Artis were identified by Bradley and Bello months after the crime, under pressure from the prosecutor's office. Brown said Carter and Artis had been arrested and were on trial only because they were black.

Brown said, "Remember what Bradley said. It will remain with me forever for a special reason. He said, 'That *Negro* over there.' What is that, an animal? Well, I will tell you . . . everything around this case revolves around that simple fact: They were Negro."

In his charge to the jury, Judge Larner noted that the prosecution never established a motive for the crime, but, he said, "Murder is murder."

"It goes without saying that the race of defendants has no significance in this case except as it applies to identification," Larner said.

Before the jury began to deliberate, the court clerk put the names of the jurors in a drum and selected the two alternates to be knocked off. The only black on the panel, the West Indian, was one of the two.

The all-white jury didn't buy Brown's defense. After deliberating for four and a half hours, they brought back a guilty verdict with a recommendation for mercy—an automatic life sentence for Carter and Artis. As soon as the foreman read the verdicts, Mae Thelma Carter screamed and started crying hysterically. She had to be helped out of the courtroom. The reporter for the *Newark News* said that most of the jurors stared at the floor as the verdicts were read. Two of the women on the panel wiped tears from their eyes.

At the sentencing, because of his prior record, Rubin got two consecutive life sentences and one concurrent. John Artis had no previous criminal record and all three of his life sentences were to be served concurrently, making him eligible for parole in 1982. Rubin would have to serve 29 years, 1996, before becoming eligible for parole.

So Rubin came back into Trenton State Prison. In some respects, I identified with Rubin. When I was a kid growing up in Trenton, my family had lived for a few years in one of the city's housing projects, the Donnelly Homes. Like Rubin, as a kid I had to learn to fight to survive on the streets and had actually done some boxing in a recreation program in the basement of the apartment building. Because of that, I always followed boxing and liked to watch the guys like Teddy and Rubin sparring in the yard.

A few days after Rubin came back, I made it a point to go into the wing and talk to him. One of the first things he said to me was that he was innocent and had been framed by the Paterson police. He also told me he didn't think much of the job Raymond Brown had done for him. He said he resented paying Brown all that money for what he considered to be a lackluster defense. Even though he felt he had been railroaded, Rubin was basically in good spirits and convinced that it would only be a matter of time until all of this got put right and he got out of prison. He was animated, outgoing and friendly. We developed a cordial relationship. Later, when he was sent back from Rahway, it was a whole different story.

Under the guidance of another inmate, Bobby "Irish" Cullen, an excellent jailhouse lawyer, Rubin studied the law and worked on an appeal. In July of 1969, the New Jersey Supreme Court reviewed his appeal and upheld the convictions. It looked like that was the end of the line for the number-one contender, the man who would be champion, Hurricane Carter.

Behind the scenes, though, a few people continued to believe in Carter's innocence and on their own initiative kept digging into the case. The hardest worker was a white former police officer who had been associated with Rubin back in the prize-fighting days, a guy named Fred Hogan. After he left the police force, Hogan had done a tour of duty in the army. Then he had taken a job as a senior investigator for the newly created New Jersey Office of the Public Defender directed by a first-class black lawyer, Stanley Van Ness In New Jersey, counties already had public defenders' offices, but this was a state-level office with a lot more clout. Rubin had spent whatever money he had on his defense, so he was now indigent and he qualified for help from the public defender's office.

Hogan said he first read about Rubin's case when he was serving as a military instructor in West Germany. He asked himself, why would Rubin Carter, making maybe $200,000 as a star boxer, get involved in a bar shooting? It just didn't make any sense. (I often asked myself the same question.)

After he was in Trenton for a couple of years, Rubin was transferred to Rahway. He said it was for political reasons, to keep him from becoming an influence on the other inmates in Trenton. But transfers to Rahway are common for inmates from North Jersey to make it easier for their families to visit. Also, back then (1969) Rahway's warden, Warren Pinto, ran a looser ship than TSP. Most inmates could have contact visits, and they could take advantage of a number of programs and activities, including an inmate newspaper, that weren't available in Trenton.

In 1972, Pinto retired and a new warden, U. Samuel Vukcevich, was named at Rahway. On Thanksgiving eve of '72, Rubin was in Rahway when Clay Thomas heaved the chair through the movie screen and started the Rahway riot. The Attica bloodbath (39 dead) had gone down in September of '72, and a couple of the saner (sober) inmates that I talked to later said they got the hell out of the auditorium and went back to their cells when Thomas started ranting. They didn't want the New Jersey State Police coming in and shooting up Rahway the way the New York troopers had in Attica.

Rubin was in the auditorium that night and tried to reason with Thomas. He said he had just about gotten through to Clay when Vukcevich pulled what I consider to be a grandstand play and did something no warden should do: he walked into the middle of the situation and tried to reason with a bunch of fired-up inmates. Bad career move.

Vukcevich pissed Thomas off and we heard that Thomas hip-threw him off the stage, causing Vukcevich to land on his tailbone on the auditorium floor. At that point there was no turning back and a full-scale riot broke out. Two of Rahway's five wings were taken over by inmates, and a call went out to all of the other correctional facilities, putting us on full alert. Rubin gave up his efforts to cool off the situation and went back to his cell to wait it out.

Vukcevich and six officers were taken hostage, and the state police were dispatched to the prison. Rubin said that the inmates released Alfred Ravenell from lockup, trying to get him to take over and lead the "revolution." (Rubin describes Ravenell as a "brother [who was] a born warrior. He was cunning as a fox, deadly as a coiled pit viper, and a man who didn't play the radio, didn't drink, didn't cuss, and didn't smoke.") According to Rubin, as soon as Ravenell sized up the situation and saw that this was about liquor and not revolution, he just sat back and watched.

The administration turned off the heat and water supply and shaped up the state police in the parking lot in front of the prison. Clay Thomas woke up the next morning with a nasty hangover. Rubin said that when his followers asked Thomas what their next move should be, he had no recollection of what had happened in the auditorium the night before. End of riot. The inmates gave up before we even had a chance to get on the buses and head north. Within a day or two, I watched as a bunch of them were brought into Trenton, all chained together like a southern chain gang, to go into Trenton's lockup.

Fred Hogan continued to work on Rubin's case. On his own, he sought out Bello and Bradley and asked them about their testimony. After he had built up a big file on the case, Hogan went to the *New York Times* and convinced one of their reporters, Selwyn Raab, that his investigation had raised serious doubts about the Carter and Artis convictions. Raab listened. In September of 1974, the *Times* broke a front-page story: Bello and Bradley had recanted their testimony and told Raab they helped frame Carter and Artis. In October, 1974, The Viking Press published Rubin's book, *The Sixteenth Round.* Things were hoppin'.

When Raab broke the story of the recantations, the New Jersey statute of limitations for perjury, five years, had been exceeded by more than two years. Raab said that Hogan and friends of Rubin came to him in September of 1973 and asked for his help in investigating the case. He agreed and he and Hogan started searching for Bello and Bradley. They found Bello in the Bergen County Jail in Hackensack, doing a nine-month sentence for burglary. Bradley was out of prison and living in New Jersey. Each of the men signed a statement saying he had lied during the murder trial. Neither of them knew that the other was also recanting.

Bello said that he was questioned by police on the night of the murders and several times thereafter in the summer and fall of 1966. He said that he had originally told the detectives the truth about where he had been and what he had seen except that he left out the part about the attempted break-in at Ace Sheet Metal. He told Raab he had stopped in the Lafayette for a glass of beer about 15 minutes before the murders, and a young black woman had come in to buy a six-pack of beer.

Bello said, "She looked at everyone in the bar, and I seen that look before and figured something would happen and I got up and walked out fast."

Bello told Raab that while he was acting as lookout for the factory break-in, he heard the gunfire and walked toward the Lafayette Grill. He was about ten or fifteen feet away when the killers came around the corner. He said he ran and hid in alley and watched them drive away in a white car that at the time he thought was a Cadillac.

Bello was at the bar when the police brought Carter and Artis to the scene. He told Raab that the two killers were dressed in dark suits, either black or brown. Carter had on a tan sports jacket and Artis was wearing a blue sports shirt.

Bello told Raab that as he was questioned in the months following the killings, he kept trying to tell the Paterson police his version of the events, but they warned him that he might become a suspect in the murders unless he identified Carter and Artis. He said the detectives referred to Carter and Artis as "Muslims, niggers, animals and murderers." Bello said the detectives told him he should get these guys off the street to protect whites and that he should help his own people.

Then, during the summer, Bello heard rumors around Paterson that Carter had committed the murders as an initiation into a black-power sect. Bello told Raab that all of the police were convinced Carter and Artis had committed the murders and they wanted him to believe it. The detectives also emphasized the $10,500 reward money. Bello said he didn't realize he would be the key witness and that the pressure finally got to him.

Bello said that Lieutenant DeSimone told him he should take the money and get out of Paterson and if he got "jammed up" with the law again, DeSimone would help him out. Bello said he finally agreed to go along.

During the course of the police interrogations, Bello told DeSimone why he was in the neighborhood that night and he told the detective about Arthur Bradley's involvement. Bello and Bradley were never prosecuted for the attempted break-in at Ace.

When Raab contacted the Paterson police to tell them about Bello's recantation and to get their reaction, they said Bello was pissed off because he hadn't gotten the full reward money pending appeals of the case. He was also angry about the burglary conviction. Bello had been picked up four times for minor offenses between 1967 and 1974 but had not been prosecuted. Bello told Raab that he had stayed silent for seven years because he figured the verdict would be reversed on appeal. He also said that he now feared reprisals from local police because of his recantation.

Raab then went to talk to Bradley after Fred Hogan had gotten Bradley's signed recantation. Bradley told Raab that he hadn't seen anything that night because he was trying to jimmy open the door of the factory with a tire iron about a block and half away when the killings took place.

Bradley told Raab he had met Bello in the early '60s while they were both doing time in Bordentown. Until Bello told DeSimone about the Ace Sheet Metal break-in, the Paterson police didn't know anything about Bradley and he hadn't been questioned. In October of 1966 Bradley was back in Bordentown awaiting trial on four armed-robbery charges when Passaic County detectives came down to question him about the Lafayette Grill murders. Bradley told Raab that most of the questioning was done by Lieutenant DeSimone.

Bradley said he was questioned frequently over a period of days and said he got a general picture of what had happened on the night of the murders. Then he said he was shown Bello's statement to help fill in the details.

Bradley told Raab, "There's only one reason I testified. That was to stop all the time. They never would have got me to talk otherwise. I saw a way out of my own mess. I was 23 years old and facing 80 to 90 years in jail. I just bought my way out."

Bradley said that both DeSimone and Prosecutor Hull promised to do everything they could to help him and that he did receive a lot less time than he ordinarily would have. He was ultimately sentenced to a term of three to five years and did three before being paroled in 1970. He had not been arrested since when he talked to Raab in 1974.

Bradley told Raab that his perjured testimony had been a burden on him for eight years and he had wanted to recant his testimony for a long time. He told Raab, "I always knew it was a matter of time before there would be a knock on the door and I would have to tell someone."

About a week after Raab broke the recantation story in the *New York Times,* his sportswriter colleague, Dave Anderson, wrote in his column about Rubin and his recently released book. Anderson interviewed Rubin at Rahway and said,

> I had known him as Hurricane Carter, who once knocked out Emile Griffith, then the welterweight champion, in the first round and who once had fought for the middleweight title. I knew about his reputation for hating whites and hating policemen. I knew about his previous prison record. I knew he was not a candidate for canonization. But he convinced me he had been framed.

Anderson said Rubin's writing style was violent, raw and unique. He said, "It's as if he typed every letter with his left hook."

Since I knew Rubin, I went out and bought his book. For one thing, I wanted to see if I was in it. I wasn't, but I was happy to see that Rubin had mentioned Teddy Roberts. After I finished reading his book, I felt that Rubin had made a big mistake in having it published while he was fighting for a new trial. I thought that some of the things he said in the book would turn off the white public and potentially tick off the members of the law-enforcement and judicial system so much that they'd be gunning for him if he did manage to win a new trial. Here are just a few of the things Rubin said in *The Sixteenth Round* that I thought hurt him:

> I wanted to destroy something, and my strange mental fog drove me towards the two cops. I wanted to get my hands around their necks and squeeze until their eyes popped out of their skins like grapes.

> Annandale had itself a matured Rube, a person who knew what he was all about, and was just that much harder to handle for the knowing. It had a man who understood what it meant to be free, who knew the consequences of selling his soul, were he to allow himself to accept the daily ration of slights and slurs dished out by its faggot, would-be-Gestapo officers.

Later in the book, when he was talking about his first bid at Trenton State Prison, this was Rubin's version of the disturbance in 7-wing that Warden McCorkle had busted up in 1953:

> I was transferred from One Wing to Seven-Right, a predominately black ghetto of the jail for hard-to-handle prisoners—and faggots—which had been the bloody arena of a riot in 1953. The Ku Klux Klan-minded guards, armed with machine guns, had stormed the tiers and killed everything in sight. The deep, mind-bending scars from the bullet holes were still visible in the repainted walls, the high ceilings, and even in the dented steel of the gates themselves. They still voiced their outrage at the holocaust that had swept through there like a mad broom, swallowing up lives like a greedy vacuum cleaner.

I had talked to the cops and cons involved in that disturbance, and Rubin's version wasn't even close to the truth. It was twisted to fit his own viewpoint. Then he went on to describe the death of Skate Jones in 1958:

> A black inmate named Jonesy was locked in the third cell down from my own. A big, bald-headed nigger whose nature was good, but whose expression was habitually wrapped up in the gloom of an embittered man's thoughts, he was set up one morning by the guards and stabbed to death by a bunch of Nazi crackers just because the prison administration was scared to death of him.

I was involved in that incident, and I know that Skate had a long history of scamming other inmates, and it finally caught up to him. Rubin is right, though, that there were also racial overtones involved.

Some of the other things he said in the book that I thought hurt him:

> Quiet rage became my constant companion . . .

> Some trigger-happy cops would kill a black man with icy calm as long as they had the law backing them up . . .

> The law! That pop-eyed sonofabitch [a Paterson cop]. . . . If there had been no one else there but me, he would have snaked his gun out and shot me down. In self-defense, he would have claimed! The nasty scum-sucking sonofabitch.

> The Paterson press, especially the *Evening News,* had consistently shown itself to be a racist arm of the law. The only time that a black resident of the community would get sufficient news coverage in Paterson was when the police had killed or arrested him, and then finally when they framed his ass and sent him away to prison for the rest of his life—with the help of the paper's vicious lies.

> And civil rights? Bullshit!
> That was just another straw on the camel's back. Isn't it strange that if a black man kills a white man, no matter what the circumstances, that ulti-

mately, if he isn't killed on the spot, he's charged with first-degree murder and sentenced to life imprisonment or death? Meanwhile, the same white man could massacre ten black men, five women, and three little children, but he would only be charged with violating the dead nigger's civil rights. A penalty which would net him only three years in prison, if anything.

So where was the justice? In a ballot or a bullet?

And he saved some of his best shots for Judge Samuel A. Larner—the trial judge and the man who, under New Jersey law, would preside over the first level of the appeal process if Rubin (and Raab) could get the case back into court:

> [Larner] appeared very irritable and in a hurry to get the mess over with.
>
> . . . it seemed like every time the defense would attempt to send an important point home to the jury, the judge would interfere and effectively neutralize the evidence with unwarranted aggression designed to divert the jury's attention, and to let them know exactly where he stood—for the state.
>
> 'We are not in the Army right now,' the judge broke in, as if he too were disgusted with a white witness 'yes-sirring' a black man who was defending two other black men against the charges of killing three white people.

On Larner's attitude toward another of Rubin's alibi witnesses, John "Bucks" Royster, whom Rubin had earlier described as "the friendly neighborhood alcoholic":

> Toward the end of [Royster's] testimony, the judge suddenly wheeled around and lashed out at him, 'How many drinks have you had this morning?'
>
> 'Who, me?' Bucks said, stunned.
>
> 'Yes, yes!' Larner growled down at him, glaring, red-faced.
>
> 'I don't know,' he answered meekly.
>
> '*You don't know,*' Judge Larner snorted with contempt, then shook his head and looked over at the jury. 'All right,' he said, satisfied. He had just snatched the credibility away from another of my witnesses.

I'm not saying that Rubin didn't have legitimate grievances against the police, the penal system and society at large. It's just that many whites reading that kind of rhetoric in 1974 wouldn't be real quick to jump to his defense if they heard Rubin was headed back to prison in a railroad car.

Shortly after *The Sixteenth Round* was published, the Carter roller coaster took another dip. Despite what Rubin said about Ravenell's staying on the sidelines during the Rahway uprising, Ravenell was shipped to Yardville with the other inmate leaders, escaped, and was hunted down and killed. Rubin was probably the most influential inmate left at Rahway, and he and a few others stepped into the vacuum created by the Yardville transfers. His efforts to cool Thomas down and head off the violence were recognized, and for a while he was a respected and outspoken member of the inmate council—too outspoken, it seems.

About a month after his book was published, Rubin was shipped back to Trenton. When he came back to The Wall, Rubin seemed like a changed man. The grind of the appeals, the events at Rahway, the number of years he had put in for a crime he said he didn't commit—all seemed to have taken their toll on him. When I tried to talk to him, he was uncommunicative. He was civil, and he would answer a question, but he wouldn't enter into any kind of conversation. I never saw him smile. Even Teddy Roberts said that Rubin had changed. He became withdrawn. He stayed in his cell, he read the law, and he wrote. He was in a shell.

After Rabb had broken the story of the recantations in September, Van Ness's office brought in two lawyers from private practice to represent Carter and Artis: Paul J. Feldman of Asbury Park for Rubin and John W. Noonan of Newark for John Artis. In late October of '74, the Bello and Bradley recantations and heavy newspaper coverage pushed the state into giving Carter and Artis a hearing on a motion for retrial. Judge Larner presided. During the week-long hearing, Bello and Bradley took the stand to explain why they wanted to recant. The Passaic County prosecutor's office came in to rebut their testimony about pressure from the police and to offer theories why the two men wanted to change their testimony.

Several times during the proceedings, Rubin got into arguments in the corridor outside of the courtroom with Noonan and Feldman over the way they were presenting the case. In his eight years in jail, Rubin had read every law book available to him in Trenton and Rahway. He knew the law, and he knew which way the wind blew in New Jersey. For example, he wanted his lawyers to subpoena prosecutors from the counties surrounding Passaic (including then Governor Brendan Byrne, who had been Essex County prosecutor in 1967) to see if they had been asked to cut a deal for Arthur Dexter Bradley in their jurisdictions. Noonan and Feldman didn't like that strategy.

The six-day hearing ended in early November. Larner said he would review the facts and render a decision in about a month.

Then, just six days after the hearing ended and while Larner was still working on his decision, Selwyn Raab dropped another bombshell. In a front-page story in the *New York Times,* Raab said he had discovered discrepancies in the handling of a key piece of evidence in the original trial. Raab said he had found out that the .32-caliber bullet Detective Emil DiRobbio said he found in Rubin Carter's car on the day of the crime wasn't turned in to the Paterson police property clerk until five days after the murders. At the original trial, DiRobbio testified that he found the bullet at 3:45 a.m. on June 17, 1966 and turned it in to the evidence room later that day. When Raab looked at the handwritten records of the property clerk, he found that the bullet hadn't been logged in until June 22—five days later. That property clerk had since died, but most clerks in police evidence rooms are, and were, extremely careful about log-in dates and times because of their potential importance in a trial.

Rubin had always maintained that the shotgun shell and the bullet had either been planted in his car or the police had lied about finding them there. Raab's discovery seemed to fit with Rubin's contention that the Paterson police waited for the results of the autopsy on the victims to verify the caliber of the bullets used. Then they went out and got a bullet to match the ones used at the Lafayette and claimed they found it in Rubin's car.

While Raab's discovery of the discrepancy didn't by itself conclusively prove anything, it did give Carter and Artis's lawyers stronger support for an appeal if Larner should turn down the request for a new trial. A private investigator working for the defense in 1966 had tried to get the property clerk's records and had been refused access. Now Carter's lawyers could argue that the prosecution had withheld critical evidence at the first trial.

Despite the efforts of Fred Hogan and Raab's extensive coverage of the case in the *Times,* Judge Larner ruled in December, 1974, that the Bello and Bradley recantations "lacked the ring of truth" and were "patently unbelievable." Therefore, there would be no new trial.

A week before Larner released his ruling, the Trenton *Times* did a feature article on John Artis, the "forgotten man" in the Carter-Artis case. Artis had just earned an associate degree from Mercer County Community College (the same school where I got my first college degree) in their Prison Education Network program. In the article the reporter said that Artis had been an outstanding high school athlete and was planning to attend Adams State College in Colorado when he was arrested on his birthday in 1966. The reporter went on to list John's achievements while in prison: writer and director of a variety show; paraprofessional instructing adult-education courses; candidate for the most valuable player award in the inter-prison football league; president of the inmate Jaycee chapter.

When Artis first came into Trenton with Rubin after the murder convictions, I remember being surprised that this kid was with a guy like Carter on the night of the murders. When I heard that Rubin had been arrested, frankly, I wasn't shocked, even though he was doing so well as a professional boxer. I always liked Rubin, but I also knew he had a mean streak that could have led him to do the crime.

But this kid . . . . he just didn't fit. For one thing, he was only 21 when he came into Trenton, nine years younger than Rubin. He was articulate, quiet, tall, handsome, smart. He came from a good family (not that Rubin didn't). Later, when I talked to him, I found out he had even started a boy scout troop at his family's church. This was no ghetto hoodlum. And he didn't seem to share Rubin's black-militant views. I just couldn't picture this kid walking into a bar with a pistol in his hand and murdering three people in cold blood.

Anyway, both Carter and Artis reacted calmly to the news that their request for a new trial had been denied. Neither one of them really expected Larner to take a position different from the one he had seven years before during sentencing when he said, "I have no hesitation in stating that the jury's verdict was fully warranted by the proofs submitted during the trial. There is not a single factor in these killings which can serve as mitigation of the heinousness of the offense."

After Larner delivered his decision rejecting a new trial, Carter made a move of his own. The case had now gotten so much publicity that Rubin was able to get rid of Feldman and Noonan and bring in two high-powered defense attorneys from New York, Myron Beldock and Lewis M. Steel. Beldock and Steel immediately jumped on Selwyn Raab's disclosure of the discrepancies in the handling of the bullet and refiled a motion for a new trial. They also asked Larner to recuse himself because he had "adopted a partisan attitude" and was no longer impartial.

In a hearing before Larner in Jersey City at the end of January, 1975, Steel accused Larner of prejudging the issues. He also said that Larner had made disparaging remarks about Carter and Artis and that Larner had improperly commented on the case in an interview with the Trenton *Times* the month before.

Needless to say, Larner also rejected the second appeal for a new trial. Beldock and Steel said they would appeal Larner's ruling to the New Jersey appellate court, and if that didn't work, they would appeal on constitutional grounds in federal court.

In September of 1975, Beldock and Steel filed a 125-page brief with the New Jersey Appellate Court, asking them to grant a new trial. In the brief, Beldock and Steel charged that the Passaic County prosecutor's office engaged in a massive suppression of evidence during the first trial and that new facts had come to light that would warrant a new trial. In the meantime, guess who had been promoted to the Appellate Division—Samuel A. Larner. In the brief Beldock and Steel were also critical of Larner for not disqualifying himself from the two earlier hearings. They said they would expect Larner to disqualify himself if this appeal were to come before his section of the Appellate Division. The major point in this appeal was that the prosecutor's office had not told the defense in the 1966 trial that Bello and Bradley had been promised reward money and favorable treatment in the consideration of their attempted break-in at Ace Sheet Metal and their other problems with the law.

In November, the New Jersey Supreme Court made an unusual move: they bypassed the Appellate Court and agreed to hear the case. Most people thought they did it because of all of the publicity.

While Beldock and Steel were fighting for Carter and Artis in the courtroom, an incredible array of sports figures and celebrities had been jumping on the "Free Rubin Carter" bandwagon. The most visible and vocal advocate was heavyweight boxing champion Muhammad Ali. When Rubin had been in the army, he had embraced Islam. In *The Sixteenth Round* he said, ". . . out of the cradle of ignorance came Saladin Abdullah Muhammad—me—the warrior and general!" I don't ever remember Rubin referring to himself by that name when he was in Trenton, but I suspect that Muhammad Ali got interested in Rubin's case partly because of Islam and partly because Rubin was a fellow "warrior" in the ring.

On October 18, 1975, Ali led about 1,600 demonstrators to the state house in Trenton for a rally in support of Carter and Artis. I remember that date so well because just two days before, I had been involved in a Muslim bloodbath in the Donald Bourne School during which one inmate was killed and several were badly wounded. When Ali came to Trenton, the original plan had been to march from the state house to the prison to let Rubin see how much support he had out in the streets. After the Muslim stabbings, state officials asked Ali not to bring the crowd down to the prison because of the incredible tension we were under and the potential for further violence. He agreed and the crowd stayed over at the state house, about a mile and a half from the prison.

As Ali led the marchers down State Street in Trenton, marching alongside him was Ellen Burstyn, a prominent actress. Joe Frazier, whom Ali had just beaten on a TKO in the "Thrilla in Manila" to retain the heavyweight title, drove up from Philadelphia and joined the crowd. The demonstration had been organized by the New Jersey and national Carter defense committees, and the 15 chartered buses used to get the demonstrators to Trenton were paid for by the Hurricane Carter Trust Fund. This effort to get Rubin and John Artis out jail was no small-potatoes affair; the heavyweights involved weren't only from the boxing world.

As the "Free Rubin Carter" movement was gaining momentum, New Jersey Governor Brendan Byrne was also looking at a couple of other options: executive clemency or a partial commutation of sentence. At first, Rubin didn't like the idea of executive clemency because it wouldn't clear him of the commission of the crime. But eventually he went along with his lawyers in officially asking Byrne for clemency.

As all of this played out, the case took a series of strange twists and turns. Rubin and three other Rahway inmates had filed suit in federal court over their transfers from Rahway to other prisons because of their activities on the inmate council. In November of '75 Rubin claimed he was offered a transfer to a medium-security men's unit located on the grounds of the Clinton reformatory for women if he would drop the suit. The state denied the charges and immediately transferred him to Clinton. In the meantime, the New Jersey Assembly set up a special committee chaired by Eldridge Hawkins, a black lawmaker from Essex County, to look into the Carter/Artis case. In December of 1975, Artis claimed he had been offered a deal by Hawkins: freedom in exchange for an admission that he had not actually pulled the trigger but had been there when the murders took place. He said he turned down the deal.

While all of this was going on, Bob Dylan revived the sixties connection between folk music and politics by hooking up part of his Rolling Thunder tour of the northeastern U.S. with Carter's cause. Dylan wrote a song about Rubin, "Hurricane," and brought the Rolling Thunder tour to Clinton to show support for Carter and Artis. With Rubin in the audience, Dylan, Joan Baez, Roberta Flack, Joni Mitchell and a number of other musicians entertained the men and women inmates in the field house at Clinton. Rubin held a small press conference at the end of the show.

Then, the next night, Dylan took the show to Madison Square Garden in a benefit on behalf of the Carter defense fund. Muhammad Ali went onstage with Rubin's wife, Mae Thelma, at his side and talked by amplified telephone to Rubin at Clinton. In the audience were U.S. Representatives Ed Koch, Herman Badillo and Charles Rangel; Newark Mayor Kenneth Gibson; Earl Monroe, Walt Frazier and Bill Bradley of the Knicks; Joe Frazier and Ali; actresses Candice Bergen, Ellen Burstyn, Dyan Cannon and Melba Moore; and Dr. Martin Luther King's widow, Coretta. The Hurricane train was rollin'.

More strange twists and turns: 1) the Hawkins report goes to Governor Byrne and says that Hurricane passed a lie detector test when he was being questioned by police; 2) information obtained by Hawkins indicates Carter and Artis weren't the gunmen but were accomplices; 3) Bello now says he was in the Lafayette when the gunfire broke out and narrowly escaped being killed; 4) Bello says Fred Hogan offered him a bribe (a piece of the percentages from *The Sixteenth Round*) if he would recant.

Finally, in the spring of 1976, the New Jersey Supreme Court unanimously ordered a new trial for Carter and Artis, saying the Passaic County prosecutor's office had concealed evidence and "substantially prejudiced" a fair trial. Beldock and Steel wanted the charges dropped, but the new Passaic County prosecutor, Burrell Humphreys, said that his office was planning to retry Carter and Artis, now ten years after the murders.

And that's exactly what happened. Carter and Artis were freed on bail, and in November of 1976 the second trial got underway. At first, Beldock and Steel had gotten a change of venue to Jersey City because of negative pre-trial publicity, but then, despite defense objections, Judge Bruno Leopizzi moved the trial back to Paterson. An out-of-town jury was brought in from Hudson County. They were sequestered for the duration of the trial in a Hudson County motel and bused to Paterson each day.

Unfortunately for Rubin and John, this trial didn't go any better than the first one. Patricia Valentine now said that the police had shown her the shotgun shell and the .32-caliber bullet hours after the killings and told her they had found them in the trunk of Rubin's car. She never mentioned this in the first trial. Then Bello recanted his recantation and said that Carter and Artis were the guys he saw leaving the Lafayette that night. Bello came into court wearing red cowboy boots. While audio tapes of his 1966 interviews with Lt. DeSimone were being played, Bello yawned, belched and stared at the ceiling. He had told so many different stories to so many different people that it was hard to believe a jury would give this guy the time of day. Unfortunately for Rubin, though, Bello's performance was counterbalanced by problems with Rubin's alibi witnesses with some of <u>them</u> recanting earlier testimony.

In the first trial, the prosecutors had never introduced a motive for the killings. In this trial, Prosecutor Humphreys painted a picture of Carter and Artis as "black avengers" for the killing earlier in the evening of June 16, 1966 of black bar owner Roy Holloway. Humphreys said Holloway was the stepfather of a friend of both Carter and Artis, Edward Rawls. The defense contended that the whole case was a frame-up engineered by Vincent DeSimone to get Carter because of his outspoken criticism of the Paterson police force.

The jury of eight white men, two white women and two black women deliberated for nine hours before coming in with a guilty verdict. On February 9, 1977, Rubin Carter was once again sentenced to one concurrent and two consecutive life terms. John Artis was given three concurrent life sentences. In passing sentence, Judge Leopizzi said that Rubin's adult history was "totally unfavorable" and that he had made little effort to rehabilitate himself. On the other hand, Leopizzi congratulated Artis for getting his associate degree and for pursuing a bachelor's degree at

The Evening Times

Con Held In Slaying Of Guard

By HERBERT KIRCHHOFF
And
GEORGE W. ROBINSON
Staff Writers

A Trenton State Prison inmate was formally charged with murder today in the stabbing death of a correction officer who was assaulted in

JAMES MONROE
. . . on way to hearing

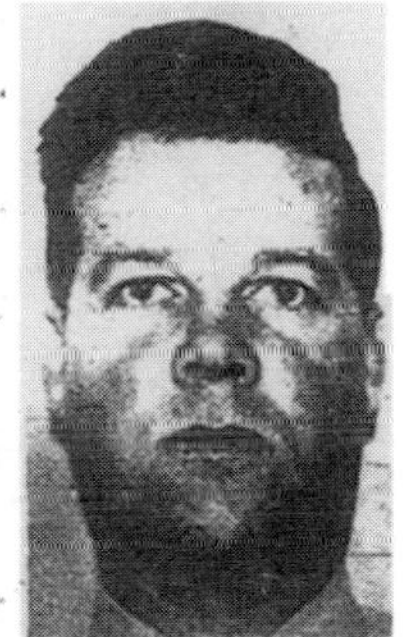

inch stab wound that punctured an artery, investigators reported.

Albert Fulling, public information officer for the New Jersey Department of Institutions and Agencies, said Monroe is serving a 12 to 15 year sentence for a May, 1970, conviction in Union County on charges of armed robbery and carrying a concealed weapon.

No Disturbance

The stabbing, Fulling said, took place while prisoners were being fed. "There was no disturbance among other prisoners, most of whom were unaware that a stabbing took place," he said.

Inmates were kept locked in their cells in the prison today as a safeguard against further violence.

Sgt. Donald Bourne (left) was struck down by a sharpened pail handle thrust into his chest simply because he was a convenient symbol of authority. (Stories, photos courtesy The Times, Trenton, NJ. All rights reserved. Reprinted with permission.)

ASBURY PARK EVENING PRESS

Belle Helps Murderer In Spectacular Escape

Press State House Bureau

TRENTON — Terrence Alden, sentenced to life imprisonment for his part in the murder of an armed guard in Middletown Township three years ago, is being sought by authorities following what has been described as his spectacular escape from Trenton State Prison Monday night.

Alden's break-out was aided by a power failure at the prison caused by Hurricane Belle which knocked the lights out along the death house roof.

The spokesman, Ed Ramsey, said it is thought Alden had a change of clothing ready when he made his escape.

Ramsey said inmates wear their own clothes rather than prison uniforms.

Alden's escape was not discovered until about 1:30 p.m. yesterday.

Ramsey said he missed the morning line-up, but guards were fooled into thinking he was still in bed by a dummy he had fashioned from old clothes and a sack and left under his covers.

and crawling through the 14-inch opening to a catwalk running behind his second-floor cell block.

He apparently then climbed 70 feet up a five-inch pipe to the top of a cell block and, holding on with one hand, used the other to saw his way through an inch-thick bar under a roof-top ventilator to reach the roof itself.

Alden's work assignment in the prison's vocational shop probably provided him the opportunity to steal the tools he needed, Ramsey

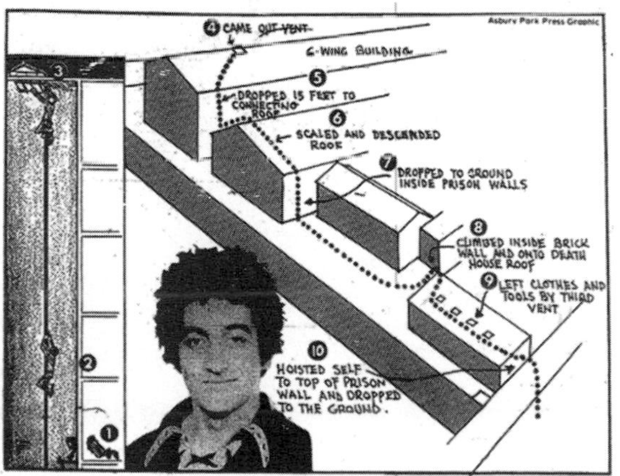

Terence Alden (insert) made his escape from Trenton State ... hoisted himself up a 70-foot pipe, and (3) left through a vent in

Terry Alden (right) followed Mario DeLucia's route out of the prison by unbolting the toilet in his cell and going out across the roof of 6-wing. Alden was dubbed "The Bionic Bandit" by Midwest newspapers when a security camera appeared to show him being shot at point-blank range by a bank guard and not even flinching. (Story, photo/art courtesy The Asbury Park Press)

Paroled Killer in Jersey Is Linked to 5 Slayings

The New York Times/Edward Hausner

Police officers roping off the area where the bodies of two teen-agers were found in a shallow grave on Staten Island.

Richard F. Biegenwald

One of Two Bodies Dug Up In S.I. Backyard Is Identified

By JOSEPH F. SULLIVAN

Special to The New York Times

FREEHOLD, N.J. April 21 — One of two bodies dug up on Staten Island was identified today as that of a 17-year-old Brick Township girl who disappeared on Halloween night in 1981, and the Monmouth County Prosecutor said he would seek a murder indictment in the case.

The Prosecutor, Alexander D. Lehrer, said the girl, Maria Ciallella, had been walking home along Route 88 when she was picked up and killed by gunshots to the head. The killer, he said, was Richard F. Biegenwald, who is suspected of slaying at least four other people in New Jersey. The two bodies were found Tuesday morning in the backyard of Mr. Biegenwald's mother on Staten Island.

Mr. Lehrer said his office had been deluged with telephone calls from relatives of missing teen-age girls. He said he would set up a special phone for inquiries if no identification of the second body found on Staten Island were made in the next few days.

Mr. Biegenwald, who has served 17 years in state prison for a 1957 murder, has been back in prison since January when Sgt. Michael Dowling of the Asbury Park police signed a complaint charging him with the murder of Anna M. Olesiewicz, a Camden teen-ager. She was last seen on the boardwalk of the resort city shortly after midnight last Aug. 29. Mr. Lehrer said that she and Miss Ciallella were each killed by gunshots to the head after being lured into a car by Mr. Biegenwald.

"It is believed that Richard Biegenwald was on Route 88 that fateful evening when Maria met her death," Mr. Lehrer said at a news conference today.

"There is no motive, in my opinion, for this senseless killing, other than that which I attributed to the other killing of Anna Olesiewicz," Mr. Lehrer said, "that of wanting to see someone die."

Three Other Murders

Mr. Biegenwald, 42, is also the central figure in investigations of three other murders — of a teen-age girl whose body was buried near that of Miss Ciallella on Staten Island and of two people whose bodies were found in Monmouth County last weekend. A body found in Tinton Falls was that of a young woman and a body in Neptune Township was that of a man about 30 years old.

After the discovery of the two bodies on Staten Island, the police have continued to dig in the backyard of Mr. Biegenwald's mother, Sally Biegenwald. District Attorney Richard D. Murphy said he believed there might be additional bodies. The searchers today uncovered some bones, but Mr. Lehrer said they appear to be those of a dog.

Two More Bodies Identified In Murder Inquiry in Jersey

By JOSEPH F. SULLIVAN

Special to The New York Times

FREEHOLD, N.J., April 22 — A 17-year-old New Jersey girl and a 34-year-old video-games operator were identified today by the Monmouth County Prosecutor as two more murder victims of Richard F. Biegenwald.

The Prosecutor, Alexander D. Lehrer, said he would seek the death penalty in both slayings, which occurred after New Jersey reinstated capital punishment last August. In all, Mr. Biegenwald has been described as a suspect in five slayings.

The victims identified today are Betsy Bacon, who disappeared near her Sea Girt home last Nov. 20, and William J. Ward of North Wildwood, N.J. The Prosecutor said Mr. Ward was killed "execution style" last September when he and Mr. Biegenwald had an argument over an illegal business deal.

Mr. Biegenwald is under 24-hour guard in isolation in Trenton State Prison. James Stabile, a spokesman for the Department of Corrections, said Mr. Biegenwald would soon undergo psychiatric examination.

5th Victim Unidentified

Mr. Biegenwald has been in the Trenton prison since January, when an Asbury Park, N.J., police sergeant signed a complaint charging him with the murder of an 18-year-old Camden, N.J., girl. He is also a suspect in the killing of a 17-year-old girl from Brick Township, N.J., whose body was discovered last Tuesday in a shallow grave behind the Staten Island home of Mr. Biegenwald's mother, Sally.

The identity of a fifth murder victim, a teen-age girl "with very identifiable dental work," is not known. Her body, with several stab wounds, was also found Tuesday at the Staten Island site.

Mr. Lehrer said he had established a special phone number, (201) 431-7916, and he invited parents of missing teen-age girls who disappeared between February 1981 and January 1983 — the period when Mr. Biegenwald was out of prison — to call over the weekend.

If the girl's identity is not known by Monday, Mr. Lehrer plans to show clothing and personal effects found with the body. He did not show them today, he said, "because I think it would be tragic for parents to learn of their daughter's death through the newspaper."

Reports to Be Studied

Mr. Lehrer said investigators from Ocean and Monmouth Counties would examine missing-persons reports over the weekend with the help of a computer. He said that there were between 200 and 250 missing-persons cases in the two counties, but that he did not know how many involved teen-age girls.

"In addition," he said, "when people who are reported missing return home, the persons who filed the original reports often forget to notify the police, so we don't konw how many cases are still active."

Mr. Lehrer has said he will seek the death penalty for Mr. Biegenwald in the murder last August of the Camden teen-ager, Anna M. Olesiewicz. According to the Prosecutor, she was lured away from the Asbury Park boardwalk before being killed by four shots from a small-caliber handgun that was found by the police in Mr. Biegenwald's home.

Mr. Lehrer has also said he will seek a murder indictment against Mr. Biegenwald in the slaying of the Brick Township girl, Maria Ciallella, who was last seen walking toward her home shortly after midnight on Nov. 1, 1981.

Mr. Lehrer said Miss Bacon, one of the victims identified today, left her home on Brooklyn Boulevard in Sea Girt at about 11 P.M. on Nov. 20 to walk to a store on Route 71 in nearby Spring Lake Heights for a pack of cigarettes.

He said she was intercepted on Route 71 by Mr. Biegenwald, who invited her into his car and killed her with two shots to the head from a small-caliber weapon.

According to the Prosecutor, Mr. Biegenwald brought the girl's body to the garage behind his apartment at 507 Sixth Avenue, Asbury Park, and the next day took it to a "secluded area" of Tinton Falls, 15 miles away, and buried it in the shallow grave where it was found by the police April 15.

The murder of Mr. Ward on Sept. 21 or 22 took place behind Mr. Biegenwald's apartment, the Prosecutor said. He said Mr. Biegenwald had shot Mr.

Continued on Page 48, Column 3

Associated Press

William J. Ward and Betsy Bacon.

The New York Times *chronicles the 12-month killing spree of Richard Biegenwald in 1981-1982. Biegenwald avoided New Jersey's death penalty twice—thirty years apart. In the 1950's, after killing a municipal prosecutor, Biegenwald escaped the electric chair when the victim's wife asked the jury to spare him. In the 1980's, after he killed four young women, Biegenwald dodged execution by lethal injection through the action of the New Jersey Supreme Court.* (Stories, photos courtesy The New York Times.)

The New York Times/John Sotomayor

State Police Officer James Suffolk using a dog to search the grounds of the former home of Richard F. Biegenwald on Staten Island.

Police Assert Friend Helped Suspect Move Buried Body

By M. A. FARBER

While police dug in vain yesterday for more bodies at the Staten Island site where two murdered teen-agers were found Monday, officials said privately that a friend of the suspect had helped him move a body from one burial place on the site to another.

Police officials said the friend, Dherran Fitzgerald, was cooperating with the authorities in their investigation of the suspect, Richard F. Biegenwald. Mr. Biegenwald is suspected of killing at least five people in New Jersey in the last year and burying some of them on the grounds of his mother's home in a rural section of Staten Island.

Mr. Fitzgerald and Mr. Biegenwald, both ex-convicts, have been charged with one of the murders, that of 18-year-old Anna Olesiewicz. Miss Olesiewicz's body was found in a vacant lot in Ocean Township, N.J., on Jan. 14, a week before the two men were arrested.

Anna Olesiewicz

Identities of 2 Not Disclosed

An official said Mr. Fitzgerald had helped Mr. Biegenwald take one of the bodies that was found Monday from a spot far in back of the Staten Island house to a spot near the garage, where it was found. Then, the official said, Mr. Beigenwald reburied it on top of the other body.

Authorities have not disclosed the identities of the two victims found Monday, both of them females, or of two victims — one female and one male — whose bodies were found in New Jersey last weekend.

An autopsy yesterday on the body of one of the teen-agers who had been buried on Staten Island showed she had been shot twice in the head.

Alexander Lehrer, the Prosecutor in Monmouth County, N.J., said there was evidence that the girl, like the other known victims, had been murdered in

20 CENTS TRENTON, N.J., SATURDAY JULY 4, 1981 TWO SECTIONS, 24 PAGES

6 break out of Trenton prison

All 4 murderers captured; two escapees still at large

Escape route

Aerial view of Trenton State Prison shows route taken by escaping inmates. (1) Milk truck commandeered by inmates is positioned inside prison wall. (2) Prisoners lob Molotov cocktails at guard tower off Second Street. (3) Six men — three of them later recaptured — go over the wall. (4) Shots fired by guards at escaping inmates strike second-floor level of neighboring house. At right, Patrolman Gregory Halpin of the Hamilton Township police department looks through woods on Duck Island.

Trenton firefighters hose down guardhouse hit by fleeing inmates' Molotov cocktail.

DARING ESCAPE FOR 6 TSP CONS; FOUR RECAPTURED

The Trentonian

Proudly Serving Historic Trenton and the Great Valley of the Delaware

Molotov Cocktail Tossed

By CHUCK DAVIS

MARVIN RUSSELL MICHAEL JONES MARK E. JONES

JESSE GUZMAN

ANDREW J. CLARK

ROBERT DAVIS

6 Prison Escapees Had Long Records

By CHUCK DAVIS
Staff Writer

Robert Davis, a Virginian serving a four-to-six year sentence for breaking, entering and larceny, escaped once before from Rahway State Prison. He was caught two months later and shipped to the maximum security prison in Trenton.

Yesterday he and five other inmates firebombed a guard tower and scaled the wall at Trenton State Prison between Second and Third streets in South Trenton and escaped.

While on morning recreation period, the six inmates held a correction officer and the driver of a milk truck at knifepoint while they climbed atop the refrigerated truck and scaled a 12-foot-high wall, officials said.

State Prison officials identified the escapees as:

—Jesse Guzman, 28, of Perth Amboy. He is serving a life sentence for murder. He was transferred from Middlesex County Jail to Trenton State Prison Dec. 1, 1977.

He is described as five-feet, seven-inches tall and weighs 180 pounds.

—Robert Davis. Born in Danville, Va. Davis has no other known address. Convicted of two counts of breaking and entering and larceny in 1975, he was paroled two years later and returned to Rahway State Prison in 1977.

In May 1980, he escaped from the prison and was captured that July 23. He was recently sentenced to 25 years for attempted bank robbery, officials said.

(Continued on Page 10)

ESCAPE FROM TRENTON STATE PRISON

Trenton police stop and search vehicles in area surrounding Trenton State Prison following escape.

The July 3, 1981 "Great Escape" was the most spectacular in the prison's history in terms of the number of inmates who got over the wall and the audacity of the plan: commandeered bread truck, Molotov cocktail; firebombed tower; broad daylight. (Stories, photos courtesy The Times, Trenton, NJ. Reprinted with permission. Headline courtesy The Trentonian)

THE NEW YORK TIMES, THURSDAY, DECEMBER 9,

5 in Jersey Family Are Found Slain

tinued From Page 1, Col. 7

00, sits on the eastern slope he Watchung Mountains. Its muters are served by the ey Central Railroad and it marked by tree-shaded ts and a busy downtown

e List house, built about years ago, is set back 100 from Hillside Avenue on oad thoroughfare lined with 000-to-$100,000 homes on acre and two-acre lots.

a desk drawer on the nd floor, Chief Moran said, police found one .32-caliber lver and one 9-millimeter l. Shots had been fired each gun.

ocked neighbors said they observed lights burning lly and throughout the day e rambling house, but had rved no activity in the last weeks. The police found, said, that the heating sys- had been turned down, but no utilities had been shut r canceled.

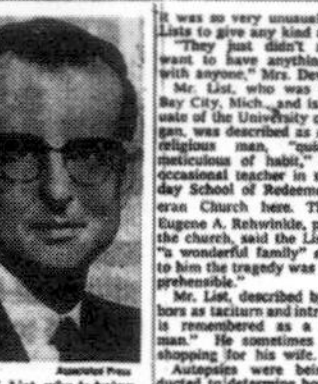

Associated Press

John E. List, who is being sought by Jersey police.

Mrs. List suffered a nervous breakdown, "and nobody saw

It was so very unusual for the Lists to give any kind of party. "They just didn't seem to want to have anything to do with anyone," Mrs. Devoe said.

Mr. List, who was born in Bay City, Mich., and is a graduate of the University of Michigan, was described as a deeply religious man, "quiet and meticulous of habit," and an occasional teacher in the Sunday School of Redeemer Lutheran Church here. The Rev. Eugene A. Rehwinkle, pastor of the church, said the Lists were "a wonderful family" and that to him the tragedy was "incomprehensible."

Mr. List, described by neighbors as taciturn and introverted, is remembered as a "family man." He sometimes did the shopping for his wife.

Autopsies were being conducted to determine how many shots had been fired into the victims. There were no other apparent wounds than the bullet wounds in the head, the authorities said. A search of the

WHERE FIVE WERE SLAIN IN JERSEY: The bodies of Mrs. John E. List, her mother-in-law and her three teenage children were discovered by the police on Tuesday in the List home in Westfield, N. J. All had been shot to death. Police have issued alarm for Mrs. List's husband.

Accountant John List (left) methodically killed his entire family, (below) neatly lining up their bodies in the ballroom of their Victorian home. He fled New Jersey and elluded capture for over 17 years until TV's America's Most Wanted *broadcast his story.* (Stories, photos courtesy The New York Times/Associated Press)

Suspect in 5 Killings in 1971 Caught With Aid of TV Show

Associated Press

John E. List in 1971, left, and in a sculptor's bust of what he would probably look like after 18 years. At right, a man said to be Mr. List in police custody yesterday in Richmond.

John E. List with his wife, Helen, his daughter, Patricia, and sons, John Jr., rear, and Frederick, in a photo taken in 1971, before all but Mr. List, who disappeared, were found dead.

Robert Stankiewicz and David Kerpen, both 21, were the first inmates to try to escape from the new prison (completed in 1983). Stankiewicz was shot and killed by a guard in one of the new "super towers" seven stories above ground that overlook the entire complex. Kerpen was wounded and fell into the razor wire on the roof of 7-wing. He survived. (Story, photo courtesy The Trentonian.)

Proudly Serving Historic Trenton and the Great Valley of the Delaware

VOL. 38 NO. 234 TRENTON, N.J., TUESDAY, APRIL 26, 1983 PHONE 989-7800 25 CENTS

TRENTON PRISON CON SLAIN IN ESCAPE TRY

Second Inmate Flees, Nabbed

By CHUCK DAVIS
Staff Writer

A Trenton State Prison inmate was killed during a desperate dash for freedom and a second was severely cut by razor-sharp barbed wire during an aborted breakout yesterday at the maximum security facility. Both were convicted murderers.

The dead inmate was identified as Robert J. Stankiewicz, 21, of Haddonfield, serving a life sentence for the murder of a Camden County woman in 1979.

The second man, David Kerpen, 21, of Atlantic Highlands, was captured several feet short of the prison roof's edge near Third and Federal streets when he

Related Picture on Page Two

became entangled in the razor wire that runs along the edge of the 147-year-old structure.

Kerpen is serving a life sentence plus 40 years for the murder of a Monmouth County woman and escape from the Monmouth County Jail, said Department of Corrections spokesman Jim Stabile.

Bloodied from the razor wire, Kerpen screamed out in agony each time four prison officials pulled and cut the wire from around his body.

He was freed after about 20 minutes and taken to the prison wing of St. Francis Medical Center with lacerations and a broken leg. He was listed in satisfactory condition last night, Stabile said.

As the prison escape alarm sounded, dozens of corrections officers and Trenton policemen, carrying

(Continued on Page 22)

Trentonian Photo By BILL RYAN

Escape Foiled

Trenton State Prison workers attempt to free inmate David Kerpen, 21, from the razor wire on the roof of the prison after he and another inmate tried to escape yesterday. Robert J. Stankiewicz, 21, the other inmate, was shot and killed during the attempted escape. Kerpen suffered cuts and a broken leg.

VOL. 43 NO. 116 TUESDAY NOVEMBER 22, 1988 25 CENTS

KILLER IS RECAPTURED AFTER 14 HOURS IN CITY

Double murderer Gonzalo Marrero (left) is recaptured after escaping and hiding out in the Trenton sewer system. (Story, photos courtesy The Trentonian)

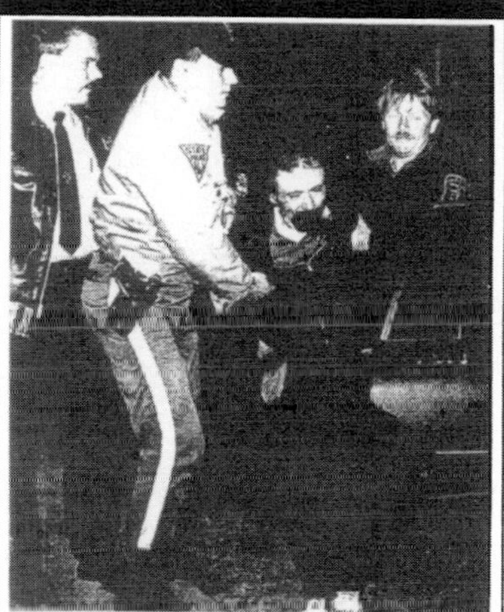

Trentonian Photo by BILL RYAN

ESCAPED KILLER NABBED — N.J. Department of Corrections Sgt. Robert Gorbe (right) and a state trooper grip State Prison escapee Gonzalo Marrero, a double murderer, while taking him into Trenton police headquarters last night following his capture by city Officer Martin Nawrock (left). Other pictures on Page Three.

Escapee Scales Prison Wall, Later Found on Lamberton St.

By ROBERT R. GRIFFIN
Staff Writer

A double-murderer who escaped from New Jersey State Prison early yesterday morning was nabbed by Trenton policemen while the convict walked down Lamberton Street in the dark, 14 hours after his unauthorized furlough began.

Marrero, a refugee who arrived in the United States in 1980 during the infamous Mariel boatlift, has been serving time at the prison since April 1986 for two murders, robbery, sexual assault and burglary convictions stemming from a break-in at a

Related Story on Page Three

Subterranean Search Is Fruitless As Sewer Sweep Comes Up Empty

By PAUL MICKLE
Staff Writer

New Jersey corrections officers and troopers crawled through several blocks of slimy sewers yesterday in search of the nimble Cuban murderer who escaped from Trenton State Prison at 3:45 a.m.

Gonzalo Marrero's clothes were wet when Trenton police captured him last evening, but officers were uncertain exactly where the escapee spent his 14 hours on the lam. Nor, police said, was Marrero cut seriously by razor wire while scaling the prison wall.

But the intensity of a search for an escaped murderer is such that when prison officers noticed what appeared to be blood at the mouth of a stormwater pipe along the Delaware River at the bottom of Federal Street [illegible], they climbed right in.

For the next several hours — through two changes of clothes and with help from colleagues, troopers and Trenton sewer workers — Corrections Sgt. Robert Gorbe and a state bloodhound named Dato followed the uncertain trail through the storm pipes.

The searchers crawled up several hundred feet of Federal before turning left up Union Street and climbing out at the manhole near the city pool on Union. Soon after, Gorbe was climbing down another manhole at the dead end of Union.

The sergeant, a member of Corrections' Special Operations Group, re-emerged from that manhole and reported there was room for only one man to climb through the pipe from that spot. Corrections Officer Joseph Nicholas and Trooper Todd Biebel then moved in to provide him support — both tactical and moral.

Lamps supplied by Trenton's sewer utility were lowered into the manholes up ahead for Gorbe to crawl toward. The sergeant later said the officers figured that if the suspect was in the conduit his frame would block the light.

It was more than a visual search, though. To make sure the suspect hadn't crawled off some side drain or was somehow hiding in the conduit, Gorbe crawled up the pipe under Union for a block to Steamboat Street and continued along two more blocks of that street before turning left and heading up Power Street.

"Everything all right down there, Bobby?" the prison officers and troopers kept hollering into the

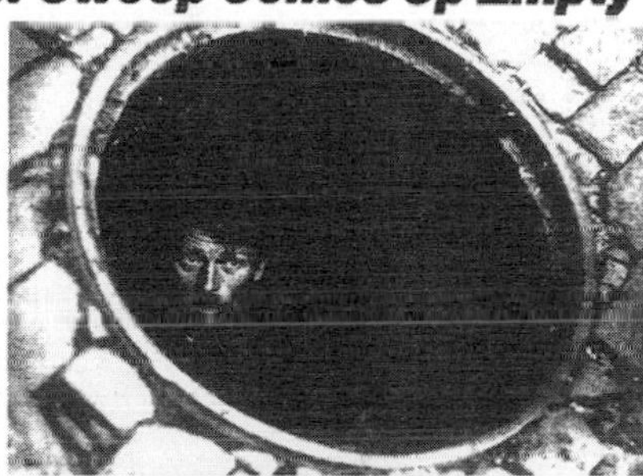

Trentonian Photos by EMMA LEE

MANHUNT IN THE SEWER — Department of Corrections Sgt. Robert Gorbe (above), looking for the escaped prisoner, climbs out of a manhole in South Trenton after a search of the South Trenton storm drains. An unidentified corrections officer (left) stands guard over a drain outlet at the Delaware River.

hole. Gorbe stayed with it, re-emerging only to consult with Nicholas and the technical expert at the scene, city utility Collection System Superintendent Andrew J. Dill.

The storm pipe widens about half up Power from Steamboat, the corrections sergeant said. "It opens up real wide. We could have sent a whole team of bloodhounds in at this end." But by 2:30 p.m., though Gorbe and Nicholas were concerned that the wiry escapee had made good a subterranean escape, the sewer search was called off.

Dill, a 48-year veteran of the city workforce, said yesterday's wasn't the first search of Trenton's sewers for an escapee from TSP. He's provided help at one or two before, Dill said, but never has an escapee been found down there.

Sgt. Robert Gorbe (above) peers out of a manhole while another correction officer stands guard with a shotgun during the hunt for escaped killer Gonzalo Marrero.

CON, GIRLFRIEND HELD IN ESCAPE ATTEMPT

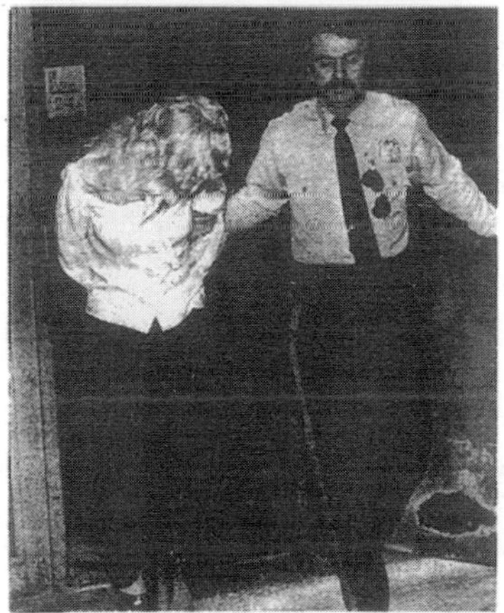

ESCAPE ATTEMPT SUSPECT — Trenton Patrolman John Guadagno escorts 23-year-old Sherry-Anne Stevens of Hasbrouck Heights to a patrol wagon after she was charged with

Robert Reldan's girlfriend, Sherry-Anne Stevens (left) tried to smuggle a sawed-off shotgun in to Reldan at St. Francis Hospital. An alert correction officer had seen her visiting Reldan at the prison. (Stories, photos courtesy The Trentonian)

The Trentonian

Vol 49 No. 124 75,255 Trenton, N.J. Thursday December 8, 1994 25¢

Escape tunnel uncovered at state prison

Inmates came within 6-10 inches of outside wall.

PAGE 3

Thursday, December 8, 1994 The Trentonian

'A little more work and they were gone'

■ A group of inmates tried to scrape a hole to the outside world.

By PETULA DVORAK

New Jersey's most dangerous inmates were a mere 6 inches from freedom this week when guards discovered a secret tunnel leading to an outside wall of Trenton State Prison.

(Continued on Page 10)

Two different groups of inmates tried to escape within a few days of each other. The discovery of the first attempt and the subsequent order of the removal of ceiling tiles by warden Willis Morton pushed the second group to speed up their work. (Stories, photos/art courtesy The Trentonian)

The Trentonian

Vol 49 No. 126 64,997 Trenton, N.J. Saturday December 10, 1994 25¢

2nd escape tunnel found at prison

Inmates chiseled through concrete

PAGE 3

Saturday, December 10, 1994 The Trentonian 3

Inmates only inches away from freedom

■ Prison officials said the near-escape probably took months of work.

By CHIP SCUTARI

For the second time in four days, a corrections officer at Trenton State Prison yesterday discovered an escape tunnel in which inmates had chiseled through a cinder block wall and were less than a foot from freedom.

(Continued on Page Seven)

Haddon Hts. cop killer suspect arraigned, jailed without bail

Surrender: *After 14 hours of negotiation, Nelson walked, unarmed, out of her house.*

By CAROL COMEGNO
and BILL DUHART
Courier-Post Staff

CAMDEN — A transsexual charged with killing two law enforcement officers and seriously injuring a third in Haddon Heights was being held today without bail in isolation and on a suicide watch in the Camden County Jail.

Wearing a gas mask and a bulletproof vest, 37-year-old suspect Leslie Ann Nelson walked out of her home unarmed at 4:34 a.m. Friday and surrendered after 14 hours of standoff and prolonged telephone negotiation with police and the FBI.

As she was escorted for a bail hearing into a courtroom jammed with police, media and court workers later Friday, the tall former go-go dancer — known as Glenn Nelson before a sex change operation — held her head down. Her long blond hair obscured her face, and the short sleeves of her orange jail jumpsuit revealed a bruised elbow.

In court, Nelson was charged with two counts of murder and one count of aggravated assault.

"She told the negotiators she was not drinking and not taking drugs. The only explanation she gave (for shooting the officers) was that she had gotten scared," Camden County Prosecutor Edward Borden told Superior Court Judge Isaiah Steinberg in asking for no bail for offenses that could carry the death penalty.

JOHN NORCROSS

JOHN MCLAUGHLIN

RICHARD NORCROSS

Borden said the murders occurred Thursday after six officers went with a search warrant for weapons to Nelson's house in the 1200 block of Sylvan Avenue. On an earlier visit that day, police had questioned Nelson about a sex allegation involving a child, but Borden declined to elaborate further and said that case is now in limbo.

Meanwhile, Haddon Heights police officer Richard Norcross continued his struggle for life Friday as he underwent a second operation for one of his four bullet wounds. He was listed in critical but stable condition at Cooper Hospital/University Medical Center in Camden.

Slain were John Norcross of Mount Ephraim, Norcross' brother and fellow Haddon Heights officer, and John McLaughlin of Cherry Hill, an investigator with the Camden County Prosecutor's Office.

It was the first time either Haddon Heights or the county prosecutor's staff had an officer killed in the line of duty. The small suburban borough is holding a town meeting Sunday to help residents cope with the tragedy involving officers well known to many schoolchildren.

"They were killed with what we believe was an AK-47 military rifle, which can penetrate through a bulletproof vest," a distressed Borden said later at a press conference. "We think some (officers) were wearing vests and some weren't, but it would not have made a difference here."

The prosecutor said he will be unable to confirm the type of weapons Nelson used until today, because the substantial amounts of tear gas used to try to force her out of her home prevented authorities from entering the house Friday. He said he also expects to

Please see SHOT, Page 3A

Correction: The suspect in the law officers' killings was mistakenly identified as Glenn Beatty in Friday's paper. The *Courier-Post* did not intend to associate this suspect with any other person. We regret any misunderstandings this may have caused.

By Tina Markoe, Courier-Post

Finally over: Leslie Nelson appears at her arraignment Friday before Superior Court Judge Isaiah Steinberg. Prosecutor Edward Borden said his office might seek the death penalty.

Feminine touch gets Nelson to surrender

By LEE MOORE
Courier-Post Staff

HADDON HEIGHTS — It took the promise of make-up and some other "things a woman would know about" to end the standoff between police and accused cop-killer Leslie Nelson on Friday.

Holed up in her parents' house on Sylvan Avenue, the former Glenn Nelson — renamed Leslie after a sex change operation more than two years ago — talked fruitlessly with male police negotiators for hours before a woman negotiator took the phone.

Shortly afterward Nelson, by most accounts a timid, part-time exotic dancer since her sex change, agreed to surrender.

"Things changed when a woman got on the line. She had a soothing voice. She convinced him (Nelson) to come out," said William Gooch, a Sylvan Avenue resident whose home and telephone police used while negotiating with Nelson during the standoff.

By Tina Markoe, Courier-Post

Enigma: Prosecutor Edward F. Borden (left) presents the case against 37-year-old Leslie Nelson (right) in court Friday.

transformation into a "brassy-looking blonde." Nelson would take solitary walks to the same park clad in mini-skirts, halter tops, tight jeans, sunglasses and a signature hot-pink jacket.

If there was a common thread in the two pursuits, it was isolation. Often seen in and around her neighborhood, Leslie Nelson was rarely heard from and never really known.

"She was always alone. Always in the park. You rarely saw her during the day. If you saw her walking, it was usually around dusk," said Rose Hudson, who lives roughly a block from where the shootout took place on Sylvan Avenue.

Said neighbor Heidi Shirley, a resident for 29 years, "I'm a regular walker in the park and I saw her often. Whenever he'd walk past you, he'd always turn away. He never spoke and he'd never make eye contact. It was obvious ... him not wanting to look at you. That always bothered me.

"Last summer he got the breasts done and wore tube tops and showed them off," the 49-year-old neighbor continued. "And

Leslie Ann Nelson, a transsexual who killed two police officers in Haddon Heights, wore her platinum blonde wig to her arraignment. She is the only woman currently on New Jersey's death row. (Stories, photos courtesy The Camden Courier Post)

SATURDAY
MAY 31, 1997

CLOUDY
High 72, Low 56
Details/A2

25 Cents

The Times

SERVING OUR COMMUNITY FOR MORE THAN A CENTURY

Many Americans still remain in strife-torn Sierra Leone A9

GOOD NEWS, BAD NEWS
Yanks sign pitcher Hideki Irabu, drop game to Red Sox C1

Verdict: Guilty of all charges

Staff photo by Frank Jacobs III
Jesse Timmendequas sits stoically as the guilty verdicts against him are read yesterday in Mercer County Courthouse

Timmendequas could face execution for Megan slaying

By EMILY J. HORNADAY
Staff Writer

TRENTON — Jesse K. Timmendequas was convicted yesterday of raping, sodomizing and murdering 7-year-old Megan Kanka in the bedroom of his home, just yards from the house where the little girl lived and played in a quiet suburban neighborhood.

The verdict, reached after about four hours of jury deliberations over two days, means Timmendequas now faces possible execution.

The little girl's death nearly three years ago ignited a national and local movement to pass laws, known as Megan's Law, to protect children from sexual predators.

Yesterday's verdict triggered quiet outbursts of approval from a packed Mercer County courtroom, where raw emotions were tightly controlled.

Megan's parents, Richard and Maureen Kanka, teared up and Maureen Kanka gasped quietly each time the jury forewoman said "guilty." A close friend held her hand.

As he did throughout the trial, Timmendequas, 36, a convicted sex offender who lived across the street from the Kanka family on Barbara Lee Drive in Hamilton, displayed no outward emotion. But he appeared glassy-eyed and nervous when the verdict was read.

Maureen Kanka was wearing a pink blouse — her daughter's favorite color. Pink ribbons have been widely used to symbolize the memory of Megan.

After the Verdict

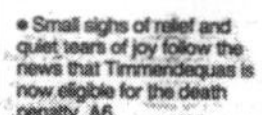

- Small sighs of relief and quiet tears of joy follow the news that Timmendequas is now eligible for the death penalty. A6.
- The reading of the verdict has some remembering back to July 30, 1994, the day Hamilton and its neighboring communities rallied to one cause — finding Megan. A7.
- An 8-foot pine planted in the park developed in memory of Megan has sprouted unusual pink pine cones — and pink was Megan's favorite color. A7.

As the court clerk took the jury through the list of charges, heads in the entire row of family members nodded in unison as each "guilty" verdict was spoken.

After the session was concluded, sheriff's officers escorted the Kankas out of the courtroom. Many ap-

• see VERDICT, A6

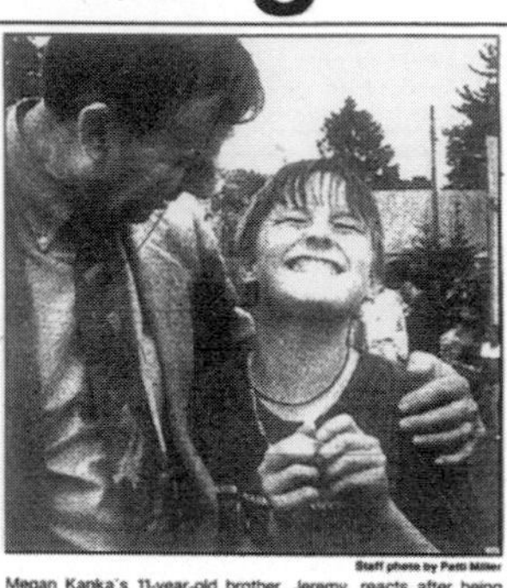

Staff photo by Patti Miller
Megan Kanka's 11-year-old brother, Jeremy, reacts after being told of the trial outcome yesterday by Sayen Elementary School Principal Hank Keller. Jeremy and his classmates were at Megan's Place park in Hamilton for a special flag-raising ceremony.

On Barbara Lee Drive, flowers and vengeance

By PETER PAGE
and MIKE JENNINGS
Staff Writers

HAMILTON — Eleven-year-old Jeremy Kanka was planting a petunia in the meticulously tended flower beds of Megan's Place yesterday when he heard the news that the man he was already certain had killed his sister had been — formally and finally — found guilty.

"Yes! My dream has come true," the young boy exclaimed with clenched fists. "I feel a lot

both to remember Megan Kanka and to obliterate the scene of her murder.

It was just a welcome coincidence that Jeremy and 50 fifth-grade classmates were visiting to plant flowers and dedicate a flagpole yesterday — the day Jesse K. Timmendequas was found guilty of murder and rape.

"What irony," said Hank Keller.

KELLER WAS the principal of Sayen Elementary School when Megan was a student there, and he's still the principal. Yes.

Tortured youth focus of defense

Plan to avoid death penalty outlined

By EMILY J. HORNADAY
Staff Writer

tortured and killed some of the

guilty yesterday of murdering 7

The separate penalty phase of the trial, scheduled to begin June 9, will involve testimony related to the ap

Jesse Timmendequas(above) was found guilty in the brutal sexual assault and murder of eight-year-old Megan Kanka in Hamilton Township, NJ. The case led to the passing of "Megan's Law" requiring notification when convicted sex offenders are returned to their communities.
(Stories, photos courtesy The Times, Trenton, NJ. Reprinted with permission.)

'Iceman' pleads guilty

Gets two more life sentences for murders

By Bill Sanderson
Record Staff Writer

By pleading guilty Wednesday to two murder charges, Richard Kuklinski, whom authorities call the "Iceman" killer, saved his wife and son from having to face criminal charges.

Kuklinski, 53, offered his plea to Superior Court Judge Frederick W. Kuschenmeister in Hackensack. In return, the state dropped a third murder charge against Kuklinski and several unrelated charges filed against his wife and son.

Kuklinski, wearing dark glasses, a red tie, and a beige jacket, displayed no emotion at the hearing Wednesday, at which he acknowledged having murdered George Malliband and Louis Masgay.

"I shot George Malliband five times," Kuklinski told the judge of the February 1980 murder. "It was due to business."

As for Masgay's killing July 1, 1981, "I shot him once in the back of the head," Kuklinski stated.

Under the terms of the plea bargain, Kuschenmeister sentenced Kuklinski to two consecutive life terms, concurrent with two consecutive life terms he already is serving for the murders of Gary T. Smith, 38, and Daniel E. Deppner, 34, both of Vernon. Kuklinski was convicted of those killings in March after a month-long jury trial.

Ultimately, Kuklinski's parole ineligibility was not changed by the guilty pleas: He would have to live to be 111 years old to be released from prison.

But because of the plea bargain, his son, Dwayne R. Kuklinski, will not have to face a minor marijuana-

See ICEMAN Page A-18

After being convicted of two murders, Big Rich Kuklinski, "The Iceman," pled guilty to two more to save his wife and son from facing criminal charges. (Stories, photos courtesy The New Jersey Record)

Glassboro State College while incarcerated at Leesburg.

Leopizzi said, "I don't have much choice, distasteful as it may be. It's not pleasant for me to tell you to spend more time in prison. But I don't have a choice."

I thought it was interesting that none of the celebrities who were involved in the case attended the second trial, and after the convictions, it seemed like they just disappeared.

Within a few hours, Rubin was back in Trenton. John Artis was sent back to Leesburg where he finished his bachelor's degree in business administration and was paroled in 1981.

End of story.

Not quite.

On November 7, 1985, Judge H. Lee Sarokin of the Federal District Court in Newark overturned the Carter/Artis convictions because, he said, the 1976 convictions were based on "an appeal to racism, concealment rather than disclosure." Sarokin found that Carter and Artis had been denied their constitutional rights on two grounds: 1) Humphreys' citing of racial revenge as the motive for the murders had "fatally infected the trial"; and 2) the prosecution had improperly withheld from the defense the results of the lie-detector test that would have impeached Bello's testimony that Carter and Artis were at the scene of the murders. In fact, Sarokin found, the lie-detector test on Bello confirmed that his recantation was true, but the prosecutor's office told the defense the results were exactly the opposite.

Rubin, back in Rahway, was released from custody on November 8, 1985. John Artis was already out, but in April of '86 he was busted again, this time for a weapons charge and conspiracy to distribute cocaine. At first John denied the charges, but then he switched his plea to guilty and was sentenced to six years.

The Passaic County prosecutor's office appealed Sarokin's judgment, but a federal appellate court and the U.S. Supreme Court refused to reinstate the convictions. For Rubin the whole thing officially died in February of 1988 when the Passaic County prosecutor's office decided not to reopen the case. The acting Passaic County prosecutor, John P. Goceljak, said the 21-year-old case had "received the attention of more courts and proceedings than probably any other case in the history of this state and possibly any other state."

The last time I saw Rubin, Ginny and I were in the Trenton train station, waiting for a train to Philadelphia. All of a sudden, Rubin stepped off an incoming train. We looked at each other in disbelief that we'd meet this way, on a train platform, after so many years of seeing each other behind the stone walls of Trenton State Prison. Rubin came over and hugged me, and said, "Harry, it's so good to see you."

He was dressed in a fashionable brown suede jacket with a white fleece collar, and he was wearing wire-rimmed glasses, a result of having lost the sight in one eye while he was in prison. Rubin told me he was living in Canada, working on a project to help overturn sentences of wrongfully convicted prisoners.

In January of 1993, Rubin Carter gave the keynote address in a two-day conference, "The Future of Habeas Corpus" at Harvard University. Judge Sarokin was in the audience.

Rubin said, “It’s a long way from Trenton State Prison to the Harvard Law School. A very, very long way.”

As I said, it’s a hell of a story.

14
CHAPTER FOURTEEN

THE MUSLIM UPRISING

On October 16, 1975, I thought my number was up; for several minutes I was convinced that I was going to die. On that day, while I was on duty as the officer in charge of the second floor of the Donald Bourne School, 20 members of the Nation of Islam, a black Muslim sect, went on a bloody rampage, killing Cleopheous Mayers and seriously wounding six other members of a rival group, the New World of Islam (Bellites). Since I was the only witness to the stabbings who was willing to testify if and when the attackers were brought to trial, my job, and my life outside of the prison, took on an added element of risk

The vicious slashing attack was the culmination of several years of internal warfare between the large and powerful Chicago-based Nation of Islam under Elijah Muhammad, and the New World group that had split off from the main body after Malcolm X was gunned down in New York City's Audubon Hotel in February, 1965. As will happen with organizations like the Mafia or street gangs, conflicts outside continue inside the prison when the members get convicted and sent to jail.

By the early 1970's, the black Muslim movement had taken hold in the prison. Their members were easily identifiable by the way they dressed—they wore their sharply pressed khaki uniforms with the shirts buttoned all the way up—and by their clannishness. In the yard, they stayed strictly with their own. A lot of us felt that the administration was giving the Muslims way too much power, to the point, it seemed to us, that the Muslims felt like they were running the jail.

In the early '70's, the prison went through a major upheaval. Part of the reason was society's focus on the prison system. When I first started as a guard, the only people interested in the inmates were their families and a few "do-gooders" (we contemptuously used the term "social worker" for anybody, cops included, who we felt were soft on the inmates). Incidents like the deaths of Speller and Hogan caused a furor in 1973; in the '50's nobody but their families would have noticed. But by the early '70's there must have been half a dozen outside prison watchdog and reform organizations: David Rothenberg's Fortune Society; the New Jersey Association on Correction; the Coalition on Penal Reform; and on and on. The administration responded to pressures from the outside by listening to inmate grievances through their leaders, like Theodore Gibson (the blacks) and David Guy

Baldwin (the whites)—both real sweethearts—and by letting the inmates form their own interest groups, like the Trenton State Prison Committee, the Inmate Legal Association (ILA) and the black Muslims.

By 1975, the Muslims had grown to be a force to be reckoned with. Every day in the yard, we watched as squads of Muslims ran around the perimeter of the yard, chanting, "Kill the whites," "Kill the Jews," "Kill the Christians." And we were under orders not to interfere with their "freedom of speech." A lot of us, the line officers, had big-time resentments over the changes we were being forced to accept.

On the surface, it looked like the Muslims in the prison were a unified force with a lot of political clout. But we were also hearing stories about in-fighting between Muslim factions out on the street. One day I was talking with a Muslim, and in the conversation I said something about Malcolm X being a respected and effective leader within the movement.

The inmate responded, "Malcolm X was a running dog who deserved every bullet that ripped his decadent body."

Oops. Wrong faction.

As new guys came in from the areas surrounding Newark, they told stories about vicious killings being carried out on the street in a power struggle within the Muslim movement. Law enforcement sources in north Jersey who were familiar with the Muslims said there were two major factions: the Nation of Islam followers (the "Regular Muslims") thought of Elijah Muhammed as a great prophet of Allah, while the New World members believed that Elijah Muhammad was Allah Himself. The Nation of Islam for years had been building an infrastructure through legitimate investments in the black community; they claimed that the New World splinter group planned assassinations and armed robberies and wanted eventually to take over the whole black Muslim movement.

Late in the afternoon of September 4, 1973, the most influential Nation of Islam minister in Newark and a prominent figure in the national organization, James McGregor (25X) Shabazz, was assassinated in the driveway of his home in the West Ward of Newark. This was seen as an attempt by the New World to take over Mosque 25, the largest in Newark. Police charged 14 members of the breakaway New World sect with conspiracy and murder in the shotgun slaying of Shabazz, who was shot in the head at close range. In piecing together the conspiracy, law enforcement officials said that Shabazz had resisted the efforts of Albert Dickens to leave the orthodox Muslims and join the New World.

Dickens was a pretty sharp guy who had been in TSP for a couple of years for killing a major Newark narcotics figure and then had been transferred to Rahway. He had been member of the orthodox Muslims, but had switched over to the New World and, according to the Essex County prosecutor's office, had helped orchestrate the Shabazz killing from inside prison. He was indicted but acquitted. Dickens was an influential force within the prison society, and he and another lifer, Frank Earl Andrews, compiled a book of stories and poems by inmates called *Voices From the Big House.*

Two weeks after the Shabazz murder, the complex situation took a couple of bizarre turns. Police discovered the bodies of twin brothers Roger and Ralph Bankston in their car in Edison. The Bankstons were captains in the New World sect and reportedly had been involved in the Shabazz killing. Then, a month later, the bodies of Warren Marcello and Michael Huff were found in a park in Newark—just the bodies, not the heads. Those were found a couple of hours later, facing away from Mecca, in a gutter near the Shabazz home. In later testimony, Marcello was identified as the trigger man in the Shabazz murder. The bizarre twist in all of these killings, though, was that apparently all four of those men were killed by New World members, not the Nation of Islam, because they had disobeyed orders. While all of this was driving Essex County law enforcement officials crazy, we were hearing about it through the prison grapevine since we had daily contact with members of both sects.

In June of 1974, several members of the New World were convicted in the Shabazz killing and were sentenced to prison terms. Among them were four men who would become victims in the October bloodbath—Ben Walton, James Coy, Albert Chavies, and Lamont Calloway. In another strange twist, Calloway and Chavies, after being convicted in the Shabazz killing, were also convicted later in 1974 in the murder of the Bankston twins. No one was ever tried for the Marcello and Huff killings.

Initially, the men convicted in the Shabazz murder were sent to the Vroom readjustment unit on the grounds of the Trenton Psychiatric Hospital to keep them away from members of the Nation of Islam who were in TSP. But, mainly through efforts of their relatives, all of the young men—all in their early twenties—demanded to be put into the general population at Trenton. By September 17, all of the Shabazz killers were in Trenton, and everybody from the custody chief on down knew it was only a matter of time before the lid blew off.

I was on the desk on the second floor of the Donald Bourne School on October 16. This facility was the newest part of the old prison, a substantial two-story cinder block structure named for Sergeant Donald Bourne who had been murdered just outside the entrance to the TSP mess hall in 1972. The Bourne School building housed the law library and a number of classrooms and offices. The building had been constructed immediately adjacent to six-wing directly across from the old death row. A door had been punched through the wall of the corridor opposite five-wing to connect the Bourne School to the rest of the prison.

After passing through this door, inmates and staff enter an upward incline that leads to the first floor of the school. Midway up the thirty-foot ramp is an officer's desk and, today, a metal detector (it wasn't there at the time this incident happened). All traffic has to pass by the officer who inspects anything carried by inmates, employees or visitors. This officer also keeps track of all inmates who are in the school or the library.

A few feet beyond the officer's desk, anyone entering the school can make a left turn and go down an eight-foot-wide corridor with classrooms on either side and ultimately reach the law library at the end of the corridor. All of the classrooms have reinforced clear glass walls, basically heavy picture windows, starting about four feet from the floor and running up to about two feet from the ceiling. These windows allow the officers in charge of each floor of the school to walk up and down the corridor and see what is going on in all of the classrooms. At the end of this corridor is the law library, a large room with metal shelving, law books, long tables, and a couple of staff offices. This room also has the heavy glass windows on either side of the doorway.

If, after coming up the ramp, those entering the school turned right instead of left, they immediately came to metal and concrete stairs, with one landing, that led to the second floor of the facility. The upper floor looks basically like the first floor except that at the far end of the second floor corridor are a couple of classrooms instead of the large open area that houses the law library directly below.

Normally, if something is going to kick off in the prison, and it's planned in advance rather than spontaneous, it's timed to happen on the second shift because fewer officers are on duty, plus the ones who are working then tend to be newer on the job without as much experience in dealing with disturbances. In this case, though, the planners realized that the only time they would find all of their victims in one place would be in the school during the day, so the violence exploded at about 9:30 a.m. while I was on duty at the desk on the second floor.

In a carefully orchestrated plan, about 20 members of the Nation of Islam managed to get passes to the school or the law library, knowing that their intended victims would all be either in class or in the library. Because these guys had been scattered throughout the prison in different wings, no one wing officer could have seen that all of them were heading for the same place at the same time, and the star officer or central control wouldn't notice it either because of the volume of inmate traffic through there each day.

At the appointed time, all hell broke loose. I was sitting at the desk, at the midway point on the second floor, when suddenly I heard the sound of scuffling feet downstairs and something that sounded like chairs being turned over. As soon as you hear running feet in a prison, your heart freezes because you know something is kicking off—nobody runs in a jail unless something's wrong. Immediately to the right of my desk was the black studies classroom; at almost the same instant that I heard the sound of the running feet coming from the stairs and turned to look in that direction, I heard scuffling behind me near the black studies room. This whole thing was so well planned that before I could say or do anything, five Muslims, all holding sharpened wood chisels, screwdrivers or shanks, had surrounded my desk.

At this point I was a hostage.

One of them said, "Don't move, Harry."

Another one said, "We don't want to kill you, Harry." And as soon as the second one said that, I spun around and hit the riot button on the wall behind my desk.

Somebody later asked me, "Didn't you think that hitting the button could cost you your life?" That's one of my problems—and, I guess, one of my assets: sometimes I don't think; I just react.

When I hit the button, one of the five said, "All right, Harry, now we're gonna have to kill you," but, thank God, another one said, "I don't want anybody to hurt Harry," and they let it go, probably because at this point four of the victims were running out of the black studies classroom, screaming and pumping blood out of their necks and heads with every step as five other guys, all with sharpened chisels and shanks, were chasing and slashing them. The guys around my desk saw that their brothers were taking care of business and that my hitting the riot button probably wasn't going to save these guys from being hacked to pieces, so they just stayed between me and the action and watched. All of the victims were bleeding profusely, blood was splattering everywhere, and the faster they ran, the farther the blood shot out of their wounds onto the windows and walls lining the corridor.

This next piece of the episode would have been comical if the whole damned thing hadn't been so horrific. Just a few days prior to this incident, the state had closed down the State Home for Girls out on Whittlesey Road in Ewing Township, just outside of the City of Trenton. As a result of the closing, several women teachers who had been teaching the girls out there for umpteen years had been transferred to the school at Trenton State Prison, and this was something like their third day on the job. Two of the women were teaching in classrooms directly across from my desk but recessed down a short corridor. Both women came hurrying out of their classrooms to see what the commotion was, and just as they reached the point across the corridor from the front of my desk, the screaming victims came running by, splattering blood all over the place, including on the two women. To add to the confusion, the older one, probably in her late sixties, fainted dead away and slumped to the floor, covered in blood but otherwise OK.

At this point, the first of the victims had reached the stairs and all were still screaming and desperately trying to avoid the slashing shanks behind them. At the same time, I could hear cops coming in downstairs in response to the riot bell, so the guys holding me at bay started to drift away to lose themselves in the classrooms. In a matter of minutes the school was flooded with helmeted officers carrying riot shields and clubs—guns never come into the prison in situations like this lest the inmates gain control of them. The officers fanned out through the classrooms and started looking for inmates with blood on their clothes. The wounded and dying were rushed to the hospital. Out of all that carnage only one guy, Cleopheous Mayers, died while six others were seriously injured but survived. After the first floor was cleared of inmates, and officers were able to get in there, they found Mayers, bleeding from multiple stab wounds, lying unconscious on the floor in a classroom.

On the second floor, as officers herded inmates out of classrooms and into the corridor, four or five other officers stood at the top of the stairs and thoroughly frisked every inmate coming by them. In a matter of a half hour, all of the prime suspects had been identified and a few of the weapons had been located (we never did find all of the weapons that we suspected had been used). Within an hour, all suspects and anyone who might be remotely connected to either side of the conflict had been rounded up and were in 1-left lockup. All of the prime suspects were defiant; none denied involvement.

The warden, Alan Hoffman, immediately ordered the prison to be put on 24-hour lockdown, which would last for several weeks. This meant that all visits were canceled, no packages for inmates were accepted into the institution, all support functions, such as school and counseling, were cut back and inmates were locked in their cells for twenty-three hours per day—one hour out for a shower each day. They were served meals, mainly sandwiches, in their cells.

Immediately after the stabbings, the chief and other upper-level officers came into the school and had me and the three officers who had been downstairs go into separate classrooms and write up a report of what had happened and what we had seen. I named as many of the inmates as I had recognized and tried to give as accurate an account as I could of what had happened on the second floor. It took me quite a while to write out the report, keeping me at the jail well beyond my normal quitting time, so I asked one of the other officers to call Ginny. I didn't want her to worry when I didn't get home at my regular time. Plus I figured she might hear something on the radio about the stabbings and be worried that I was hurt, especially if they reported it happened in the school.

When I came into work the next day, I was in for a couple of nasty surprises—something that still bothers me to this day. It seems that the three officers on the first floor of the school "didn't see," or "couldn't identify," the inmates who had been involved. I found that to be a little strange since I had been surrounded face-to-face by five armed inmates standing only a couple of feet from me, and I sure as hell knew who they were and what part they had played. But for whatever reason, the three cops downstairs couldn't help in the investigation.

I also heard the next day from one of the cops who had responded to the alarm and rushed to the school, Sergeant Frank Bowlby, that one of the three cops downstairs had said, "Don't go up there, man, they've got knives."

And my brother officer who said this to Bowlby knew I was up there all alone, unarmed and helpless.

Then came the investigation. Hoffman and the rest of the administration were really concerned about this incident not only because it involved a murder but also because it signaled the breakdown of the delicate balance between inmate power groups in the jail. It was viewed as an insurrection as well as a murder. Since the other officers on the first floor and I had been taken hostage, even though only for a few minutes, the administration pursued that angle while the Mercer County prosecutor's office did the murder investigation. State police detectives and investigators from the prosecutor's office were in and out of the prison during the next several weeks, interviewing witnesses to build a case to present to a Mercer County grand jury for indictments.

This bloodbath had such far-reaching implications that the head of the state police, Colonel Clinton Pagano, personally took charge of the initial stages of the investigation.

When Colonel Pagano heard that the officers who had been on the first floor were saying that they were unable to identify any of the killers because of all of the confusion, he sought me out and said, "Harry, if they give you any trouble over this, don't hesitate to call me."

I always appreciated him for doing that, and later when things did get sticky, I almost took him up on his offer, but a subsequent change in administrations, which I'll explain later, solved the problem.

When I heard that the other three guards weren't willing to name names, my role in this whole mess started to get to me. While the incident had been going down in front of me, and I know this is an old cliché but it swear it's true, my life had basically flashed in front of my eyes. As those guys stood there in front of me with those sharpened chisels, it seemed like a thousand images flashed through my mind. I thought about my wife, my kids, our friends, my parents—all kinds of rapid-fire mental pictures. Now that the immediate danger had passed, my thoughts had shifted and I started dwelling obsessively on the potential danger to me and my family, of getting shot down in the street, of one of my kids being abducted or otherwise harmed.

Every day I worried about the effect that my testimony in open court might have, especially on Ginny and the kids. This incident was so serious and these guys so vicious—and with no death penalty not much to lose—that I was going crazy with worry. The killings in Newark, especially the shotgun slaying of Shabazz in his driveway and the decapitations of Marcello and Huff, were in the back of my mind every damned day. I knew that I could easily be marked for death on the inside, or even on the outside, to keep me from testifying. The Muslim movement had so many complicated cross-connects inside and outside the prison that I couldn't begin to know where an attack might come from. I became depressed and withdrawn.

In December a Mercer County grand jury indicted 20 inmates for the attacks. The 32-count indictment included charges of murder for the death of Cleopheous Mayers, assault with intent to kill, conspiracy, and aggravated assault and battery. When the news of the indictments put the glare of the spotlight on me again, Alan Hoffman did something that really pissed me off—and made me almost mad enough to call Colonel Pagano to take him up on his offer to help.

Shortly after the news of the indictments, Hoffman called me into his office and said, "Harry, we need to get you out of harm's way until this Muslim thing blows over. I want you to go on third shift."

I hit the ceiling. Sure, I was going to get shafted and go on midnights while the guys who refused to testify would still be on first shift, sleeping in their beds at night. I had been at the prison for 25 years at this point and had worked hard to build enough seniority to be able to pick the good assignments—which almost always meant working first shift from 6:20 a.m. until 2:20 p.m. Now Hoffman was asking me to piss all that away and disrupt my lifestyle.

I flat out refused.

So Hoffman said to me, "Well, then, you'll have to go into a tower."

While not as bad as the third shift, tower duty was not my cup of tea, either. First, as I found out way back in 1950, it's boring. Second, for a gregarious guy like, me it's sheer torture to be away from the ebb and flow of the life inside the prison and my fellow officers and the inmates. Hoffman was adamant, though, so I went out into three tower for a few months, hating every minute of it.

In the meantime, two investigators from the Mercer County prosecutor's office, Paul O'Gara and Kevin McGrory, were coming into the jail every night for weeks, working from around five in the evening until five the next morning—when activities and movements were at a minimum—interviewing witnesses and even shooting video footage of the crime scene. As I've said before, crimes committed inside the prison are difficult to prosecute (like the Darryl Curtis murder) because it's so hard to get inmate-witnesses to talk. They know that if they open their mouths, they're dead, so O'Gara and McGrory had a tough job.

As the investigation proceeded into 1976, someone sent the prosecutor's office a copy of a letter written by one of the Muslim inmates, Herbert X. Johnson, to his brother Barry at Annandale State Prison. In the handwritten letter, Herbert told his brother that the rival New World of Islam Muslims had planned a mass execution of Nation of Islam members and "were actually planning to kill every follower of the chief minister in this prison, so God told us to move first and that's what we did." Johnson's letter also indicated that the violence was motivated by the slaying of Minister Shabazz in 1973.

In his letter to Barry, Johnson went on, "Well in short, we tried to kill all them hypocrits but unfortunately we only killed one and more is expected to die in the hospital." He also said that it "was not a wise thing to do" when the Department of Corrections transferred the New World members out of protective custody in the Vroom Building into Trenton. Four of the wounded guys were in prison because they had been convicted of the murder of Shabazz, and Mayers was the leader of the New World in the prison.

When I read the letter in one of the local newspapers, my blood ran cold, especially when I read this: "Brother when they finish their investigation and the stool pigeons get through talking all they have to tell, I will be in lock up for God knows how long, and I'll have God knows how many charges and detainers. But praise be to Allah." And then, "Brother things just started the worst is yet to come, many people will loose their life if they are not careful." As I'm sitting in the officers' dining room at the prison reading this in the paper, I'm thinking that I'm still the only witness from the prison staff willing to testify.

While the Muslim investigation continued, Alan Hoffman was coming under a lot of fire for the job he was doing as warden. One of the big changes that had come about in the early '70s had been the establishment of an inmate furlough program. Rumors had been circulating around the jail for months about certain inmates getting favorable treatment, including ineligible inmates getting furloughs, because they had something on Hoffman. In April of '76 the *Sunday Times Advertiser* ran a story about Hoffman with the headline "The warden Ann Klein wants to dump." (Ann Klein was the commissioner of Institutions and Agencies, which had jurisdiction over the prisons.) Later, there would even be allegations by an inmate that Hoffman hired him to kill another inmate and got a furlough as a part of the deal. The inmate, Robert Darby, then escaped while he was out on the furlough.

Finally, in April, Hoffman was "kicked upstairs" and Gary Hilton, an administrator from Yardville, was brought in as the new warden. This was my chance! As soon as I could, I went into Gary's office and told him how inappropriate it was for an old veteran like me to be out in a tower. Gary was a terrific administrator, and he understood my position completely.

Gary said, "Harry, having you in a tower is a waste, but at the same time I can see why Hoffman wanted to keep you away from contact with the inmates for a while until the Muslim trial is over."

Then he told me he needed an officer for the halfway house that had been set up across Third Street from the prison in the big brick duplex that used to be the chief's and doctor's residences.

Gary said, "There's a social worker in there now, but we've been having some problems. We need an officer to help out. Would you be interested?"

I said, "Absolutely."

Then I asked him if I could get Teddy Roberts (who now had 18 years in and had minimum-custody status) to help me. Gary said he would look into it, but that it was probably OK. And that's exactly what happened.

When Teddy and I went across the street to the halfway house, it was like a dream assignment for me. My mother, Rose, was still alive and living in the old family home on Third Street, about two blocks away from the front door of the prison. The halfway house was just about a three-minute walk to her house.

The first day that Teddy and I were at the halfway house, I said to him, "Hey, Bull, let's go see Rose and get some lunch."

When I walked into Mom's house with the Bull tagging along behind, I thought she'd have a heart attack. A black man in her house! Not only black, but a convicted murderer?! I think she thought that her Harry had lost his marbles. But within a few minutes, Teddy, as rough and tough as he is, had charmed the old lady and she was falling all over the two of us, making us pasta and telling me, like she always did, "You're too skinny, Harry, *mange, mange.*"

As the year, and the behind-the scenes maneuvering in the Muslim investigation, went on, I felt a lot less apprehension about testifying, but I was still constantly watching my back on the street. Any time a car cut me off or something looked suspicious, I was on the alert. In fact, the tension built up so much that even Gary Hilton was concerned about his own family. It got to a point that for a few months in the spring of '76, Gary took me off the halfway house assignment and had me serve as an armed escort for his kids, who were attending Trinity Episcopal School on West State Street in Trenton, about three miles from the prison. Since I was still concerned for my own safety, carrying a .38 while driving Hilton's kids to and from school made me feel a little more secure.

In July of 1976, the newspapers reported the Mercer County prosecutor's office had requested that the 20 indicted inmates be split into two groups of ten for trial. Superior court judge George Schoch said, "It seems ludicrous to attempt to try ten persons in this courtroom," and split the defendants into three groups: seven, seven and six.

It was becoming apparent that his trial was going to be a security nightmare—and it was going to be expensive. Needless to say, the Mercer County freeholders (the county legislators) were not happy. Just because the prison happened to be located in their county, they felt, shouldn't make them financially responsible for trying a bunch of prisoners from North Jersey. One of the freeholders, Joe Tighue, said that the difficulty and high cost of providing adequate security should be enough to justify moving the trial to a courthouse in New Jersey with more modern security facilities. The court said this would be illegal.

"The crime was committed in Mercer County, so it has to be tried in Mercer County," the Mercer County executive told the freeholders.

By the end of the year, the two local newspapers were predicting that the trial would cost anywhere from $1 million to $ 2.5 million.

Meanwhile, Mercer County officials looked to California for guidance. The year before, six inmates at San Quentin had gone on trial in Marin County for the murder of three prison guards during an escape attempt. That 16-month trial had cost Marin County $2.3 million, partly for increased security, including sensitive metal detectors at the entrances to the courtroom to spot handguns; closed-circuit TV; a bulletproof Plexiglas shield to protect the judge, jury and spectators; and special chairs to shackle the defendants while they sat through the trial. Mercer County was seriously considering adopting all of those precautions. Other expenses would include a lot of overtime pay for hundreds of corrections officers, sheriff's officers and state police in the courtroom as well as for local police to control traffic around the courthouse.

A banner headline in one of the local newspapers read, "MUSLIM MURDER TRIAL MAY COST $2.5 MILLION." Fiscally speaking, things were not looking good for Mercer County.

Then, just as the judicial and financial picture looked bleakest, the whole thing ended with a whimper: the Muslims copped a plea.

On January 25, 1977, 15 months after the bloodbath, at 4:15 p.m. three of the Muslims were driven in a Department of Corrections van from the Vroom Building (where they had been transferred a year earlier) to the Mercer County courthouse. They conferred with their lawyers, the judge and the prosecutors and then demanded to meet with three of the other defendants. These guys were brought to the courthouse, and at seven o'clock in the evening, the six Muslims pleaded guilty, and the murder charges against the others were dropped. The freeholders breathed a sigh of relief, and everybody went back to business as usual.

Then a few weeks after the plea bargains, just as the dust seemed to have settled, one of those remarkable coincidences occurred that got the pot boiling again—and got me back on center stage. At about 12:30 a.m. on a Sunday morning, one of the guards who had been on the first floor of the school the day of the stabbings (and wasn't slated to testify at the trial) was standing outside a bar on Lamberton Street with his brother, who was also a corrections officer. Suddenly, an unknown assailant appeared, fired on both of them with a handgun, and disappeared. One of the officers was hit in the stomach and his brother took one in the jaw. That Monday, everybody in the jail was talking about the shooting of the two officers, and the immediate assumption was that this was retaliation on the part of the Muslims against the one who had been in the school on the day of the stabbings. Armed corrections officers were stationed outside both officers' hospital rooms.

Then the administration thought about it a little more and figured if the Muslims had gone after an officer who <u>wasn't</u> going to testify, what did that mean for old Harry, who <u>was</u>? The immediate response was to throw a 24-hour armed guard around our house on Centre Street. Armed Department of Corrections officers escorted our kids to school, stayed with them throughout the school day and brought them home. Our son Vance was fourteen at the time and loved all of the attention, but when my older daughter Kim's boyfriend stopped by unexpectedly one night to visit, five armed SWAT-types swarmed around him in the dark and almost gave the kid a heart attack.

Vance was a good student, and Ginny had managed through a lot of hard work and arm twisting to get him enrolled on a scholarship in a local prep school, Princeton Day School. We never could have afforded to send him there on my salary, even combined with the little extra money that came in from the flower shop. When the cops started escorting the kids and staying at school with them, we were terrified that Princeton Day would revoke the scholarship and throw Vance out. Thank God, they were understanding about it and Vance eventually finished and went on to the University of Pennsylvania.

Within a few days after the wounding of the two correction officers, the Trenton police said they were following leads that had nothing to do with the Muslim trial. I knew the two officers liked the Trenton night life and figured all along that the shootings had more to do with something that happened in or around the bar than the trial. In fact, one source told a newspaper reporter that the officers might have been shot in connection with a crap game that had been going on outside the bar that night.

Even so, the Department of Corrections didn't want to take a chance that there might be a relationship between the trial and the shootings, so they left the guard on Ginny, the kids and me for several weeks. After about a month and a half there had been no indications of any attempts on any of us, and the guard was withdrawn.

Just about the same time the two officers were shot, the other 14 Muslims went back to court for sentencing on assault and conspiracy charges. A few of them got time tacked onto their sentences, but almost unbelievably, most of the sentences handed down ran concurrent with time they were already serving. In my view, most of the perpetrators got away with no more than a slap on the wrist.

A few weeks after the sentences had been reported in the newspapers, one of the Muslims approached me, smiling. He said, "See that, Harry. That's how powerful we are. They're so afraid of us that they let us get away with murder."

I looked him in the eye and said, "I don't see it that way, X. The way I look at it, they just don't give a shit when you kill each other."

15
CHAPTER FIFTEEN

THE 7-WING SHOOT-OUT

During the several months following the Muslim uprising, the Department of Corrections and Parole, the state police and the Mercer County prosecutor's office were investigating the causes and dealing with the aftermath. At the same time, the prison administration was trying to cope with the sudden breakdown of what had been for the past several years the delicately balanced division of power among the inmate interest groups.

Prior to the Muslim attack, the administration and the two to three hundred inmates who were vocal (out of about 1,000 total inmates) and had political agendas had come to a basic understanding: "You don't make waves and keep your members in line, and we don't hassle you."

By this time, there were probably some 20 to 25 inmate groups, each with some kind of political goals, usually connected with conditions inside the prison. These groups were tolerated—and watched—within the population. Easily the biggest and most powerful had been the Muslim sects with about 200 followers among them and strong ties to the Muslims on the street. The administration informally recognized the leaders of the many groups as an unofficial leadership caucus and periodically met with them to work together on a number of issues, including meeting space, disciplinary proceedings, food, and so on.

The Muslim violence had shattered the calm and left everybody wondering who had the power among the inmate population. Immediately following the attack, the first priority of the administration was to get some inmates into protective custody and to segregate and lock down others to prevent further violence. For several weeks after the stabbings, the whole prison was locked down with inmates being served meals in their cells and allowed out only an hour each day for a shower. At the same time the administration was trying to tap their sources in the population to find out which groups were jockeying to fill the vacuum caused by the rift between the Muslim factions.

The atmosphere in prisons throughout the state was incredibly tense. The word was out that it was open season on members of the law enforcement community in New Jersey, and everybody was uptight. A few years before, somebody had fired a shotgun blast at Rahway's warden U. Samuel Vukcevich while he was sitting on his enclosed porch watching TV in his house across the street from the prison. Correction officers started carrying guns to and from work. That same kind of tension was in the air again.

By early December of 1975, the administration had put together a picture of who was planning what, and it didn't look good—the word was that several of the groups vying for power were planning to use violence to get into the driver's seat. The warden and his staff put their heads together and came up with a solution based upon a technique that had been used in Soledad Prison in California: a Management Control Unit (MCU). This was basically the same concept as 1-left lockup except that the inmates targeted for the MCU hadn't *yet* done anything violent (to get sent to 1-left, an inmate usually had to commit a violation and get sent there after a court-line hearing). The guys singled out for the MCU were viewed as potential troublemakers or political leaders who needed to be segregated to keep them from influencing the rest of the population. This was a new, and controversial, concept in New Jersey.

Since virtually every inmate at Trenton had been sentenced to at least 20 years for a crime involving some degree of violence, concentrating these street and prison-hardened inmate leaders in one section of a wing to keep an eye on them and keeping them locked in their cells twenty-three hours a day seemed to make sense. The administration reviewed all of the housing wings and settled on a section of seven-wing to be designated as the MCU.

Seven-wing is a five-story, ten-tier brick building constructed in 1905-1907, making it the "newest" housing unit in the prison. When it was built, its outer wall became the outside wall of that section of the prison complex, the only housing unit where this is the case; its windows looked directly out onto Third Street with no yard or twenty-foot wall in between. In retrospect, putting these hardened convicts so close to the street probably didn't make much sense, but inside, 7-wing was a pretty secure unit, so it seemed like a reasonable move at the time.

The interior of 7-wing looks like the typical cell block of any older American prison that everyone has seen in movies and on TV. The barred cell doors are controlled by levers at the end of each tier. By dropping pins into numbered slots, one officer can open and close individual cells or all of them at once. In the event of trouble, the tier officer can seal off the cells just by throwing the lever, though it isn't easy—it takes some real effort to move that lever to close all of the doors simultaneously. When I was wing officer in there, I had to hold the lever with both hands, lock my arms and jump up slightly to bring all my weight down onto it to throw all of the doors closed at once (and they make a hell of a racket as all that metal slides along a track and then hits and engages the big lock on the metal door jamb). The wing officer also carries a large metal ring with a number of keys on it, one of which is a master key to open individual cell doors.

What made 7-wing different from the other housing units was the heavy steel mesh that screened in each of the tiers to prevent inmates from throwing things like garbage cans—or each other—down onto officers below. Unlike tiers in other wings, each 7-wing tier was an enclosed cage with a barred door at either end. Theoretically, if the wing officer is walking a tier and has a problem, he can run to the end of the tier, unlock the door, jump through, and slam it behind him, isolating the inmates on that tier even though they're out of their cells. Each of 7-wing's five tiers of 34 cells (except the flats) is enclosed in this mesh "cocoon."

Given all of that security, it made perfect sense to put "the baddest of the bad" in seven-wing. But, what the administration couldn't predict nor plan for was the ingenuity of a couple of those "political prisoners" in coming up with a fantastic escape plan that turned violent and deadly.

In December of '75, I had had the confrontation with Hoffman and was out in 3-tower on first shift, so when all of this action kicked off, I wasn't in the jail. A good friend of mine, though, CO Vernon Stockton, was in 7-wing that night, and he filled me in on the details.

To understand what happened in 7-wing on the night of January 19, 1976, we have to go back to the early-morning hours of May 2, 1973 on the New Jersey Turnpike. A little after midnight, a 30-year-old New Jersey State Trooper named James Harper called in to the dispatcher at Troop D headquarters in New Brunswick, reporting that he was following and planning to stop a 1965 white Pontiac with Vermont license plates and faulty tail lights. He also said that the car was slightly exceeding the speed limit. The trooper, traveling in the southbound lane, had just passed Exit 9 of the turnpike, within sight of the Troop D headquarters building that sits at the top of a slope, overlooking the roadway.

Suddenly Harper said, "Hold on—two black males, one female," and, following state police procedures, he called for backup.

When trooper Werner Foerster arrived on the scene a couple of minutes later, both officers got out of their cars and approached the 1965 Pontiac LeMans. Harper noticed a discrepancy in the vehicle registration and asked the driver to get out of the car. While Foerster was questioning the driver at the rear of the vehicle, the two other occupants of the car suddenly opened fire with automatic handguns, hitting Foerster in the chest and head and Harper in the shoulder. Before Foerster went down, he managed to draw his weapon and fire four times into the car. Harper, in shock from being hit, started to crawl up the embankment to Troop D headquarters, about 200 yards away, to get help while Foerster was dying on the shoulder of the road.

The driver jumped back into the car and took off down the turnpike as the state police radio alerted three patrol cars in the southbound lanes above New Brunswick and toll booths to the south. The three suspects pulled over and stopped their car on the shoulder of the road about five miles down the Turnpike, probably to try to tend to the wounds they sustained in the shootout. Trooper Robert Palentchar, the first officer to arrive on the scene, spotted the car and saw one of the male suspects standing about fifty yards away in a field. As Palentchar jumped out of his car and ordered the man to halt, the suspect ran off into a wooded area; Palentchar emptied his gun at the man, but wasn't sure whether he had hit him.

As he was reloading his pistol, Palentchar saw Joanne Chesimard walking toward him from 50 feet away, her bloody arms raised in surrender. Palentchar then found the body of James Costan, also known as Zayd Malik Shakur, in a gully along the shoulder of the road where he had fallen and died as a result of wounds from the shots fired by Foerster back at Exit 9.

Chesimard was taken into custody and transported back to Middlesex County

General Hospital in New Brunswick where Foerster had earlier been pronounced dead and where Harper was being treated for his wound. Chesimard was suffering from gunshot wounds in the left shoulder and both arms.

At the time of the turnpike shoot-out, police in the New York-New Jersey-Pennsylvania corridor had been searching for two years for members of the Black Liberation Army, especially Joanne Chesimard, to question them about a number of violent crimes. The BLA had been linked by law enforcement officials to bank robberies and ambushes of police patrols in Philadelphia, Atlanta, St. Louis and North Carolina over a period of about four years. Chesimard, who had been tagged "the soul of the Black Liberation Army" by law enforcement officials, was being sought for suspected involvement in at least six major crimes.

Police traced the origins of the BLA to a militant band of Black Panthers who, in the spring of 1971, had broken with the Panther leadership of Huey Newton in California and allied themselves with Eldridge Cleaver, then in Algiers. The new group coalesced around Richard Moore and began living more or less collectively at a two-story house in the Bronx. According to law-enforcement authorities, they also went on a three-year rampage of bank robberies and murders of police officers in the New York City area.

In the first of the attacks on police, in May of '71, the BLA shot and seriously wounded two New York City police officers outside the Manhattan District Attorney's home on Riverside Drive. A note sent to newspapers said the shooting was done by "the righteous brothers of the Black Liberation Army." When Richard Moore was arrested for involvement in the shootings and sent to jail, Chesimard took over the leadership of the BLA. A couple of days after the attack on the DA's house, two NYPD officers, Waverly Jones and Joseph Piagentini, were ambushed and killed. Six members of the BLA were arrested and after a hung jury in the first trial, three of them were convicted of the murders in a second trial.

Even though these killings happened outside of New Jersey, we were fully aware of them because they were nearby and because black militancy was becoming a big issue inside the walls. A lot of black inmates identified with organizations like the Panthers and the BLA, and some claimed to be members (not likely). Instead of being just an armed robber or a rapist, it was now fashionable to be a revolutionary and a political prisoner. So the activities of the BLA in New York City were followed closely by our inmates, and we heard about their exploits constantly in a derisive way: "Hey, Harry, did you hear about the pigs who were offed in the City yesterday by the BLA?"

It was the prison version of black pride.

After the two cops were killed, the police think that Chesimard was then directly involved in two BLA bank robberies—one in Queens in August of 1971 and one in the Bronx in September. She was also wanted for attempted murder of two NYC police officers when she and a companion allegedly threw a hand grenade at a police car pursuing them through Maspeth, Queens, in December of '71. The grenade exploded and demolished the car, but the two officers inside were not seriously injured.

Chesimard was also wanted for questioning about the ambush murders of two more NYPD officers, Gregory Foster and Rocco Laurie, who were shot and killed on the Lower East Side in January of 1972. In January of 1973, four patrolmen were wounded in two ambushes of police cars in Brooklyn and in Queens, and Chesimard and five other members of the BLA were being sought for that crime. You could almost hear a lot of our inmates cheering every time these crimes hit the front page.

So with a BLA track record like that, when Harper pulled over that 1965 LeMans, he was dealing with three of the most dangerous people in America: Joanne Chesimard, James Costan (Shakur) and Clark Squire.

After the turnpike shoot-out, while Chesimard was being treated and questioned at Middlesex General (now Robert Wood Johnson) Hospital, Squire was on the run in the East Brunswick area surrounding the turnpike. For 36 hours 400 law-enforcement officers searched for Squire after he got away from Trooper Palentchar.

At about 3:15 p.m. the day after the shoot-out on the turnpike, a couple of East Brunswick patrolmen spotted someone wearing a light tan safari jacket and fitting Squire's description walking along some railroad tracks. When the suspect disappeared, a helicopter was called in and Squire was again sighted. An hour after he was first seen by the officers, Clark Edward Squire, 36 years old, surrendered. He was soaked from off-and-on rain showers, had no shoes and was obviously weak.

All he said was, "I give up, man."

Squire was convicted of being the trigger man in the death of Trooper Foerster and was sentenced to life plus 25 to 30 years (there was no death penalty in effect). He came into Trenton State Prison in 1974, and from the time he arrived, the administration was concerned that the BLA, with their history in New York, would try something spectacular to get him out. Chesimard had been remanded back to New York to stand trial in federal court on the bank robberies, so her trial had been split off from Squires'. She had gotten pregnant while on trial for the bank holdups with Fred Hilton (both were acquitted), so she was still on Riker's Island waiting to be returned to New Jersey for trial in Middlesex County in the Foerster killing when Squire came into Trenton.

To our black inmates, Squire was a hero and a celebrity, and a fair number of them started identifying themselves as BLA members. Rumors circulated constantly around the prison about how the BLA members in New York and Newark were going to get Squire out of Trenton and Chesimard out of the Middlesex County jail.

Late in 1974, our administrators were given information about an elaborate plan to free Squire. BLA members on the outside were supposed to use high explosives to blow open the front doors to the prison while members inside would use smuggled-in guns to blast their way down through center and out into the lobby. In the meantime, according to the plan, 1-tower across from the front entrance to the prison and other towers with a field of fire on the front door were supposed to be either blown up or placed under automatic weapons fire. The plot sounded utterly fantastic and unworkable, especially since the inmates would have to breach the locked door on the wire mesh surrounding the seven-wing tiers, travel 150 yards down stairs and through corridors, all the while exposed to gunfire from officers, and get through four more locked gates, including the two well-covered grille gate doors, before getting out into the lobby. But, because of the grenade attack on the police car in Queens and the murders of the police officers in New York, the administration couldn't afford to take the plot too lightly. So, security was beefed up, including putting an officer with a Thompson submachine gun and a pistol in the warden's office near the front door during second and third shifts to cover the last twenty feet of lobby between the grille gate and the front entrance.

Periodically over the next year, while Chesimard was awaiting transfer to New Jersey for trial in the Foerster killing, rumors would circulate through the prison about another BLA plot. Then, on Monday evening, January 19, 1976, just after 8 p.m., the rumors became fact.

Joe Macaluso was a relatively new, young (22) officer on the second shift. That night he was walking down the catwalk in front of the MCU cells on tier 5, the topmost block of cells, in 7-wing on his way to get John Clark for his daily shower.

John Clark was an interesting character. He was 30 years old and had been convicted of killing a bartender in Newark. When he first came into the prison, he was just another violent armed robber. While he was in Trenton, Clark started reading a lot and developing a political philosophy. Apparently, he had not been a member of the Black Liberation Army on the outside, but while he was in prison, he was constantly reading books about leftist/Marxist interpretations of history, economics and warfare. He talked frequently about the white man's repression of blacks and described himself as a political prisoner and a revolutionary. It's likely that John Clark had been recruited into the Black Liberation Army in the prison, probably by Clark Squire.

When Clark and The Mole Dovan dug the tunnel back in '74, everybody who knew the two of them commented about how strange it was those two would get together since each hated the other's race. One theory about why they clicked as partners was they both viewed themselves as political prisoners being held by a repressive government.

As Macaluso opened Clark's cell, Clark stuck a .25 caliber pistol in Macaluso's belly and pulled the trigger, shooting him without warning at point-blank range. Macaluso staggered back against the wire mesh enclosing the tier, and Clark rushed him, grabbing at Macaluso's key ring. Just as Clark succeeded in wresting the key ring from him, Macaluso recovered his balance and took off running toward the open door in the mesh enclosure down at the end of the tier. Vernon Stockton said apparently Clark was so startled that the shot hadn't killed Macaluso that he let the officer get a several-yard head start down the catwalk before he went after him.

Some of the other officers who were there that night speculated later that since Clark had Macaluso's keys, he might have stopped chasing Macaluso at the end of the tier to throw the lever to release the other cell doors on the tier. We also don't know why he didn't shoot Macaluso again, but the most likely explanation is that when Macaluso took off running, Clark, taken by surprise, hesitated and then chased Macaluso, planning to tackle him and take him hostage. Whatever his reasons, Clark's hesitation turned out to be a fatal mistake because it gave Macaluso enough time to get down to the next level and hit the riot button, alerting central control . . . and Captain Simmons.

Glenn Simmons was 39 years old at the time, a tough, single ex-marine whose whole life was corrections and the prison. He had worked his way up to chief of security, making him the second most powerful administrator in the jail. He was such a strict disciplinarian that almost all of the inmates either hated him or were afraid of him—or both. After the Muslim uprising, Simmons had orchestrated the segregation and transfer of the various Muslim inmates, and all of them wanted to see him dead. Because of his personality, he didn't have many friends among the officers either, but everybody knew that if something serious went down, they wanted Simmons to be in charge of the operation.

Back on the tier Stockton said he first heard there was trouble in the wing when an inmate runner, Leroy "Duke" Snyder, came sprinting down the steps from 7-up yelling, "They crazy, man! They got guns up there, they got guns up there!"

After hitting the riot button, Macaluso, wounded and bleeding, sagged into the arms of another officer, CO Nate Manning. Manning was helping Macaluso down the steps to ground level to get medical help as the alarm went in to center. The second-shift officer in charge of center that night was Lieutenant Fran Menschner. Sensing that this was a serious disturbance but not yet knowing that a gun was involved, Menschner and another officer grabbed batons and headed into 7-wing. Stockton met them and said, "They've got guns. Macaluso's been shot."

Menschner headed back toward center to draw guns out of the armory and to alert Simmons, who was spending a lot of time in the prison because of all of the rumors of impending violence. Stockton and CO Leonard Camiso headed back toward 7-up. At the foot of the stairs leading up to the top tier, Stockton got hit in the chest with a pineapple type grenade that either fell or was tossed from above. The device rolled under some desks and went off, burning Camiso. It's likely that the grenade was either a homemade bomb or a phosphorus grenade since it didn't send shrapnel all over the area—it exploded and moved the desks, but it didn't put a hole in the floor.

Menschner alerted Captain Simmons, who grabbed a Thompson submachine gun from the armory just to the rear of center and headed toward the wing with another officer, Wilson, who had drawn a shotgun.

Just as Simmons got to the top of the stairs of the uppermost tier and was assessing the situation, Clark fired and hit him in the side, the bullet lodging near Simmons' spine. As Simmons' knees buckled, he fired a burst from the Thompson; then it jammed. Before Clark could fire again, Wilson stepped around the falling Simmons and fired the shotgun at Clark, hitting him in the chest at close range with at least one charge of double ought buckshot. Clark went down, fatally wounded. Another inmate, a runner named John "Gunner" Douglas, was apparently hit by a ricochet and knocked out when Simmons fired the burst from the Thompson. Douglas was lying in a pool of blood near Clark.

Other officers who had come running up to the tier behind Simmons pulled the wounded chief down the stairs out of the line of fire as Wilson covered them and backed down the stairs.

For a while it looked like a battleground high up there on the tier, five stories from the ground. This was obviously no spontaneous uprising over some grievance; it was a well-planned revolt, and nobody knew how many inmates were involved. It looked at the time like the inmates, led by John Clark, had armed themselves with a cache of weapons. Since Clark Squire locked down at the end of this tier and John Clark had been identifying himself as a black revolutionary, everybody assumed this was the beginning of the long-rumored BLA breakout attempt. Two officers were down, including the chief, and nobody had any idea how many weapons, or what kind, were in the jail.

What exactly happened over the next few hours is still not known. The inmates that Clark had released from their cells, including Clark Squire, were out on the tier, but it isn't clear how many of them, if any, were armed besides John Clark. What is known is that prison officials believed that several of the inmates in the MCU were armed with hand guns and were reported to be firing at officers responding to the riot bell. It also appeared that they were shooting out of the windows down into Third Street in the front of the prison.

With the wounded Simmons and Camiso pulled to safety and Macaluso's stomach wound being tended to out of the line of fire, all prison personnel were accounted for—no hostages. The administration believed there was a group of armed inmates in control of the tier. About twenty second-shift officers armed with riot guns and Thompsons were clustered around the stairs at either end of the tier, waiting.

An alarm went out from central control shortly after 8 p.m. to the Trenton police and the state police, but it was originally broadcast as a "small disturbance" at the prison. When the city police pulled up in front of the complex, they were greeted by the sight of shot-out windows and the sound of gunfire coming from seven-wing. As the police jumped out of their cars, they could hear the thud of bullets hitting the ground across from the front of the prison near 1-tower. State police cars were also converging on the prison as the seriousness of the disturbance began to become apparent through the police radio transmissions. Squads of both city and state police fanned out among the surrounding neighborhoods, telling residents to turn off their lights and to stay away from windows.

Within a half an hour, by about 8:30, the situation had settled into a stalemate; two groups of heavily armed corrections officers, supplemented by state police, were stationed on and around the foot of the stairs leading to either end of the top tier of seven wing, and the inmates were huddled in their cells. Some officers said that inmates were reaching around out of their cells and "popping" at them with hand guns, but this was never confirmed. Macaluso, Simmons and Camiso had been taken out and rushed to St. Francis Hospital. John Clark's body lay in a pool of blood and the unconscious John Douglas was nearby, also lying in a pool of blood. Finally, invoking his position as an inmate leader, Theodore Gibson said he would go in and get Douglas out. Prison officials gave their OK and Douglas was carried out by Gibson and rushed to St. Francis. About 9 p.m. a .25-caliber semiautomatic handgun was kicked down the concrete floor toward one end of the cell block. Sporadic firing continued over the next several hours, but it was unclear who was doing the shooting.

As the standoff continued, an antique red Trenton Fire Department hose truck that had been converted to a searchlight platform was driven down the roadbed of a railroad track about 100 yards across Third Street from the front of the prison. At the same time, a Trenton cop suddenly bolted out from the cover of the alcove at the front entrance of the prison where he and a couple of other police officers had been huddled for warmth and protection, raised his shotgun and blew out three of the street lights across the street from the jail.

About forty yards from the lights being shot out, five TPD vehicles were grouped in the parking lot directly across from seven-wing, with eight or nine Trenton police officers taking cover behind them. Someone on the fire truck gave the order to switch on the searchlights, and the officers in the parking lot suddenly found themselves and their vehicles brightly silhouetted from behind by the powerful lights, making them perfect targets for the inmates inside. They yelled at the cops manning the truck to cut the lights, but after a few minutes when nothing happened, they shot the lights out. It was widely reported that the inmates firing from seven-wing had taken out the lights on the fire truck, but Lieutenant Frank Capasso of the Trenton police later told a reporter that he had ordered the lights shot out.

The shooting continued sporadically until about 1 a.m., and when it seemed as if the last shots had been fired, corrections officers in full riot gear and state police in flak jackets set up a searchlight at the end of the tier. Using a bullhorn, the officers ordered the men in the cells to strip and to come out onto the catwalk, get down on all fours and crawl toward the searchlight. Two state police marksmen kept M16 rifles trained on the inmates as they crawled to the end of the tier where their hands were checked for gunpowder residue. Then they were handcuffed and hustled down to empty cells on the tiers below. The last one out, from cell 29, was Clark Squire. He surrendered without resistance and was taken down to the first floor with the rest of the inmates.

When John Clark's body was taken off the tier, officers found a note in his pocket that said, "Truck waiting on Furman Street." State police had no trouble finding the 1972 Ford van parked several blocks from the prison on Furman. Armed with a search warrant, they opened the getaway vehicle and found several fully loaded handguns, loaded shotguns, including one sawed-off shotgun, a large quantity of ammunition for the weapons, food, blankets, a first aid kit, 10 gallons of gasoline, false identification papers, and clothing.

By 7 in the morning of Jan. 20, the last of the inmates had been moved down and locked into the cells in the flats. Later in the morning, when John Clark's cell was searched, prison officers, investigators from the Mercer County prosecutor's office, and state police detectives found three dozen new hacksaw blades, a 12-foot rope fashioned out of strips of blanket and the makings for several incendiary devices. Over the next several days corrections officers scoured seven-wing looking for the other weapons. Not finding any, they theorized the other handguns were broken down and stuffed down toilets (this was commonly done with shanks after a stabbing or during a shakedown of cells). The other weapons were never found even though officers went into the utility space between the backs of the cells on the tiers in seven-wing and broke open waste pipes there and down below the wing.

In the weeks following the shootout, the official story was pieced together as follows: Somehow, up to three or four handguns were smuggled into the prison in one of three ways—brought in during contact visits by relatives and friends of the BLA members and sympathizers in the prison (doubtful, given the care usually exercised when searching visitors from the outside); hidden in a TV or some other appliance sent in through the prison mail room (also doubtful since all appliances must come from the retailer in a sealed carton and are usually searched carefully); brought in by a lawyer, a volunteer worker or an employee (most likely, especially since in 1973 a .38-caliber pistol had been smuggled in by a civilian cook who had been paid $1,000 and since these people are generally not searched that thoroughly).

The next piece of the theory was that John Clark, Clark Squire and other BLA members in the MCU were going to shoot their way out of seven-wing, taking guards as hostages and either blast their way through center, out into the lobby of the prison and out the front door or out into a yard and over a wall. The next step was to get to the van parked on Furman Street and then to parts unknown. Unfortunately for John Clark, the theory goes, he—for some unknown reason—chose to start the escape attempt during second shift rather than third when there would be fewer officers in the jail. In another piece of bad luck for Clark and Squire, Chief Simmons happened to be in center that night and responded quickly and courageously. The most significant piece of the foul-up on the part of the inmates was Clark's letting the wounded Macaluso get off the tier and make it to the riot button downstairs. If Clark had managed to take Macaluso hostage and get the rest of his comrades out of their cells, the whole incident might have had a very different outcome—probably a lot bloodier.

I've never been comfortable with the official version. I do believe that it was an attempt to get Squire out and that John Clark was an unwitting dupe of the BLA, but I don't believe that more than one gun was in the prison that night. I think that most of the gunfire the Trenton police heard out there was coming from us, shooting at what we believed was a much larger armed force than was really there. I believe that once that .25-caliber pistol got kicked down the tier floor, the rebellion was over and the escape attempt, along with John Clark, was dead.

As a footnote to this piece of the history of Trenton State Prison, Joanne Chesimard was returned to the Middlesex County jail in 1977. She was tried and convicted for the Foerster murder and sent to the Clinton Reformatory for Women about forty miles north of Trenton. Then in November of 1979 she escaped and is currently living openly in Cuba. Clark Squire was transferred to a federal prison several months after the escape attempt and as far as I know is still locked up. Since Squire was taken out of circulation and Chesimard escaped to Cuba, no more police cars have been blown up in Queens and no more NYPD officers ambushed and killed, so it looks like the Black Liberation Army is a closed chapter of American history.

Courtesy of the Trentoniana: Local History and Genealogy Collection, Trenton Public Library

Aerial photo of the old prison complex taken from the south, 1970's.
Seven-wing is in the upper right-hand corner.

16
CHAPTER SIXTEEN

THE BIONIC BANDIT

Mario DeLucia went over the wall in the 1950's; Bill Van Scoten went over in the 1960's; now it was the 1970's . . . . Fifteen years after Bill Van Scoten's 1961 escape, Terry Alden got out and over the wall in August of 1976. Terry, like most cons, figured he was smarter than the guys who had gone before, and he could do what DeLucia and Van Scoten had done but not get caught. He would be the 15th inmate to get out since the beginning of the century.

Alden was convicted of felony murder in 1974. When his appeal was denied and he was faced with 25 years in Trenton, he engineered a spectacular escape out of 6-wing and over the wall.

Alden was from Keansburg on the Jersey shore. For some reason, for a town that small, Keansburg seemed to send a lot of convicts to Trenton. Alden had a wife and son and a steady job as a carpenter. He was well-known in the shore area as a talented athlete.

I liked Terry Alden—most people who met him did. He was tall—six feet—well-built, athletic, soft-spoken and intelligent. He was the type of guy other guys are jealous of . . . the good-looking guy who walks into a bar and every woman in the joint, including your girlfriend, turns to look at. He walked like a cat, or a jock, and with his blue eyes and 200-pound muscular frame and good looks, it seemed like he could have his pick of the women he would be likely to run with. That's why I could never figure out how he managed to get charged with assault with attempt to rape before he did the armed robbery that brought him into the prison.

While he was on probation for the attempted rape charge, Alden was involved in a holdup that went wrong in Middletown Township, not far from Keansburg. In June of 1973, Alden and a friend of his, Leroy Fix, were in the Two Guys store on Route 35 in Middletown buying canoe paddles when they saw an armored truck pull into the parking lot to pick up the day's receipts. Fix said that Alden told him if they wanted to rob the armored truck, "it could be done."

A couple of weeks later, Fix, Alden and another friend, John Nelson, were having a few beers in the Shamrock Bar across the street from Alden's apartment in Keansburg. The three of them talked about the feasibility of robbing the armored truck.

The following Friday night, Fix spent the night at Alden's apartment. The next morning, while Fix and Alden were watching Saturday-morning cartoons on TV, Nelson came in. Fix said that he thought Nelson was "sick on drugs." The three of them talked again about sticking up the truck. According to Fix, Nelson said, "I'm ready to rob anything. I need money for drugs."

Alden, Fix and Nelson went across the street to the Shamrock, drank beer, and worked out the details of the plan. By three o'clock in the afternoon, they were ready to roll.

Alden and Nelson dropped Fix off at the Foodtown market in Port Monmouth a couple of miles away from the Two Guys shopping center. Nelson wrote down the number of the pay phone outside the market, and he and Alden drove off. An hour later, the phone rang. Fix picked it up and a voice said, "Call." Fix dialed the Middletown police, told them a bomb was about to go off behind the Foodtown market, hung up and walked away from the area.

Nelson's girlfriend, who was an assistant manager at Two Guys, said Nelson came into the store a short time before the robbery and told her that he and Alden were out in the parking lot, "waiting for a truck." She cut him short and said she didn't want to hear any more about it.

Around 4:30 the armored truck arrived to pick up the day's receipts. As the driver walked out of the store, he was ambushed and shot six times by a gunman wearing a ski mask and a poncho with the hood up. The bandit then yanked open the passenger-side door and yelled at the other guard, "Don't move or I'll blow your head off."

Before the guard, Alfred Johnson, could react, he said he heard "Pop! Pop!" and felt a sensation in his stomach. The bandit reached behind the seat and grabbed a couple of money bags. Then he shot Johnson one more time and took off running as people in the parking lot ducked for cover.

Inside the store, Roger Moldenhoff was shopping with his four children when he heard the shots. He said people came running in from the parking lot yelling, "He's got a gun!"

Moldenhoff looked outside and saw a 6-foot man wearing a green poncho and red ski mask fire several shots from a handgun into the cab of the armored truck and then run away. Moldenhoff said the shooter appeared to have a "heavy Afro" protruding from under the hood of the poncho.

Donald Ross was crossing the Two Guys parking lot with his little girl when he heard what he thought were the sounds of balloons popping. As Ross was putting his daughter into his car, the robber sprinted by. Ross started his car and followed the bandit around one end of Two Guys toward the rear parking lot of a Howard Johnson motor lodge behind Two Guys. Ross said the gunman dropped an empty money bag and a red mask as he loped around the corner of the store. Ross stopped his car, jumped out and tried to get to a pay phone to call police as he watched the getaway car shoot out of the parking lot, run a red light, and head north on Route 35.

When the two men in the car ran the red light, they just missed colliding with a car driven by an off-duty Middletown Township cop, Steven Xanthos, who recognized Nelson behind the wheel. Xanthos knew Nelson because of Nelson's prior record of arrests in the township. Xanthos couldn't identify the passenger, noting only that the man had a "frizzy sort of Afro style" haircut.

Back in the parking lot, as bystanders and witnesses lifted the wounded Johnson out of the truck, a doctor passed by. The doctor took one look at the driver lying on his back on the ground and shook his head, indicating that 51-year-old Richard Huizenga was already dead. Then the doctor tended to Johnson, who was shot in the stomach, hip and shoulder but survived after being rushed to Riverview Hospital in Red Bank. When police arrived, they found the unopened money bags in the parking lot. The bandit had killed one guard, badly wounded the other, and stolen three empty bags.

Nelson and Fix were arrested the day after the botched robbery. That night, a Middletown Township detective spotted Terry Alden in the Shamrock, but Terry hadn't yet been connected to the robbery. By the next day, he was a suspect, and an all-points bulletin went out for Terry Alden. When police searched Alden's apartment, they found a .45 caliber pistol and shell casings with markings that matched spent cartridges found in the Two Guys parking lot. They had also found a Colt .357-caliber Python revolver alongside Route 35 shortly after the robbery

Alden managed to evade capture and get out of New Jersey. He stayed on the lam for five months, making it onto the FBI's 10-most-wanted list. While he was on the run, Alden worked as a circus roustabout in the Midwest, climbing poles and rigging tents. Finally, in November of 1973, Terry was captured by the FBI in Indianapolis. One of the agents told reporters that when they confronted Alden, he took off, leading them on a high-speed foot chase, vaulting over fences and leaping over garbage cans and other obstacles.

"When they caught him, he wasn't even breathing hard," Alden's lawyer said. "He looked like Bruce Jenner." (Jenner was a track and field champion who would go on to win the decathlon in the 1976 Olympics in Montreal).

Who actually pulled the trigger in the parking lot that day was never determined. Several witnesses said they saw only one man in a ski mask fire the shots into the truck and then run away with the money bags. Two young women shopping in the store picked Nelson, who had long, brown hair, out of a lineup as the gunman. Other eyewitnesses said the shooter had a "heavy Afro" (at the time, Terry Alden wore his hair in a "white man's Afro"). Another witness said the bandit was built like and moved like an athlete.

When Nelson went on trial in October of 1973, he took the stand and fingered Terry Alden as the shooter. He claimed Alden told him they were going to the shopping plaza to get some pot and maybe rip off the dealer. That's why they had guns with them. He said he had no idea Terry was planning to hold up an armored car. Nelson said he was sitting in the car when Alden ran up and said, "Jesus Christ! I just shot two guys, and all I got was three empty bags."

Under New Jersey law it doesn't really matter who pulls the trigger if someone gets killed during an armed robbery; everybody involved is guilty of murder. The jury took only 2 1/2 hours to bring back a guilty verdict against Nelson, and he was sentenced to life.

When Alden went on trial, his lawyers pointed the finger at Nelson, who was already in Trenton, as the triggerman. That jury took 20 1/2 hours to come to a decision, but the outcome was the same: guilty, life sentence.

Terry Alden came into Trenton in the spring of 1974 at the age of 24. Because of his background in the building trades, the PCC (prison classification committee) first assigned him to the repair shop where he got to know the other inmates on the repair crews. He also got to know what tools were available and where they were kept. After a few months Alden requested a transfer to the law library, partly because he was working on an appeal of his conviction. PCC granted the request.

Whenever I would see Terry, he was either on his way to the yard to lift weights and run or to the library to work, study law and draft the appeal. When the appeal was rejected in November of '75 and he was looking at 25 years before parole eligibility, Alden started planning his escape.

(After Alden was recaptured and sentenced to Leavenworth federal pen, he was interviewed for a book by Pete Earley, *The Hot House*. A few of the details here come directly from Terry through the interview with Earley. The rest we know from the investigation by the prison staff.)

Alden locked on the second tier of 6-wing, the same cell block that Mario DeLucia had gone out of, so his escape would start the same way Mario's had—through the toilet. Like everybody else in Trenton, Terry had heard the story of Mario's escape; it was part of the folklore of the prison. Alden figured if Mario could do it, he could do it too, but there was one important difference: Mario was a tiny guy—maybe five foot, five and120 pounds soaking wet. That's how he was able to fit through the opening in the back wall of the cell and get into the utility space after he unbolted the toilet. Terry was six feet tall and weighed over 200. He would have to shrink by about 40 percent to go out the way Mario did, but, hey, looking at 25 years in Trenton makes almost anything seem like it's worth a shot.

After his appeal was turned down, Alden sat on his bunk on the second tier and studied that toilet and back wall. He knew that Mario had spent years slowly, quietly working the bolts that held the toilet in place; Terry was 25 years old and didn't have that kind of time to waste. With his mechanical skills, he knew he could get the toilet off the wall, but he also knew, being nearly twice the size of Mario, there was no way he could fit through an opening that small. There had to be another way. Then Terry noticed the ten-by-twenty-inch metal plate next to the toilet that the pipes ran through. There was the answer. Even with an opening that big, it would be a tough fit, but . . . .

Alden knew if he had the right tools he could get through the welds around the plate, but it would be noisy. And he'd have to take a big risk. He'd have to let somebody else in on the plan—usually the kiss of death for any escape attempt. As soon as another con gets a piece of information like that, it becomes a valuable commodity that can be traded for a lot of things, including a transfer to a minimum-security facility or an early release.

Terry had no choice but to take the chance. One morning in the late spring of '76, when he went out into "Big Dusty," the main prison yard, for his daily exercise, Terry arranged a deal with one of his buddies who worked in the repair shop—a bag of marijuana for a hammer and chisel. It took a while but Terry finally got the tools and a piece of scrap wood. He tapped a sliver of the wood into the lock on his cell door and broke it off, jamming the lock open.

The wing officer notified center about the broken lock, and the repair shop sent over the same inmate who had stolen the tools for Terry. The other inmate had to chisel the bolts off the broken lock to replace it; another bag of marijuana, another favor—take your time getting the lock off. While the inmate from the repair shop hammered at the bolts, Terry worked on the welds around the plate. Every time the guy from the shop hit the lock, Terry hit the weld. When the lock came off the door, the plate came off the wall.

Terry had bought some sticky candy in the inmate store and after chewing it to form a putty, he put the plate back in place. He smeared the candy mixture on the welds and using some silver paint, also stolen from the repair shop, he covered the gaps in the welds in case any guard took a close look at the plate.

After Terry established that he could get the plate on and off and get access to the utility space, he started going out into the big yard and running on the worn path around the perimeter of the ball field and the handball courts. He also went on a crash diet of sardines, crackers and oranges. He was losing about three or four pounds a week, and every few weeks he would take the plate off late at night to see if he could squeeze through the opening. Finally, when he had lost about thirty pounds, he was able, with a lot of effort, to force his shoulders through and reach into the utility space, grab a pipe, and pull himself into the space between the back walls of the cells.

The first time he pulled himself into the utility area, Terry struck a match and looked around. (After Terry's escape, doors with portholes at the ends of each tier and lights left on twenty-four/seven were installed in the utility space.) Mario had been small and agile like a monkey. Terry was bigger and stronger and had the experience of climbing up tent poles and working with one hand while he held on to the pole with the other. He had also worked for his father in the TV antenna business when he was a kid, so he was used to heights. Terry found a five-inch toilet waste pipe that ran up to the top of the cell block and used it to shinny up near the louvered ventilation openings in the roof.

Mario's escape made Terry's a lot more difficult. When Mario had gone out, a catwalk under the vents had given him a platform to stand on while he sawed through the single set of bars covering the inside of the vent opening. Maintenance workers had removed the catwalk and replaced the original bars with new ones an inch-thick and with stronger welds. Then, they had come down a few feet and run another set of bars from side to side between the backs of the cells on the uppermost tier. And, to really make sure nobody could follow in Mario's footsteps, they had rerouted the pipes coming out of the backs of the cells on the top tier so there was nothing to stand on . . . nothing between that lower set of bars and a 70-foot drop to a concrete floor at the bottom of the utility space, maybe bouncing off some water pipes on the way down. Terry was stymied. He climbed back down and squeezed through the hole into his cell.

Alden went back to his buddy in the maintenance shop who had covered for him while he was chiseling through the weld and traded more marijuana for some hacksaw blades. That night he climbed back up to the new set of bars between the back walls of the cells and, going hand over hand, swung out until he was directly under the vent. Terry held on with one hand, dangling seven stories above that concrete floor, and tried with the other hand to cut through one of the bars. Impossible. He climbed back down and squeezed into his cell.

With nothing to stand on up under those bars, Alden had to figure out some way to support himself while he cut. One day while he was doing some typing in the law library, he had to free a jammed ribbon. While he was working on freeing the ribbon, he had a sudden inspiration from his circus roustabout days: the roller in the typewriter was about the size of a trapeze bar. Bingo! If he could steal the roller (no problem) and suspend it from the bars under the vent, he'd have a perch to sit on while he sawed. Still working on the jammed ribbon, Terry made another important discovery: those ribbons were incredibly strong, impossible to break by pulling on them. He stole the roller and started stashing away typewriter ribbons.

As Alden walked through the jail later that day, he kept his eyes open for something to use to suspend the typewriter roller from the bars. When he got back to 6-wing, he spotted a Gurney parked against a wall with inch-wide canvas straps dangling from one side. Problem # 2 solved. When he got back to his cell with the belt, he sewed a loop in each end. That night, he stuck the canvas belt and the roller into the waistband of his pants and made the climb up to top of the utility space. He threaded the belt over a couple of the bars, slid the roller through the loops and secured the ends so they couldn't pull out. Straddling the roller, he steadied himself with one hand and sawed with the other.

Alden allotted himself half an hour each night to work on the bars to lessen the chance of being discovered out of his cell during random bed checks. Like all the other inmates, Terry hung a blanket on the inside of the barred door of his cell, but he knew the third-shift cops routinely pushed the blanket aside with their flashlights as they made their rounds. No sense in tempting fate.

Terry needed to cut through only one of the bars in the lower set to open enough space to slide through. After a week of work, he was through the first set of bars and able to pull himself up inside the vent. Using the intact bars from the first set to support his weight, he worked on the second, heavier, set. Now that he was closer to the louvered vent opening, Terry could see that he was still too big to squeeze through; he would have to lose even more weight, so he cut his daily intake to half an orange and four crackers and kept on running.

When he wasn't cutting bars, Terry was braiding his stolen typewriter ribbons into a 50-foot lightweight rope and studying *The Farmer's Almanac* in the library to see which moonless nights would coincide with his last cut with the hacksaw. His calculations pointed to August 10, 1976. An act of God in the form of Hurricane Belle moved his exit date up by one day. On the night of August 9, Belle's 50-mile-per-hour winds and driving rain hit Trenton and made for ideal escape conditions. When he heard that the storm had knocked out the mercury floodlights that normally lit up the tops of the perimeter walls, Terry knew it was time to go, even though he still had a little more cutting to do on the last bar. He stuffed some of his clothes into a laundry bag and made a dummy to put under the blanket on his bed. Then he wrapped the ribbon rope around his torso, loaded up with two shanks, pliers, a wrench and a screwdriver, and pulled on his favorite cowboy boots.

Alden waited until a little after 11 p.m. to give the incoming third-shift cop a chance to make his first bed check. After the officer had gone through, Terry took the plate off the wall and pulled himself into the utility space for the last time. It was a lot easier now that his weight was down to around 160. After Alden got up inside the vent, he reached back down and, using a piece of straightened coat hanger and some tape, reattached the lower bar. He figured if they discovered he was gone and shined a light up toward the roof in the utility space, it might buy him some time if they thought the bars were still intact. Terry still had a little more sawing to do on the last bar before he could get to the opening in the roof. The strength of the wind outside made an incredible racket as the louvers clattered and the rain pounded off the roof.

Alden cut through the last bar and pushed one of the louvers up against the force of the wind. He got his head out, but his shoulders and chest were still too big to get through. Using the bars below for leverage, he gave one last all-out shove and heaved his body out onto the windswept tin roof. As he headed for the hospital roof adjacent to 6-wing, the wind and rain hit him full blast; he slipped and almost slid off the roof, a six-story drop to the yard below. He took off his boots for better footing and abandoned them on the roof where they were found the next day.

Fighting the rain whipping into his face, Alden worked his way to the end of 6-wing where it connected to the three-story prison hospital. He slid down the metal surface toward the edge of the gabled 6-wing roof until he was about 15 feet above the flat roof of the hospital. Jumping down and crouching low, he ran across the hospital roof to the far edge overlooking the old death row, a separate building several feet away from the hospital. Using the pliers, Alden twisted and broke six strands of barbed wire strung on the hospital roof, then secured one end of his typewriter-ribbon rope and threw it over the edge. He lowered himself to the ground, and using the screwdriver and wrench, removed bolts on a barred gate, cut through some more barbed wire and got access to the narrow alley between the hospital and the death row building. Using his athletic ability, he shinnied back up onto the roof of the empty two-story building and crouched on the catwalk that ran along the roof to guard tower # 10.

Inmates had been moved out of death row some years before, and the building had been converted to a contact visit hall used only on weekends, so the guard in 10-tower no longer patrolled the catwalk onto the death house roof. This was the most critical point in the escape: Terry would have to go along that catwalk and pass within eight feet of the guard in the tower to get to the top of the outer-perimeter wall. He knew, though, on a night like this, the cop wouldn't step foot out of the shelter of that tower.

The mercury lights attached to the tower were out, so for the time being Terry was safe, hidden under by the darkness. He pulled off the prison clothes he was wearing over his street clothes and piled them along with the tools on the death house roof. Still in bare feet, Terry slid along the catwalk, ready to use the shank if the guard happened to come out of the tower. The wind-driven rain was so heavy that Terry couldn't even see the cop inside the tower, so he figured the cop couldn't see him either.

It was now about 2 a.m. Sliding on his belly to the end of the catwalk, Alden pushed up the bottom strand of a little barbed-wire fence along the outer edge of the wall, swung his body over and dangled 15 feet above the ground. He let go and dropped onto the rain-softened earth below, leaving two perfect footprints that would be found later that afternoon, some twelve hours after he made his getaway.

The newspapers had a field day with Alden's breakout—especially when the Department of Corrections spokesman, Ed Ramsey, had to admit that the escape wasn't discovered until 1:30 p.m. when the 6-wing officer finally discovered that the lump in Terry Alden's bed was a sack of dirty laundry. I have to give the local newspapers credit, though; they did acknowledge that the looser regulations in the prisons since Attica and Rahway in '71 had played a significant role in Alden's escape. Prior to the '70s, an inmate never would have been allowed to lie in his bunk all morning; now, a lot of inmates chose not to work ("idle" status), and they could sleep all day if they wanted to. So the first-shift wing cop didn't see anything unusual about a guy spending half the day in bed.

Also, inmates were now allowed to have radios and TVs in their cells, not like the old days when all they had was the internal AM radio hookup with earphones. Having all of that noise coming from the cells, even late into the night, helps cover the sound of undercover activities. And now that inmates could wear civilian clothes in the jail, if they got out, they'd look just like everybody else when they hit the street. It's a sure bet that Terry had street clothes on under the prison dungarees and tee-shirt he left on the death house roof along with the stolen tools. When he got to the corner of Third and Cass Streets, with his mustache and civilian clothes, he would have looked like any other late-night partier of the '70s walking by the jail—even in bare feet.

This escape had everything the newspapers loved: a young, good-looking, athletic bandit overcoming all odds to get out of the century-old fortress lockup and making a clean getaway. The details made for great copy: the trapeze act under the vent, dangling high above certain death; the barefooted trek across windswept roofs, battling the elements; the danger of slipping past a tower only eight feet away from a guard with a shotgun loaded with double ought buck shot—wow! It also helped that Terry hadn't definitely been identified as the triggerman in the armored car robbery—maybe he wasn't really such a bad guy after all. One of the most popular movies at the time was *Bonnie and Clyde;* Terry Alden was the Clyde Barrow of Trenton State Prison.

After he got over the wall, Terry headed west again, and, just like Clyde, he started robbing banks. In five robberies in the St. Louis area, he netted some $72,000. The Missouri newspapers started calling Alden "the Bionic Bandit" when he was caught on video tape leaping over the counters of the banks to get to the cash drawers. The image of the indestructible man was reinforced when one tape showed Alden being shot in the back at point-blank range by a security guard with a .38—and not even flinching. (At first, police thought he was wearing a bullet-proof vest; they later found out Alden checked into a Las Vegas hospital the day after the robbery for treatment of a gunshot wound he said he got while target shooting out in the desert.)

In August of 1977, exactly one year after Alden escaped from Trenton, under-cover St. Louis PD cops watched as Alden and John Givens stood near a car and exchanged two magnum handguns and two shotguns. When a plainclotheswoman approached the two, Alden took off running and vaulted over a six-foot fence. The other undercover cop, George Venegoni, along with an off-duty officer who happened by, went after Alden and, after a two-block sprint, caught up to him. Alden spun around with a .44 magnum in his hand. Venegoni grabbed Alden's gun hand, and as Alden spun loose, the off-duty officer leveled his gun at Alden and said, "Drop it or I'll shoot."

Alden said, "Go ahead, kill me," and turned away.

The two officers grabbed Alden and handcuffed him.

A few days before he was scheduled to go on trial in federal court, Alden tried one more time to bust out, an unsuccessful attempt to escape from the St. Clair County jail in Illinois. The jury found Alden guilty of four of the five bank robberies. When they said they were unable to reach a verdict on the fifth and the judge ordered them to resume deliberations, Alden said, "Cut the bullshit. I'll plead guilty to the other one."

Terry drew a sentence of five consecutive 25-year bids and was sent to Leavenworth. I read somewhere that New Jersey wants him back to complete his sentence here after he does the federal time, but I don't know where they'll put a 110-year-old man.

****

One of my least-favorite inmates is Robert Reldan, though I do have to admit that he has perseverance.

I always tried to be up front with the inmates. As long as they didn't try to screw me, I tried to look beyond what they were convicted of and establish a relationship based on mutual respect and trust. As far as I was concerned, what they did to get sent to Trenton stays outside the front door, and our relationship was based on what happened inside the jail.

One evening in the late 1970's when I was on duty in the inmate library, I walked into one of the offices and found Reldan taking apart the air-conditioning unit in the window. I asked him what in the hell he was doing, and he told me he was taking out the fan to take back to his cell.

He said, "What do you care, Harry? It's just state property. It isn't yours."

I said, "That's bullshit. I'm responsible for everything in here while I'm on duty here. Put it back."

It really bothered me that Reldan would do that while I had responsibility for the area; I take that personally. After that incident I never trusted Reldan. The odd thing about him is that this guy had everything in the world that I didn't have—he's tall, he's handsome and he comes from a wealthy family. His uncle, Col. Ferris Booth, was an investment counselor who made a lot of money as one of the early investors in IBM. I always thought Reldan looked like a golf pro. He's about 6',1", has finely chiseled features, silver hair and wears beautiful v-neck sweaters. In fact, he's so good looking and photogenic that when he got "rehabilitated" in the sex-offenders' unit at Rahway back in the mid '70s, the shrinks there got him on national TV as a "completely rehabilitated" sex offender.

Reldan first got into trouble with the law in 1958 at the age of 18 when he was convicted of stealing five cars. In 1963 he was arrested for stealing 30 purses from women in elevators in New York City. Even though he was from a wealthy family, Reldan seemed to have a thing about challenging the law.

Colonel Booth's widow, Mrs. Lillian Booth, sent her nephew Bobby to Europe a few times and paid for his flying and scuba-diving lessons. Even with all of these advantages, Reldan continued to get into trouble with the law, mainly for offenses against women, and was convicted in 1967 of raping a Teaneck mother of two. He went into the sex-offender treatment program at Rahway Prison, getting out on parole in late 1970.

Five months after he was paroled, in the spring of 1971, Reldan went to a hospital to visit William Prendergast, the clinical psychologist who ran the Rahway program. Prendergast was recuperating from surgery. As Reldan was leaving the hospital, he assaulted a woman in the parking lot, threatening her with a knife. He was arrested, convicted and sent back to Rahway.

This was the '70's and the buzzword in corrections was "rehabilitation." The recidivism rate nationally for state prisons was estimated to be a little over 70 percent and society wanted changes. We no longer "warehoused" inmates; we gave them services (education, counseling, meaningful vocational training) that would make them productive members of society when they were released. In the age-old conflict between custody and services, the "social worker" side had the upper hand. It was now a lot more common to see upper-level administrators, including wardens, coming up through the ranks from the education department or the social services staff rather than custody.

This new attitude was reflected in New Jersey's treatment of sex offenders. If a man was convicted of a sex offense, he was given a choice: take the straight sentence and go into the general population at one of the adult male prisons or take treatment in the special unit at Rahway with an indeterminate sentence. The downside to choosing the treatment program was the indeterminate sentence—they could hold the guy until they said he was ready to return to society, even if that exceeded the fixed maximum of the regular sentence. Conceivably, indeterminate could even mean life if the shrinks said so. Some guys didn't want to take that chance. The advantages were that the indeterminate sentence could also be a lot shorter than the fixed if the guy responded well to treatment—or could con the shrinks into believing he was "cured." The other advantage was being in a population of like offenders. Sex offenders are at the bottom of the prison pecking order and are often victims themselves of rape or assaults when they're in general population. A lot of inmates look at sex offenders as depraved trash, potential attackers of members of <u>their</u> families, and they go out of their way to make the sex offender's life miserable.

Toward the end of his "rehabilitation" on this bid for the attack in the hospital parking lot, Reldan was trotted out as a "model graduate" of Rahway's sex-offender treatment program. Prendergast thought Reldan was so completely rehabilitated that in May of 1975 he and Reldan went on a nationally syndicated television show in a segment called "Rape: the Unspeakable Crime" hosted by David Frost, one of TV's most popular personalities at the time. During the interview, Reldan pleaded for more support and understanding of the sex offender. Reldan was paroled shortly after the show was aired, in July of 1975.

A few months later, in October of 1975, two young women disappeared in North Jersey. While the search was on, Reldan was picked up for an unrelated breaking and entering charge and remanded to the Bergen County jail as a suspect in the burglary and as a possible parole violator. While Reldan was behind bars, state law enforcement officials and the FBI zeroed in on him as the prime suspect in the murders of the two women, Susan Heynes, 26, and Susan Reeve, 22. The body of Heynes, a newlywed and British citizen, was found on October 27 in a wooded area in Rockland County, NY; Reeves' body was found the next day a few miles away. Both women had been strangled, and one showed signs of sexual molestation. The investigation pointed to Reldan.

When Prendergast found out that Reldan was a suspect in the murders, which had gotten wide publicity in the local area, he said, "Bob Reldan is a brilliant man. He has studied how psychological tests are administered until he knows all the angles. If he's guilty, he conned the Rahway officials who paroled him and he conned me."

Since Reldan was a parole violator and had been convicted on the B & E charges, he was sent back to Rahway. Then, in January, 1977, he was indicted by a Bergen County grand jury for the murders of the two young women. (The Bergen County prosecutor's office moved slowly on Reldan's indictment because he was already in custody.) Because of the seriousness of the charges against him, Reldan was shipped back to us in Trenton. While in Trenton waiting to go back to the Bergen County jail for the murder trials, he was indicted again, this time for plotting to have his wealthy aunt killed because he knew he was named as an heir in her will.

When he had been sent back to Trenton, Reldan had gotten hooked up with Albert Barber, a 37-year-old bank robber from Atlantic City and had enlisted Barber in the plot to kill Mrs. Booth. Barber had put Reldan in touch with a guy on the outside named Nicholas Gallo, who, Barber said, would be willing to kill Mrs. Booth for a fee. Gallo came down to the prison and met with Reldan a couple of times. Reldan told Gallo that his aunt was worth $50 million and that he would pay Gallo $100,000 to $150,000 to whack her.

Reldan told Gallo, "If you do like I tell you, it's one, two, three, in and out, pop."

Reldan gave Gallo detailed directions to Mrs. Booth's home and described the house and grounds in detail. He also told Gallo that Mrs. Booth and the man who had been her long-time companion after her husband's death, Mischa Dabich, would be easy targets. "When you pull in, you got 'em right in the car. They can't even get out, run, nothing. Bang, right through the window of the car."

What Reldan didn't know was that Gallo was not an assassin-for-hire but an undercover Bergen County detective who had duped both Reldan and Barber—and he was wired when he met with Reldan. Even with her Bobby's voice on tape plotting her death, Mrs. Booth refused to believe that her nephew wanted her dead. She testified as a defense witness for Reldan and said that she didn't believe that the voice on the tape was her nephew. When the prosecutor told her that Reldan had admitted that the voice was his, she said in a muffled voice, "I guess I wasn't in court that day."

Reldan took the stand and testified that the whole thing was an elaborate hoax, that he knew all along Gallo was an undercover cop. He said that he was sick of being hounded and maliciously prosecuted by Bergen County DA Joseph Woodcock so that Woodcock could advance his political career. He claimed that he and Barber had concocted this plot to make Woodcock look bad. The jury didn't buy it and convicted Reldan and Barber after deliberating for just over four hours. Back he came to TSP.

In October of 1979 Reldan was sent back to the Bergen County jail to stand trial for the murders of Heynes and Reeves. This was his most spectacular stunt yet. While he was being guarded by a sheriff's deputy in a holding area off the courtroom on the third floor, he suddenly whipped out a can of Mace, sprayed the deputy in the face and jumped out of a window, falling 35 feet to the ground. He landed on a patch of grass surrounded by concrete and, uninjured, took off running. About a block away, he confronted a lawyer who was just getting out of his car, squirted Mace in this guy's face and stole his Cadillac. He drove north on Route 17, stopped in Paramus long enough to snatch a woman's purse, and headed into New York State. New Jersey and New York police picked up his trail and finally nailed him in Tuxedo, NY when, after an hour-long high-speed chase, he flipped the lawyer's Cadillac over—not far from the spot where police had found the bodies of Heynes and Reeves.

Reldan was convicted in the murders of the two women, partly on the fact that he had tried to pawn one of the victim's rings at a department store, and he was sent back to Trenton with a sentence of life plus seventy-two years.

But wait. It doesn't end yet.

In April of 1981, on a Sunday, Reldan was out in the big yard when he claimed to have fallen on a pile of rocks and cut himself. He kept insisting that he was badly injured and that he needed x-rays, meanwhile knowing that no x-ray technicians are on duty at the jail on weekends. Reldan finally convinced custody that he needed to be transported to St. Francis Hospital for x-rays, but because Reldan was considered an extreme escape risk, they wisely sent a couple of officers on ahead to check out the area. Sure enough, one of the officers noticed Reldan's girlfriend, Sherry-Anne Stevens, sitting in the lobby of the hospital. Even though Stevens was wearing sunglasses and a bandanna, the officer recognized her from having seen her visiting Reldan at the prison every Sunday.

The officer, sergeant Michael Voight, found two Trenton police patrolmen in a nearby room writing a report on a minor assault. Voight asked the two police officers to check out Stevens. One of the cops asked Stevens if he could talk to her in another room, and when he looked into the plastic shopping bag she was carrying, he found a loaded sawed-off 20-guage shotgun and several rounds of ammunition wrapped in a sweater. The cops arrested Stevens and hustled her out the front entrance just as Reldan was being brought in through the emergency room door. She was charged with abetting an escape attempt, possession of a sawed-off shotgun, defacing a firearm and possession of a hollow-point bullet.

I may not like Bob Reldan, but I'll say one thing about him: he never quits.

****

Shortly after Rich Biegenwald went out the door on parole in 1975, I was offered one of the sweetest jobs in the jail: court officer—driving inmates to and from county jails for hearings, appeals, resentencings and so on. With time allowed for my two years in the army, I now had 26 years in, and this assignment usually went to senior officers. Despite what had happened to Vic Vittorito way back in the early '50's, this job was a dream come true for me. It got me out of the jail and out on the road. I met a lot of new people in just about every county in New Jersey. And it gave me a chance to get to know several of the inmates a lot more personally.

On one such occasion I had driven an inmate to a hearing in Camden County, and the judge and the attorneys were discussing setting a sentencing date for some armed robberies that this guy had done and hadn't yet been sentenced for. In the course of the back-and-forth in the courtroom, one of the public defenders said, "Your Honor, before you set the date for sentencing, may I remind you to keep in mind Yom Kippur."

All of a sudden, the inmate got highly upset and belligerent. I was sitting near him, and I didn't want to have to drive him all the way back to Trenton while he was in such a hostile mood, so I asked him what the problem was. He said, "These assholes are trying to put one over on me, Harry. They're tryin' to tag me with one I didn't do. I done a lot of robbin' but I never stuck up no one named John Kipper."

Another candidate for the Trenton State Prison chapter of the Mensa Society.

Aerial photo from the west of the new prison with the old prison complex in the foreground.

17

CHAPTER SEVENTTEN

THE EIGHTIES: GREAT ESCAPES

Three convicts went over the wall in the 29 years that I was a correction officer from 1950 to 1979: DeLucia, Van Scoten, Alden. Not that there's any connection, but in the ten years after I retired as an officer and came back as a civilian employee, the number of escapes and attempts skyrocketed. I remember the '80's mainly for three things: a lot of escapes; the conviction of several officers for beating inmates; and being taken hostage for the second time.

I graduated from Mercer County Community College with an Associate in Arts degree in 1974 and was still working on my Bachelor of Science in education at Trenton State College when I retired in 1979 (I got the degree in 1984). After I took several months off for accrued sick days, I went to the central office and talked to Gary Hilton (who was now an assistant commissioner) about a job as a civilian employee. He liked the idea and hired me as a Teacher II, assigning me to Trenton State Prison. The warden at the time was Elijah Tard, a former officer I had worked with who had gone up through the ranks to the top job. I had known him for over twenty years. He was surprised to see me when I came back in wearing a sport jacket and tie, but he knew he could put me to work immediately with no break-in period.

My last job as a prison guard had been officer in charge of the prison wing at St. Francis Hospital in Trenton. This was good duty, especially for an old guy like me (50), because there was nowhere near the everyday danger of The Wall, though I still had to be alert (look at the Reldan and his girlfriend incident).

For my first three years as a Teacher II, I traveled around the state to all of the adult-male penal institutions, administering GED tests while finishing my degree at Trenton State College. The decade of escapes had already started in January of 1980 when Alexander Stewart, an armed robber from Paterson, escaped from officers at the Mercer County Courthouse. Stewart sort of set the tone for the decade. He had tried to escape twice before—once in 1978 by slipping out of handcuffs and diving through an open window of the state car he was being transported in. He was recaptured quickly in that attempt as well as another one two years earlier.

This time, it looked like he had set up the escape and might have had help from the outside—prosecutors later indicted his mother and his twin brother for helping him escape. In the week before he got away, Stewart called the office of a Mercer County judge six times from the prison, telling the judge's staff that he wanted to plead guilty to an assault-on-an-inmate charge. When he got in front of the judge, Stewart said, "I don't know what I'm doing here," so the judge ordered him held over for trial and sent back to The Wall.

When he got outside of the courthouse, Stewart took off from his two escorts, who weren't armed, and sprinted into a high-rise apartment building across the street. Despite a floor-by-floor, apartment-by-apartment search, Stewart got away.

None of this is all that remarkable except that Stewart then started calling various people—judges, prosecutors, newspaper reporters—to remind them that he had gotten away and to generally bust their chops. He called one Passaic County judge's office, identifying himself as the state's public advocate, Stanley Van Ness. Then he sent a postcard to an assistant Mercer County prosecutor with "Ha, ha, ha, ha, ha," written on it.

Stewart was out for about nine months when he was snagged in Phoenix, Arizona on a robbery charge. It turns out he had been arrested in Las Vegas in March, but they let him out on his own recognizance because he didn't have a record in Nevada. Phoenix authorities were also about to let him go when the Mercer County prosecutor's office found out they had him and started extradition proceedings. He came back to the prison in May of '81 to face a lot of new charges.

Two months after Stewart was returned to The Wall, the most spectacular breakout in the history of the prison, complete with exploding Molotov cocktails and gunfire from a tower, erupted on the Fourth of July weekend in 1981. On the morning of Friday, July 3 as people in the South Trenton neighborhood around the prison were getting ready to celebrate the Fourth, six inmates went over the wall.

At 8:55 a.m., a Johanna Farms milk delivery truck was backing slowly up the narrow driveway alongside the wall between the prison and Second Street, making its daily run to the rear of the mess hall. About 400 inmates had already had breakfast and were outside in the yard nearby when six of them suddenly broke out of the group and rushed the driver and the officer who was riding in the passenger seat. Two of the inmates, holding homemade knives to the throats of the driver and the guard, commandeered the milk truck and forced the driver to turn it perpendicular to the 22-foot-high wall and back it up to the base. The delivery truck was one of those big six-wheelers, like a soda or beer truck and was about 15 feet high.

As the two inmates forced the driver to position the truck against the wall, the other four ran toward 6-tower and lobbed Molotov cocktails made of paint thinner high on the wall at the base of the tower. The firebombs exploded, preventing the tower guard, Yvonne Cabell, from seeing clearly what was happening or from firing her weapon. (Tower guards are under standing orders to "shoot to kill" whenever an inmate starts to climb an exterior wall.)

As the flames from the firebombs drove Cabell—the first female officer hired at Trenton State Prison—back away from the prison side of the guard tower, all six inmates scrambled up onto the roof of the milk truck. They helped each other grab on to the top of the wall and hauled themselves up. The guard in 4-tower, about 100 yards away, saw what was happening and fired one shot from his shotgun loaded with 00 buckshot. One pellet hit one of the inmates in the back. The other pellets hit the upper floors of a couple of houses on the other side of Second Street, one pellet breaking a bedroom window and lodging in the wall of one of the houses.

Civilian contractors had been working for several days refurbishing 5-tower and installing razor wire along the top of the wall. They got a front-row seat as the six guys, four of them murderers, scrambled up and over. The workers and their equipment were between 4-tower and the escaping inmates, so the tower guard had to hold his fire after the first shot. While civilians on the street and the construction workers watched in amazement, the inmates dropped down onto the grassy strip between the base of the outer wall and the street and took off running. They scattered down alleyways and into back yards, peeling off and throwing away their prison-issue pants and shirts as they ran. Each of the inmates had prepared for the escape by dressing in civilian clothes and then putting on his prison khakis and tee shirts over the street clothes.

The guard in 4-tower signaled center that an escape was in progress (Cabell had headed down the stairs toward the street, to escape the flames, a move that would later result in disciplinary charges being brought against her), and the alert immedi ately went out to the Trenton and state police. Within the next several minutes, more than 60 local and state police officers responded and began searching the area around the prison.

Meanwhile, Balbino Morales, the president of the El DePortino Social Club on Centre Street, was sweeping the sidewalk in front of the club when he heard a friend of his, Alberto Velez, yelling for help. Velez had been turning his Ford station wagon around in an alley near the club when three of the inmates, including Michael Jones, the inmate hit in the back by the shotgun blast fired from 4-tower, came running up and tried to drag Velez out of his car. While Jones and a second inmate tried to open the locked door on the passenger side, 6-foot, 300-pound Marvin Russell opened the door on the driver's side and tried to yank Velez out of the car. Velez grabbed hold of the steering wheel, honked his horn and yelled for help.

As Morales dropped the broom on the sidewalk in front of the club and ran toward his friend's car, Jones and the other inmate took off running toward the Delaware River, about six blocks away. Russell got Velez out of the car and had just climbed into the driver's seat when Morales came running up. Seeing blood on his friend's shirt, the 5-foot, 9-inch 180-pound Morales thought Velez had been stabbed in a carjacking attempt and went after the 300-pound Russell. Russell pushed Morales away, hauled himself out of the Ford and took off running. Morales chased Russell for two blocks, finally catching him at the corner of Lamberton and Federal Streets; he grabbed Russell by the back of his shirt, spun him around and threw him to the ground.

Russell yelled, "Let me go, man. I just escaped from prison."

Morales said, "No way," and held Russell in a headlock for a few minutes while other neighbors alerted police and correction officers to come and get the convict. Russell was doing 30 years for murder, robbery and weapons possession.

While Russell was being subdued, 23-year-old Joe Winicki was awakened by his mother downstairs yelling that a stranger was in the yard of their Lamberton Street house. Winicki jumped out of bed, grabbed his .22 rifle and pointed it at a man in the driveway of their home and told him not to move. Winicki said the man froze and stayed still for a couple of minutes while Winicki's mother called the police. When the man (probably Michael Jones) heard the sirens, he took off running. Winicki didn't shoot at him because he said he didn't want to put a hole in his boat parked in the driveway.

Meanwhile, the other three escapees had run to the rear of the Brittain & Parnell Sign Shop on Cass Street and jumped into the company's Ford panel truck parked behind the shop. The owner, William Parnell, heard the engine start and ran outside to investigate. He chased the truck a little way down the alley, but when he saw that the driver was "pretty big," he decided to let it go. The truck was found a little while later abandoned in a ditch about two miles away from the prison in a marshy area near the Delaware River.

Around 11 a.m., Trenton patrolmen John Collins and David Johnson saw a man dressed in a jogging suit throw a gym bag off the Route 1 toll bridge into the Delaware River. Witnesses told the two Trenton cops that a few minutes earlier the man had been trying to flag down cars in the southbound lanes of Route 1 (heading toward Philadelphia) by waving a 20-dollar bill and gesturing for them to stop. While the cops were questioning the man, the officers noticed he had a wound in his back and arrested him. He was Michael Jones, the inmate who had been hit going over the wall. Jones was a 28-year-old Philadelphian who had been convicted in April of 1980 of shooting Moorestown police sergeant Frank Fullerton three times, fatally wounding him, following a liquor store holdup in Hammonton and a high-speed car chase. He was serving a life sentence.

At 9:15 p.m. that night, as the manhunt continued in the area surrounding the prison, residents around Furman and Centre Streets, a few blocks away, alerted two foot patrolmen that a man dressed in a black and red woodsman's jacket was acting suspiciously. When patrolmen Walter Kirstien and Ed Rios spotted the guy, he ran into a garage where the two officers found him hiding under a car. The officers told him to come out or they would call in a K-9 unit. When Mark Jones, 22, of Newark crawled out, the two officers disarmed him of a 10-inch shank. Jones, serving a life sentence for murder, was one of the Muslims indicted for killing Cleopheous Mayers in the Bourne School violence of October, 1975.

The fourth escapee captured was Jesse Guzman, 28, of Perth Amboy, one of the guys who had stolen the truck from the paint shop on Cass Street. He managed to hide out in a wooded area near the Delaware River despite intensive search efforts, including a state police helicopter, in that area throughout the day. He was spotted at 1 a.m. on the morning of the Fourth walking on Clinton Street near Yard Avenue, about eight blocks from the prison, by Trenton police officer Richard Nicholson who was patrolling in a paddy wagon.

"You got me, I give up," Guzman told Nicholson.,

Guzman, who was covered with mosquito bites, was also serving a life sentence for murder.

The two who got away were Andrew Clark, 36, from Newark, serving a 45-year sentence for two counts of rape and one count of robbery and Robert Davis, originally from Danville, VA, who was serving a 25-year sentence for attempted bank robbery. Most people around the prison figured Davis was the brains behind the plan since he had escaped earlier from Rahway (that's why he had been sent to Trenton) and after his recapture in this escape would engineer another one in December.

Davis was recaptured in September after he and a female accomplice flashed some kind of badges to gain entrance into the apartment of 37-year-old Geraldine Jones in Newark. Once they were inside, Davis and his partner pulled out guns and told Jones they were robbing the place. They ripped out the phone wire and used it to tie up Jones' 14-year-old daughter and then ransacked the apartment. When Davis found a bank book for an account at Fidelity Union Bank, he forced Jones to take her three-month-old daughter with him to the bank to withdraw the money.

Davis waited out in the car with a .38-caliber pistol and the baby while Jones went into the bank. When she got to the teller's window, Jones became hysterical and started yelling, "He has my baby!"

The bank manager and a security guard, both armed with handguns, ran outside and found Davis holding the baby. Davis crouched and fired a shot at the two men, dropping the baby. The security guard and the manager fired 14 shots at Davis, nine of them coming from the bank manger's 9mm, while Davis returned their fire from his .38- caliber Colt Special.

The owner of a delicatessen near the bank said, "Bullets just came through the door and ricocheted all over. Three cans of hair spray exploded after they were hit, and a bottle of shampoo burst. There were five employees and six customers in here, and we all hit the floor."

Another guy was on a ladder fixing an electrical sign for the bank when the shooting started. "I saw these guys running out and heard a sound like firecrackers," he said. His truck was hit several times and had to be towed from the scene.

As Davis turned to run, he was hit in the leg and fell to the sidewalk, dropping his weapon. He was arrested and returned to Trenton after he got out of the hospital in Newark. (New Jersey note: police said they intended to question the bank manager closely about possessing the 9mm pistol.)

Andrew Clark was able to stay out for two and a half years before he was finally recaptured and returned to Trenton in January of 1984.

On December 4 of '81, Davis did it again. He hooked up with Marvin "Walking Tall" Ellison (6ft., 5 in.) and Carson Edwards and escaped from the hospital. Davis was still recuperating in the prison infirmary from the removal of a pin that had been put in his leg after the Newark shoot-out. Using a hacksaw, the three men sawed through bars on the window of the infirmary, got out onto a ledge and jumped down into the yard between the infirmary and the perimeter wall. Just before dawn, they scaled the wall and wearing several layers of clothes and mittens to protect themselves from the razor wire, the three convicts lowered themselves to the ground on a rope made of bedsheets.

I don't know what the tower guards were doing when these guys got up on the wall, but for some reason no one saw them. (Three officers, one in the hospital and two in the towers were immediately suspended when the escape was discovered.) Ellison and Edwards were recaptured within an hour and a half about ten miles away from the prison out in Lawrence Township north of Trenton. People driving to work heard about the escape on the radio, saw the two men and called police. As far as I know, Davis has never been recaptured.

I was out on the road doing GED testing when these escapes occurred, and it looked to me like security had really gotten lax. When Davis and the five other guys went out in July, the construction workers on top of the wall who obstructed the tower guard's field of fire were working on the first phase of a multi-million-dollar upgrade of the prison, supposedly to make it more secure.

When Davis went out the second time, in December, it was construction workers putting up the housing units for a new prison who spotted the bed sheet dangling from the wall and turned in the alarm. They were building a brand new prison immediately in front of the old one. Even though just about every New Jersey governor since the late 1940's has vowed to tear the old prison down, when it comes down to it, the state needs the beds, and they left the 150-year-old compound basically intact (they tore down the old death house). Instead of making the old jail a parking lot, as Gov. Driscoll had said in 1947, they built a huge brand new red-brick prison on top of Third Street and connected the old front house roof to the new structure with glass skylights. The new building is divided into a north and south compound and houses approximately 1,000 inmates. Another 900+ men still lock in the wings that were built from 1835 through 1907.

By October of 1982, the first half of the new structure, the North Compound was finished. The South Compound was completed in April of 1983. Along with the new razor wire strung along the top of the perimeter walls of the old prison, other security features included two 92-foot "super towers" overlooking the entire complex.

Almost as soon as guards with shotguns and M-16s went into the new towers, two inmates decided to test them out. In late April of '83, 21-year-old Robert Stankiewicz, a convicted murderer from Haddonfield, and 21-year-old David Kerpen got out onto the roof of chapel/rec and headed for the roof of the old front house. Where they thought they were going is anybody's guess since the new eight-story prison stands directly in front of the old four-story front house; basically they were heading for a brick wall. Guards in the super towers saw Stankiewicz and Kerpen running along the roof about 1 p.m. and ordered them to halt. The two inmates kept running, and the guards opened fire. Stankiewicz was hit immediately and fatally wounded as he ran onto the front house roof. Kerpen kept going despite the gunfire and fell into the razor wire on the roof of 7-wing.

When officers got to Kerpen, he was covered in blood from trying to free himself from the wire. Every time an officer wearing heavy gloves would cut through a ribbon of wire and pull it away, Kerpen would scream out in agony. After about 20 minutes, four officers were able to get Kerpen out. He was taken down a ladder on a stretcher and driven to St. Francis with lacerations (lots of them) and a broken leg. He survived.

* * * * * * *

A couple of days after Stankiewicz was killed, Teddy Roberts and I were in the lobby of the new section of the prison, looking at the new building and talking about the escape attempt. Teddy had gotten out on parole in the late 1970's and even though his family was in Elizabeth, he decided to stay in the Trenton area. During most of the time he had been an inmate, Teddy had worked in the repair shop. By the time he finished his life bid and got paroled, Teddy knew more about the physical plant of the prison than the civilian maintenance staff did—so they offered him a job. Now, this bad-ass killer who had hidden shanks in a couple of cigars and had thrown a corrections officer down a flight of stairs in 4-wing, was working on the state payroll. Sometimes prisons actually do rehabilitate, even if it takes a lot of years.

So Teddy and I were standing in the lobby, talking, when a young mother and her little boy came in for a window visit with an inmate. All of a sudden, Teddy and I heard a ruckus behind us at the counter in the front of the new mail room. The kid, probably no more than three years old, had been making a lot noise, so a guard in the lobby walked over to him and asked him to quiet down.

When the cop asked the kid to quiet down, the kid yelled at him, "You motherfucker!" and threw his bottle—nipple and all—at the cop.

The cop started toward the kid, and the kid went into a boxing stance and said, "Come on, asshole. I'll punch you right in your cock."

That kid must be about 21 or 22 now. I sometimes wonder if he's in the prison somewhere and I just don't know it.

* * * * * * *

In May of 1984 I got my bachelor's degree and was switched from the GED testing assignment to a classroom position back at The Wall. I had just started teaching adult basic education classes (ABE, the elementary school level program that leads into the GED courses) when I began hearing rumors about a problem during a prisoner transfer. The word was that 15 inmates had been transferred from one of the state's new prisons, Southern State Correctional Facility in Leesburg, to Trenton after they created a disturbance over having liver for dinner. Now they were claiming to have been manhandled by corrections officers on the way to Trenton and after they got into the prison.

When I was an officer, all of us had an "understanding" about how we would act when a situation like this came up. It was commonly known as the "blue wall of silence"—nobody rats out a fellow officer. It looked, though, like this incident was too big with too many people involved to manage. The inmates had filed charges, the commissioner of corrections, William H. Fauver, had ordered an investigation, and the newspapers had gotten hold of the story. This wasn't the old days of gauntlets at Rahway or ass-whuppins in 1-left. The times weren't a'changin'—they'd already changed, and eight corrections officers were caught in the crosshairs.

As I see it, there was a big difference between what we had done at Rahway back in '61 compared to this. For starters, the whole country's attitude toward prisons and inmates had changed big time in those two decades. Inmates now had a lot more "rights" inside the jail as well as within the law itself. On the street, police officers had to be much more careful in documenting their causes for searches and in their handling of suspects, including reading them their Miranda rights. In the prison, we now had an office of Internal Affairs that spent the majority of its time investigating inmate complaints against officers. Unlike the old days of the goon squad rushing into a bad-ass inmate's cell at 3 a.m. to subdue him (often with a few "payback" shots), wrapping him in a wet sheet and bundling him off to the Vroom Building, now—1984—Internal Affairs was video taping all inmate transfers for possible use in court in the event the inmate filed suit. Needless to say, there were no video cameras around when this Southern State transfer took place.

The other difference was that at Rahway in '61 we had been ordered to Rahway to put down a mini-riot involving injured officers and damage to state property. These Southern State guys had only led a food boycott to protest the administration's choice of menu selections. At Rahway the operation was directed by the commissioner himself, and we had been ordered to set up the gauntlet and run the inmates through—with the commissioner watching. The officers in the Southern State beatings had acted on their own late at night, without the knowledge of even the warden, and then had filed false reports to try to cover up the incident.

The version of events that I heard was that the inmates had provoked the response from the officers by a non-stop string of verbal abuse from the time they were taken from the mess hall until they had finished the 90-minute drive from Leesburg to Trenton. It's probably difficult for someone who has never been inside a prison to understand how inmates, with words alone, can goad an officer into physical violence. But when you're screamed at non-stop with things like "What kind of man are you anyhow? What kind of man looks up real men's assholes for a living? You know what, motherfucker? When I get out of here, I'm gonna find out where you live, and I'm gonna come to your house and fuck your wife. And your daughter if you were ever able to get it up long enough to have any kids, motherfucker. And when I'm finished, maybe I'll fuck you up your ass you goddamned faggot."

Multiply this by 15 inmates by 90 minutes and you can see how it can rub an officer's nerves raw. The officers that I talked to felt that these inmates wanted to provoke an incident so that they could file charges. If so, it worked.

A few days after the inmates were brought into the jail and locked up, they got together and filed complaints against the officers who had transported them and processed them in. The inmates alleged that on the drive up from Leesburg they had been verbally assaulted and threatened. When they got to the prison, they said, they were ordered out of the vans and forced to walk down a long, dim hallway between two lines of 15 to 30 officers who yelled insults at them, forced them to call themselves derogatory names, hit them with night sticks and punched them. They said the abuse went on for about two hours.

Commissioner Fauver ordered a full investigation, and the Mercer County prosecutor's office got involved. Meanwhile, the warden, a guy I had known for over 20 years, Elijah Tard (the first black to be named warden of TSP) was transferred to the central office, and Gary Hilton came back to run the jail on a temporary basis. Eventually, eight officers—two captains, a lieutenant, a sergeant and four guards—were indicted for official misconduct.

The eight officers went on trial in the fall of 1985. The attorneys for the eight acknowledged that force had been used and that some striking of inmates had occurred. But, one of the attorneys said, the violence was only a form of initiation into the toughest maximum-security institution in the state. The attorney said that the violence was intended to let the inmates know who would be running this jail.

After five weeks of testimony, including a trip to the prison by the judge and jury so they could see the intake area and the corridor, seven of the eight officers were found guilty. One of the officers was acquitted of all charges. The seven who were found guilty were immediately fired.

In March of 1986 Superior Court judge Judith Yaskin handed out sentences ranging from three to five years. The sergeant who was pinpointed as the ring-leader was sentenced to five years on misconduct with concurrent one-year terms for tampering with evidence and conspiring to file a false report. Other guards had testified that after the beatings the sergeant had told them, "You know how to write the reports—now write them."

A captain who was there that night and saw what was going on but didn't stop it got the same sentence as the sergeant. The others got three-year terms for official misconduct.

I have mixed feelings about the whole incident. While I can't fully condone what the officers did, I was on the receiving end of inmate verbal abuse enough times to know how it can get to an officer. Sometimes the attitude that a few inmates display toward officers can be infuriating, especially when you know they've committed a particularly nasty crime, like a sadistic sexual assault/murder. And here they are standing in front of you, acting as if they're some kind of superior being and telling you what a lowlife asshole you are. It's not easy to listen to that crap.

Combine that with the ever-present threat of a punch in the mouth from some guy who's been pumping iron out in the yard for several years or the sudden shank in the heart, like Vic Vittorito or Don Bourne. So, sometimes we do have lapses. The officers involved in this case probably should have been disciplined, maybe suspended, but firing them? Prison terms? No way.

But that's coming from someone who has had to put up with 50 years' worth of abuse from some of the meanest, nastiest scum buckets (who, thankfully, are in the minority) in New Jersey. So take it for what it's worth.

* * * * * * *

Back when Eddie Sheffield tried to escape and fell asleep on the roof of the front house, I said I would never plead guilty to a crime or plea bargain. I would take a chance with a jury of my peers every time. Here's my second big reason why.

A month after the Southern State beatings, in June of 1984, three more inmates tried to make it out the back door. These guys, all lifers, must have been watching *The Late Movie* on TV and figured they'd try the same technique that worked for

Alan Ladd and William Bendix in the movie *Escape*—by hiding on a food truck leaving the prison grounds.

The three guys all worked in the kitchen and on this June morning had helped load a Department of Corrections truck with food trays being taken out to Jones Farm. When the civilian employee who drove the truck slammed down and fastened the rear door of his vehicle, he had more than bread and pastries aboard. The driver made one stop inside the walls and then headed out through the vehicle gate on the southwest corner of the jail. The guards on duty at the gate opened the rear door and checked for stowaways, but to do a thorough job, they would have had to remove about 300 trays. They waved the truck through.

The driver then pulled the truck around to the front of the prison to pick up two Jones Farm trusties who were sitting near the front entrance, waiting to ride back to the Farm. As the truck went over one of the speed bumps in front of the jail, one of the trusties thought he heard a food cart tip over, so he told the driver to pull over while he checked in the back. When the trusty opened the door, two inmates leaped out and took off running. An alert tower guard saw them and turned in an alarm. Both would-be escapees were recaptured within the hour, and the truck was driven back onto the grounds. A count was taken and 26-year-old Harry James, a multiple armed robber serving a life sentence came up missing. Internal Affairs investigators unlocked the back door of the truck and did a more thorough search and *voila!* there was Harry James (the inmate, not the band leader).

Now here's why I say I'll take my chances with a jury any day. When the three guys were indicted and went to court, James told the jury he had a gambling problem and was <u>not</u> trying to escape. On the contrary, he told the court, he was running a numbers operation between Jones Farm and The Wall and he was simply making a trip out to the Farm to pick up betting slips. He basically said he was just an entrepreneur trying to achieve the American dream. Any bets on what the jury decided? The only way I could figure it was 1) either this was the dumbest jury in the history of Mercer County or 2) they figured any guy with *chutzpah* enough to come up with a story like that deserved a break. They let him off.

* * * * * * *

In September of 1984, a little over ten years after the chance meeting between my daughter Kim and me and Frank Bisignano on the campus of Trenton State College, I persuaded Kim to come to work at the prison. Kim had gone on to get her master's degree in speech pathology at Trenton State and had gotten married shortly thereafter. She worked in her field for a few years and then she and her husband Larry had their first child, Clint. Kim told me she wanted to stay out of the workforce for several years and raise a family before she went back to work. I told her I thought she was making a big mistake and that she should at least work part-time to keep her hand in. After going back and forth about this for a while, we agreed that I would talk to some people and see if I could get her a part-time job at the prison, working one day a week.

At the time, a number of inmates that I knew of had speech problems, and no one on staff had the qualifications to help them. One guy, for instance, had been shot three times in the head, almost totally destroying his ability to speak. Another guy, Jimmy Stewart (I always remembered his name because of the movie star) stuttered badly, and another one had what they call "tongue thrust," so there were a number of inmates who needed help in speech.

After I told Kim about these guys who badly needed speech therapy, she was convinced she ought to take the job. Working there would help the inmates and it would look good on her résumé. But what happened on the day she started in September of 1985 probably gave her the record as the employee with the shortest career in the history of the prison.

That morning in September '85 Kim met me in the lobby of the new part of the jail, and we headed inside together. I took Kim into the old prison to the Donald Bourne School to meet with Yvonne Frayer, the education department secretary, to do the paperwork for Kim's new job. I also introduced her to one of the teachers who would fill her in on her responsibilities and show her the files of the inmates she'd be working with.

I said to Kim, "I'll leave you with Yvonne to get squared away and come back for you around 11 for lunch."

Then I went off to do my work for the morning.

I found out later that while I was teaching an Adult Basic Education class in the Bourne School, my boss, Doug Heil, was having an argument in the vocational school in the south compound with an inmate named Eugene Jones. I knew Jones slightly; he was in his mid-twenties and had been convicted five years before of shooting and killing a gas station attendant during a holdup near Englewood in Bergen County. In Doug's capacity as director of education, he also served as chairman of the PCC (prison classification committee). The PCC was responsible for reviewing inmate files, interviewing the men, and assigning them to the appropriate level of schooling, work details and special programs, like behavior modification.

Jones had originally been assigned to the inside sanitation detail, going through the jail picking up trash, spraying and cleaning dirty surfaces and so on. Inmates liked this detail because it allowed them the freedom to roam the jail without a pass. Nobody put a lot of pressure on them to get their work done, so they could visit with their friends and be in on all the news and scuttlebutt making the rounds. Being on inside sanitation gave a guy a little bit of jailhouse status.

Jones had an attitude problem: he had been screwing up on the job, giving officers a hard time when they asked him to clean particular areas and generally being a pain in the ass. He had been warned a couple of times about his attitude, but nothing had changed. When Jones was called before the PCC that morning and Doug told him he was being reassigned to food cart pusher in the cafeteria, Jones went ballistic. He started yelling at Doug, insisting that he be left in his current job. But Doug had had too many complaints about Jones and wouldn't give in on the reassignment.

Doug later told me about the meeting with Jones. Jones would say something like, "I demand to be heard! I have a right . . ." and Doug would cut him off.

"This decision has been made, Mr. Jones, and you're going to abide by it."

"You can't do this. I have rights. I . . ."

And Doug would cut him off again. "This decision is not going to be changed, Mr. Jones. You're going to the new job effective immediately."

"But I want you to listen to what I have to say . . ."

"That's the end of the discussion, Mr. Jones."

"But . . ."

"End of discussion. Leave the room before I have to write up a charge."

Doug knew Jones was furious with him, but that goes with the territory. He never thought that Jones would take the action he did.

A little after 11 a.m. the men went back to their cells for the mid-day count and to get lunch, so I met Kim, and we left the jail and went to a nearby restaurant to have lunch. I told Kimmy she would be working that day until about 3 or 3:30 and that I would be right downstairs in a classroom and not to worry—she was going to be fine. The two of us walked down to the school. After we went up the ramp and through the metal detector, she went upstairs and I walked down toward the classrooms on the first floor.

I finished my class at about 1:45 and was heading for the stairs to see how Kim was doing when I looked down the incline toward the entrance to the school and saw Jones coming up the ramp. In his hand was a shank about ten inches long—the handle from a kitchen ladle with the scoop part broken off and the tip sharpened down to a point. The cop sitting at the desk next to the metal detector, Fred Swank, had turned to say hello to me as I passed by and didn't see the shank until Jones grabbed him from behind, took his keys and said, "OK let's go. You're coming with me."

Then, pulling Fred up out of the chair and pushing him in front of him, Jones started coming up the ramp, yelling, "Where's that guy? Where's that PCC guy?"

Even though I hadn't yet heard what happened at PCC that morning, I put two and two together and knew that Jones was talking about Doug Heil. I turned and ran back down the corridor and ducked into Doug's outer office. As I burst in, one of the librarians, Pat Singleton, was standing in front of Yvonne Frayer's desk talking to her; Doug was in a meeting in his office with two of the prison psychologists, Dave Parish and Richard Cevasco. Yvonne looked startled as I blew by her desk and pushed open the door to Doug's office.

I said, "Doug, there's a guy out here with a knife heading this way. Let's get the hell out of here."

Before anybody could make another move, Jones appeared in the doorway holding the knife to Fred Swank's throat.

Jones pointed at Doug and said, "You, you son of a bitch. That's why I'm in here. You wouldn't listen to me. All I wanted you to do was listen to me."

Jones had closed the outer office door and as I looked over his shoulder through the narrow window in the door, I could see that a bunch of cops had gathered outside and the other inmates were being herded out of the school; somebody had called center and told them there was a hostage situation. Jones saw where I was looking and glanced back at the door. Pushing Fred aside, he grabbed Yvonne and put the point of the shank under one of her breasts.

He turned and yelled through the door to the cops, "Anybody comes in here, she's dead! Stay away from that goddamned door!"

Then, still holding the shank up against Yvonne's rib cage, Jones turned back to us and said, "Any of you try to move or get cute and she's dead. Get in there," and he waved the shank toward Doug's office.

At this point, I'm thinking, "I don't need this shit. We don't need any heroes."

And I'm looking around at everybody, hoping that nobody is going to say anything. I thought then, and I still think it's true, the best thing to do in those situations is keep your mouth shut. I thought that anything I might say could really set this guy off, and we'd all be in trouble.

So we all sat down quietly in Doug's office and listened to Jones go on about how he had been screwed over and how all he ever wanted was a fair hearing and on and on. After we had listened to Jones' monologue for about ten minutes, the phone on Doug's desk rang, and Jones picked it up. On the other end of the line was the prison's chief psychologist, Dr. George Saxton. He asked Jones if he needed anything, and Jones told him he was thirsty. Saxton offered Jones water if he would let one of the hostages go. Jones told Saxton to stuff it, that he wasn't going to fall for that shit.

The negotiations on the telephone went nowhere, and after a few minutes, Saxton appeared at the narrow window in the door leading out into the corridor. Saxton slowly pushed the door open and stuck his head inside. He asked Jones for permission to come in, and Jones said it was OK. I heard later that Saxton caught hell for doing this, mainly because he didn't wait for the hostage negotiating team to get to prison from the central office out in West Trenton. Saxton opened the door and came in.

Jones was babbling irrationally and after repeating several times how nobody would listen to him and all he wanted was a fair hearing, he started going into a whole list of complaints about the prison—the food, visits, telephone privileges, job assignments and on and on. Saxton just listened calmly and nodded his head, looking directly into Jones' eyes.

Then Jones went off on a different, chilling tangent. He said, "I'm going to die anyway, and then they'll know I was right. Then maybe things'll change around here."

He said, "I'll take a couple of these people out and those cops'll shoot me and it'll get in the newspapers and everybody on the outside will see how bad things are in here. Then the other guys will see that I did this for them."

Saxton didn't blink. He spoke calmly and quietly: "You're right, Eugene. Killing some of us will definitely grab some headlines, and those cops probably will shoot you, but you know what? Afterwards everybody will say, 'Oh, he was just a murderer who went crazy,' and in a day or two they'll forget all about you and nothing will change."

Saxton went on, "Look, Eugene, you've already made your point. The whole jail is locked down, waiting for this to end. All the other guys know what you've done for them. If you work with us on this, we can work together to make some real changes."

Saxton continued to talk calmly to Jones and told him he would testify for him in court and say that he, Jones, was under a lot of stress and that he wasn't in his right mind when he did this thing.

Saxton told him, "Naturally, I can't say that we're going to let you go free, but I will go to court and testify in your behalf."

Slowly, after a couple of hours of talking with him, Saxton won Jones over. We could see the tide had turned when Jones asked Saxton if he would be hurt by the cops if he surrendered.

Saxton said to Jones, "If you don't hurt anybody here, I guarantee nobody will hurt you."

It worked. Little by little we could see that Jones was calming down and coming to his senses. Saxton repeatedly told Jones he wouldn't be harmed when the officers came in to take him into custody and that he would be treated with respect. Finally, at about 5 p.m. Jones laid the knife on Doug Heil's desk, and Saxton signaled the officers out in the corridor to come in and get the surrendering inmate.

While all of this had been going on in Doug's office, officers had spread out through the school and moved everybody out. They had gone from room to room on the second floor, ordering everybody out of the building but not telling them there was a hostage situation on the first floor. Kim told me later that when she got out into the lobby, Mike Nawrocky happened to be up on the second level looking down into the lobby.

He yelled to Kim, "Are you all right?"

Kim said "Yes, I'm fine," but she had no idea why he would ask her that other than the fact that they had grown up together and he was just generally asking her how she was doing. She left the jail and drove home to Bordentown.

After the officers moved into Doug's office and handcuffed Jones, a medical team came in and checked each of us out, taking our blood pressure, listening to our hearts and asking us if we were feeling any palpitations or pains. Then Internal Affairs came in and debriefed us. They told us we should report to work the next day as if nothing had happened unless we started to feel any physical or emotional reactions in which case we were to call a certain telephone number. They told us reporters would probably be waiting outside and that we were free to talk to the press if we wanted but that it was probably best if we said as little as possible because Jones would have to go to trial on this.

Ginny was working in Princeton at Educational Testing Service at the time, and I always, like clockwork, got home before she did. The first clue she had that something was wrong was my not being there to greet her. Then her brother-in-law, Jim Wallace, came in and told her he had heard something on the radio about hostages being taken at the prison.

Ginny said to Jim, "Did they say any women were involved?"

When Jim told her he thought there were, she knew immediately that the incident was in the school since, at the time, that was the only area inside where women worked. Before she even had time to process the implications, though, the phone rang. It was Kim. Mike Nawrocky had called her at home and told her all about Jones and that I had been held hostage but that the incident was over. Kim told Ginnny that I was OK, so Ginny found out I was a hostage but that I was all right all in the same phone call.

That night, Kim called me up, crying, and said, "Daddy, I can't work there. I can't work in that place."

She asked me to tell them that she wasn't coming back. Under the circumstances, I didn't even try to talk her out of quitting. So, that was the end of her career at Trenton State Prison—a total of about three hours (she got a check in the mail for one day's pay.) Darryl Curtis holds the record for the shortest stay as an inmate, and Kim Camisa Walker probably owns the record for the shortest career as an employee.

As for Jones, he went to court and got another 20 years tacked on to his 30-year murder bid. In New Jersey, taking a hostage falls under the kidnapping statute with an automatic 20-year sentence. Saxton kept his word and did testify on Jones' behalf, but my understanding is that the statute doesn't leave any room for bargaining. Jones is still at Trenton and we would run into each other occasionally, but we never talked about the incident.

****

The next attempted escape was one of the strangest. In October of 1986 somebody dropped a dime (the way most escape attempts are discovered), and internal affairs scooped up six inmates. Gary Hilton, who was now assistant commissioner, told the press, "It was a unique attempt."

The six guys, "heavy hitters" with long sentences, worked in a big shop building near the back wall of the prison. Just on the other side of the wall in that section of the prison is the niche where the original 18th century jail—now the warden's house—sits.

The inmates had built a crossbow powered by compressed air. Then they made several short arrow-like projectiles out of scrap metal. They had also accumulated material for some kind of incendiary device. When internal affairs checked out the second floor of the shop building, they found several wooden planks rigged with nuts and bolts obviously designed to be fitted together to bridge the gap from a shop window to the top of the wall behind the warden's house. The guys in internal affairs figured the six planned to either firebomb the tower or kill the guard with a projectile fired from the crossbow—or both. There was also evidence that people from the outside would be waiting in cars on Second Street near the warden's house to pick up the inmates after they got over the wall.

Except for the danger to the officer in the tower, I almost would have liked to have seen this one go down just to see how far they would have gotten with that 30-foot bridge suspended 20 feet in the air.

****

Things seemed to quiet down in the escape department for the next few years, and then in November of 1988, another killer got over the wall. Gonzalo Marrero, 37, was one of the criminals that Castro sent us in the Mariel boatlift of 1980. Like a lot of those guys that came over when they emptied out the Cuban jails, Marrero was a real sweetheart. He was convicted of a double murder in Hudson County in the spring of 1986 and had been in Trenton for a little over two years when he broke out. Marrero reminded me a lot of Mario DeLucia: he was just about the same size, five feet, four inches tall, 125 pounds, and he seemed like another born loser.

In December of 1985 Marrero and two others invaded a restaurant in Union City. They tied up and killed a man and a woman execution style with a bullet to the back of the head. The woman was sexually assaulted.

When he got to Trenton in April of 1986, Marrero was assigned to a cell in 4-wing, the oldest cell block in the jail, with two other killers: Jorge LaBrada and Andrew Bisesi, both 28. LaBrada was from Elizabeth and was serving a 45-year sentence for aggravated manslaughter and robbery; Bisesi was from Passaic and was serving a life sentence for murder.

The walls in 4-wing, the "Andrew Jackson Wing," are constructed of stone blocks, 30 inches thick by 16 inches wide and ten inches high. Marrero and his two partners accumulated a variety of little chipping and digging tools: old broken chisels that had been thrown away in the repair shop, a butter knife, shanks, ten-penny nails, you name it. They worked for weeks, maybe months, on the mortar surrounding one of the blocks. When they stopped working each night, they stuffed the gaps around the stone block with cardboard and painted it white with paint they had smuggled in from one of the shops.

Marrero had also managed to get a friend of his in one of the shops to build him a wooden modular bookcase for his cell. Marrero designed the book case so that it could be broken down into sections. He told officers and inmates who commented on the design that he had it built so that it could be taken apart in case he was moved to another, smaller cell.

At about three o'clock in the morning of November 22, Marrero and his two buddies drew straws to see who would go over the wall first. Marrero won. They agreed that once they were over the wall and hit the street, it was every man for himself. One of the men broke the "bookcase" down while the other two worked on pushing that huge block out into the alley between 4-wing and the mess hall. Marrero went out first and dropped the few feet down to the ground. The other two passed the wood and the hardware to him through the hole in the wall, and then they crawled out. Using open-ended wrenches they had made from toothbrushes, the three guys put together a 19-foot scaling ladder from the pieces of the bookcase. They used the same wrenches to unscrew bolts from the hinges on a gate in a chain-link fence between them and the perimeter wall.

Dragging the ladder behind them, the three convicts worked their way over to the base of the wall between towers 4 and 5. Working quickly and quietly in the dark, moonless night, they leaned the ladder up against the wall and Marrero went up. Just as he reached the top of the wall and was working his way through the razor wire, getting cut in the process, Marrero was spotted by one of the tower guards. The guard turned on the tower searchlight and trained it on LaBrada and Bisesi, still standing at the bottom of the ladder. They knew they were caught with no place to go and gave it up. While the tower guard was covering the two men still on the inside of the wall with his shotgun and ordering them to surrender, Marrero finished negotiating the razor wire and dropped down onto the grassy strip on Second Street at the base of the outer wall. He was off and running as soon as his feet hit the grass.

Corrections officers and Trenton police were on Marrero's trail within minutes, but he had enough of a head start to lose himself among the row houses and backyards of the working-class neighborhood around the jail. He worked his way down toward the Delaware River, about six blocks away. Trenton is an old city with a lot of storm drains and sewers running down and emptying into the river in that section of town. When he got down to the river bank, Marrero crawled into one of the storm drains to wait out the search.

Blood on the ladder, the razor wire and the sidewalk on Second Street indicated that Marrero had been cut up when he went over the wall. More than 100 officers and bloodhounds fanned out through the surrounding neighborhood and found a blood trail leading down to the river bank. They followed the trail to an old fishing wharf near the end of a storm sewer system that empties into the river. Figuring that Marrero had either crawled up into the sewer or was hiding in the heavy brush along the riverbank, the Department of Corrections set up a command post on the wharf. As police and corrections officers were shining lights into the sewer, somebody spotted what he thought was a bloody handprint on the side of the pipe in a system that runs about a half mile under one of the neighborhoods near the prison and has seven manholes.

Sergeant Robert Gorbe of the Department of Corrections special operations group followed by a state bloodhound named Dato crawled several hundred feet up Federal Street through the narrowing pipes, then made a left turn and crawled up Union Street—in the dark several feet under the pavement. Up ahead, workers from the city sewer utility lowered lamps into manholes, hoping to silhouette Marrero and giving Gorbe a target to crawl toward.

"Bobby! Everything all right down there, Bobby?" yelled correction officers and state police into the open manholes.

No Marrero. They pumped water in to try to flush him out. Nothing. The tide came up, pushing river water into the big pipes down near the banks of the Delaware. Still no sign of the elusive fugitive.

Throughout the day, officers searched trains leaving Trenton and posted warnings and descriptions of Marrero in the emergency rooms of city hospitals. State police helicopters flew low over the river, searching along the river bank while marine police boats cruised back and forth watching for Marrero to try to swim over to Pennsylvania. Armed corrections officers and Trenton police stood guard on street corners in the neighborhoods around the prison as other officers went door to door, asking if anyone had seen anything suspicious.

Around six o'clock in the evening, Trenton police officers Marty Nawrock and Richard Czyz were patrolling in their paddy wagon on Lalor Street about four blocks from the prison when they saw a short Hispanic man, soaking wet and dressed in dark clothing, walking rapidly along the street. As they hit the guy with their high beams and slowed down to take a closer look, the man put his hand up alongside his face and did a quick 180-degree turn. Czyz jumped out of the wagon while Nawrock gunned the engine and shot ahead to cut Marrero off farther up the block.

Marrero took off and sprinted up the street, turning the corner onto Lamberton but Nawrock careened around the corner and drove the van onto the sidewalk, blocking Marrero while Czyz caught him from behind.

"When we grabbed him, he went real quick for the front of his pants, but we pinned his arms real fast and cuffed him," Nawrock said.

When Nawrock and Czyz searched Marrero, they found a sharpened screwdriver blade with a masking tape handle and a butter knife. Marrero had dropped another shank on the top of the prison wall when he went over. LaBrada and Bisesi were also carrying shanks when they were caught.

Nawrock and Czyz also found $200 in cash and a plastic baggie in Marrero's pockets. At first, they thought the baggie contained marijuana, but it turned out to be filled with ground pepper to throw off the bloodhounds. Gary Hilton said he was concerned that Marrero had that kind of cash on him when he was caught since inmates aren't supposed to have any money inside the prison.

"He told us someone gave him the money while he was on the street," Hilton said, "but he spent most of the day in the sewer, and there aren't many people down there."

Hilton also said, "While it's true that people do occasionally get out of maximum security prisons despite our best efforts otherwise, it is my personal and professional belief that people do not escape if everyone is doing their job."

Marrero later told correction officers that he had hidden in the sewers throughout the day, moving farther and farther back up from the river as the tide pushed the river level higher. Finally, he had moved back from the river bank about three blocks and had come up through a manhole into the street just before he was spotted.

Marrero was hustled in front of municipal court judge Paulette Sapp-Peterson who charged him with unlawful possession of a weapon and set bail at $50,000. Marrero was back at The Wall in time to catch the announcement of his capture on *The News at 11*.

18

CHAPTER EIGHTEEN

RICH, JOHN AND 'THE ICEMAN'

Around the time that Bob Reldan was being paroled out of Rahway in 1975, Rich Biegenwald, the killer of the Union County municipal prosecutor, was notified that his application for parole had finally been approved. Rich was now in his mid 30's and had served 17 years, a typical life sentence under state statutes in effect back then. Now, under the 2C law, a life sentence for a conviction for first-degree murder in New Jersey is a minimum 30-year sentence with no provision for parole.

I occasionally ran into Rich around the jail, and he hadn't changed much from when he was sentenced in '57. He was still a quiet, hard-talking tough guy, giving off an air of "Don't screw with me or you'll get hurt." When he told me he had gotten a date, I told him I was happy for him and that I hoped, no offense, that I would never see him again.

After he was paroled in '75, Biegenwald settled in Perth Amboy until December of 1976 when he moved to Teaneck. In 1980 he committed a technical violation of parole when he moved out of New Jersey and into a house owned by his mother on Staten Island without getting permission from his parole officer. He was picked up by the NYPD on suspicion of rape, but the charges were dropped. New York sent him back to New Jersey as a parole violator. He did a few months in Rahway and was released from there in February of 1981. Rich moved to Point Pleasant where he was contacted by a guy he had been friends with off and on for 15 years in the joint, 50-year-old Dherran Fitzgerald. Fitzgerald, who had also been paroled recently, had been in and out of New Jersey prisons since 1955, mostly for robbery. Rich and Fitzgerald started hanging out together. When Fitzgerald got a job managing an apartment house on Sixth Avenue in Asbury Park in February of 1982, he invited Rich to move into the building.

This apartment house must have been an interesting place, to say the least. Clustered under one roof were Fitzgerald and his girlfriend in one apartment; Rich in another; and in a third apartment, a 34-year-old drug dealer, William Ward, who supposedly used Fitzgerald to "solve business problems" (i.e., kill people) for him. Quite a collection. Rich was 42 years old at the time and shared his apartment with 21-year-old Theresa Smith, who later testified that she and Rich were "very, very close friends." Ward, an operator in a video games arcade, had a long police record.

According to a chronology compiled by the Monmouth County prosecutor's office, starting in the fall of 1981, Biegenwald and Fitzgerald went on a 12-month killing spree that resulted in the murders of four young women and William Ward.

The killings began on Halloween eve, October 31, 1981. At 6:30 p.m. Maria Ciallella, 17, of Brick Township asked her father for a dollar and said she was going out for a while. She didn't say where she was going, but she told her parents she would return about midnight. At 20 minutes after 12, a Point Pleasant patrolman, Michael Whittles, was responding to a call, and he saw Ciallella walking along Route 88 toward her home. He made a mental note to go back and pick her up and take her home after he had completed the call. When he came back, less than ten minutes later, she had disappeared.

Biegenwald and Fitzgerald had driven by the teenager and lured her into their car. Then, Biegenwald shot her twice in the head with a small-caliber handgun, "just to watch her die," as the Monmouth County prosecutor said later. Ciallella had not been sexually assaulted. Her body was cut into three pieces, put into plastic bags and then buried in the side yard of Biegenwald's mother's house on Sharrotts Road in the Charleston section of Staten Island, about a mile from the Outerbridge Crossing bridge into New Jersey.

About six months later, on April 5, 1982, 18-year-old Deborah Osborne and her girlfriend left the motel in Toms River where Osborne was staying and working as a chambermaid and the two went to the Idle Hour Tavern on Route 88 in Point Pleasant. After they had been there for a while, Osborne's girlfriend went to the restroom, and when she came back, Osborne was gone. Prosecutors said that Osborne left the bar and was hitchhiking back to the motel when Rich Biegenwald picked her up. Her body would be found a year later also buried in the yard of Biegenwald's Staten Island house near Ciallella's remains. Osborne died from multiple stab wounds.

On August 27, 1982, Anna Olesiewicz, a 19-year-old woman from Camden was lured from the boardwalk in Asbury Park to Biegenwald's car by the offer of a marijuana cigarette. After driving around for a while, Biegenwald shot Olesiewicz four times in the head with a small-caliber handgun. He and Fitzgerald dumped the body in a lot in Ocean Township.

A few weeks later, the killings continued when Fitzgerald and William Ward got into an argument over a contract killing that Ward wanted Fitzgerald to do for him. Biegenwald and Fitzgerald jumped Ward and beat him badly in the backyard of the Asbury Park apartment house. Then Biegenwald shot Ward five times in the head execution style with a handgun equipped with a silencer. Biegenwald and Fitzgerald buried Ward's body six feet behind Mount Calvary Cemetery in Neptune Township.

The fifth victim was Betsy Bacon, 17, from Sea Girt. At about 11 p.m. on November 20, 1982, Bacon went out for a pack of cigarettes. She was walking along Route 71, heading for a convenience store in nearby Spring Lake Heights. Biegenwald got her into his car and killed her with two shots to the head, again from a small-caliber gun. Biegenwald brought her body to the garage behind the apartment on Sixth Ave., and the next day he took it to a secluded area about 15 miles away in Tinton Falls and buried it in a shallow grave.

On January 14, 1983, two months after the Bacon murder, a couple of kids playing in the wooded area behind a Burger King on Route 35 in Ocean Township discovered Anna Olesiewicz's body. Theresa Smith had moved out of the Biegenwald apartment and was living with a boyfriend whose estranged wife, Bonnie Curtis, was a Monmouth County probation officer. When Smith heard that Olesiewicz's body had been found, she told Curtis that she knew something about the murder. Curtis contacted Ocean Township detective Sgt. Robert Miller, and Miller persuaded Smith to give a statement to police.

Based on Smith's statement, police went to the Asbury Park apartment house and arrested Rich and Fitzgerald. When they searched the apartments, police found drugs and a variety of weapons, including revolvers, a .45-caliber machine gun, a sawed-off shotgun, cigarette lighters that fired bullets, silencers, inactive grenades, pipe bombs, and, in Fitzgerald's apartment, a .22-caliber pistol.

Almost as soon as he was arrested, Fitzgerald started cooperating with police. Fitzgerald talked to his lawyer, Jon Steiger, and gave him information about Biegenwald's string of murders. Steiger went to the Monmouth County prosecutor's office with the information and made a deal for Fitzgerald—a lighter sentence in exchange for Fitzgerald's testimony against Biegenwald.

Rich was indicted for the murder of Anna Olesiewicz and went on trial in Monmouth County Court in Freehold in late November of 1983. In his opening remarks, Assistant Monmouth County Prosecutor James Fagan said that Anna Olesiewicz and her friend Denise Hunter had gone to the Asbury Park boardwalk in August of 1982 "to have fun and hunt for drugs."

Fagan said "Richard Biegenwald was also hunting, but not for drugs. He was hunting for someone to kill."

When Biegenwald's lawyer, Louis Diamond, opened, he said, "You could take the same case and change the defendant's name to 'Fitzgerald.'"

Diamond told the jury that Fitzgerald was the one they ought to be looking at for the murder of Anna Olesiewicz. Diamond said that Fitzgerald listed his occupation as a murderer and that he was a hit man for a drug dealer. Diamond also said that Fitzgerald was a despicable man who had "necrophiliac habits."

Prosecutor Fagan's first witness was Denise Hunter, Anna Olesiewicz's friend who was with her on the boardwalk the night Olesiewicz was killed. Hunter testified that she and Anna had driven up from Camden to visit Hunter's uncle in Neptune and had ended up on the boardwalk.

Hunter told Fagan, "If somebody came up and said, 'Do you want to smoke a joint,' we would do it."

Hunter got separated from Olesiewicz, and that was the last time she saw her friend alive.

Fagan then called Theresa Smith to the stand. Smith told the jury about her relationship with Biegenwald and that Biegenwald had been after her to participate in the murder of a random victim with him. She said that in the early morning hours of August 28, Biegenwald came into her bedroom, woke her up and wanted her to come out with him. Smith said she couldn't remember the exact conversation because she was half asleep, but she recalled that Biegenwald got angry because he had picked out a victim for her to kill and she wasn't going along with it. Smith testified that she looked out the window and saw the shadow of a passenger sitting in Biegenwald's car parked in the driveway.

The next day Biegenwald picked Smith up from her job in Brick Township and when they got back to the house in Asbury Park, Rich told her, "I have something to show you—if you have the stomach for it."

Biegenwald took Smith to the garage behind the house. He unlocked the padlock on the door and they went inside. Smith said that all she saw at first was a mattress, but when Biegenwald lifted the mattress she saw the body of a girl with a large green trash bag over her head secured with a cord around the neck.

Smith said Biegenwald told her this was his victim from the night before, and the trash bag was there because she had been shot in the head. Then Rich asked Smith if she had ever felt a dead body. When Smith said, "No," Biegenwald told her to pick up the leg. She picked up the leg.

Biegenwald told Smith that he had picked Olesiewicz up on the boardwalk, smoked marijuana with her and brought her back to the house, telling her he wanted to get some more. Biegenwald said that he shot Olesiewicz in the head with a .22 short. Rich knew from his days in the joint that the .22 was ideal for shooting people in the head because the bullet didn't exit from the skull, instead rattling around inside and doing a lot more damage. It also limited the amount of blood splash, especially desirable when someone is shot inside a car, as Olesiewicz was.

When Fagan asked Smith if Biegenwald told her why he shot Olesiewicz, Smith said, "She was there, so he just shot her."

When Dherran Fitzgerald took the stand, he said that he got back to the apartment house in Asbury Park about 5:30 a.m. after a night in Wildwood. Fitzgerald said he found Biegenwald walking around in the yard.

"He told me he had a problem. He said there was a body in the garage he had to get rid of," Fitzgerald said.

"I asked him the whys and wherefores—why he killed her—but he wouldn't give me a straight answer. All he would say is something about this being a training exercise for Miss Smith."

Fitzgerald said he decided to testify for the state as a matter of "self-preservation" and "because I thought the murder was senseless."

Fitzgerald testified that Biegenwald and Smith drove over to Staten Island to visit Rich's mother, Sally, on August 29, and on the way back, Biegenwald spotted the wooded area behind the fast-food restaurant on Route 35. When they got back to Asbury Park, Rich and Fitzgerald loaded Olesiewicz's body into the trunk of Rich's car and drove to the spot. They took the body out and Fitzgerald drove around to make sure Biegenwald wasn't spotted while he dug the grave. When Fitzgerald picked Biegenwald up, Rich told him that the area was too marshy for a grave, so he just dumped the body.

Fitzgerald also said that he had the murder weapon, the .22-caliber pistol, in his apartment the day he was arrested because he had a fascination with guns and he was going to clean it.

Diamond presented his defense in one day. He tried to shift the blame onto Fitzgerald, who, like Biegenwald, had been returned to Trenton for parole violation, by calling in three TSP inmates to testify. Terry James said he worked in the inmate kitchen with Fitzgerald.

James said, "Fitzgerald showed me a clipping about this victim Anna and he told me this was one of the girls he killed. He said he shot her."

Charles Layton testified that Fitzgerald told him he would like to watch a girl die while he was having sex with her. He would kill the victim by shooting her in the head. Layton described Fitzgerald as "a sick person."

Marcus Albuquerque testified that Fitzgerald also told him about a fantasy of having sex and killing the partner. He said, "One day we were discussing sexual fantasies. He said he enjoyed killing women while having sex with them. He said he would blow their heads off."

All three of the inmates said they wrote to Diamond to tell him about Fitzgerald without any prompting from Biegenwald. But when the prosecutor asked them how they got Diamond's address to write to him, Layton and Albuquerque said Biegenwald had given them Diamond's business card with the address, and James said Biegenwald gave him an addressed envelope. Look at it this way: they got out of prison for a day and took a nice ride over to Monmouth County for a change of scenery while the state picked up the tab.

The jury deliberated for less than an hour. When Rich was found guilty, Olesiewicz's boyfriend, Michael Knoblauch, who had been in the courtroom during most of the six-day trial, said he would like to administer the lethal injection if Rich got the death penalty because "he did that to my girlfriend, and the way he did it—no reason behind it at all."

The next day the same jury deliberated for six hours in the penalty phase of the trial before recommending the death penalty. When Judge Patrick J. McGann asked Biegenwald if he had anything to say before the sentence was pronounced, Rich just said quietly, "No, your honor."

Biegenwald was shipped back to Trenton and became the second guy to go into the CSU (Capital Sentences Unit) under New Jersey's recently reinstated death penalty statute. Thomas Ramseur, 44, had been the first person sentenced to death under the new law about six months before and was already on death row when Rich came back into Trenton. Up until the killing of Anna Olesiewicz, it seemed like Rich was leading a charmed life: he wasn't killed in the shootout with Maryland police in '57; he didn't get the death penalty in the Sladowski killing; he killed Ciallella and Osborne while New Jersey had no death penalty. Now, though, it looked like his luck had run out—the new death penalty statute had gone into effect August 6, 1983, and Rich had killed Anna Olesiewicz in the early-morning hours of August 28. Ramseur had stabbed his girlfriend to death in Irvington on August 25, so he won the race to be the first New Jersey murderer eligible for execution under the new death penalty. Rich finished second.

Monmouth County still had four more Biegenwald murders to prosecute, and they started with the next one that qualified under the new death penalty statute: William Ward. Judge McGann granted a change-of-venue motion to Burlington County because of the publicity surrounding the Olesiewicz case, and Rich's next trial was held in February of 1984 in Mount Holly.

During the three-day trial, Rich's attorney, Louis Diamond, again attempted to shift the blame for the killing onto Dherran Fitzgerald, who testified for the prosecution. Theresa Smith testified that Biegenwald had told her that he killed

Ward, and a tenant in an upstairs apartment said she saw Biegenwald with a gun with a silencer standing over a man with a bloodied face who was screaming for help. (As I said, this must have been an interesting apartment house).

Fitzgerald told the jury that Ward had hired him to kill a member of Ward's criminal organization for a payment of $25,000. Ward was involved in the large-scale manufacture of amphetamines and wanted Fitzgerald to kill someone who was stealing from him and generally "fouling up the organization."

Fitzgerald testified that he and Ward got involved in an argument over the contract. Fitzgerald said Ward wanted to watch the killing and Fitzgerald refused, telling Ward he didn't want any witnesses. The argument developed into a fight that spilled out of the kitchen into the yard of the Asbury Park house. Biegenwald got involved, and he and Fitzgerald beat up Ward, bloodying his face and dragging him onto the front porch. Then, while Fitzgerald held Ward face down on the front porch, Rich knelt in front of Ward and Fitzgerald and shot Ward five times in the head with the .22-caliber pistol. Fitzgerald said he thought Rich shot Ward twice on the left side of the head and three times on the right side of the head. The Monmouth County medical examiner, Dr. Stanley M. Becker, testified that Ward was shot once on the left side of the head and four times on the right side at the base of the brain.

After a three-day trial, the jury took another three days to find Rich guilty. During the death-penalty phase, the jury was shown a video tape of the testimony of Dr. Azariah Eshkenazi during the Olesiewicz trial. In my many conversations with Rich over the years, he had told me several times about how his mother had had him sent to mental institutions at a young age and that he had been given a lot of shock treatments.

He also told me that Sally had called the cops on him once and he had told her, "If you ever do that again, I'll kill you."

I remember looking at him and saying, "Aw, come on, Rich, you don't mean that. You wouldn't kill your own mother."

I'll never forget the look on his face and in his eyes when he said, "I sure as shit would."

Eshkenazi testified that Rich's records showed he had had a troubled childhood. He had been in and out of mental institutions starting when he was eight years old and had been given 20 shock treatments. Eshkenazi said that Rich had an anti-social personality with paranoid traits, and that he could intellectually understand the nature of his acts but not emotionally or morally.

In his closing argument during the penalty phase, Diamond made the same request he had in the Olesiewicz trial. He asked the jury to keep Rich alive so that society could study the mind of a sociopath.

Diamond said, "Alive, Mr. Biegenwald can be studied and treated. If you take Mr. Biegenwald and bury him, you're burying society's mistakes instead of treating them."

The jury recommended a life sentence.

Monmouth County started preparing for the next trial, but in September of '84 Rich went back to the courthouse in Freehold and pleaded guilty to the Ciallella and Osborne murders. Since those murders had occurred before the new death penalty took effect, the most Rich could get was life for those crimes. Biegenwald was still facing trial in the Betsy Bacon murder, committed after the new death penalty law had gone into effect. Diamond said his client had pleaded guilty for two reasons: the first was that the Monmouth County prosecutor agreed not to introduce the Ciallella and Osborne murders as aggravating factors in the death-penalty phase if Biegenwald were tried and convicted in the Bacon murder; the second was that Diamond and Biegenwald felt that the publicity that was bound to come with a Ciallella and Osborne trial would remind people that Rich was a cold-blooded serial killer and make conviction (and death penalty) in the Bacon case that much easier.

In the courtroom, Judge McGann asked Rich if he had killed Maria Ciallella and if so, where he had done it. Rich said he couldn't remember exactly where he had killed the 17-year-old but that it was near the beachfront in Point Pleasant. He also said he couldn't remember if he had used the same .22-caliber pistol he had used to kill Olesiewicz and Ward.

McGann said, "Do you remember how you killed [Ciallella]?"

Rich said, "She was shot."

McGann asked him, "Did you shoot her?"

Rich said, "Yes."

Biegenwald then admitted he had stabbed 17-year-old Deborah Osborne to death, and he had buried both bodies, Osborne's on top of the dismembered Ciallella corpse, in a shallow grave in Sally's backyard on Staten Island. McGann sentenced Rich to two consecutive life terms, making a grand total of death by lethal injunction, three lifes, and 10 to 20 years on weapons and drug charges.

At the end of the Olesiewicz trial, McGann had sentenced Rich to die by lethal injection on January 26, 1984, even though everybody knew it would take years before the sentence was carried out because of the appeals process. But Rich's luck was holding. The New Jersey Office of the Public Defender had tied the Ramseur and Biegenwald cases together in an attempt to have the death penalty statute overturned. In March of 1987 the New Jersey Supreme Court upheld Ramseur's conviction but said the judge's instructions to the jury in the death-penalty phase were so prejudicial that Ramseur couldn't be subjected to the death penalty. So Ramseur was off the hook. Rich's conviction was also upheld, but the Supreme Court overturned the death penalty phase and ordered Monmouth County to hold that part of the trial again. They did and Rich was again sentenced to death.

He appealed, and in August of 1991 his <u>second</u> death sentence was overturned once more on a 4-3 vote of the New Jersey Supreme Court (he was the first person in New Jersey to be sentenced to death twice for the same crime). So Rich went back to Freehold for a third death-penalty trial, and this time, one juror held out for life, so that's what the judge had to give him. A 4-3 vote by the Supreme Court. One juror holds out. Does this guy lead a charmed life or what?

When Rich came back to the prison and went into the general population, I went to the classification committee and asked if I could have him to work in the typewriter repair shop, which I was now supervising. They thought I was nuts, but they agreed. As I said, Rich and I had always gotten along, dating all the way back to when his mom used to visit him and I was in the mail room in the late 1950's.

So he came to work for me in 1991.

To this day, Rich will talk freely about the crimes he was convicted of and pleaded guilty to. But he will never discuss the Betsy Bacon case. Because his death sentence in the Olesiewicz case became the test case of the death penalty statute in New Jersey and went on for so many years, the state held off on bringing him to trial for the Bacon murder. Then, when all the smoke had cleared, the prosecutors must have figured it wasn't worth the taxpayers' money to go for another death sentence since Rich will never see the street again. But they could try him if they should ever decide it was worth the effort. So Rich will not talk about Betsy Bacon. I've told him many times he's crazy, but that crazy he's not.

Rich is not a big guy, about five foot, seven, balding, with a red beard, a pot belly, and very prominent dark circles under his eyes. He smokes a couple of packs of cigarettes a day and was recently diagnosed with lung cancer. He's basically arrogant and loves to talk about two things: the old days in the jail and how he beat the system.

He told me that when he came back on the parole violation in 1982, it was a totally new world in here. For one thing, he said, when he got back, the word had gotten around about him, and he found that almost everybody was afraid of him. When he first came back, he went into the general population because he hadn't yet gone to trial and gotten the death penalty in the Olesiewicz case. His take on all of the appeals and retrials was that he had very good lawyers and because the prosecutors, and the judge, were so anxious to get him, they made mistakes.

He said to me, "Look, Harry, everybody has to follow the law. I made a mistake. I committed a crime—I killed somebody and got caught. That was <u>my</u> mistake —killing somebody . . . ."

He paused for a minute and said, ". . .or getting caught, depending on how you look at it."

Then he said, "I got caught, so I had to go through a trial to establish my guilt or innocence. The legal process has its own rules and regulations; that's the law. If <u>they</u> make a mistake, then they have to pay the price for it."

We were sitting in my office during this conversation. At this point, Biegenwald took a deep drag on his cigarette and said, "During the trial, the police made mistakes, the prosecutors made mistakes, and the judge, especially the judge, made mistakes. The judge knew better but that's how bad he wanted to get me. He told the jury things he shouldn't have told them, so my lawyers appealed, and the high court looked at this and said, 'Yeah, well, Biegenwald was found guilty, but they made a mistake when they sentenced him to death. They shouldn't have done it that way. They're not allowed to do it that way, so we have to grant him a new death penalty trial.'"

Biegenwald told me that one juror held out for life in the third death-penalty trial in the Olesiewicz case, and one in the Ward trial.

"And that's all it takes under New Jersey law," he said as he blew smoke toward the ceiling.

So now Rich Biegenwald spends his days repairing the hundreds of manual typewriters used by the inmates for their correspondence and appeals, and I imagine that some of the Monmouth County prosecutors spend a part of their day

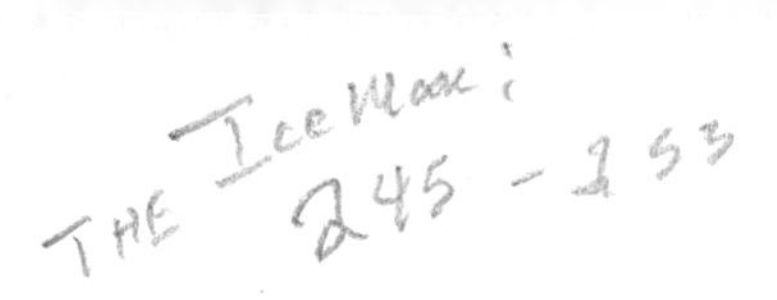

hoping to hear that he has died a lingering, painful death from lung cancer. So far, Biegenwald is winning.

****

I first met "The Iceman," Rich Kuklinski, shortly after he came into Trenton with two consecutive life sentences in March of 1988. He had just been convicted of killing two small-time hoods by lacing their food with cyanide and strangling them. A couple of months later he would go back to the Bergen County courthouse in Hackensack and plead guilty to two more murders. From what Rich has told me and others, he has killed at least 100 people, "for business reasons."

When I heard that this guy the press was calling "The Iceman" had come into the prison, and I heard his last name "Kuklinski," I wondered if he was related to Joe Kuklinski, an inmate I had known for years. Joe Kuklinski is a big guy—about six-foot, three and well over 200 lbs. In the time he's been in Trenton, Joe has been losing it mentally to the point where one day he tried to escape out of the big yard during a recreation period (good luck), and punched a sergeant in the process. For the last few years Joe has been confined in 1EE, the "nut wing."

The first time I saw Rich Kuklinski, I knew immediately that he and Joe were brothers. Rich is also a big guy—about 6 ft., 4 in. tall, around 270 lbs. When I first met him sometime in the spring or summer of 1988, Rich had just been assigned to work as a clerk in the inmate law library. I had heard about his trial in north Jersey through the grapevine and in the newspapers. When we met, we hit it off right away. I told him I had known his bother for years, and that seemed to establish an immediate connection between us. Rich is soft spoken and witty with a good sense of humor. I always enjoyed kidding around with him.

One day he and I were in the law library with several other inmates and I said to him, "You know, Rich, it's hard to believe that a nice guy like you could have done all those things they say you did."

He laughed and said, "Keep saying things like that, Harry, and maybe they'll let me out of here some day."

He knows damned well that he'll never see the street again, but he can still kid about it. I should mention that I would never ask someone like Rich specifically about his crimes—it's considered poor jailhouse etiquette. Plus it could be dangerous. If an inmate volunteers the information, that's fine, but unless you know the guy real well, you normally stay away from that topic.

One aspect of Rich Kuklinski's makeup that surprised me recently was his lack of aggressiveness, (Should I say his "coolness?") in a confrontation. I had read and heard that Rich could be a raging bull when he was pissed off, and at six-four, 270, he had the size and strength to do some damage. One day, Rich and another smaller inmate (6 ft, 200 lbs.) got into an argument that led to the smaller guy taking a swing at Rich. Rich has huge hands. He just put his open hand up in front of him and blocked the guy's punch.

I thought, "Uh oh, here it comes. Rich is gonna mop the floor with this guy's ass."

Nothing. He just defended himself by deflecting the punch and backing away—which is a smart move in jail. Number one, you don't know if the other guy has a shank, and number two, if you start swinging back, somebody's going to hit the riot bell and flood the area with cops. Then you **and** the other guy are going to court-line and probably to lock-up, even if the other guy started it. So even though Rich could have easily kicked the other guy's ass, he stayed cool. The Iceman.

Rich is a celebrity around the jail because of an article about him, "Tracking the Iceman," by Reynolds Dodson that appeared in the September, 1996 issue of *Reader's Digest* and two half-hour profiles that HBO did on him in 1998 and in 2001.

The case against "Big Rich" began as a routine investigation in 1981 when an informant tipped the NJ State Police that a burglary ring was operating in North Jersey. The informant showed a state police detective, Patrick Kane, more than 40 houses that had been burglarized and said that he could identify the members of the gang that had robbed them. Kane built a case resulting in a 153-count indictment in November of 1982 against the gang members. Then he went looking for them. When Kane asked the informant how the gang had managed to fence all of the loot, the guy didn't know for sure. All he knew was that a guy named "Big Rich" Kuklinski and a place known only as "the store" in Paterson were involved.

The first member of the gang to be captured, in December of 1982, was the foreman of the house-robbing crew, Percy House. House was locked up in the Passaic County jail while police continued to search for two of the other crew members, Daniel Deppner, 34, and Gary Smith, 38. On December 27, North Bergen police were called to the York Motel where they found Smith's body stuffed under a bed. He had been strangled.

A week later, the Franklin, NJ police called Kane. They said they had picked up Danny Deppner's wife, Barbara, and she was scared out of her wits. Kane went to Franklin police headquarters and talked to Barbara Deppner. She told Kane Danny had called her and said that after House was arrested, Rich Kuklinski had gotten a room for him and Smith at the York Motel. Kuklinski had ordered them not to leave the motel because the heat was on for the burglaries. Rich would bring them food and anything else they needed. Danny Deppner told his wife that Smith got tired of being cooped up in the motel and decided on December 23 to pay a Christmas visit to his daughter in a nearby town.

Danny Deppner told his wife Kuklinski showed up while Smith was out and went into a rage when he found out what Smith had done. Kuklinski said Smith had to die for exposing them to discovery by the police. When Smith got back to the motel, Kuklinski went out to get food for everyone. He returned with three hamburgers, two with pickles, one without. Smith got the one without the pickle and within minutes after eating it, he was choking and thrashing around. Deppner told his wife that Kuklinski ordered him to finish Smith off and, being too scared not to obey, Deppner strangled Smith with a lamp cord.

After calling and telling his wife about the killing, Danny Deppner disappeared again. Kane couldn't figure out why this guy Kuklinski would kill one of his partners over such a simple error in judgment, especially since the crime they were involved in, burglary, wasn't serious enough to justify a murder. Kane also figured that Deppner could be next on the hit list.

Kane did some digging and found out a few things about Rich Kuklinski. Number one, Kuklinski had no criminal record. He seemed to be a "Joe Average" businessman who lived with his wife and three kids in a split-level house in suburban Dumont. Dumont police said they had once picked up Kuklinski on suspicion of passing bad checks, and he had been photographed and fingerprinted, but the case had been dropped. Number two, Kuklinski had once listed his occupation as a film distributor. Kane found out the films he distributed were pornography.

The police didn't yet have enough solid evidence to go after Big Rich for Smith's murder, and the trail on Danny Deppner had grown cold. Meanwhile, Percy House was still in jail, awaiting trial on the burglary charges. Then, on May 14, 1983, a bicyclist riding down a lonely dirt road near a reservoir in West Milford saw a turkey buzzard pecking at some garbage bags. Taking a closer look, the cyclist saw the bones of a human arm sticking out of a hole in the bags.

When an assistant state medical examiner, Dr. Geetha Natarajan examined the corpse, she found that it was the body of a man, about 6 ft., 2 in. who had weighed over 175 lbs. Natarajan speculated that the man had been murdered because he had been so carefully wrapped in the garbage bags, but she couldn't find any evidence of wounds, other than a bruise on the victim's neck. Through motel receipts and family photographs in the man's wallet, police established that the body was Danny Deppner. Barbara Deppner confirmed the identification.

Kane heard that Percy House was getting antsy in jail, so he went to see if House might cooperate with police. House was a tough hood, but he agreed to help with the investigation in exchange for some consideration in his own problems with the law. House told Kane that he had heard through the grapevine that Rich Kuklinski might have been involved in three other murders.

One was Louis Masgay, a store owner from Forty Fort, PA, who had disappeared July 1, 1981 after leaving home with $90,000 in cash to meet Kuklinski in a diner in Little Falls. When Masgay didn't return home, his wife filed a missing person report. Police found the van Masgay was driving, but there was no trace of him or the money. When police had questioned Rich Kuklinski, he denied knowing Masgay or ever meeting with him.

House then mentioned another possible Kuklinski victim: Paul Hoffman, a pharmacist from Cliffside Park, who disappeared in April of 1982 along with $25,000 in cash after meeting with Kuklinski to buy some pharmaceutical supplies. Kuklinski had been questioned in that case also and denied knowing or meeting with Hoffman. Police couldn't prove otherwise.

When Kane talked to an assistant DA whose office was working on Hoffman's disappearance, the prosecutor told Kane that he was familiar with Kuklinski's name, but not from the Hoffman case. The prosecutor said that Kuklinski's name had come up during an investigation in 1980 of the murder of a big-time gambler, George Malliband, rumored to be in trouble with loan sharks. Malliband had been shot, dismembered, stuffed in a drum and rolled off a cliff behind a chemical factory in Jersey City. His body was found February 1, 1980. Before he disappeared (with $27,000 in cash), Malliband had told his brother he was going to meet with Richard Kuklinski. No one had seen Rich with Malliband, and there was no other evidence connecting Rich with the murder.

Now, though, Kane was beginning to get the impression that he was dealing with something more than a "Joe Average" who lived quietly with his wife and family in a split-level in suburbia.

But still there was no hard evidence connecting Rich Kuklinski with any of the killings—only hearsay.

Because of George Malliband's involvement with loan sharks and the way he was killed, Kane thought there might be a Mafia connection, so he contacted the NYPD and sent them the mug shot of Kuklinski from the bad check incident. One of their informants recognized Rich as "The Polack," a hit man known to be an expert at getting rid of bodies. The Polack had worked closely with Roy DeMeo, another Mafia enforcer who had been murdered.

Then, in September of 1983, Louis Masgay's body was found in a park in Orangetown, N.Y. Like Dan Deppner, Masgay had been carefully wrapped in garbage bags. He had been shot once in the back of the head. When police examined the body, they found that Masgay was still wearing the clothes he had on when he told his wife he was headed out to meet with Rich Kuklinski in July of 1981—26 months earlier. The body should have been a skeleton by now. The medical examiner also found ice crystals in the tissues of Masgay's body, an indication that he had been stored in a freezer to hide the time of death.

Storing a body in a freezer. Coolness under questioning. A hit man with ice water in his veins. To New Jersey police, Rich Kuklinski wasn't "The Polack"—he was "The Iceman."

Kane could now connect Kuklinski with five murders, but he still didn't have the hard evidence to arrest him.

Through the office of the New Jersey Attorney General, Detective Kane hooked up with an experienced undercover agent from the federal Bureau of Alcohol, Tobacco and Firearms (ATF), Domenick Polifrone. Polifrone infiltrated "the store" in Paterson and gained the confidence of the guys in Kuklinski's gang. Meanwhile, the state police had gotten permission to tap Kuklinski's telephone lines and were slowly obtaining evidence that way.

Eventually, by December of 1986, Kuklinski trusted Polifrone enough to join him in a plot to rob and kill a "drug dealer" (another undercover agent). Polifrone told Kuklinski that he had a rich kid on the line who wanted to buy a couple of kilos of cocaine for $85,000. Polifrone and Rich agreed that the two of them would meet the rich kid at a service area on the turnpike, kill him and split the money.

On the morning of December 17, Rich and Polifrone met at the Vince Lombardi service area to set the plot in motion. Polifrone gave Rich a bag of three sandwiches and a vial of "cyanide" (actually powdered quinine prepared in a state police lab). Rich headed home to lace the sandwich and to pick up a windowless van that would be used in the murder. Polifrone and Kuklinski would meet back at the service area later in the day and wait for the rich kid to show up.

After Rich left the service area, he went home, "poisoned" the sandwich, and got ready to take his wife to a doctor's appointment. He was moving so calmly and deliberately that the cops tailing him panicked—they thought he might be on to them and wasn't going back to the service area. They decided to go with what they had and bust him.

As Rich and his wife drove down the quiet suburban street, a squad of vehicles containing plainclothes investigators, uniformed state police and federal agents converged on his car. When Rich realized he was being cut off, he gunned his car over a curb and across a neighbor's lawn, around some police cars and back into the street. One of the plainclothes cops further down the street stood in the middle of the road and aimed his pistol at Kuklinski as Rich accelerated toward him. The officer didn't budge, coolly drawing a bead on Rich's head.

Kuklinski stopped the car, and before he could get to the pistol he had under his seat, the police yanked open the car door and dragged him out. Kane tried to handcuff Rich, but Kuklinski's wrists were so thick that Kane couldn't snap the 'cuffs closed. Finally, with a lot of effort, Kane was able to pull Rich's hands behind his back and cuff him. The Iceman's carefully maintained double life came to a screeching halt on December 17, 1986.

Rich went on trial in February of 1988 at the Bergen County courthouse in Hackensack for the Smith and Deppner murders. In this trial Rich was charged with eight offenses, two of them capital murder. Another trial was scheduled for later with 24 additional charges, including three more murders.

The newspapers picked up on "The Iceman" tag that police had started using after they found the ice crystals in the tissues of Masgay's body, and typical headlines in the New Jersey *Record* and *The Star Ledger* during the trial were, "'Iceman' phoned slaying site, cop says," "Ex-fiancee of 'Iceman' daughter tells of helping dump body in woods," "'Iceman' accused of threatening witness," "'Iceman' knew for years he was being investigated."

Nailing Rich had been a long and tricky operation, requiring cooperation among local and state police along with the ATF (one of Rich's "enterprises" was trading in guns). The lead prosecutor for the trial was Robert J. Carroll from the New Jersey Attorney General's office along with another state Deputy Attorney General, Charles E. Waldron. They were assisted by the staff of Bergen County Prosecutor Larry McClure. The state wasn't taking any chances with this one.

Carroll said he would show that Richard Kuklinski, a 52-year-old businessman from a quiet New Jersey suburb with no prior arrest record, was actually a cold-blooded killer who was remarkably good at his trade. In this trial, Carroll said, the state would prove that Kuklinski was the brains behind a burglary ring and was helping to hide Daniel Deppner and Gary Smith when police found out about the gang. According to Carroll, Kuklinski and Deppner killed Smith when Smith jeopardized their hideout by telephoning his wife and hitchhiking home. Carroll said he would show that Kuklinski then killed Deppner to cover up the Smith murder. Rich's attorney, Assistant Public Defender Neal Frank, said there were no witnesses to the murders, and the state had no hard evidence to link his client to them.

In opening testimony Sgt. Ernest Volkmann of the NJ State Police testified that phone records showed that in late December of 1982 Kuklinski frequently called the York Motel where Smith and Deppner were holed up. Rich called the motel five times on Dec. 22 and 23, the day before and day of Smith's murder.

The star witness for the state was Percy House, the "foreman" of the house-robbing crew in the series of burglaries that first focused police attention on Rich. House was testifying against Rich in return for immunity from prosecution for his part in the crimes.

When House stepped up to the witness stand on February 24, 1988, Rich stared hard at his former accomplice, and House, also a tough nut, stared right back at him. Midway through his testimony, during a recess, House told prosecutor Waldron that Kuklinski had mouthed the words, "You're dead," at him. Waldron told the judge and asked that Rich be removed from the courtroom so that he couldn't intimidate the witness.

Judge Frederick Kuechenmeister warned Rich not to make gestures or comments to any of the witnesses and let him stay in the courtroom.

House told the jury that he and Kuklinski were involved in a group that stole cars, passed bad checks and received stolen property. House said that Kuklinski was the boss, he was the foreman, and Smith and Deppner were workers. House said that Deppner's ex-wife, Barbara, was also involved.

House said that the gang's problems began when the police started to put heat on them in November of 1982, and Gary Smith said that he wanted to leave the gang and get a job. House said that he and Rich discussed Smith's leaving the gang, and Rich said, "Gary knows too much about what's going on. If he doesn't want to be in anymore, then that's it," meaning that Smith would have to be killed.

Detective Kane's investigation led to the arrest of House in December of '82. House testified that Barbara Deppner came to visit him in the Passaic County jail, and he told her to tell Kuklinski that Smith needed to be killed. At the time, Smith and Danny Deppner were holed up in the York Motel in North Bergen.

House said that he found out several days later that Kuklinski had poisoned Smith's hamburger and that Danny Deppner had strangled Smith, and the two of them had stuffed Smith's body under a bed in the motel.

House made bail and got out of jail in February of '83. When he got out, he thanked Rich for taking care of the problem.

Rich said, "Let's not talk about it. Keep your mouth shut."

Then House and Rich discussed what to do about Danny Deppner. Rich told House that Danny would be "taken care of" and later said that Danny "wasn't going to be a problem to anyone anymore." House and Kuklinski decided that Barbara Deppner was OK because she was under House's control. At the time he testified at Rich's trial, House had been living with Barbara Deppner for five years, and prosecutors had put the two of them in a witness-protection program.

When Neal Frank cross-examined House, he noted that House had been granted immunity to help convict his nephew in another murder case. Frank said that House was a liar and was once again "trying to get away with murder."

Patrick Lane, the state police detective who had started the ball rolling in this case, testified that House had, in fact, initially lied to him and had taken him to a trailer park where House said that Danny Deppner had been killed. House told Lane that Kuklinski killed Deppner by injecting air into his veins with a hypodermic needle and then wrapped the body in garbage bags while House went out to get a pickup truck. Lane testified that House couldn't find the spot where he and

Kuklinski supposedly buried Deppner's body and that House later recanted the whole story. House said that he had "ordered" Kuklinski to kill Deppner but didn't know where, when nor how it was done.

Other than House, the most damaging witness against Rich was his daughter's former fiancee, Richard Patterson. Patterson testified that he helped Kuklinski dump a body in the woods in Passaic County in 1983.

Patterson said he basically lived in the Kuklinski house in Dumont for several years while still maintaining an apartment in Bergenfield and that over the years he and Rich had grown close. He said that Rich kept a key to the apartment. Patterson said that he and Rich's daughter had gone on a hunting trip to New York State in February of 1983, and when they got back to Dumont, Rich asked him to take a ride with him. While Rich and Patterson were in the car, heading toward Patterson's apartment, Rich told him he had been hiding someone in the apartment and had told the man not to go out, make any phone calls or stand near windows. Rich told Patterson he had been bringing the man his meals.

Patterson then testified that Rich told him the man had apparently called someone, and when Rich went to the apartment to bring the man a meal, he found the man dead on the living room floor, shot in the head.

Rich then told Patterson that the man's body was in the trunk of the car.

Rich directed Patterson to drive to a wooded area in West Milford where he asked Patterson to help him get the body out of the trunk. Patterson said he couldn't do it and got back into the driver's side of the car, reaching over into the glove box to pop the trunk lid. Patterson said he heard a couple of thumps and watched in the rearview mirror while Rich dragged something heavy out of the back of the car.

Patterson said the body was wrapped in brown plastic secured with silver tape and that Rich left the body lying on the snow-covered ground. Police recovered Danny Deppner's body about three months later, in May of 1983. Patterson said the incident didn't damage his relationship with Rich, that they still had "a lot of closeness."

Rich told Patterson never to speak about what he had seen that day. A few days later Patterson left his apartment and moved into the Kuklinski home in Dumont where he lived for the next few years. He moved out after his relationship with Kuklinski's daughter ended.

The medical examiner who did the autopsies on Smith and Deppner testified that both men had eaten shortly before they were killed and Smith's stomach contained ground meat. Dr. Geetna Natarajan said the condition of the bodies fit with the prosecution's theory that both were poisoned with cyanide before they were strangled. The absence of defensive wounds in two relatively young, healthy men indicated they had been incapacitated before they were killed. Dr. Natarajan testified she found no traces of cyanide in the bodies, but that wasn't surprising. Unlike most poisons, cyanide dissipates quickly from human tissue, and both bodies had decomposed long enough to eliminate all traces. Smith's body was in a warm motel room for four days before it was discovered, and Danny Deppner's was in the woods for three months.

Dominick Polifrone, the undercover agent from the ATF who plotted with

Kuklinski to kill the "rich kid" in a mythical cocaine deal, followed Dr. Natarajan to the stand. Polifrone told the jury that Rich Kuklinski had told him he often used poison to kill his victims and asked Polifrone to get some pure cyanide for him.

Polifrone laughed and told Rich to go to a garden store. Rich said he needed a higher grade of poison, "the kind of stuff you get from a laboratory." Then he had grinned and said, "I got some rats that need exterminating."

Kuklinski got serious and told Polifrone he had "to take care of somebody"—that he had a "personal problem." Prosecutors figured he was probably talking about Percy House or Barbara Deppner . . . or both.

Polifrone told the jury he posed for months as a New York wise guy named "Dom Provenzano," complete with pending fugitive warrants in case anyone should check his background. He even drove a big black Lincoln Continental to fit the role. Polifrone taped all of his phone conversations and meetings with Kuklinski. When the tapes were played in court, they sounded like a lecture on how to be a hit man for fun and profit.

In one telephone conversation, "Dom" asked Rich why he used poison, why he didn't just shoot his victims.

Rich said, "Well, it's quiet, my friend, and not as messy. I'm not averse to a little lead, but there's more than one way."

Kuklinski told Polifrone the cyanide could be mixed with ketchup and put on a hamburger, and the victim would be dead in seconds.

Polifrone asked Richie, "Doesn't it taste?"

Rich replied, "Naw, not if you mix it right. And even if he tastes it, he's already dead from it."

In her testimony, Dr. Natarajan had said cyanide is so powerful that 30 to 60 milligrams can kill someone instantly (a typical aspirin weighs between 325 and 500 milligrams).

Rich also told "Dom" that the cyanide could be administered as a mist from a nasal sprayer and when the victim collapsed, people would think it was a heart attack. Rich told Polifrone he once killed a man with a cyanide spray on a crowded street.

"The best effect is to hit him right in the nose," Rich said. " Got to hit him in the nose and where he inhales it. Then, once he inhales it, he's done."

Polifrone asked Rich if his method was "guaranteed."

Rich told him, "My friend, you can see it happen if you like because I've done it already. The way we do it, he has no way of knowing what it is till you get past him. Once he's got it, you know where he's going to go. It's in his system. He's done. He's gone."

In his summation, Kuklinski's lawyer, Neal Frank, conceded that Rich talked about cyanide in his conversations with Dominic Polifrone. But, Frank said, that wasn't enough to convict his client of being a murderer. Frank said if Kuklinski was really a hit man, would he ask his daughter's boyfriend to help him dispose of a body? Then he tried to undermine Percy House's testimony, saying, "Percy House wouldn't know the truth if he fell over it."

The jury went with the state's version and convicted Rich after about four hours of deliberation. They recommended against the death penalty, and Judge

Kuechenmeister gave Rich two consecutive life terms.

Two months later, in May of 1988, Rich pleaded guilty to the murders of George Malliband and Louis Masgay in exchange for the dropping of criminal charges against his wife and son. The state also agreed to drop a third murder charge against Rich in the death of Paul Hoffmann, though prosecutor Robert Carroll said in court that Rich had "confessed and implicated himself" in the killing.

When the judge asked Rich if he was guilty of murdering George Malliband (the gambler whose body was found in a drum in Jersey City), he said, "I shot George Malliband five times. It was due to business."

Then he admitted killing Louis Masgay, the guy police say he had kept in the freezer for a couple of years. Rich said, "I shot him once in the back of the head."

Under the plea-bargain agreement, unrelated drug and weapons charges against Rich's son, and weapons and resisting arrest charges against his wife were dropped. Rich will be 111 years old when he comes up for parole in 2047. I'll probably be retired by then.

****

John List was convicted on April 12, 1990, of killing his mother, his wife and his three children. He started working for me a couple of years later and was an exemplary employee from the time I hired him. He meticulously kept track of all of the paper we used in the print shop, kept the storeroom in apple pie order, and maintained accurate and detailed records of all supplies coming in and jobs going out. From everything I've read and heard about him and from the NBC TV Sunday Night Movie about his case in 1993, this is the same kind of methodical behavior he exhibited in murdering his family in November of 1971 and in evading capture for nearly 18 years.

The investigation into John List's deviation from the norm—big time—started on the night of December 7, 1971, when his neighbors in Westfield noticed the lights that had been burning continuously in the Lists' three-story Victorian mansion for a month were going out, one by one. Somebody called the police, and when they got into the old house on Hillside Avenue in this well-to-do community, in the ballroom they found the bodies of List's mother, Alma, 85; his wife, Helen, 45; and their three children, Patricia, 16; John Jr., 15; and Frederick, 13. All had been shot in the head with a .32-caliber revolver and a 9-millimeter pistol that investigators found in a desk drawer. Police also found a five-page confession addressed to the pastor of the Lists' church where John List sometimes taught Sunday school.

The bodies were discovered December 7, but investigators figured the murders took place on November 9 because List, always the meticulous planner, disappeared on that day after calling Westfield High School to tell them he was taking the kids on an extended vacation. He also stopped mail and newspaper delivery. A few days after the bodies were discovered, List's car was found in a parking lot at Kennedy Airport on Long Island, about an hour's drive from Westfield.

And that was the last anybody in New Jersey saw of John List for the next 17 1/2 years.

After years of dead-end leads, early in 1988 the head of the homicide division of the Union County prosecutor's office, Frank Marranca, asked the managing editor of *America's Most Wanted* TV show, Margaret Roberts, to take on the List case. Roberts accepted and asked Frank Bender, a Philadelphia forensic sculptor, to do a bust of List. Bender had demonstrated an uncanny ability to project what unidentified murder victims would have looked like in life, based only upon their skulls found years after the murder. He could also project from early photographs what a person who had disappeared would probably look like after aging for twenty years. Working with Michigan prison psychologist and profiler Richard Walter, Bender aged List's face and created a bust of what List would probably look like 18 years after the crime. The TV show also predicted that List would likely be working in a profession related to accounting (he has a bachelor's and master's degree in business administration from the University of Michigan); he would be an active member of a Lutheran Church; and he would be remarried with a family. The List case was one of three featured on the May 21, 1989, broadcast of the show.

Eleven days after the show was aired on the Fox television network and 300 phoned-in tips were followed up, the FBI arrested a mild-mannered, college-educated, churchgoing married man named Robert P. Clark at his office in Richmond, Virginia. The 63-year-old suspect denied he was List, but when his fingerprints were run and authorities found a telltale concave scar behind his ear from a mastoid operation, Robert Clark was positively identified as John List.

The murders had caused shock waves in New Jersey because Westfield was a stable, relatively affluent community and because John List was such an average type guy—the last person in the world anyone would think of as a killer. Besides having the bachelor's and master's degrees, List had served in the army in WW II and Korea, reaching the rank of first lieutenant. He had been vice president and controller of the National Bank of New Jersey in Jersey City. He was a CPA who sold insurance and did people's taxes. List was really "Joe Average" in almost every way. In fact, after he was captured, one of his neighbors in Midlothian, VA, outside of Richmond, told the FBI that List went to work Monday through Friday, cut the grass on Saturday, went to church every Sunday, and went back to work on Monday.

"The guy was so average," the neighbor said.

After List was captured, Union County prosecutors pieced together the story of his successful flight from prosecution and evasion of capture for 18 years. After the murders, List flew to Colorado and established himself as "an American John Doe." He settled in Denver and assumed the identity of Robert P. Clark. He resumed his profession as an accountant, lived in modest homes, went to work every day, worked in the yard on weekends and stayed active in St. Paul's Lutheran Church, serving as treasurer. He met a woman at a church social, married her, contributed to the local Fraternal Order of Police and stayed out of any trouble that would have caused his fingerprints to be checked.

In August of 1988, List and his wife Delores moved to Virginia to be closer to her family, and then in May of 1989 he was featured on *America's Most Wanted.* For months after his arrest, List maintained that he was Robert Clark, even though the FBI had matched his fingerprints. After he was extradited to New Jersey, John steadfastly maintained his assumed identity until February of 1990 when, to allow his lawyer to make motions to suppress certain evidence, he had to finally admit that he really was John List.

At his trial in Elizabeth, List's attorney argued that John killed his family "with love in his heart" to protect them from threats by society to their salvation and to shield them from the humiliation of going on welfare. He had been siphoning money from his mother's $200,000 bank account to meet growing financial obligations and was afraid that the family was running out of assets. It was also alleged that his daughter had become interested in witchcraft, which helped push him over the edge. Two Lutheran ministers were called to testify about how deeply religious John was. Dr. Sheldon Miller, a psychiatrist, testified for the defense that List saw only two options when financial and health problems burdened his family: 1) go on welfare; 2) kill his mother, wife, and three children to send their souls to heaven. The psychiatrist for the prosecution said that List was suffering from nothing more than a mid-life crisis.

He was convicted in April of 1990 of all the killings and, since the new death penalty statute wasn't in effect in 1971 at the time of the crime, he was sentenced to life in prison.

A couple of years after List had come into the jail, I was given responsibility for the print shop. When I started the job, my boss told me that I was going to have to keep track of all of the forms used in the prison, reprint them when requested and keep an accounting of all the paper in the storeroom.

I thought to myself, "Jeez, Harry, you're gonna need an accountant to help you on this job."

Bingo! The first guy I thought of was John List. I knew from the publicity about his case that he had been an accountant on the outside and that, if nothing else, he was meticulous and reliable. I filled out a personnel request form and called John in for an interview. Within a few minutes I knew that he would be ideal for the job. It was clear that he was an introvert and would thrive working alone in the storeroom. It was also clear that he would be extremely conscientious, and not one sheet of paper would go out of that room without being strictly accounted for.

For the most part, John is a quiet, studious type who likes to stay by himself. I found out one day, however, that he does have a temper. I had gotten a change order for one of the forms that we do and had forgotten to log it in with John. When he found out about the change in the form, he flared. I was sitting in my little office when he suddenly appeared at the door. John was then about 70 years old. He's about five feet, ten inches tall, a little bit stooped with age, and has thinning white hair. His face was red and I could see that he was agitated.

He pointed his finger at me and said, "Don't you <u>ever</u> change a form again without letting me know about it."

I said, "Whoa. Who do you think you're talking to?"

I looked him straight in the eye and said, "Don't <u>you</u> ever raise your voice to me like that again. Now get the hell outa here."

He came back by my office several hours later and apologized. I could see, though, that he had a volatile side to him, and I understood how he might have snapped before he killed his family.

On the other side of the coin was the relationship between John List and Rich Biegenwald. When those two were near each other, I was always afraid that Rich was the one who was going to snap and do something to List. John's storeroom office was in the back of a large work area, and Rich's workbench where he repaired typewriters was toward the front, just across the hall from my office. Every day, in the course of his job John wheeled a cart stacked with reams of paper from the storeroom, through Rich's work area and across the hall to the print shop. The cart had very squeaky wheels.

One day Biegenwald said to me, "Harry, do me a favor. Get the wheels fixed on that cart, or I'm gonna kill that son of a bitch the next time he comes through here."

Knowing Biegenwald, I was afraid he meant it, so I got some WD-40 and personally lubricated the wheels.

19
CHAPTER NINETEEN

THE NINETIES

The last significant attempt to escape from the prison (up to this point—there'll no doubt be more) has the greatest significance to me because I spotted it and received a commendation for stopping it. Even though I have been a civilian employee for twenty-one years, I think I still have the instincts developed over twenty-nine years as an officer. I spotted the attempt just as the inmates had reached the last layer of bricks before being able to break out. In one of the local newspapers, the warden, Willis Morton, was quoted as saying, "They probably had less than two hours of work to do before they were gone."

Today, as you approach the new section of the prison, you see a massive red brick front wall eight stories high and a city block long with a lobby area located approximately midway. The lobby separates the south compound, to the left, from the north compound to the right (the old prison complex, in the back, is now known as the "west compound"). As you come up to the large plate glass windows and four glass swinging doors of the lobby, you'll notice four five-foot-high concrete "flower pots" spaced about five feet apart sitting near the curb in front of the prison. The "pots" are actually barriers to prevent a large vehicle from being driven through the glass windows and doors into the lobby.

Above the lobby is a three-story cathedral ceiling with offices and meeting rooms running around the lobby space on the second level. Looking up to the third floor, you will see darkened windows. Behind those windows, the custody officers who are running the prison for that shift are watching you and, on closed-circuit TV, about forty critical areas throughout the prison. Turning to your right, within a few feet you will encounter an officer sitting behind a high desk with an airport-type metal detector arch right behind him or her. Behind and to the left of the officer is a large glassed-in, darkened control booth. Keeping the control booth dimmed makes it look foreboding, but it has a practical purpose: it allows the officer inside to always be looking out from dark into a brighter area so that he's quick to see anything that looks suspicious.

Entering the north compound, after you have gone through a series of electronically operated heavy steel doors, you'll eventually come to a large contact-visit hall. Today, as you walk along the corridor on the way to the visit hall, looking up, you'll see exposed water and heating-system pipes running alongside electrical conduit.

It wasn't always so stark and factory-like. When this part of the prison was built, the architects attempted to make a more pleasant atmosphere by putting all the electrical conduit, pipes and duct work above dropped ceilings. Naturally, it didn't take the inmates long to discover that the space between the dropped ceiling and the actual concrete ceiling, about four feet, gave them plenty of room to do some remodeling work in a secure environment.

The story of the escape attempt that I discovered actually started four days before I spotted some pushed-up ceiling tiles and an on-again, off-again florescent light and called Internal Affairs. On December 6, 1994, two officers on patrol on the top floor of the south compound saw what looked like mortar dust on the floor of a corridor. They looked up and saw a couple of the dropped-ceiling tiles out of place. (This was the same hallway where, in April of '83, Stankiewicz and Kerpen had managed to cut their way out and get down onto the roof of the old front house where Stankiewicz was killed by a blast from a tower guard's shotgun.)

In this first attempt in December of 1994, after the officers saw the ceiling tiles, they got a short stepladder and pushed the ceiling tiles up. They found pieces of metal pipe and small sticks being used to methodically scrape away the mortar around a heating duct and a fresh-air vent that opened out onto the roof. The vent opened out onto the east side of the prison over the main driveway. The officers alerted the administration and steps were immediately taken to repair the breach.

In the few days after this escape attempt was discovered, prison officials took a lot of heat from the local press because 1) everybody, from the commissioner's office on down to the warden, first denied that anything unusual was going on, even though they had set up searchlights out in the street trained on the upper floors of the south compound; and 2) nobody had alerted the Trenton Police Department to increase patrols in the neighborhood around the prison in case somebody did manage to get out. When the newspapers finally pried some of the details out of corrections officials, Trenton Police brass, particularly Deputy Police Chief Joe Constance, were angry, and the people in the neighborhood were scared and concerned.

Constance said, "Whenever there is an escape attempt, according to policy, we should be told about it."

Over the next few days, correction officers with rubber mallets went along the corridor walls in the south compound all the way up to the ceiling on all floors, pounding the bricks and listening for hollow spots. Gary Hilton, who was now Department of Corrections Chief of Staff, told the press the situation was "under control." He said that the department had been reluctant to release details because they didn't want to give other inmates a "show-and-tell" on how to get out. He also praised the guards who spotted the attempt (officers are usually not named publicly in these cases to minimize the chance of reprisals) and said, "That's what's expected of them; they're trained to be students of their environment."

Hilton told the press that all of the vents to the outside were being inspected and strengthened, certain hidden areas were being spray painted white to make them more visible and all of the dropped ceilings were being removed on all levels. It was that last statement by Hilton that gave "my guys" the incentive to speed up their work and caused them to get careless.

After all the attention the first escape attempt got, everybody in the jail was more alert to anything that looked even a little bit suspicious. Hilton was right: when you work in a prison, you do learn to become a "student of your environment." Sometimes that's the only thing between you and a shank in your heart.

A couple of days after the first escape attempt had been discovered, we were doing an orientation for new fish in the contact visit hall on the north side. I was there, as usual, representing the education department to fill the new guys in on the educational opportunities available to them. The contact visit hall is a large room about forty feet long by twenty-five wide with a guard booth set about six feet up in the wall next to the door that the inmates use to come in for visits with their families. A bathroom for visitors and inmates is over on one side of the room—the side closest to the corridor and outside wall of the prison.

On this particular day, the session got underway, and the other speakers were telling the new guys about custody rules, services available from the social work department, religious services and so on. I noticed that the nurse who usually talked about medical services hadn't come in yet, and since the hospital is just down the corridor from the contact visit hall, I decided to walk down the hall and get her while someone else was giving his spiel. After I went through the "airlock" (a 7' x 7' area where the door from the visit hall locks behind you before the other one opens into the corridor), I made a left and headed toward the hospital. I happened to glance up and saw that a ceiling light was out and the plastic cover that refracts the light was lifted up slightly in one corner. I got the nurse, and as we were walking back, I saw that the light was on and the plastic cover was back in place.

I said to myself, "Whoa, wait a minute, now. I came through here only a couple of minutes ago, and I didn't see anybody from the repair shop heading this way with a ladder. I didn't see anybody changing that bulb. Something's wrong here."

I went back into the visit hall, got to a phone and called Internal Affairs. I said, "Hello, this is Harry Camisa. I want you to come down here and look at this ceiling tile. And when you look up in there and you don't find anything, I don't want you goin' around the jail sayin' 'Harry's gettin' old; he's lost it and goin' senile. He's been here too damn long.' I don't need that bullshit, I'm tellin' you that right now."

I said, "Maybe there's nothing up there, but I want you to come down and look."

So one of the guys from IA, Terry Dillar, came down and got one of the inmates from the repair shop to bring a ladder. Terry climbed up, pushed aside the ceiling tile and looked in.

"Jesus Christ, Harry," he said, "this looks like somebody workin' on the ceiling of the Sistine Chapel."

Three inmates working on the inside sanitation detail (floor waxing, dusting, general cleaning) in the contact visit hall had made a rope from sheets and had looped two pieces around a heating duct. Then they suspended a piece of plywood under the duct to make a platform. One of them would lie prone on the piece of plywood while he chipped the mortar out from around the cinder blocks. They had also stolen bleach from the laundry and were using that to help soften the mortar. After the ceiling tiles were taken down around this work of art, officers found pillow cases full of cement chips, a screwdriver, a drill bit, a guitar string (keep at it long enough and drawing a guitar string, even a piece of thread, across metal will cut it), and a lamp. These guys had a second home up there. And, as Willis Morton had told the newspaper, they just had a little bit more mortar to get through before they penetrated the outer wall, opening a hole that would allow them to drop down into the parking lot in the front of the prison.

But to even get to where they were now working, first they had had to get through an interior concrete block wall between the bathroom in the contact visit hall and the corridor. After they finished that project, they set themselves up on the suspended plywood platform in front of the double block wall going to the outside and started working on that.

Using the bathroom in the contact visit hall as their base of operation was perfect. First, it was out of the line of sight of the cop in the booth who monitored the visits. Also, the bathroom had a fold-down baby-changing table that gave them a step to use to haul themselves up into the ceiling area. Then, they had the toilet to get rid of the mortar and dust.

These guys were supervised by an officer, Morara, who went with them into the visit hall, but we were short-staffed at the time and it was felt that this was a relatively low-level security matter, so he was routinely called away to do other duties. Whenever Morara would be called away, he'd leave "the boys" cheerfully mopping the floor and doing a bang-up job. As soon as he was out the door, one of them would slip into the bathroom, jump onto the changing table and crawl up into the ceiling to work on his part-time job while the other guys listened and watched for Morara to come back.

I should point out that contact visits are usually held in the evenings and on weekends, so on most weekdays the visit hall is deserted except for the cleaning crew. During the week, though, inmates do get window visits (just like in the old jail) held in a long narrow room next to the contact visit hall. The officer in the booth has to monitor those visits as well as watch traffic and electronically open and close doors out in the corridor, meaning his/her back is often turned away from the contact visit area for extended periods.

After Gary Hilton issued the order to remove the ceiling tiles following the first escape attempt, the guys in the visit hall got worried. Maintenance crews had started taking the tiles down on the top floor and, day by day, were working their way down to the first floor. These three knew they were working against the clock. They figured they had to go that night or not at all, and they were making one last, desperate push to get the job done. That's when they got careless. Even with a bunch of employees and fish out in the visit hall, one of the guys was up in the ceiling going for the gold. At first, whoever was up there didn't notice he had knocked out the light and kicked up the corner of one of the ceiling tiles in the corridor. Then, he must have noticed it and fixed it. If he had left it alone, I probably wouldn't have been suspicious.

In the December 6 attempt, the prison administrators weren't able to tell for sure which inmates engineered it (though they had a pretty good idea who they were) because a fair number of inmates had access to that corridor. In this attempt, we knew exactly who the perpetrators were because the inside sanitation crew were the only ones with the access and the unsupervised time to get the job done. They were brought up on institutional charges, but, you know, I can't remember whether or not they were indicted.

Maybe I am losing it.

* * * * * * *

On Sunday, July 31, 1994 one of those heartbreaking stories that everybody, especially a parent, dreads hit the front pages of the *Trentonian* and the *Trenton Times*—the rape and murder of a little girl.

Seven-year-old Megan Kanka of Hamilton Township, a suburban area just outside Trenton, disappeared from in front of her home on a Friday evening. When Megan hadn't come in from playing outside by 7 p.m., her parents, Maureen and Richard Kanka, started searching in the quiet, middle-class residential neighborhood about ten miles from our house in Ewing Township, another suburb of Trenton. They were unable to find their daughter at any of their friends' or relatives' houses. The Hamilton Township police responded immediately, bringing in five tracking dogs from the Department of Corrections and other agencies. An all-night search produced no sign of Megan.

Throughout the next day, Saturday, in one of the largest searches in Mercer County history, 500 volunteers from 39 fire companies and several police agencies combed a three-mile area around the Kanka home. They looked in yards, sheds, garages, swimming pools. Nothing. In the meantime, as Hamilton Township police questioned neighbors in the immediate vicinity, they discovered that the house diagonally across the street from the Kankas' was occupied by three men who had all done time for sex offenses. The home was owned by the mother of one of the men, and he was sharing the house with two other guys he had met in the Adult Diagnostic and Treatment Center (ADTC) in Avenel.

Police said as they questioned the three men, one of them, 33-year-old Jesse Timmendequas, who had been out on the street helping neighbors distribute missing-person fliers with Megan's picture, seemed nervous. He started to sweat profusely and chain smoke. As Timmendequas gave the Hamilton police details about his past, they put in a call to Middlesex Borough police and talked to Detective Sgt. Robert Schwartz. Schwartz remembered Timmendequas well: as a patrolman in 1981 he had arrested the suspect for attempting to rape and strangle a five-year-old girl in a wooded area near a public pool and tennis courts in the borough.

Sgt. Schwartz drove the 25 miles to Hamilton Township to participate in the questioning of Timmendequas. He said that the suspect, who is a slightly built, withdrawn man, seemed almost glad to see him—relieved to see a familiar face. Within a few hours of Schwartz' arrival, around 7 p.m. Saturday evening, Timmendequas admitted he had killed Megan and agreed to take police to her body. A little while later, a caravan of police vehicles pulled into a parking lot near a soccer field in Mercer County Park, about a five-minute drive from the Kanka home. Timmendequas led police to Megan's body dumped in some weeds near a portable toilet.

When police told the Kankas Megan's body had been found in the park, Richard Kanka went out onto his front porch and, looking at the house across the street, yelled, "Someone ought to burn that house to the ground!"

As the word of Megan's death spread through the neighborhood, people immediately began to express outrage that these convicted sex offenders could be living across the street from the Kankas without anyone knowing about their past histories.

One of Megan's aunts, Barbara Driscoll, asked a Trenton *Times* reporter, "When is it going to stop? When are we going to have laws which protect the victims, which protect the children all over?"

Another aunt, Monica Mohan, said, "When they do their time and come out, we should know that. We have to know that for the sake of the kids in this neighborhood. What are we supposed to do, keep the children on our front lawn?"

At the Five Points intersection in the middle of the township where the Mercerville Fire Co. had served as a command post during the search, one of the volunteers, Keith Owens, said, "I'm sick of it. The convicts' rights supersede the rights of the victims. It's insane that they're living in a neighborhood with a bunch of kids."

Hamilton Township's mayor, Jack Rafferty told a reporter, "I know this is an old cry, but these people like this Jesse Timmendequas should not be allowed on the street. They should be incarcerated forever or executed. You just can't fool with them."

The anger in the community really escalated when details of Timmendequas' past came out. As a kid Timmendequas lived in a rundown apartment building in Piscataway with his mother and four of her other children. Most of the people who knew him, if they could remember him at all, knew him as someone who was just "around," who never seemed to fit in. He was friendly with kids much younger than he was—as a 17-year-old, his friends were in the 10-13 age range.

When Jesse was 18, he rode his bike past two kindergarten girls playing a few houses away from where one of them lived. He persuaded the girls to go down an embankment across the street and help him search for ducks in a nearby stream. At the bottom of the hill, one of the girls suddenly changed her mind and ran back up the embankment to find an adult. Jesse knocked the other girl down and pulled down her pants. The next day when he was confronted by police, he said that he just wanted to look at the girl's vagina. The little girl said he smelled her.

Timmendequas pleaded guilty to attempted aggravated sexual assault and was given a suspended sentence on the condition he attend counseling sessions. He didn't like counseling and failed to live up to the terms of the sentence. He was sent to the Middlesex County Adult Correctional Center for nine months.

By the end of June, 1981, Timmendequas was out of jail and living in an apartment in Dunellen not far from Piscataway. About a quarter-mile from his apartment was a patch of woods and Middlesex Borough's public pool and tennis courts. Timmendequas approached two 7-year-old girls playing in the area and asked them if they wanted firecrackers for the Fourth of July. One of the girls got scared, jumped on her bicycle and took off to look for their mothers. The other girl went with Jesse.

The two of them walked down a trail into the wooded area. Then 19-year-old Jesse grabbed the little girl by the throat and pulled her into the woods. When she turned blue and passed out, he let go of her and ran away. The girl's mother found her daughter lying unconscious and called the police. As Timmendequas walked out of the woods on the Dunellen side, headed toward his apartment, Patrolman Robert Schwartz was waiting for him in a patrol car.

When the little girl was examined at a nearby hospital, doctors found no evidence of sexual contact, but she had blue marks on her neck and a black and blue handprint on her stomach where Jesse had grabbed her.

Timmendequas was charged with five felonies, including kidnapping and attempted murder. In cases involving young children, prosecutors know that it's often difficult to make the charges stick. In this case, the little girl's parents wanted to avoid a trial, so the prosecutor's office plea bargained. Jesse agreed to plead guilty to attempted sexual contact and attempting to cause serious bodily injury. He also agreed to be sentenced to the ADTC at Avenel.

Most experts seem to agree that sex offenders are extremely difficult to rehabilitate, especially if they don't get with the program. Apparently, Timmendequas never got into the therapy at Avenel. One of the therapists there, Dr. Edward Balyk, said that when Timmendequas would get upset in a session, he would pout.

"Then he'd go hide," Balyk said. "He spent a lot of time in bed."

While he was in the ADTC, Timmendequas met the two other sex offenders he would end up living with in Hamilton Township. When they were released from Avenel, Jesse and the son of the woman who owned the house got jobs in nearby Princeton Township mowing lawns in parks and playgrounds. That's where he was employed when he attacked Megan Kanka.

Within hours after Megan's body was found in Mercer County Park, her family, friends and neighbors were circulating petitions and spearheading a campaign for tougher laws for convicted sex offenders. Another high-profile case a few months before Megan's death—the sexual assault and murder of 6-year-old Karen Wengert in Manalapan Township by a neighbor with a record of sex abuse as a juvenile—helped light a fire under the seats of New Jersey legislators. In record time (three months) the New Jersey legislature wrote, debated and passed—and Governor Christie Whitman signed—a nine-bill package of new laws known as "Megan's Law." Maureen and Richard Kanka and the Wengerts attended the bill-signing ceremony.

The keystone law of the package requires police to notify a neighborhood, nearby schools and other institutions when a convicted sex offender intends to move into the area. The rest of the package included requirements for convicted sex offenders to report their addresses to the local police or state authorities every 90 days; lifetime supervision for convicted sex offenders, making it possible for parole officers to track them after normal prison and parole terms expire; and notification of county prosecutors by the Department of Corrections 30 days before a sex offender is released (we had already been doing this since 1989 as a matter of policy).

Naturally, civil libertarians immediately attacked the new laws, and some have been modified or struck down. I know, though, that the core of Megan's Law, the notification of the community, is something that the vast majority of the citizens of New Jersey agree with and want.

While Timmendequas was in jail awaiting trial, a *New York Times* reporter, William Glaberson, wrote a profile of him in May of 1996. In the article Glaberson said, "Megan's death has become part of the national psyche."

Megan Kanka's death at the hands of Jesse Timmendequas would result in more than a dozen states passing laws named for her and President Clinton's signing of a federal Megan's Law in May of 1996. That same year the Random House *Webster's College Dictionary* added "Megan's Law" as a new term in the English language.

Even though he had confessed and led police to Megan's body, Timmendequas' lawyers entered an innocent plea, and he went on trial in the Mercer County Courthouse in Trenton May 5, 1997. The murder had been committed July 29, 1994, but because of the incredible amount of publicity surrounding the case and the political ramifications, it took nearly three years to bring Timmendequas to trial. The trial was held in the Mercer County Courthouse (Hamilton is in Mercer County), but the jury was selected from nearby Hunterdon County and jurors were bused in each day.

The state's case was presented by First Assistant Prosecutor Kathryn Flicker and Assistant Prosecutor Lewis Korngut. Defense attorneys were Roy B. Greenman and Assistant Deputy Public Defender Barbara R. Lependorf. Superior Court Judge Andrew J. Smithson presided.

Day by day the prosecution presented a carefully constructed case of physical and forensic evidence. A forensic dentist, Dr. Haskell Askin, testified that a bite mark on Jesse Timmendequas' hand fit perfectly with a mold of Megan's teeth that Askin had taken after the little girl was murdered. As the jurors were being shown the mold and a life-sized color photo taken by police of the mark on Jesse's hand when he was arrested, one of the jurors moved closer to the railing of the jury box. When the juror saw how the mold fit exactly with the bite mark on the defendant's hand, he breathed out sharply, uttered a sound like, "Whew!" and made a sweeping thumbs down gesture to a juror behind him. During the lunch break, prosecutors, defense attorneys and the judge met in Smithson's chambers and discussed the incident. Smithson removed the juror who made the gesture, leaving 14 still on the panel (two more would be excused later when deliberations began).

Richard and Maureen Kanka stayed in the courtroom throughout the trial and listened to almost all of the testimony. The most difficult witness for the Kankas and the jurors to hear was Mercer County Medical Examiner Dr. Raafat Ahmad. Before Ahmad took the stand, Judge Smithson told the jurors they could ask to take a break any time because of the potentially emotional nature of her testimony. Both Richard and Maureen Kanka teared up several times during Ahmad's first day of testimony, but they stayed in the courtroom. Meanwhile, Jesse sat at the defense table, expressionless and somewhat glassy eyed. (Defense attorney Greenman later told the jury that throughout the trial Timmendequas had been under "heavy medication" to control an anxiety disorder.) When Lependorf cross-examined Ahmad during a second day of testimony, Maureen Kanka had to leave the courtroom.

Dr. Ahmad said that all of Megan's injuries were inflicted on her before she died, though Ahmad couldn't say whether the little girl was conscious or not. Ahmad said that the autopsy on Megan's body, which was covered with "innumerable" insects when police located it in Mercer County Park, showed that Megan died between 6:30 and 7:30 p.m. on Friday and that she had eaten shortly before she died. Maureen Kanka had testified earlier that her daughter had eaten dinner about 6 p.m. the night she disappeared.

Dr. Ahmad testified that Megan had deep bite marks on her tongue, consistent with being strangled; the corner of Megan's right eye was bruised and swollen, indicating she had been punched or slapped; the wide ligature marks on Megan's neck fit with Jesse's confession that he had strangled her with a belt; and a cut on Megan's right ear lobe was consistent with a missing teddy bear earring being ripped out of her ear. Dr. Ahmad also testified that bruises on Megan's colon and kidneys indicated she had been punched in the body, and severe head injuries showed she had either been hit in the head or had fallen and hit her head against a blunt object. Bleeding and other evidence indicated Megan had been raped and sodomized. An earlier witness, a state police forensic scientist, had testified that anal swabs taken from Megan's body had seminal fluid on them but no semen was found on vaginal swabs. Dr. Ahmad said that injuries to the little girl's vagina were evidence of rape, but the blood from the injuries had probably washed away the semen.

When Lependorf challenged Ahmad's testimony that Megan had been sodomized, Ahmad said she had noted two "fresh" tears in Megan's anus, and the semen on the anal swabs found by the state police scientist confirmed her conclusions. In his first confession to the Hamilton police Timmendequas had said he killed Megan, but he didn't confess to raping her until he was confronted with the autopsy results.

Following Dr. Ahmad's testimony, Hamilton police detective Sgt. Charles Stanley took the stand and read Timmendequas' fifth and final confession into the record. Timmendequas had given police several statements over a period of days, each time giving more pieces of the story as he was confronted with new evidence, including the autopsy report.

Sgt. Stanley testified that when the Hamilton police got the autopsy results showing Megan had been savagely sexually assaulted, he said to Jesse, "It's important we learn the truth, exactly what happened."

Stanley said Timmendequas paused, looked down at his lap, and said that he had been "slipping," and his obsession for little girls had been eating at him for months before he killed Megan. Then he described exactly what went on in his bedroom that day.

Timmendequas said he lured Megan into the house shared by the three men by promising to let her pet his new black Labrador puppy. When he got her upstairs to his room, at about 6:30 p.m., the other two men were out running errands. Timmendequas said he started fondling Megan and trying to pull down her pants. She started screaming and tried to run out of the room.

Timmendequas grabbed the waistband of Megan's shorts and attempted to pull her back into the bedroom. Then he grabbed a belt hanging from a hook on a closet door and looped it around Megan's neck to help pull her into the room. Megan fought desperately for a few minutes, kicking, screaming, and biting. Timmendequas was bitten when he put his hand over her mouth to quiet her. Using the belt, Timmendequas brutally swung Megan headfirst into the door jamb and then into the side of a dresser. While she was lying on her back on the floor, Jesse slapped Megan hard in the face, causing blood to trickle out of the corner of her mouth.

While Megan was lying dazed and barely conscious on the bedroom floor, Jesse continued to choke her with the belt until she stopped struggling. Then he ripped her shorts off and spent about two minutes raping her. At some point he also sodomized her. (In one of his earlier statements Timmendequas denied sodomizing Megan but acknowledged he might have "slipped" while he was raping her.)

When he was finished, Timmendequas got a plastic shopping bag and a plastic garbage bag, put them over Megan's head and tied them tightly around her neck. He told police that Megan was still bleeding around the mouth from being slapped, and he didn't want the blood to get on the bedroom rug.

Sgt. Stanley said that throughout this confession, Jesse's "tone was very flat and unemotional. The only emotion he ever displayed was when he was upset about his hand wound, and he blamed Megan for inflicting that upon him."

Timmendequas said after he raped and strangled Megan, he went down to his truck and dumped the tools out of a plastic toy chest he was using as a toolbox. He told police that the little girl "fit nicely" into the chest. As he carried the box containing Megan's body down to his pickup, he said he heard a "faint cough" from inside.

Timmendequas drove to Mercer County Park, opened the toy chest, sexually molested the corpse and then dumped the body into some high weeds near a soccer field. On the way back home, Timmendequas stopped at a convenience store to buy cigarettes and a newspaper. When Maureen Kanka came by the house looking for Megan, Timmendequas told her he had seen Megan earlier in the day and she had told him she was on her way to see a friend. Later, Timmendequas splashed ammonia inside the toy chest and on the front porch of the house because he knew the police had brought in dogs to try to track Megan's scent.

Hamilton police started to suspect Timmendequas within hours of Megan's disappearance. The next day, after police had questioned all three men living in the house, based upon the evidence and interviews, they concentrated on Timmendequas. When they brought the men back to headquarters Saturday evening and told them what they knew, one of Timmendequas' roommates started yelling at him, "They got you, they got you, they got you."

The jury deliberated for four hours before finding Timmendequas guilty on all eight counts against him, including the capital crime of knowing, purposeful murder by his own conduct. The same six-man, six-woman jury who heard the murder case would hear arguments in the penalty phase and decide whether Timmendequas should live or die. The announcement of the verdict was carried live nationally by the Court TV cable television network.

In a capital case in New Jersey one trial is held to determine guilt or innocence. Then a second hearing is held in which the prosecution presents aggravating factors to support the death penalty followed by a defense presentation of mitigating factors to argue for a sentence of life imprisonment.

During the mitigating factors argument, defense attorneys Barbara Lependorf and Roy Greenman portrayed Jesse Timmendequas' childhood as a life of living hell. Greenman told the jury that Jesse's mother, Doris Unangst, was "an alcoholic," "promiscuous," and "mentally retarded." He said Jesse was born and raised in an atmosphere of alcoholism, domestic violence, criminal activity, neglect and severe physical, mental and sexual abuse. According to Greenman, Jesse's mother frequently drank alcohol while she was pregnant with him, causing him to suffer a birth defect, fetal alcohol syndrome.

Greenman said Doris was promiscuous, having ten children by seven different men. Seven of her kids were given up for adoption or taken by the state, and she and the rest of the family were always on welfare. When Jesse reached school age, he was classified as retarded with emotional problems, but, the defense claimed, the schools never followed up with appropriate counseling or further psychological evaluations.

Lependorf said that Jesse's father, "Skip" Timmendequas, drank excessively, engaged in criminal activity, demonstrated a total disregard for his family and was in and out of jail. Whenever Jesse's father was sent to jail, his mother would hook up with a boyfriend, and Jesse often witnessed violence between his mother and these men. Lependorf said the mother and the siblings rejected Jesse because of his physical resemblance to his father.

When Skip wasn't in jail, he subjected Jesse and the rest of the family to physical and sexual abuse, according to Lependorf. She said that when Jesse was eight years old, he saw his father brutally rape a little neighborhood girl. Skip then threatened to kill Jesse if he told anyone, and to get his point across, he killed a couple of Jesse's pets in front of him. The defense also claimed that Skip Timmendequas subjected Jesse to beatings and sexual abuse including fondling, forced oral sex and sodomy. They said that Jesse also witnessed sexual and physical abuse of his brother and sister, and the mother once beat Jesse so badly she broke his arm.

The defense pointed out that the family moved 21 times before Jesse was 17 years old, forcing him to change schools frequently and that he suffered head injuries in two separate automobile accidents. They also pointed out that Jesse's mother and several of her children, including Jesse, had been classified as mentally retarded.

The defense played a video-taped interview with Timmendequas' younger brother, Paul, in which he talked about the physical and sexual abuse the two boys were subjected to when they were young. When talking about their father, Paul cried and said, "He raped Jesse."

When he talked about watching their father rape the neighbor girl, Paul said, "She musta been about 7 years old," and then he started sobbing uncontrollably, unable to continue for a couple of minutes.

When he resumed, Paul said that after raping the little girl, Skip killed their dog Bullet in front of them by forcing the dog's head into a bucket of water. He also killed Jesse's pet rabbit and then fed the rabbit to the boys for dinner, laughing when he told them what they were eating.

Paul said that soon after the father came home from a jail term, he started to sexually abuse the two boys. Paul was around four or five years old and Jesse was six or seven. According to Paul's testimony, Skip would take both boys into the bedroom and force them to perform oral sex on him; then he would push Paul away and sodomize Jesse while Jesse screamed. This abuse went on for about four years, Paul testified. Skip left New Jersey and went to California in 1972 to escape charges of stabbing a man in the stomach. He never returned.

After playing Paul Timmendequas' video-taped testimony, the defense called to the stand Carol Krych, a "forensic social worker." Krych said she spent 2 1/2 years compiling a detailed social history of Jesse Timmendequas and his family. One state evaluator said the history sounded like *Tobacco Road.*

Krych said she went to California to meet with Skip Timmendequas, whose real name was Charles Wilbur Hall. He used a number of aliases, including Charles Howard and James Howard. Jesse's mother, Doris, told Krych that Hall started using the name "Timmendequas" when he saw it on the tombstone of a Native American and liked the sound of it.

Krych said she was "quite nervous" being around Skip when she met with him in California. He told her he lived on a property with 12 other families and that nine of the families were members of the Ku Klux Klan and the others were members of white supremacist groups. Skip said he belonged to the "Sons of the Confederates" and flew a Confederate flag outside his trailer. He was remarried (though it was unclear whether he was still legally married to Jesse's mother) and had another son named Jesse. Skip said he liked the name "Jesse" because Jesse James was his hero.

Krych said Jesse II was 22 years old but had the mental capacity of a seven-year-old.

Skip told Krych he was dishonorably discharged from the Army because he refused to sleep in a barracks with blacks. He said all of the families in the compound were armed, and he lived by the motto, "If it ain't worth killing over, it ain't worth fighting over."

When the prosecution cross-examined Krych, the assistant DA, Kathryn Flicker, asked her if she was a mitigation specialist for the defense in death penalty cases. Krych answered that she was a "forensic social worker."

Flicker then produced a note in which Krych called herself a "capital mitigation expert." Krych acknowledged that she had described herself that way in her notes concerning a meeting with one of Jesse's sisters.

Flicker pressed the point and suggested that Krych's job was to present a sympathetic picture of the defendant to the jury.

Krych said, "No, not sympathy—it's mitigation."

At the end of Paul's video-taped testimony, he had been asked how he felt about his brother. Paul had said, "I love him. I love him."

When he was asked if he thought his brother should get the death penalty, he shook his head and said, "No."

Flicker asked Krych if she was aware that Paul had changed his opinion since the taping and now believed that his brother should be executed.

Krych said, "I'm aware he's said those kinds of things."

Under further questioning, Krych said she was paid $60 per hour plus expenses and that she had worked about 250 hours on the Timmendequas case.

While the defense was presenting testimony from Paul's video tape and putting Krych on the stand in the penalty phase, a *New York Times* reporter went out to California to interview Skip Timmendequas. The reporter, Evelyn Nieves, said she caught up to Skip in the southern California desert a half an hour on a dusty road from the nearest town. Nieves said Skip knew he was all over the news back in New Jersey as a sexual predator and sadist who turned his son Jesse into a pedophile and murderer.

Skip told Nieves, "It's all lies. All of it."

He said that Paul made up all of his testimony because they had a falling out during a reunion 12 years before. Skip said that Paul had told him he and Jesse used to have sexual relations with their half-sister, Linda, in their attic bedroom. Skip said that was unforgivable.

"I nearly took him out," Skip told Nieves.

Now, Skip said, Paul was making up all of these stories about the rape of the neighbor girl and the killing of the pets just to save his brother Jesse from the death penalty.

Skip said, "He [Jesse] should definitely be killed."

Then he said, "Let's suppose for argument's sake that all of what they say happened, really happened. Does that excuse what he did? My dad kicked the hell out of me from the time I was able to walk. I didn't kill a baby. When they say that it's mommy's fault or daddy's fault, it's just an excuse."

Skip said that as far as he knew, Jesse was never classified as retarded nor diagnosed as suffering the effects of fetal alcohol syndrome. He said his former wife, Doris, liked men, but she was neither an alcoholic nor an abusive mother.

He said, "She drank, but in moderation. We used to go to barn dances, and she'd have a few."

And the burglaries that put him in prison were motivated by his desire to help his family, Skip said.

"I was stealing food to feed my starving family."

While he was in prison, Skip said, Doris became pregnant by another man, and he told her he would raise the child as his own to save the family name.

"I took Linda," he said. "I didn't even know who her father was. I said, 'Let's call her Timmendequas to preserve the family.'"

Skip said he left Doris and the kids and took up with another woman, a "slightly retarded" 21-year-old daughter of a neighbor. She became pregnant and bore his daughter. Then they broke up. A little while later he had a fight with a man in New Jersey, stabbing the man in the stomach, and then fled to this California no man's land on the Arizona border.

"He got me by the throat," Skip said, "and I got my butcher knife in him. I was a fugitive for 15 years."

Skip talked freely to Nieves because he knew the statute of limitations had run out on the stabbing and any allegations of sexual abuse on Paul and Jesse.

But he said he was still ready for trouble. Nieves said Skip had two shotguns and two pistols on the counter in the kitchen of his trailer while she was interviewing him.

"We've got rattlesnakes out here," he said. "Two-legged and the other kind."

Skip said the people he lived around in California were isolationist and racist, himself included. Nieves said Skip flew the Confederate flag on one flagpole and an upside-down American flag on another.

After several days of testimony for both sides, the jury rejected the defense claims and sentenced Jesse to death by lethal injection. He came into our Capital Sentences Unit the day after he was sentenced to death.

I've said before that despite witnessing 13 executions, I've always been ambivalent about where I stand on the death penalty. This is one of those cases that make it hard for me to go one way or the other. Like just about everybody else in Mercer County, after I read Dr. Ahmad's testimony in the newspapers, I wanted to stick the needle in this guy's arm myself. I even thought I might go to the warden and volunteer to be a witness at his execution if he got sentenced to death. Then the defense tells what happened to Jesse as a kid, and I start to have doubts again. Add to that the times I've seen Timmendequas, looking like a pitiful, scared rabbit, and it's a tough call.

Whenever I have seen Timmendequas being escorted through the jail, he has struck me as trapped, frightened animal. My impression of him is that he's definitely retarded. He's a small, skinny guy, about five feet, seven inches, maybe 140 lbs. Whenever I've seen him, he's been turned at a 45-degree angle facing into the wall, like he's afraid to see anyone or have anyone make eye contact with him. I think he's mainly trying to shield himself because he knows that 90 percent of the population would kill him in a heartbeat if they could get at him. A guy who committed a crime like his rates about a .0000001 on a scale of 1-10 (with a Rubin Carter or Teddy Roberts being a 10) in the prison caste system.

This is going to sound like I've lost it and I'm an old man going off on a tangent, but bear with me. Several years ago a nice-looking, young Hispanic kid (whose name I won't use because of what happened to him) came into the jail. He had a slight build and delicate features—prime meat. I think he was in on a drug rap. Within a few weeks the predators got him. They trapped him in a stairwell, beat the shit out of him and then 10 or 12 of them took turns raping him. When it was over, he was bleeding so profusely from his rectum that he had to be rushed to the hospital and given blood transfusions.

After this kid came back into population, whenever he had to go someplace in the jail, he looked terrified. He walked next to the wall with his head tucked down into his shoulder, his eyes constantly darting around, watching for attackers. If an officer stopped him to talk to him, he would squint and cringe like he was being slapped. Trembling, he would cup his hands and draw them up over his mouth and nose, peeking out at the person who was speaking to him. This kid was in bad shape for months after he was assaulted. Whenever I see Timmendequas, I think of that inmate. Jesse isn't quite at that level, but he's close.

Should we kill him? I honestly don't know.

****

New Jersey executed two women in the 1800's. Bridget Durgen, a domestic who killed her mistress, was hanged in the Middlesex County courthouse yard in 1867. Martha Meierhoffer was hanged in Essex County in 1874 for killing her husband. Three women were sentenced to death in New Jersey in the 20th century: Harriet Evans (1931); Marguerite Dolbow (1937); and Marie Moore (1984). All three had their sentences commuted to life imprisonment. A fourth is currently on death row, but I'm not 100 percent sure "she" counts as a woman.

On a pleasant Thursday afternoon in early spring, April 20, 1995, Leslie Ann Nelson (formerly known as Glenn Nelson) rocked her quiet Haddon Heights neighborhood when she opened fire on three law-enforcement agents, killing two of them and critically wounding the third. John McLaughlin, an investigator for the Camden County prosecutor's office, and two Haddon Heights police officers, Richard Norcross and his brother John, had gone to the 37-year-old transsexual's home to serve a weapons warrant when a gunfight erupted.

Earlier in the day police had gone to the house where Nelson lived with his parents to investigate a report of possible sexual abuse of a three-year-old girl. While the officers were inside the house, Nelson told them she had weapons in her bedroom, but she refused to let the officers see them. When the investigators got back to headquarters, they ran a check and found out Nelson had a 1988 conviction for possession of a firearm and hollow-point bullets. The police obtained a search warrant for Leslie's bedroom and six officers returned to the house around 2 p.m. to talk to her about the guns. After Leslie's mother let the officers into the house, McLaughlin started up the stairs.

The other officers heard McLaughlin yell, "Drop it! Drop it! Drop it!"

Then they heard gunfire and saw McLaughlin fall. Officer Richard Norcross was behind McLaughlin and was also hit, but he managed to get back out through the front door with the help of another officer, Detective Sgt. Bob Griffith. A couple of teenagers on bikes saw Norcross stagger out the door and collapse.

Norcross yelled, "I'm hit! Get an ambulance!"

The teenagers watched from a safe distance as other officers pulled a blue cover off a swimming pool and used it to carry Norcross across the street, through a stream to safety. He was picked up a few minutes later by an ambulance responding to calls to police from neighbors who heard the gunfire and saw Norcross stagger out of the house.

Meanwhile, Nelson had switched from the 9mm handgun she had used to shoot Norcross and McLaughlin to an AK-47-style semi-automatic rifle with a telescopic sight. Looking out of her bedroom window, Nelson spotted John Norcross peeking around the corner of a house across the street where he had ducked for cover. She hit him with one shot in the temple, killing him instantly. Then she went back to the top of the stairs and fired 20 more shots into McLaughlin's body, even though she knew he was dead.

Police cordoned off several blocks around the house and evacuated some of the neighbors while a police helicopter circled overhead. Other neighbors were warned to stay under cover in their homes. Leslie's mother had run out of the house when her son/daughter started shooting.

A command post was set up in a house across the street from the Nelson home, and police and an FBI negotiating team talked with Nelson on the telephone, trying to convince her to surrender. Around 8 p.m. Nelson dragged McLaughlin out onto the front porch, but she refused to let police get near enough to retrieve the body. She also tossed some weapons outside, but nobody knew how many more she still had inside the house.

The police negotiating team on the scene brought in a woman negotiator whose soothing voice eventually got to Nelson. Haddon Heights police dispatcher Melissa Bastien spoke calmly and gently to Nelson and promised her she could have her make-up in jail and other "things a woman would know about" if Nelson would surrender. Nelson was promised she would not be harmed if she surrendered, and police tossed a bullet-proof vest and gas mask onto the porch for her. At 4:30 a.m., 14 hours after the standoff had begun, Nelson came out and surrendered, wearing the mask, vest and a sequin-studded go-go costume under her street clothes.

After Nelson was in custody, a picture of her began to emerge. As a skinny young, long-haired boy, Glenn Nelson could be seen in a park near his house building forts and wearing military-style camouflage outfits. A 1976 graduate of Haddon Heights High School, Nelson was described by classmates as an excellent student but a remote loner. He drove around town in a brown Ford van with a porthole window in the side. Neighbors said that when he was growing up, Glenn Nelson seldom played with the other kids in the neighborhood. He was always polite when adults spoke to him, but he would never initiate a conversation. He had two brothers and a sister.

Sometime in the early '90s Nelson underwent four surgical sex-change procedures that cost $34,000. Now in her mid-thirties, Nelson still lived at home with her parents. She seemed to come out of her shell and was frequently seen around town wearing tight, revealing clothes like halter tops, tight jeans and hot-pink short shorts along with a shoulder-length platinum-blonde wig. Neighbors said Nelson obviously liked the attention she got with her new look.

One of the neighborhood teenagers told a reporter from the Camden *Courier-Post,* "One day he was walking down the street and he had tits."

The kids around the neighborhood called Nelson "shim" for she/him.

Nelson later told her lawyers that she felt the sex-change operations would bring her financial, personal and social success. She said she had three goals as a woman: to be a go-go dancer, a prostitute and a star in porn films. She accomplished two of her goals, working as a go-go dancer and later as a prostitute. After her sex-change operations, she told acquaintances she wanted large breasts, hoping eventually to achieve a 50-inch bust. As a dancer, she got bookings in New York City, Philadelphia and Camden.

After her arrest, Leslie decided not to contest the charges against her and instead entered into a plea bargain agreement with the Camden County prosecutor's office. Nelson admitted murdering John McLaughlin, the investigator for the prosecutor's office, and John Norcross, the Haddon Heights patrolman. She also admitted shooting John's brother, Richard Norcross. The agreement included dismissal of other charges, such as attempted murder in the shooting of Richard Norcross, but it allowed the prosecutor to continue to seek the death penalty.

The death penalty phase started in late April, 1997 and, because of all the local publicity surrounding the shootings, was heard by a jury bused in each day from Mercer County. The defense called to the stand a psychotherapist who described herself as an expert in sexuality, especially trans-gender concerns. She said that Glenn Nelson (male) had been a nail biter and a bed-wetter well into adolescence. She also said he had to be taken out of kindergarten because he wasn't socially ready and didn't get a job until 4 1/2 years after graduating from high school.

Another witness, a Haddon Heights police sergeant who talked with Nelson on the telephone during the standoff, told the jury that Nelson said she was "scared and felt as though they [the police] had barged into her home."

Probably the most effective witness for the defense was a criminology professor from Indiana University in Pennsylvania, R. Paul McCauley, who said the police had to take some of the responsibility for the officers' deaths. McCauley basically said the officers were not properly trained to react to the situation and didn't know how to plan a raid of this type.

McCauley said, "It's not the officers' fault. It's the agency's fault to allow them to go in with minimal protection."

McCauley said the Nelson home, with its enclosed stairway to the second floor, created a "killing zone" for Leslie Nelson to trap and kill the officers.

McCauley said, "To get to the bedroom, to where you want to search, you have to funnel through a tunnel, an area particularly volatile because it's solidly closed off."

"The person up there, Leslie, knows where the police are. They're in the tube. She has only to aim at the steps," said McCauley.

McCauley said that the officers had heard Leslie say she would kill herself if she was put in jail, so they knew they were dealing with an unstable person. Instead of sitting down and carefully planning out how to go back and get the weapons out of Leslie's bedroom, they returned within ten minutes of getting the search warrant. McCauley said because of their lack of training in dealing with these situations, the officers took no time to plan, to rehearse, to even think about the potential danger of entering the house.

McCauley said that some of the officers on the raid had no idea about how narrow the steps were or that they were enclosed. He also said that after the police got inside the house and heard Nelson upstairs yelling, screaming obscenities and threatening to use her guns, they should have pulled back and considered other options. Instead, they tried to rush up the stairs and confront her, with fatal consequences.

McCauley said that when the officers heard Nelson threatening to use her guns, they should have "closed the door to the second floor and isolated Leslie inside the house."

Under cross-examination by the prosecution, McCauley said he saw no particular urgency to serve the search warrant after Nelson had told the investigators about the two guns in her room earlier in the morning. And, making matters worse, McCauley said, neither the police department nor the prosecutor's office had a policy in place at the time of the shootout to cover the serving of high-risk warrants.

Toward the end of the penalty phase, Leslie read a prepared statement to the court, asking the jury to spare her life.

"I would just like to be clear that I do now wish to live. I have come to realize it is possible for me to have a useful and productive life, even confined inside a prison," she said in the 3 1/2 -minute statement.

The jury disagreed.

When Leslie Ann came into the Capital Sentences Unit in May of 1997, the problems started almost immediately. Rich Biegenwald (who has the best ear in the jail for news on the prison grapevine) was the first one to tell me about the ruckus she was causing.

One morning Rich said to me, "Hey Harry, have you heard what that she-male up in CSU is doing?"

I told him I hadn't heard anything, so Rich filled me in. First, she put in a request to the administration for a dildo. They went bananas. Their attitude was, "Who is this fruitcake who thinks she can come in here and turn the place upside down with a request like this?"

As strange as it may sound, Leslie's request for the dildo was actually based on a medical need. Since her sex-change surgery had removed her male apparatus and replaced it with a vagina, she told the administration, she needed the dildo to keep the orifice from closing up. She said that, like a pierced ear lobe, if the opening was not used, it would eventually form scar tissue and close. She told the administration that without regular use of the dildo, she would eventually be unable to urinate. She even was able to produce a doctor's prescription for the "appliance."

This went all the way up to the commissioner's office, and they were as adamant as the warden: no dildo. So Leslie went to court and won. The last I heard, she has a dildo in her cell for "medicinal purposes."

Rich also kept me up to speed on the next incident. The next problem occurred a couple of months after she came into the jail on a hot day in August when she went out into the yard for her allotted hour. (In the CSU, each inmate is given one hour per day, alone, out in a private courtyard.) She decided to sunbathe so she took her shirt off. Remember what the kid in Haddon Heights said? "One day he was walking down the street and he had tits"?

Well, Leslie definitely has 'em. And the guys in the unit whose windows look down into the CSU yard—four tiers worth—were loving every minute of the show. An officer went out into the yard and told Leslie she had to put her shirt back on or he was going to give her a charge and have her sent to lockup. Rich told me that in her case, lockup consisted of a stripped cell next to hers that the administration keeps vacant to put her in when her cell is periodically searched.

Leslie Ann's response to the officer was, "Why? All of the other inmates who use this yard are allowed to strip down to their undershorts. Why don't I have the same rights?"

The cop tried to reason with her, but she stuck to her guns, so he wrote her up. When Leslie went to courtline, she said she was being discriminated against. She said as long as she was in this jail, the same rules that applied to all of the other inmates had to apply to her as well. The board agreed, and Leslie is allowed to sunbathe topless, just like the fellas.

I distinctly remember the first time I went into the CSU after Leslie had come in. For over 20 years I've worked in the education department with a wonderful art teacher named Dorothy Masciotti. A few months after Leslie came into the CSU, Dorothy got a request from a condemned inmate, Robert Marshall (a businessman convicted of having a hit man kill his wife for the insurance), for some art supplies. Dorothy had put together a package of supplies for Marshall and asked me if I wanted to take a walk with her up to the CSU unit.

Whenever I went into the Capital Sentences Unit, I thought back to the old days and the old death row. What a difference. In the old death house, the cells were large, about eight feet wide by eight feet deep with a big barred door running across the entire eight-foot wide opening. The condemned inmate had no privacy, especially with the lights kept burning 24-7. Suspended over each cell door was a 100-watt bulb enclosed in a "bird cage" like over the back door of a retail store or in a factory. The large opening plus the light bulb made it easy for the cop on duty to keep a constant watch on death row inmates, looking especially for suicide attempts. The building (torn down in the '80s when the prison was expanded) was a stark grimy red brick structure that added to the oppressive atmosphere of guys waiting to go to the electric chair.

The new CSU is entirely different. The cells are comfortably large, about eight feet by about six feet, but instead of that big barred door, these units have a gray metal solid door with by 10-inch by 40-inch vertical window running down the left side. The cells are arranged on two tiers with a cop-booth directly across facing them. The officer inside the booth monitors the whole pastel-colored concrete block area by looking through his large window, by watching TV screens fed by cameras placed at strategic locations throughout the cell block and by frequent walks along both tiers, looking into the cells through the window in the door.

I'm also struck by how expensive it is to maintain a capital sentence unit these days. In addition to the electronic surveillance equipment, it takes a lot of manpower to maintain the CSU. Every time a lawyer comes to see a condemned inmate, it takes three officers to escort the inmate to one of the lawyer-inmate conference rooms outside of the CSU. If the lawyer stays two or three hours, these officers are tied up for the entire time. When the inmates go into the yard for their two hours a day, it takes another four officers to complete the movement and, of course, these inmates have to be served meals individually by the officers. Visitors to the CSU have to be confirmed by the administration, and then they're escorted to the unit by an officer where another officer is tied up monitoring inmate and visitor all during the visit.

It's also interesting to watch the way the inmates react to hearing the entrance door open and close: it's like watching fish being fed in an aquarium. Almost every one of the condemned convicts immediately comes up to the window in the door and peers out at the visitor—it's like a knee-jerk reflex in these (I almost said "guys," but I have to remember Leslie).

That day I went up there with Dorothy, as soon as we got buzzed in and the metal door to the unit slammed behind us, the piranha fish all rushed to the narrow windows to see who came in. I sometimes wonder if they're expecting a squad of cops to come in to take them to the death chamber. As Dorothy and I headed toward Marshall's cell, I was startled when I saw Leslie, over six feet tall with her long, spectacular platinum blonde hair hanging in her face, peering out of her window. I was fascinated. I took a long look at her as she stared back at me. I'll tell you one thing—as a woman, she makes a better man. Maybe it's because I know that she used to be a man, but, to me, she is definitely not attractive. Seeing her standing there in her cell, I couldn't see anything feminine about her except maybe for the long hair. She's tall, she has a thick man's body, and her facial features are coarser than most women's.

Leslie is appealing her sentence on the grounds that the police who came to her home that day were not properly trained and that the whole incident could have been avoided if the officers had used a different approach when they came back to question her about the guns. After looking at the news stories about Leslie's crime, once again I have reservations about using the death penalty. To me, in a different way from Jesse Timmendequas, Leslie is a pathetic case where I'm not sure killing her serves any purpose.

Ultimately, in both cases, the New Jersey Supreme Court will say thumbs up or thumbs down.

20
CHAPTER TWENTY

FIFTY YEARS OF CHANGE

Well, it's been quite a run. I'm now 75 years old and retired after fifty years in the system. I've seen a lot of changes over those years—some definitely for the better and some for the worse.

Probably the most significant change, to me anyway, is the difference in the attitude of today's inmates. For one thing, they're younger and meaner. We've always dealt with the cream of the crop in Trenton when it comes to tough guys, but these young inmates today are a totally different breed. A lot of the younger guys I see now don't seem to have any moral restraint whatsoever. In the old days, you could usually count on the inmates to follow some kind of code. It was a case of one hand washes the other—as long as they didn't get too far out of line and you didn't hassle them with petty bullshit, everybody got along (Monroe killing Don Bourne was an exception). Today these younger guys look, talk and act as if they could snuff someone with no more thought than you or I might give to killing a fly. In the old days, if one inmate killed another, there was usually a reason, like an unpaid gambling debt. Today, it can be something as simple as looking at someone the wrong way.

I even heard an inmate oldtimer say one day, "Damn, I'm glad I'm in here. When I see on TV what these young kids are doing out in the street today, I feel safer in prison."

Another change that often gets me thinking is society's attitude toward gambling. Look back at the '50's and '60's and Joe Adonis and Newsboy Moriarity. Those guys did time in a maximum security prison for doing something that today brings thousands of people to Atlantic City and puts millions of dollars per year into the state's pocket. I sometimes wonder whether our attitude toward drugs will eventually go through a similar change.

Of course, I've seen a lot of other less significant changes as well. In the '50's, inmates wore blue wool pants with a gold stripe down the leg in the winter and brown khaki cotton pants with a black stripe in the summer. Beginning in the '60's, inmates began wearing the khakis with black stripe year around, and they had short haircuts, like the military, with no facial hair. In the 1970's all of that changed, and it seemed like overnight the jail looked like a giant disco palace—shoulder-length hair, bell bottoms, sideburns, mutton chops—you name it. The short hair, the clean-shaven look and the prison khakis have a legitimate security basis, though. Think about it. If an inmate did manage to get out, it would take him some time and effort to get rid of the khakis and into civilian clothes, making it easier to spot him. Plus, if you have short hair and no mustache or beard, you're not going to be able to grow all that hair to disguise yourself as soon as you hit the street. BUT if you have real long hair and a big beard, and you manage to get over the wall, a razor and scissors and a few minutes will make a new man of you. At least a different one from the photo they'll have up in center as soon as they know you're gone. For that reason, the pendulum has swung back, and inmates are back in khaki and there are more restrictions on clothing, hair length and facial hair.

Another big change occurred in the early 1970's. Until around 1972, inmates were allowed window visits only, and they could see visitors for only one hour per month. Now, inmates and loved ones can meet in contact-visit halls and actually touch each other—and a lot more than touching goes on. This, of course, has also led to more smuggling of illegal substances into the jail. Around the same time, we stopped censoring outgoing mail. We still open incoming mail to check for contraband.

Eating utensils have changed, and I think that's been one of the positive moves. Now, instead of tin cups and metal utensils, which were easy to convert into weapons, we have plastic utensils and Styrofoam cups and dishes. That one change has made the mess hall a much safer place than it used to be.

Another positive change is one that has caused more work and frustration for the officers, but has made life better for the inmates. The changes in disciplinary hearings that first began in the late '60's and picked up steam in the '70's have made it more difficult for officers to arbitrarily punish inmates. In the old days, the hearing was held by a captain and another correction officer. Now, a civilian employee, usually a teacher or a social worker, sits on the disciplinary committee, and the inmate has the right to be assisted by counsel, usually another inmate who has made good use of the law library.

Related to that change is the elimination of bread and water as punishment. Inmate lawsuits over the years have pushed the administration into making changes like limiting the length of time an inmate can be kept in lockup

The ethnic and racial makeup of the population has changed considerably since I started in the early 1950's. When I first went to work at the prison, most of the inmates were white with a lot of Italians and Irish in the cells, and all of the guards were white. Now, about 70 percent of the inmate population is nonwhite, and probably a little over half of the officers are African-American. We also have women officers now, something that nobody in his wildest dreams would have imagined in the 1950's.

We had civilian employees in the old days, but most of them ran the state use industry shops, like the tag shop (license plates) or the tailor shop. Now, we have a lot more teachers and social workers—"do-gooders" we used to call them. We have many more employees on the service side of the house as opposed to custody. Custody still runs the jail, but the presence of so many civilian employees has taken away some of custody's traditional power.

State use has also changed. When I started, the prison system was pretty much self-sufficient with staples like milk and bread coming from prison farms and institutional bakeries. We also made clothing, shoes and even furniture. That was always a sore point with organized labor, and today a lot more of our goods and services are purchased from outside vendors.

And the mental hospitals have just about gone away. Up until the mid-1960's, inmates who lost it, like Barney Doak, got shipped to Trenton Psychiatric. Today, those inmates are retained in the prison and usually heavily medicated. We now have "nut wings" to house these guys, and the officers assigned to those wings need to be more aware of mental disorders. And that has led to another change: a lot more of the officers have some college courses under their belts. I don't think I could name one officer in 1950 who had a college degree. Now I could probably name several (though a lot of officers use their degrees to move over to the services side of the house). It's also possible for inmates to earn college degrees while they're in jail, with local colleges sending professors into the institution.

Last but certainly far from least is the whole capital punishment issue. We stopped electrocuting in the 1960's and switched over to lethal injection in the 1980's. But no one has been executed in New Jersey for more than 30 years. In the 1950's, when the death penalty was handed down, the sentence was usually carried out within 24 months. Theodore Walker was executed less than a year after the crime. Today, no one can predict when the first inmate on death row will go to the death chamber. Some inmates have been there for eight years or more.

And here are some things that haven't changed: we still use goon squad tactics to "extract" inmates from cells (except now we video tape the proceedings); we still shoot inmates off the top of the wall and the roofs of buildings; inmates still punch out guards and guards, excuse me, correction officers, still get their revenge. Women were shipped out of Trenton prison sometime in the 19th century and sent to Clinton. Now we have a wing in the new section set aside for bad-ass women.

It goes around, it comes around.

And so it goes . . . .

APPENDIX

A Guided Tour of Trenton State Prison

Probably the best way to describe the Trenton State Prison of the fifties, sixties and seventies that I worked in would be to go back to that day in July of 1950 when I was hired. After the interview with Captain Fleming and Mr. Page, Fleming made a phone call to get a white hat to come out to the front house and take me on a tour of the prison.

That day in 1950 I got my first look at the inside of Trenton State Prison, after all those years looking at it from the outside and wondering what it was like to be in there. After Mr. Page made the call, a lieutenant named John (Jack) Malkin showed up at the warden's office.

After the warden introduced me to Malkin as a new hire, the sergeant and I left Page's office and went out into the lobby. Over to the right were doors to offices and the mailroom. Along the left wall was a high semi-circular desk, like the sergeant's desk in old police stations, where an officer sat on a stool, helping direct visitors to the appropriate offices and generally overseeing the traffic flow through the lobby. Beyond that desk, along the left wall, were more offices and the visitors' entrance to the window-visit area. Directly in front of Malkin and me was a six-foot wide, eight-foot high metal door with a big lock, the "grille gate" door. The door opened into a 10-foot square air-lock-type area with another six-foot by eight-foot door that led into the prison itself. For obvious reasons, when that big grille gate door opening into the front house lobby was unlocked, the one that led into the prison was locked and vice versa; those two doors were never open at the same time.

As Malkin and I approached the lobby-side of the first grille-gate door, the officer stationed inside looked out, recognized Malkin, unlocked the door with a huge brass key (I later found out the cops called them *paracentric* keys) and pulled it open to let us in. Inside the grille gate, the officer who had opened the door looked at me, memorizing my features so that he would recognize me when I came out. I looked up and posted on a board over the inner grille gate door were several mug shots. Malkin explained to me that these were the "bad asses" who were either cop-killers, troublemakers, or inmates deemed likely to escape. If an inmate did escape, his photo was prominently displayed on this board. To our right was a door into a large room that the lieutenant told me was the armory where the Thompson submachine guns (vintage 1920's), shotguns, .38 caliber revolvers, shields, helmets, batons and other equipment were stored.

After we went through the second grille gate door, we were in center, the half circle that formed the hub of the prison with the housing wings radiating out. As the grille gate door slammed and locked behind us, we were in the interior of the prison with the central control booth directly to our right. Inside this steel-walled booth with thick glass windows, I could see maybe four officers watching what was going on in center, talking, laughing, and answering phones hanging on the back wall.

Bob Harris photograph, 1976

Central control, "Center," the command and communications hub of the prison. The armory is located behind the rear wall. The grille gate and the star officer are to the right, just off the right-hand corner of the glassed-in booth.

In front of us facing the entrances to the wings was an officer standing on a 10-inch brass star embedded in the concrete floor; Malkin told me this was the star officer, the guy who directed all traffic passing through this central crossing point of the prison. To go from one part of the prison to another, all traffic had to pass through center and wait for the star officer to indicate when to move—just like a traffic cop at a busy intersection on the street.

Bob Harris photograph, 1976

Star officer directs traffic through center. Entrance to the mess hall is straight ahead through the metal detector. Central control is behind the star officer.

The noise level was incredible. Inmates standing in the necks (the entrances to the various wings) who were waiting to cross the fifty-foot semi-circular center area were yelling out to each other. Behind them, I could see other inmates milling around inside some of the wings, also yelling to other guys high up on the tiers. The officer in front of us was pointing at the entrance to wings, motioning inmates and cops out, holding up his hand to stop traffic. Steel doors were slamming. It looked and sounded like a nut house.

I followed Sgt. Malkin as he moved to his left, and we came to a big barred gate, the entrance to 5 and 6-wings. Malkin said, "I'm going to take you through the jail moving from left to right. The numbers of the wings aren't going to make sense to you, but don't worry about it—you'll get used to it."

As we waited for the star officer to signal the wing cop, giving him the OK to open the barred gate, Malkin pointed to another door that looked like it would lead out into the lobby. He told me that it was the door into the inmate side of the window visit area and a thick wall separated the inmate side from the visitors' side.

As the gate opened and we stepped through, inmates in khaki uniforms with black stripes down the pants, passed us going out into center, looking curiously at me and with what I took to be pure hatred at Malkin. I started to feel better; I figured he despised everybody equally and they felt the same way about him. In a strange way, I felt more empathy with the inmates than I did with this cop who was showing me the jail—after all, most of the convicts looked like the guys I hung around with in the Burg.

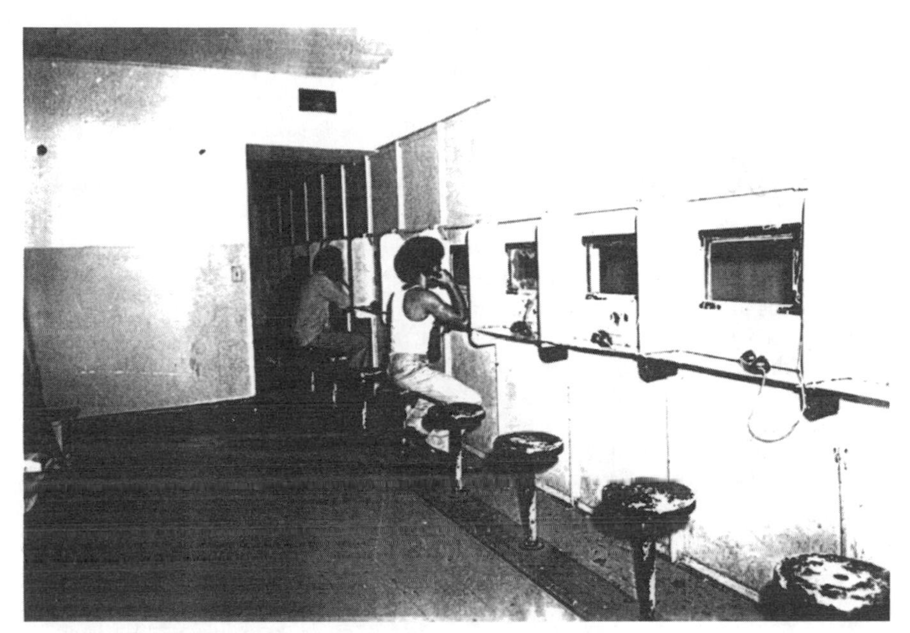

Inmate side of the window visit area.

Malkin and I entered a corridor with high ceilings and smooth, light blue plaster walls. Down at the far end, about 50 yards away, I could see a big opening into what looked like another building with a cell block running down the middle. As we walked down the corridor, Malkin suddenly steered me toward the left to a steel door recessed in a doorway a little larger than in a house—about three feet wide by about eight feet high. Malkin used a big ring of keys that he had picked up in the rear of central control to rap on the steel door. The officer inside looked through a round porthole; recognizing Malkin, he stuck a huge key into the lock and pulled the door open. Malkin told me this was 5-wing. and that security was tight here because this was where all the bad guys who had broken institutional rules were confined. He called it lockup.

We stepped several paces inside the area. To my right I could see three tiers of 20 cells (60 cells total) facing the opposite wall of the brick building. High up in the wall opposite the cell block, about on the level with the second tier of cells, were 20-foot-high windows looking out onto a yard and the inside of the prison compound's front wall that ran along Third Street.

Sergeant Malkin showed me the lever-operated locking system that opened and closed the cell doors. He said that this system was used in all of the housing areas except 4-wing. It consisted of a heavy steel rail running along the wall over all of the cell doors with a sliding mechanism controlled by a large lever down at one end of the cell block. By dropping pins into slots and throwing the lever, the wing officer could release certain doors and not others, or he could lock or release all doors simultaneously. At night, all of the cells were individually locked and this system double-secured them. During the day when inmates were moving in and out of their cells, the cell doors were manually unlocked, but the wing officer still controlled access by using the locking system.

Since the guys in this wing were locked in their cells twenty-two hours a day (one hour for yard, one hour for a shower), we had to find a "house" where the inmate was out for his shower so that Malkin could show me a typical cell. We found an open one on the first level, an area that Malkin called "the flats" (the first floor of any cell block). The cell was about seven feet wide, 11 feet long and seven feet high. Malkin said that inmates in cells of this size usually "double-locked" (two inmates to a cell) but because these guys were disciplinary problems, only one man occupied each cell. The walls were brick, the floor concrete. In the front right corner of the cell was a small sink and next to that was a dirty-looking toilet. In the middle of the concrete ceiling was a single naked light bulb.

As we left the cell block and went back out into the corridor, Malkin told me that 5-wing had originally been built to house women sometime back in the last century. That's one thing I'll say about "Cap Jack" Malkin (he had that on a vanity license plate later on in the late 1960's, early '70's when was promoted to captain and made chief of custody): he knew a lot about the history of the prison. Across the corridor from 5-wing were some fairly good-sized rooms; one was a barber shop for officers and staff, and a few feet further down the corridor

Bob Harris photograph, 1976

The interior of a typical TSP cell in wings of the old prison—still fully occupied. Most cells are seven feet wide by seven feet high and 11 feet long.

was an inmate store. We continued on and went into 6-wing, the large open area that I had seen from the barred gate when we first came into the corridor.

This wing consisted of a large brick building with an all-metal cell block running down the center of the building; the cell block was divided into 6-right with four tiers of 25 cells, and backed up to it, 6-left, also four tiers of 25 cells—total 200 single-lock (one man per cell) units. At each end of the large block were metal stairs, like on a ship, going up to catwalks that ran in front of the cells on the upper tiers. The stairs and the catwalks all had pipe railings running along them. Unlike 5-wing, where the cells were all along one wall of the building, these cells

Bob Harris photograph, 1976

Interior of 6-wing. Most of the wings in Trenton State Prison, except the old 4-wing (the "Andrew Jackson" wing) and 7-wing look like this.

sat in the middle of the building and did not come in contact with either the side walls or the end walls of the building itself. The tiers of cells to the right and to the left backed up to each other but were separated by a six-foot-wide utility space with catwalks, wires and pipes running the length and height of the cell block. Access to this space at each end of each tier was through a metal door with a round porthole in it so that the wing officers could look in to see if anyone was in there. Bare light bulbs burned constantly, keeping the area well-lit.

Lieutenant Malkin pointed out a door down at the end of 6-wing that he said led out to the hospital, and then we turned around and retraced our steps, walking back through the corridor next to 5-wing and back to center. At the barred gate, we waited for the star officer to see us, and when, after a minute or so, he still hadn't noticed us, Malkin yelled at him to open the gate, something like, "Open five!" or "Comin' out of five!"

Once we were back in center, we moved to our left and came to another similar barred gate. Again I heard a click as central control activated the lock, and Malkin led me into another wing. "This is four, the oldest wing in the jail," he said. "It was built when Andrew Jackson was president."

I could believe it. This wing looked totally different from the other two we had been in. Instead of a bunch of steel cages piled on top of one another, this wing looked more like a long horse stable on an estate. Instead of a big metal cell block with tiers running down the middle of the building, the cells in this building were against the outer walls. This made for a wide central corridor, and since the cells in the flats had wooden doors covering the entrances, it looked like a big horse barn, especially with the high vaulted ceiling. There were only two tiers here, with the second level recessed back and a balcony type of walkway running in front of those cells rather than a catwalk. Also, instead of metal stairways, the second level was reached by concrete and brick staircases built along either wall with wrought iron side railings topped with a wooden handrail. This wing really looked like it was from another century.

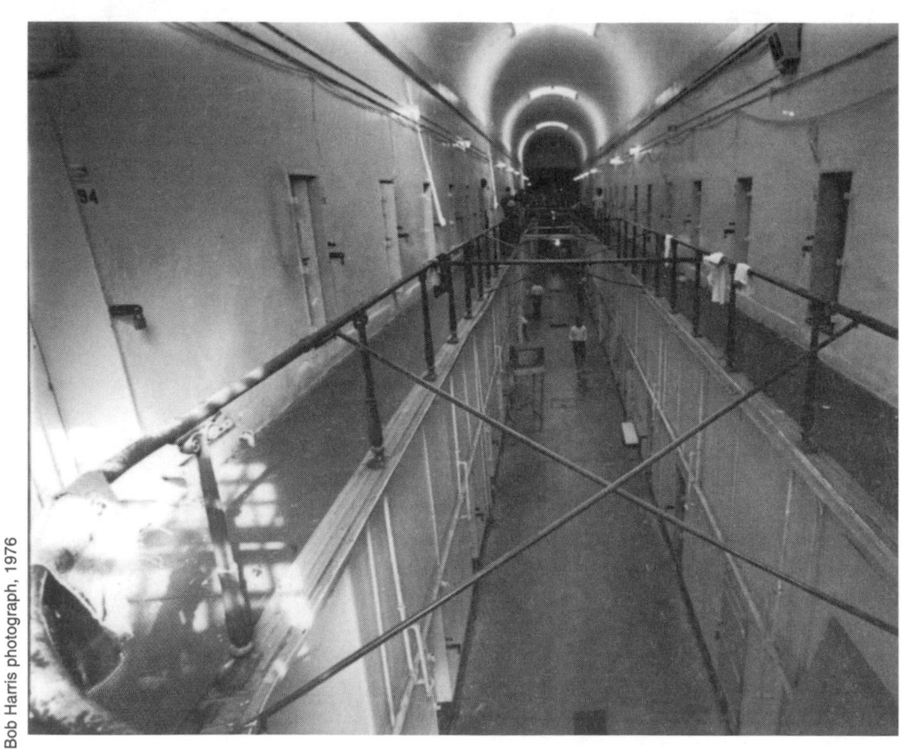

Bob Harris photograph, 1976

The upper level of 4-wing, the oldest housing wing in the prison.

Up above, the balconies in front of the second-level cells were connected by several iron or steel crossovers that looked like gangways on a ship. These allowed officers or inmates to go from one side of the wing to the other at the second level without having to go all the way down to the end, go down one set of stairs and up the other. Two-inch pipe railings ran all along the second level and along the crossovers.

The lieutenant pointed out that each of these cells had to be opened manually with a large key—there was no lever-operated locking system in here. This was definitely an old part of the jail. When Malkin took me over to one of the cells in the flats, I couldn't believe the size of the doorways: 20 inches wide by about five feet high. I'm five, eight, and I had to duck down to look into the cell.

The thick wooden doors, with a six-inch square hole about three-quarters of the way up, completely covered the opening in the wall. The walls were about a foot thick and on the inside of the doorway was a barred door, also operated by a manual lock, that swung into the cell. The floor of the cell was recessed down about ten inches so we had to first duck and then step down to get into these cells.

The cells themselves were huge compared to the other ones I had seen: about 16 feet deep, eight feet wide and ten or eleven feet high. A sink hung on the back wall, and a toilet sat in the right rear corner. Unlike any of the other cells in the prison, these had windows—about two feet long by about eight or ten inches high—in the back wall.

Bob Harris photograph, 1976

The flats in 4-wing. Cell entrances were covered by heavy wooden doors with barred doors a few paces inside. This is where Daniel Hogan scalded to death.

Malkin said that these cells had originally been designed for one man, but they were so big that years ago, as the population grew, the prison administration had put two double bunks in most of them. With 70-some cells in the wing and four guys in a cell, nearly 300 inmates locked in this wing.

Bob Harris photograph, 1976

The inmate mess hall—one of the most dangerous places in the prison. Chapel/ rec auditorium is on the floor above.

We moved back out into center and went into the next area. Malkin told me that this originally had been a housing wing, but about thirty years ago it had been converted to a dining hall on the first floor and an auditorium on the second—he called the upper floor "chapel/rec." The mess hall didn't seem big enough to me to accommodate over 900 inmates, but Malkin told me they ate in four shifts. The mess hall was reached by going through a wide barred door and down some steps. Two narrower barred doors on either side of the wide mess hall gate led to steps going upstairs to the chapel/rec area. This was a large auditorium with a stage at the far end. Malkin told me the inmates got a fairly current movie in here every Tuesday night. He also said that sometimes they got more action in the audience than on the screen once the lights went out. I was afraid to ask him what kind of action he meant.

The next housing unit, 2-wing, was divided into 2-left and 2-right. This was really the oldest wing in the jail Malkin said, but it had been gutted out in the late 1800's and rebuilt; otherwise it would have looked just like 4-wing. When they redid it, they built a four-tier brick cell block down the center with the cells backing

Bob Harris photograph, 1976

Steps leading down into the inmate mess hall. Sgt. Donald Bourne was stabbed to death here in February of 1972.

up to one another like 6-wing. Instead of those huge 4-wing-type cells, these were only five feet wide by eight feet deep and seven or eight feet high. They also had a sink and a toilet in the back, and only one man locked in them. With 33 cells per tier times four tiers per side (132 cells) the total capacity of the wing was 264. The cell doors were opened and closed using the lever-operated locking system.

The next wing, 1-wing, was a lot like 2-wing—a cell block running down the middle of a building and divided into 1-left and 1-right. The cell block was steel, like 6-wing, and consisted of four tiers of 22 cells each tier, 88 per side, total capacity 196 inmates. The large locking system was also used in here.

As we approached the last wing, I could see that we had come around the center in a semi-circle and each of the wings radiated off of and fed into the center through a large barred doorway that Malkin called a neck. When we got to the barred door to enter 7-wing, we were back near the central control booth, down at the far end away from the grille gate door. An officer inside looked at Malkin and nodded and the lock clicked open. We went through the barred gate, Malkin letting it slam shut behind us, and made a right turn. We walked down a slightly sloping concrete floor, bringing us into a low-ceilinged area with another barred door that an officer inside unlocked with a big brass key. Malkin said this was the last of the housing units—7-wing.

This was a big wing—a five-story building with 340 cells. It wasn't like the other cell blocks, though. In those other wings (except for 4-wing), the cells were stacked up in tiers with pipe railings in front so that when we stood down in the flats and looked up, we were looking at all of the cells on that side of the cell block. When we went into the first level of 7-wing, it was more like going into a low-ceilinged room with a couple of desks for the officers, some lockers, and the levers for the locking system. The whole area seemed to be enclosed in steel and heavy wire mesh so that the impression was more like being below decks on a battleship rather than in a big, high-ceilinged building. Regular cell blocks are depressing enough, but to me, this one was downright claustrophobic. Looking down the tiers was like looking into a low, narrow, dark tunnel running in front of the cells. Even though the outer walls had those high windows like the other wings, the mesh enclosure and the steel decks where the wing officers worked, connected by metal stairways, gave the wing a more horizontal feel—like each tier was a self-contained unit. Malkin told me that even though this was the biggest wing in terms of the number of cells, it was one of the easier ones to control because of the way the tiers were enclosed by mesh with barred doors at either end of the tier. In this wing, in case of trouble, each tier could be isolated by closing those two doors.

After we left 7-wing, we went back through center and into 4-wing again. Malkin explained that this was the easiest way to get out into the yard area. We walked through 4-wing, down to the far end, where the wing officer unlocked a steel door leading to the

Bob Harris photograph, 1976

The interior of 7-wing, with its self-contained tiers, where new inmates ("fish") were initially housed; later the site of the MCU (Management Control Unit).

outside of the building so that Malkin could show me the yard.

We went out into the bright sun of the hot July day and Malkin began to walk briskly, almost, it seemed to me, defying me to keep up with him. We were in a long alleyway behind 4-wing and the mess hall with the rear wall of the prison compound over to our right. On the other side of that 20-foot-high wall was Second Street. I looked up at the tower sitting up on top of the wall.

Without breaking stride, Malkin said to me, "That's 5-tower. They're called SB for sentry-base. The one you saw outside the front door is called SB-1 or 1-tower. SB-2 is on the corner of Third and Federal and so on around the perimeter wall. You'll get used to the tower numbers just like you will the wing numbers. It takes maybe a week to get to know this place."

As Malkin strode, and I trotted, he rattled off a lot of details about when certain wings were built, what the shops we were passing were originally built for, when a certain section of the wall was broken through to add space for buildings and so on. I got the impression that this place was this guy's life—this big, ugly mish mosh of buildings was like a part of his family.

"That's good for you," I thought to myself, "but I'm sure as hell not gonna spend the rest of my life in this shithole." Fifty years later, . . .

I followed Malkin as he skirted old stone buildings and we worked our way toward the front wall of the prison complex; he kept up a continuous round of

Jack Boucher photograph, 1979

The exterior of 7-wing, scene of the BLA shootout in January of 1975. This is the only wing that fronted directly onto a street with no intervening perimeter wall.

Bob Harris photograph, 1976

Inside of "The Big Yard." Third Street is to the left, Cass Street down at the far end. Bill Van Scoten went over the wall in the far corner in June of 1971.

chatter: "This is the tag shop; we make all of the license plates for the state here. That's the paint and repair shop; we keep this place running using skilled inmates. We have a lot of plumbers, carpenters, masons and electricians in here. Over there is the tailor shop. Inmates make all of their own clothes as well as for other prisons, reformatories and mental hospitals around the state. That's all coordinated by State Use Industries . . ."

He was walking and talking so fast that my head was spinning.

Malkin wheeled to the right around the corner of one of the largest of the old brown stone shop buildings and headed for a high concrete wall. I thought this was the outer perimeter wall on the south side of the prison that fronted on Cass Street. Malkin must have read my mind because he said, "This used to be the south perimeter wall and this was the yard, but after they built those shops, the hospital, and the death house, they extended the outer wall along Second, Third and Cass Streets for a new yard and punched a hole for a gate in this wall."

The two wide metal gates that led into "the big yard" were closed, but I could peek through a gap between them and watch as inmates played baseball, jogged or just stood around in groups, talking.

We turned around and headed for the front perimeter wall. Malkin pointed out the exterior of the hospital building attached to the south end of 6-wing. He said this building was erected around 1900 as a free-standing structure, but was connected to the south end of 6-wing sometime in the 1920's or 30's so that sick or injured inmates wouldn't have to go outside to get medical help. A few feet behind

Death row cells with the continually lit light bulb in front of each cell.

the hospital was another small cell- block building.

Once again Malkin rapped on the door with his ring of keys, and an officer looked out through a porthole before swinging open the heavy metal door. Malkin led me inside and explained that this was death row, the last stop for inmates condemned to die in New Jersey's electric chair. I swear a cold chill came over me as I looked to my left at those two tiers of nine cells each; I felt like I was looking at a set of cages containing some kind of animals waiting to be led out and slaughtered. I didn't have any strong feelings one way or the other about the death penalty, but the atmosphere in that building was . . . I don't know how to describe it . . . it just seemed like the chill of death hung over that wing like an oppressive, suffocating blanket. And unlike the rest of the prison, this cell block was quiet. All I could hear was the buzzing of the florescent lights and some muffled voices—a couple of the inmates talking quietly between the locked cells.

Malkin impressed me again with his wealth of historical detail about the prison. He told me this building was constructed in 1907 and originally accommodated six inmates. In the 1930's it was enlarged to its present capacity of 18. He told me that before the New Jersey legislature voted to authorize electrocution as the method of execution, the counties carried out the death penalty by hanging, usually in a courtyard at the local jail. He said that something like 140 men had been electrocuted up to that time (this was July, 1950) and that the next execution was scheduled for March of '51.

Malkin asked me if I wanted to see the actual death chamber. I wasn't real hot to see the chair, but I figured if I didn't, Malkin would spread the word that I was gutless. So I tried to look tough and said, "Yeah, sure."

We walked to the far end of the cell block and Malkin asked the wing officer to open the metal door. The officer produced another one of those huge metal keys, turned it in the lock and pulled the door open. Malkin stepped through the doorway first and switched on the overhead fluorescent lights. Directly in front of us was the chair facing to our right. I stared at it for several long seconds, trying to imagine what an inmate would look like the instant he was hit with the electricity. Then I turned to my right and looked over toward Malkin, who was standing in the area where witnesses sat on execution night. Lined up neatly and leaning against the side walls were stacks of wooden folding chairs. Directly behind Malkin was

The electric chair. Built by Carl F. Adams, an electrician, it was first used December 11, 1907 to execute 31-year-old Sereris DiGiovane from Somerset County. The last man electrocuted in New Jersey was Ralph J. Hudson, 43, from Atlantic County, January 22, 1963.

another metal door, almost identical to the one the officer had opened to let us into the death chamber from death row. Malkin explained that this door opened out into a sally port through which the witnesses left the prison after an execution.

The brick walls of windowless room were painted light green. I was surprised by how small and close the room was. It seemed to me to be about the size of the living room in an average-size house.

Behind the chair was a control panel with an eight-to-ten-inch diameter wheel in the center surrounded by dials and heavy armored cables going from the top of the panel, through the wall into a smaller room behind the chair. Malkin said this was a kind of utility room with more electrical cabling and a Gurney used to transport the corpse to the morgue on the second floor of the hospital after the execution.

As we left death row and headed back to the front house, Malkin flashed a grim smile at me and said something like, "Who knows, maybe you'll be one of the lucky ones and draw death squad duty. Hell, it's a good way to pick up some overtime."

After watching 13 men die in that chair, I sometimes think back to Malkin's words and how significant they turned out to be.

COPYRIGHT ACKNOWLEDGEMENTS

Trenton Evening Times/ Sunday Times Advertiser/ The Times of Trenton

Police Comb 'Spooning Area' for 'Mad Killer' Clues, p. 1 Trenton *Evening Times,* Nov. 18, 1940

One of the Duck Island Victims, p. 1 Trenton *Evening Times,* Jan. 31, 1944

Duress Alleged By Hill; Hill at Scene of Duck Island Slayings p. 1 Trenton *Evening Times*, Dec. 22, 1944

Hill Guilty, Gets Life p.1, Trenton *Sunday Times/Advertiser*, Dec. 31, 1944

Fugitive Convict Caught After Kidnapping Trooper, p. 1, Trenton *Evening Times*, Aug. 2, 1946

Convict Kills Guard, Stabs Another In Attempted Break On Auto Ride, p.1, Trenton *Evening Times*, Mar. 1, 1951

Tear Gas, Water Fail to Rout Rioting Prisoners From Wing; Firemen Try Water Chaser On Prisoners; Ready For Anything, p. 1, Trenton *Evening Times*, Mar. 3, 1952

58 Rebellious Convicts Still Hold Prison Shop; Prison Riot Ringleader, p. 1, Trenton *Evening Times,* Apr. 16, 1952

General Scene of Precaution Outside Prison, p. 3, Trenton *Evening Times,* Apr. 16, 1952

Cool Con Stages Classic Escape, p. 1, Trenton *Evening Times*, June 12, 1961

Defiantly Flings Lit Cigar At Death House Witnesses As He Walks To Electric Chair, p. 2, Trenton *Evening Times*, Jan. 5, 1955

Mild Little Man Who Staged Risky Jailbreak, p. 2, Trenton *Evening Times*, Dec. 12, 1956

Gift for Acquiring Money, No Knack For Enjoying It, p. 2, Trenton *Evening Times*, July 5, 1962

Pickets March. . . . p. 3, Trenton *Evening Times*, Jan. 23, 1963

Con Held In Slaying Of Guard, p. 1, Trenton *Evening Times,* Feb. 29, 1972

Dying Pusher Names Attacker At State Prison, p. 1, Trenton *Evening Times*, May 25, 1973

Raymond Dozier, 26, an inmate at Trenton State Prison being returned to the institution p. A-3, Trenton *Evening Times*, Oct. 17, 1975

Jailbreak foiled, 1 dead, 4 hurt, p. A-1, Trenton *Evening Times*, Jan. 20, 1976

Two killers played key roles, A-5, Trenton *Evening Times*, Jan. 20, 1976

Seven Wing failed as ultimate answer, p. A-4, Trenton *Evening Times*, Jan. 20, 1976

6 break out of Trenton prison: All 4 murderers captured; two escapees still at large p. 1, *The Trenton Times,* July 4, 1981

Escape From Trenton State Prison: Four murderers on list of escapees; Trenton's prison the end of the road p. A-11, *The Trenton Times*, July 4, 1981

Verdict: Guilty of All Charges/Tortured youth focus of defense/On Barbara Lee Drive, flowers and vengeance, p. 1, *The Times*, May 31, 1997

The Trentonian (Reprinted with permission. All rights reserved.)

Prison Security Tight After Bloody Battle, p. 1, Oct. 17, 1975

Gunbattle Rips NJ State Prison, p. 1, Jan. 20, 1976

Con, Girlfriend Held In Escape Attempt: Guard Foils Try At City Hospital, p. 1, April 20, 1981

Daring Escape For 6 TSP Cons; Four Recaptured: Molotov Cocktail Tossed, p. 1, July 4, 1981

Escape tunnel uncovered at state prison, p. 1, p. 3, Dec. 8, 1994

2nd escape tunnel found at prison, p. 1, p. 3, Dec. 10, 1994

The New York Times (Reprinted with permission. All rights reserved.)

5 in Jersey Family Are Found Slain, p. 43, Dec. 9, 1971

Jersey Police Scour Suburban Area For 2d Woman to Vanish in 8 Days, p. 39, Oct. 17, 1975

Paroled Killer In Jersey Is Linked To 5 Slayings, p. 1, April 20, 1983

Police Assert Friend Helped Suspect Move Body, p. B-3, April 21, 1983

One of Two Bodies Dug Up in S.I. Backyard Is Identified, p. B-1, April 22, 1983

Two More Bodies Identified In Murder Inquiry in Jersey, p. 25, April 23, 1983

Suspect in 5 Killings in 1971 Caught With Aid of TV Show, p. 1, June 2, 1989

Newark Evening News (Courtesy Newark Public Library. Reprinted with permission. All rights reserved.)

Schultz Dying of Gun Wound, Two Aides Slain in Gang War, p. 1, Oct. 24, 1935

Asbury Park Press (Reprinted with permission. All rights reserved.)

Belle Helps Murderer In Spectacular Escape, p. A-3, August 11, 1976

New Jersey Record (Reprinted with permission. All rights reserved.)

'Iceman' pleads guilty, p. A-1, May 26, 1988

Camden Courier-Post (Reprinted with permission. All rights reserved.)

Haddon Hts. cop killer suspect arraigned, jailed without bail/Feminine touch gets Nelson to surrender, p. 1, April 22, 1995

The Associated Press (Reprinted with permission. All rights reserved.)

SURRENDER IN GAMBLING INQUIRY: JOE ADONIS, *NEW YORK TIMES*, p. 1, Nov. 1, 1950

John E. List in 1971, *New York Times*, p. 1, June 2, 1989

PHOTO CREDITS

Page

iv — Aerial photo of the old prison complex taken from the southeast, *circa* 1930. Library of Congress, Historical American Buildings Survey (HABS, NJ,11 - TRET, 13-18)

v — Diagram of the prison complex in 1974. Original drawing by Lt. Donald Fiscor

vi — The front (east) wall of the old prison complex. View down Third St. from Cass St. Jack Boucher, photographer, 1979. Library of Congress, (HABS, NJ, 11 - TRET 13-2)

x — Front entrance of the 1835 prison. Jack Boucher, 1979. Library of Congress, (HABS, NJ, 11 - TRET, 13-6)

204 — Aerial photo of the old prison complex taken from the south, Trentoniana: Local History and Genealogy Collection, Trenton Public Library

218 — Aerial photo of the new prison from the west, Paul Savage, 1995, *The Times*, Trenton, NJ. Reprinted with permission. All rights reserved.

281 — Central control. Bob Harris, 1976.

282 — Star officer directs traffic. Bob Harris, 1976

283 — Inmate side of the old window visit area. Harry Camisa.

284 — The interior of a typical cell. Bob Harris, 1976.

285 — Interior of 6-wing. Bob Harris, 1976.

286 — The upper level of 4-wing. Bob Harris, 1976.

287 — The flats in 4-wing. Bob Harris, 1976.

288 — The inmate mess hall. Bob Harris, 1976.

289 — Steps leading down into the mess hall. Bob Harris, 1976.

290 — The interior of 7-wing. Bob Harris, 1976.

291 — The exterior of 7-wing. Jack Boucher, 1979. Library of Congress, (HABS, NJ, 11 - TRET 13-8)

292 — The big yard. Bob Harris, 1976.

INDEX

C

D

G

H

I

J

K

L

M

N

O

P

T

U

V

W

X

Y

Z